THE WORLD THAT FDR BUILT

Vision and Reality

Edward Mortimer

CHARLES SCRIBNER'S SONS
NEW YORK

Charles Scribner's Sons
Macmillan Publishing Company
866 Third Avenue, New York, NY 10022
Collier Macmillan Canada, Inc.

Library of Congress Cataloging-in-Publication Data
Mortimer, Edward.
The world that FDR built / Edward Mortimer.
p. cm.
Includes index.
ISBN 0-684-18687-X
1. World politics—1945- 2. Roosevelt, Franklin D. (Franklin Delano), 1882–1945—Influence. I. Title.
D843.M714 1988
909.82—dc19 88-21997 CIP

10 9 8 7 6 5 4 3 2 1

Printed in the United States of America

One of the fundamental principles of the education of our youth is not to let it forget the Great Patriotic War. In this connection some people accuse us of militarist education, that is of educating youth in some kind of militarist spirit by constantly reminding it of the events of the Great Patriotic War. That is not so. I will give you an example. In 1918, when the Versailles Peace Treaty was concluded, all of Europe was dancing, rejoicing, everybody was singing and all were convinced that there could not be another war. It was then that a Swiss scientist was asked in an interview, "Do you think there will be a Second World War?" and he replied, "Yes, there certainly will be." It was taken as a weird reply—nonsense—and they asked, "If you are so sure the war will happen, perhaps you'll tell us which year exactly?" And he said, "Yes, of course. In 1939." By then the journalists were nonplussed, and asked him a third question: "And why do you think so?" He said, "It is all very simple. By 1939 there will have grown up a generation which did not know the First World War, which has forgotten it, and the second one will start."

We are trying not to permit that.

—Viktor Mironenko, Soviet youth leader (born 1953)

Sometimes I have the impression it is between peoples and countries a bit like with children. My experience as a mother of two small children is that we can tell them all our experiences—we say, "Don't put your fingers on these things," but they have to do it, and then they feel, "Oh! I have cut it" . . . and sometimes I have the impression that people and countries have to make their experiences, too. But the problem is that concerning nuclear weapons we are not allowed to make the experiences—and perhaps it will be a chance that we are wiser than our parents.

—Ingrid Matthäus-Maier, West German politician (born 1945)

This book is dedicated to my own children,
and their contemporaries,
in the hope that they will get that chance.

CONTENTS

PREFACE

This book is based on a series of interviews commissioned by Channel 4 Television, London. As I explain in the Introduction, the idea for the series was worked out jointly by me and the producer, Michael Wills. I am deeply grateful to him, and to Channel 4, both for making the interviews possible and for making transcripts of them available for use in the book. (They are not, of course, responsible for the opinions expressed, or for any of the errors of fact that the alert reader will no doubt discover.) A word of thanks is also due to those who undertook the immense labor of transcribing the interviews, foremost among them Alison Selwyn.

The ideas in chapter 1, and to a lesser extent in chapters 8 and 9, are derived in part from the weekly seminar I was privileged to organize jointly with Professor (now Sir) Michael Howard and Mr. (now Professor) Adam Roberts, at All Souls College, Oxford, in the fall of 1985, on the theme "The Partition of Europe, 1945–1985." The speakers at that seminar included two people who subsequently agreed to be interviewed for the television series and are extensively quoted in the book—Sir Frank Roberts and Lord Franks—but there were many others from whom I learned a great deal and who were most helpful in informal discussion as well. I would mention especially Timothy Garton Ash, who suggested two of the best German interviewees, and whose spoken and written views on Germany and Eastern Europe I have found immensely illuminating as well as entertaining. He has done much to save me (though perhaps not to his own full satisfaction) from the perils of imposing a false symmetry on the relationship between Europe and the two superpowers.

Others who gave invaluable help in selecting and contacting potential interviewees included Christopher Hitchens, Sir Julian and Lady Bullard (who also most graciously entertained me on a preliminary visit to Bonn), Diana Geddes, Sir James Craig, St. John Armitage, Sir Robert Wade-Gery, Galina Orionova, and Richard Owen. Some of these efforts bore fruit, others in the end did not, but certainly not for lack of goodwill on the part of those named. In Japan we were helped enormously, over and above his own direct contribution, by Hitoshi Seki of the Japan Productivity Center; also by Miss Tokiyo Kuromiya of the Liberal Democratic party; and by our magnificent guide and interpreter, Mayumi Kawasaki. Similarly invaluable help was given in Moscow by the "guardian angel" mentioned on page 222, Pavel Tsarbulanov.

For help in arriving at an analysis of the relationship between American power and the world monetary system I must acknowledge a deep debt to Professor David P. Calleo, whose book *The Imperious Economy* is frequently quoted or referred to in chapters 6 and 11, and who was most helpful and friendly in elucidating various points in conversation. His wisdom was supplemented by discussion with Stephen Marris, of the Institute for International Economics in Washington, D.C.; Peter Oppenheimer of Christ Church, Oxford (then working at the Shell Centre in London); Samuel Brittan and Anatole Kaletsky of the *Financial Times;* Rupert Pennant-Rea, editor of the *Economist;* my sister Kate Mortimer and Richard Katz, both of N. M. Rothschild and Sons. (It should be said that these authorities disagree with each other on many points, and probably none of them will recognize their views in anything I have written.)

On the Third World and the United Nations I acknowledge gratefully the help and advice not only of Sir Brian Urquhart but also of his successor, Marrack Goulding; of Ambassador Stephen Lewis of Canada; and of Professor Fred Halliday of the London School of Economics.

Special thanks are due to all the interviewees, only one of whom received any remuneration, and nearly all of whom submitted with great patience to questioning at great length, as well as to the various delays and inconveniences involved in recording interviews on film (in this case, actually, on videotape). Even greater patience was shown by the film crew—Steve Haskett, Adam Alexander, Julia Richards, and Ian Hughes—who had to listen to the same line of questioning over and over again, and did so with remarkable good humor.

Finally I must thank Irene Andreae for most generously lending me her house as a place of seclusion to write in and her car to enable me to come and go between her house and mine; and, of course, I thank my wife and children for putting up, for several months, with such an unsociable husband and father.

THE WORLD THAT FDR BUILT

INTRODUCTION

Of Memories and Men

I was born in 1943. I grew up in the England of the 1950s and 1960s: the age of the Cold War, of decolonization, of full employment and rapidly growing prosperity in the West. Like most of my generation, I took these things more or less for granted. Nuclear weapons, the United Nations, the dollar as the main international currency, the division of Europe into East and West: all those were part of what seemed a largely static world political landscape—the only dynamic element being provided by the movement of the colonial peoples toward freedom. This last seemed both inevitable and desirable, as did the rapid economic and technological progress—the spread of television, jet aircraft, antibiotics—that was taking place all round me, against this political backdrop.

Just over the horizon of memory, but constantly audible in the conversation of my elders, visible everywhere in books, films, comics, and the bomb sites that disfigured my hometown, lay The War: an exciting but obviously dangerous and on the whole unpleasant experience, which a more adventurous child might perhaps have been sorry, but I was definitely grateful, to have missed. Obviously it had disrupted people's lives severely. I had a godfather who had been killed before he set eyes on me, an uncle who was captured by the Japanese, an elder brother and sister who had endured six years of childhood without seeing a banana or a jar of marmalade. I myself can just remember what a ration book looked like. But I thought of the war as a grim trial that my world had been through and survived. That my world was in many ways a product of that war was something that occurred to me only much later.

I discovered it by accident and by degrees, through following a series of threads that all led to the same intriguing tangle. When I was eighteen I was sent by Voluntary Service Overseas—similar to the Peace Corps—to Senegal, a West African country, then newly independent from France. What I heard about the history of that independence was so unfamiliar and confusing that I decided to find out more about it. The thread led back to the end of World War II, when France, herself newly liberated from Nazi rule, decided to give her African colonies a new deal, making their inhabitants—in name, at least—citizens of the French Republic. I found a phrase in a poem by Senegal's poet-statesman, Léopold Sédar Senghor, that seemed to capture perfectly the spirit of that remarkable moment when a fresh start had to be made with so many things: "the World's rebirth."[1]

That took me to France, where I lived in the late 1960s and became intrigued by the size and importance of the Communist party—one of the factors that made French politics strikingly different from British. This, too, I found, dated from the Liberation and the Resistance, in which Communists had played a leading role, emerging from it as *"le premier parti de France"* in terms of votes, prestige, and influence. For nearly three years they served in the government. Many people at the time, it transpired, had feared or hoped that France would become a Communist state, as the countries of Eastern Europe were in the process of doing.[2] Until then, the fact that Eastern Europe was Communist and Western Europe was free, like the fact that America was our ally and Russia our adversary, had seemed to me self-evident. Now it dawned on me that as recently as 1945, within my own lifetime, these things had not been evident at all to many highly intelligent people.

Later still, in the 1970s, I found myself writing editorials for the London *Times* about the Middle East, and particularly the Arab-Israeli conflict—another aspect of the world scene that I had grown up with, and vaguely assumed to be part of the eternal order of things. But here, too, I discovered that everything had really been decided in the immediate aftermath of World War II. There was no political entity called Israel before 1948, and had it not been for the combination of Hitler's treatment of the Jews and the exhaustion of British power in the war there might well never have been one.

Once you think of it, and look around the world, it becomes obvious. A world war is like a furnace of extraordinary heat: it melts the world down and makes it malleable, so that populations and frontiers can be shifted this way and that at the push of a statesman's thumb, and patterns of behavior that have set over centuries can be suddenly changed overnight. Lord Franks, who lived through this period and played a significant part in its events, uses the same metaphor.

> FRANKS: The world was malleable. It had no set shape. There was this vast vacuum of what had been Germany, and the occupation forces looking at each other across the middle of Germany. Nobody knew what the shape of things was going to be. It was worked out step by step, and these great adventures in policy were taken one by one, against perceived need.

It happens because certain things can be done very quickly by force that can be done only very slowly, or not at all, if human beings have to be persuaded to accept change; and even those who disapprove in principle of the use of force are anxious to make the best use of it once they have been driven to take up arms in their own defense. It happens because war subjects people to extremes of fear and discomfort, so that remedies that themselves seemed extreme and unrealistic come to be grasped as necessities of common sense. And it happens because war, more effectively than any other political device yet invented, concentrates the energy of a people in the service of the state, and thereby greatly increases, for both good and ill, the scope of political decision-making in national and international affairs.

It lasted only a few years. By 1950 the earth had cooled again and the new structures were as rigid as the old ones had ever been. Perhaps more so, because, as our German contemporaries—the children of defeat and partition—have understood, it can never happen again. They cannot hope to reverse the process that split their country between the two halves of a divided Europe, because after a nuclear world war there would be nothing left to reshape. Volker Rühe, a Christian Democratic politician, talks about the future.

> RÜHE: [In future,] the changes in European history will be more gradual because no longer changes by force are possible. The nuclear bomb has changed everything—I think to the advantage of Europe, but it also slows down this historical process, or it puts it in a kind of icebox.

So that short period, coinciding almost exactly with the period between my birth and my earliest memory, was a unique moment in human history. The Second World War was indeed a *world* war: much more literally than the First, which was really the last great European war, with the usual colonial sideshows. While Germany's destruction left Europe split down the middle, Japan's defeat inaugurated the nuclear age; in its aftermath the Chinese Communists completed their long struggle for power, and the Vietnamese Communists began theirs; Indonesia achieved independence from the Dutch, and India was partitioned. All the great European overseas empires (though not, for some reason, the Russian overland empire) were to break up within the thirty years that followed.

Of all the continents, only South America was not profoundly transformed. The United States was transformed not, like every other belligerent, by being devastated or exhausted, but by emerging as unquestionably the strongest world power and taking on the main responsibility for the new world order. This was an unfamiliar experience for a young nation whose foreign policy hitherto had been based on the avoidance of entangling alliances. But Americans were prepared for their new role by the tireless pedagogy of their longest-serving president, Franklin D. Roosevelt. He had been a disciple and supporter of President Woodrow Wilson, the architect of the League of Nations, and he was convinced that America's failure to join the League was partly responsible for the breakdown of the Versailles settlement and the rise of aggressor states in Germany, Italy, and Japan. He was determined that this mistake should not be repeated, that this time the alliance that would defeat the aggressors must remain in being to organize and preserve the peace in the postwar world, with America playing her full part. He was determined, too, that the new world order should do away with the old evils of imperialism and economic nationalism: it should be a world of free peoples, trading freely with each other.

This outlook contrasted with that of his allies. Churchill was anxious as far as possible to keep the British empire in being, while Stalin was trying to reconstitute, and if possible extend, the empire of the czars. Both were more practical, less visionary, than Roosevelt. They concentrated more on securing the immediate interests of their own states, and less on devising general systems and principles to be applied to the world as a whole. Roosevelt perceived no contradiction between American national interests and those of the international order, and in a sense he was right: the United States would emerge from the war so much the most powerful nation, in economic and military terms, that in an international system of free and equal opportunities its influence, and its commercial interests, were bound to prevail.

So it was Roosevelt who devoted most thought to the postwar world order, and who set his stamp upon it, even though he himself did not live to see the end of the war. Besides being the political father of the atom bomb (since it was on his orders that the top-secret Manhattan Project was set up and the necessary funds allocated to it), he is the undisputed progenitor of the United Nations Organization, and he gave a powerful boost to the movement of decolonization, through his influence on American and world public opinion, and through the constant pressure he maintained on his wartime allies. He also convened, on the advice of his close friend Henry Morgenthau, Jr., secretary of the treasury, the Bretton Woods conference of July 1944, which drew up the rules of the new world monetary system. And by his participation in the summit meetings with Stalin and Churchill, at Teheran in November 1943 and Yalta in February 1945, he helped to determine the future shape of Europe and the relationship between what would become known as the two "superpowers"—though here the eventual outcome was very different from what he had hoped and envisaged.

So we who grew up in the postwar world are all, in a sense, "FDR's children"—but more especially those of us who grew up in the "Free World," which for this purpose includes the "Third World," as it has come to be known, as well as the First. For the Third World is composed essentially of former European colonies which have found themselves part of a world economic system dominated by the United States, and which have become such enthusiastic participants in the world political system devised by Roosevelt that they have virtually taken it over. Only the inhabitants of the Second World—the Communist bloc—have been fenced off from full participation in the Rooseveltian order. They, perhaps, should be considered "Stalin's children."

When I began thinking about this subject I meant only to investigate the origins of the world I grew up in, by studying those crucial few years in which the great decisions were taken and the decisive events occurred. But after a while I was persuaded that, being a journalist rather than a professional historian, I should do better to try and analyze what had happened to the world system that was then set up: how far it was still functioning, where it had gone wrong, how much longer it might last.

Apart from all the local issues, it seemed to me that three crucial things had been decided in those years, which affected the world as a whole. First, Europe, which had dominated world history for the previous three or four centuries, was destroyed by its internal conflicts and devoured by its own children—ending up dominated by, and divided between, two powers that are both products of European civilization transplanted to or imposed on another continent, drawing from that alien soil both a new character and a new strength.* These two powers were generally seen as the world's new masters. That state of affairs may be called, symbolically and schematically, the legacy of Yalta. Secondly, the foundations were laid for an unprecedented expansion of prosperity throughout the world—which, again symbolically and schematically, can be called the legacy of Bretton Woods. And, thirdly, a new world political order was also founded, in which the authority of the new masters was to be contested by (metaphorically speaking) the freed slaves of the old—what we have come to know as the North-South conflict. Since the main arena of that conflict has been the United Nations system, we may perhaps call this third inheritance the legacy of Dumbarton Oaks, after the conference of August–September 1944 at which FDR's blueprint for the UN was accepted, with some modifications, by the three powers he expected to associate with the United States in the maintenance of the new world order: Britain, the Soviet Union, and China.

With Michael Wills, one of Britain's most talented young television producers, I began to explore the idea of a documentary series that would examine "the world that FDR built" under these three headings. But it soon struck us that what mattered was not so much what we thought about the postwar world order, but the attitudes of those who would inherit, or were already inheriting, the task of making it work. What was interesting about my relationship with it was that I belonged to the first generation that had grown up in this world, and could not remember any other. But if that was true of me, it must also be true of people far more influential and important than I, who happened to be roughly the same age.

Commissioned by Channel 4 Television in London, we undertook to identify a group of such people around the world: children of FDR's world order who might plausibly be expected to play some part in shaping its future—in deciding what kind of world order, if any, our own children will inherit; and to interview them at length about their memories and experiences of the international system, from childhood onwards, and about the feelings and beliefs that these experiences had left them with. One of them, the British politician Chris Patten, himself summed up rather well the premise on which the exercise is based.

> PATTEN: We're all the products of our backgrounds. We carry round a knapsack of prejudices and opinions which, to a great extent,

*Geographically, the Soviet Union is partly in Europe, while the United States is an ocean away. But culturally the former is more Asiatic than the latter is "American" in any pre-Columbian sense.

> I think, are shaped by experiences, recollections—events when we're growing up. I think in some way most of the events which have shaped me have far more to do with domestic than international events, but nevertheless I would imagine that international events had an impact on the sort of person I am, and the sort of political opinions I have as well.

Or, as Kenneth Adelman says, "The experiences the person brings into . . . office, I think, are far more important than what he learns on the job."

Of course, memory plays tricks. As another of our interviewees, Congresswoman Pat Schroeder, puts it, "When you are very young you can't remember if you remember, or if you remember being told about it so much you think you remember." But what is important in this context is not so much the actual event as the residue left by the event in the conscious or unconscious mind of the speaker.

Starting from that premise, this book is essentially a record and an analysis of those interviews, and an attempt to build up from them a kind of collective oral self-portrait and autobiography of a generation of world leaders. It is too early yet to say which, if any, of these people will achieve supreme power. But many of them already hold or have held high government office, while others have hopes of doing so, which depend on the outcome of elections or other political processes in their countries. They can be said to be reasonably representative of the pool of talent from which tomorrow's world leaders will be drawn. In Japan, where economic leadership may be as important to the rest of the world as, if not more so than, political leadership, we interviewed a number of prominent businessmen of the same generation, as well as two rising politicians of the ruling party. In several countries we also interviewed a leading political commentator with extensive international experience—drawn again from the same generation—allowing them to fill the gaps left here and there by the politicians' reticence and to attempt to sum up the collective experience of their contemporaries. In the same spirit I have interwoven my own memories and comments with those of the people interviewed.

Regrettably we found ourselves obliged to exclude China from the exercise. The difficulty, as well as the expense, of identifying and approaching suitable Chinese leaders was simply too great. FDR himself would, of course, have been outraged by this decision not to include the leaders of one quarter of the world's population among those of "tomorrow's world." It was entirely at his insistence, and to the considerable annoyance of his other allies, that China was involved in the great wartime conferences and became one of the permanent members of the UN Security Council. But it has to be said that Chinese history in 1949 took a turn that he did not foresee, and that China, preoccupied with her own vast internal problems, has not so far played anything like the role in the international system that he expected, or which her demographic weight would justify.

By far the largest number of interviewees are drawn from six countries: the United States, the Soviet Union, Japan, West Germany, France, and Britain. This reflects not only convenience but also the fact that, for at least two of the topics discussed—the Yalta and Bretton Woods legacies, it is the leaders of these countries who have the major decisions to take in the next twenty years or so. The Third World point of view is represented by two Africans, two Arabs, an Iranian, and a Mexican. We hoped also to interview one or more leaders from South or Southeast Asia, but unfortunately were unable to do so in time to incorporate the results in this book.

In the first part of the book I have grouped the early memories of my generation under the three general headings, and then, in each case, have attempted to go back behind these memories to establish what the ideas and actions were that brought about that aspect of the postwar system: for this purpose a number of elder statesmen were interviewed who had attended the great wartime conferences or otherwise participated in what Dean Acheson called "the creation" of the postwar world. In Part II I have gone on to recount what seem to have been the most important formative experiences of my generation during the sixties and seventies. In Part III comes the discussion of the present and future, with two chapters devoted to each of the three aspects of the world order: chapter 8 deals with the future of the East-West relationship, and chapter 9 with that—closely related, of course—of the Atlantic Alliance. Chapter 10 analyzes the challenge to the postwar economic order posed by the rise of Japan as an economic power, while chapter 11 looks more generally at the consequences of the breakdown of the Bretton Woods system and the possible remedies. Chapter 12 deals with the frustrations of the Third World peoples, to whom Roosevelt's liberal international system has not delivered the benefits they hoped for, and chapter 13 with the consequent disorder prevailing in the world political system, and the frustration of the Americans at the world's increasingly sour response to their leadership. In the Conclusion I have tried to draw all these threads together, suggesting that the new generation of leaders, particularly in the West, may have been too much impressed by the failures of various attempts at international management that they have witnessed, and too little aware of the extent to which the stable and hopeful world of their adolescence was the product of deliberate state intervention and international cooperation; and that unless something of FDR's belief in and commitment to a global order can be recaptured, we are in danger of repeating the fatal drift of the 1930s, with even more catastrophic results.

PART I

"An American Peace": The World We Grew Up In

CHAPTER 1

Legacy of Yalta: The European Frontier

MEMORIES

For as long as I can remember, Europe has been divided into East and West. Did I already know about it before 1956? I'm not sure. If so, it can't have meant very much to me. But the Hungarian revolt, which happened when I was twelve—nearly thirteen—was something real. I was aware of a great stirring among my immediate elders, undergraduates at Oxford and Cambridge. Money was collected, and one or two intrepid souls actually went to help. Not to help fight, of course—the fighting was over very quickly—but to help people escape.

Refugees: it may have been the first time I heard the word, certainly the first time I took in its meaning. Refugees poured over the border into Austria. Camps were set up. A friend of my mother's was there, working for the Save the Children Fund. The children who arrived had been drugged by their parents so they shouldn't make a noise and alert the border guards. So they arrived very sleepy, but they had to be awakened and kept awake until the effect of the drug had worn off. That must have been in a letter to my mother from her friend.

Neil Kinnock, now leader of Her Majesty's opposition, is two years older than I am. He has a Welshman's ear for the musical cadences of the English language, and a strong sense of the emotional wellsprings of political attitudes. Consequently he responded with relish to my invitation to describe his formative political memories. For him, too, Hungary was an important one.

KINNOCK: We relied upon photographs of immensely evocative situations: people literally jumping on the back of tanks, using Molotov cocktails, and I must say that the event made much more of an impression on me physically than politically—because the issues to me seemed so stark and so straightforward and so simple. And after all it was only eleven years after the world war. I was part of a generation brought up on the memories of the war, whether they appeared in the form of the conversation of relatives or the wounds of people I could see in the street, amputees and so on, or people who were said to be shell-shocked, and you saw once or twice a year when they came out of a mental hospital. And it was also to be seen in the comics and the endless adventure stories that fabricated events in the war. But that was the evocation: they were the partisans, they were the *maquis* . . . people who with nothing but what they stood up in were taking on might . . . that was the connection I made at the time.

David Owen, six years older than I—and a much tenser, more cerebral character than Kinnock—was to become foreign secretary in a Labour government at the age of thirty-eight, and later, as leader of the breakaway Social Democratic party, the dominant figure in the middle ground of British politics. He has a very clear memory of "the Hungarian episode."

OWEN: I was eighteen, just going to university, and that was easily the most traumatic incident in my life: listening to the cries for help and not really knowing why we couldn't . . . I felt the strong yearning to give up my medical studies and go out to . . . some of my friends did, in fact a very few of us were able to get into Hungary. . . . Night after night we argued as to whether or not we should go, and there was a great sort of . . . I suppose the same feeling that people felt in the Spanish Civil War, the feeling that you should go out and help them fight fascism. Bit unrealistic now, but that was one's feeling, and the feeling was: "Something's got to be done, this can't be allowed to happen!"

How much did I know or understand then of what the Hungarians were revolting against, or what they were fleeing from? I'm not sure. But from then on, if not before, I must have known that Hungary was part of "Eastern Europe," and that Eastern Europe was under Russian control. I must have known that between Eastern and Western Europe was a frontier, the "Iron Curtain," which was in some way more difficult and dangerous to cross than the English Channel, or even the Atlantic Ocean. And while at that stage I probably had no very clear picture of what life on the other side was like, at least I knew that people who wanted to change it were prevented by force from doing so, and that we on our side were safer and freer than they on theirs.

What I didn't know, in any detail or with any clarity, was how, why, and when that state of affairs had come about. Like Neil Kinnock, I knew about "the war" from innumerable films and novels and from endless reminiscences by parents, uncles, and teachers. That's to say I knew about a war between Britain and Germany, in which the Americans were our allies—well-meaning but clumsy. (The French under German occupation, I remember being told, were delighted to have their cities bombed by the British, but dreaded an American raid!) Was I told that Russia had been our ally, too; had destroyed many more German fighting units than Britain and America combined; and had had many times as many casualties? Perhaps I was, but it was not a point that figured much, either in the films and novels or in the reminiscences.

I suppose soon after 1956, if not during it, I must have known that Russian control of Eastern Europe was the result of Russia's victory over Hitler, and therefore was something that had come about (just) within my own lifetime. I knew it, that is, in the sense that if someone asked me the question I would probably have produced the right answer. But I don't think I can really have integrated this knowledge into my overall picture of the world. Certainly I never thought about the creation of the Communist states in Eastern Europe as a process. It was simply a fact.

The line between Eastern and Western Europe seemed very clear, absolute, permanent. What about Berlin? I think I was aware quite early on of West Berlin's enclave status. I'm not old enough to remember the airlift of 1948, but I must have heard it talked about, as a significant event of the recent past. I knew, I'm sure, that Berlin was a divided city. I had heard of Checkpoint Charlie and the Brandenburg Gate—the latter blended in my adolescent mind with the Mandelbaum Gate, another crossing point in another divided city that was mentioned from time to time in the news. I think I remember being a bit puzzled by all the fuss about the Berlin Wall, which was built when I was seventeen, since what this did was to make Berlin conform more exactly to the mental image I had had of it all along. In all this I was probably fairly typical of my generation in Britain, though some, like Neil Kinnock, were closer to the event than I was.

KINNOCK: Quite by coincidence I was in Germany, with a youth club soccer team, at the time that they built the Berlin Wall. And what was interesting was the way in which the German people that I was with reacted, and the way in which people were reacting back home. A lot of the Germans I was with had come from East Germany and understood it to be a necessary action in Soviet terms, in terms of that system, because they were willing to believe any excess was possible, and of course they were right. Back home, whilst it was evidence of that, it was also treated, if you recall, as a demonstration of the weakness of the system, that had to build walls to keep people in—I've always thought that was the case.

But young Germans of the same age must have been more aware than we were of the novelty and anomalousness of the division of Europe, and of the fact that it resulted directly from Germany's defeat by Russia. Josef Joffe, now a leading West German commentator on defense and foreign affairs, was, like me, four years old at the time of the 1948 Berlin airlift. But as he was living actually *in* Berlin, he does remember it.

JOFFE: I remember lots of candlelight, because there was no electricity; lots of dried milk and dried potatoes; lots of American planes flying in low over Tempelhof Airport, and feeding and heating the city for over a year.

Of course, the war itself is liable to be a much more traumatic and vivid memory for Germans, whether they are old enough to have some fragmentary direct memories of their own, or only to have heard their elders talking about it and to have experienced its immediate aftermath.

Norbert Gansel, now a leftish, mild-mannered member of the Social Democratic opposition, is just old enough to remember British and American bombs dropping on Kiel, the city of his birth.

GANSEL: We spoke of Christmas trees when, in the night, these lights were falling down from the sky to mark the aim of the bombers. I remember the nights when I was carried by an old man who lived nearby, in his arms, into the shelter. I remember that my mother was always in panic—but also I remember nice things, like balancing next morning in the sun on a bomb which had not exploded and was lying in the sun. . . . And of course the most traumatic event was when my teddy bear became a victim of the war. Well, these are typical memories of a child, which stick to your mind, which you don't forget—and later on you see it in a different light. . . .

I remember the British troops coming into Kiel. The sun was shining and the tanks were passing the house where we lived after the bombing:

the earth was trembling. And the next picture is my father coming back —I didn't know him—and now I don't know whether that is my memory, or whether it is what my mother told me after a while, that my sister came and said, "There is a man downstairs who says he's Father!" And he had come on foot from the Netherlands, all the way to the north of Germany, with a group of soldiers and a group of German women who had been in the army, and always being wary not to become prisoners of war, and not to be carried by the waves of war into the direction of the east, to the Red Army.

I remember two, three, years of hunger and poverty, when there was no bread in the house, and no shoes, and I was forbidden to play football. But also nice memories like when my father had managed to get things on the black market—like a parcel of butter. One day he had got cigarettes from the English—he worked in those days for the English occupation army, repairing cars and wheels as an unskilled laborer, and so he had access to British cigarettes: that was the real currency in those days. I know that we collected cigars and cigarette ends in the streets. We tried them ourselves, of course, six or seven years old. I know that the first English phrases I learned were, "Have you chocolate? . . . Do you have chocolate? . . . Have you chocolate, mister?"

I remember soldiers giving us sweets or chewing gum—and I remember the first time, so to say, the reality of the Soviet Union entered into my life. It was 1947: I was already able to read. . . . We had a dog called Blackie (named by my sisters, who were older and pro-English). One day Blackie had disappeared. We searched the whole area. . . . Blackie was not there, and my parents said, "Well, we have not seen him either." But we were suspicious about the whole thing, and we remembered that people from the Russian ship had been in our house in the evening, and some changing of things—black-market goods—must have happened in the kitchen. And then we found in a cupboard a tin with strange letters—Cyrillic letters, as I now know—and it rattled, and obviously that was coffee—and we knew that that was what was left of our dog Blackie. And later on our parents confessed—yes, they had given the dog to the Russian captain, who liked it very much, and they had got the coffee in return. But such was life in those days.

It sounds rather romantic when I tell it, but it was a hard time, especially for the parents, of course. And now, as a politician, I consider myself very lucky to have these experiences. In my generation of those who participate in politics, those like me who were born in 1940 are the last to remember what hunger really meant and how it feels, how it looks when the last slice of bread is shared among five members of the family and when you have no butter—of course, you have no butter, but no margarine—to put on it and it's put in the hot pan to give it some color—well, it's a good thing to be able to remember that.

David Owen, who is just old enough to remember what it was like being on the *winning* side in World War II, also thinks that it must make a difference.

OWEN: If you don't remember the bombing, going underneath the stairs or down into the cellar and hearing the bombs, if you don't remember the rationing, the luxury of eating any meat other than corned beef, the absence of fresh fruit—or much more traumatic experiences were those of us whose fathers were away during the war. I mean, I remember my mother—I can't remember what was said on the news, but I remember her listening at six o'clock every night to the news, and she was, of course, listening to how the battle was going in North Africa or in Europe; and not knowing your father, having your fundamental relationship really with your mother—my father was away all the years of the war—and coming up to him, when he was demobbed, with my sister and my mother, and shaking him by the hand, saying, "Good afternoon, sir": I didn't recognize my own father, because he'd grown a mustache! I'd barely seen him, just from photographs.

But Germans, even those younger than Norbert Gansel, had also to cope with the fact that their country was the only one in Europe that the Cold War had actually split in two. Many young West Germans had relatives on the other side. For some, like Volker Rühe, now a fast-rising member of West Germany's ruling Christian Democratic Union and a valued foreign policy adviser of chancellor Helmut Kohl, it was largely a matter of chance which side they themselves were on.

RÜHE: I always try to think of somebody my age in East Germany, you see, because when we were bombed out in Hamburg my mother first took me to what is now East Germany. And fortunately when the Soviets came she took me to what is now West Germany. So I might have been brought up also in what is now East Germany.

An early memory for many West Germans, of my age or a little older, is the workers' revolt in East Berlin in 1953.

RÜHE: It was a human event, you see. You don't understand all the political implications, but people throwing stones against tanks . . . And we also, I think, got some understanding that this is very unusual in

German history. I mean, we haven't had a revolution—or a semirevolution—and we didn't have much of a resistance . . . and so in school I think we saw it in this relationship, and that impressed us a lot. Because it's very extraordinary in German history that such things happen: people throwing stones against tanks, and fighting a fight they never have a chance to win.

This memory is shared by Karsten Voigt, Rühe's opposite number in the Social Democratic party—a man as voluble and scintillating as Rühe is careful and stolid.

VOIGT: In 1955 I came to Hamburg, and in my school class more than 50 percent were refugees who left the GDR* as youngsters after 1953, and when they told me about all the events, which I had seen at the time on television or by radio . . . when they told me about all these events which happened over there and how little we could really do about it, this was very impressive. And later on the 1956 Hungarian uprising is deeply rooted in my memory: how much the Western forces promised, how much they could do with military force and military strength, and how little they really could do and how much those people finally suffered who expected too much.

MORTIMER: What political conclusion did you draw from that?

VOIGT: I think that, deeply, I feel that suppression in the East is a problem for me, but that changing something in the East by military strength is not possible; and that in one way or the other this led to the later détente policies.

One senses that for Germans the Berlin Wall remains an open wound—a source of pain that has somehow to be relieved. Here is Volker Rühe's version of Kinnock's experience. (Could it, one wonders, have been the same soccer tournament?)

RÜHE: We went to Berlin with our class from Hamburg and we just walked over to East Berlin and played soccer with friends over there —we just crossed through the Brandenburg Gate. And so this was a very big shock—I mean the building of the Wall. . . . On that very day —that was a Sunday, you know—I was playing in a soccer team in West Germany, you know, at a tournament, and there were teams from East Germany—young people, you see, like myself, eighteen, seventeen, nineteen—and when the news came in you could feel their tragedy and their problem: do they want to go back? If they go back, they may never have a chance to come to the West again.

*German Democratic Republic (East Germany).

But for many non-Germans the Wall is either just an unpleasant event in the past, attributable to Western weakness, or a kind of grisly morality play that forms a useful part of one's political education: evidence, as Kinnock says, at once of the barbarity and of the weakness of the Soviet system. That, at least, is how such robust anti-Soviet commentators as George Will in the United States and Pierre Lellouche in France describe their own experiences of it.

WILL: The first vacation I took as a student at Oxford in the spring of 1963 I went to Berlin . . . and went and saw the Wall, which was still a fairly young wall at the time, and that's a sobering experience. I mean, there was no doubt about the stakes of politics in the twentieth century after you'd seen the Berlin Wall. . . . A few yards from Checkpoint Charlie was the grave—it's still marked to this day, I assume—of . . . the young East German who'd been shot trying to scale the Wall and they'd just let him bleed to death. That's a very good educational experience to see that.

Pierre Lellouche is a Parisian leftist of the sixties who turned rightward in the seventies and is now France's most influential civilian commentator on defense and security matters.

LELLOUCHE: The last and most important turning point, if you believe it, was going to Berlin. When I went to Berlin and I saw the Wall —which I had heard about, like everybody—I saw that Wall and I saw the *mirador* [watchtower], then I saw the minefield on the other side . . . I—I just couldn't believe it. This was a monument to human monstrosity. I mean, to put a whole city in jail behind barbed wire and a wall was—is—completely abstract, until you see it. And you see that wall all over that city. And you begin to think, what do they have to fear so much, that they have to wall in a whole city?

Richard Burt—now U.S. ambassador to West Germany—describes the effect of the Berlin Wall on young people who hadn't actually seen it.

BURT: [The Berlin Wall was] less of, I would say, a strategic crisis than a kind of moral crisis: the recognition that there was a clear difference between what we stood for and what the other side stood for —that here was a society, the German "Democratic" Republic, closing in its own people, and that was a graphic illustration of the difference between the two sides. But I wouldn't say the Berlin Wall crisis had the same impact on me and my friends in that period as, say, the Cuban missile crisis. . . . To have Soviet missiles ninety miles away [from the United States] had a tremendous psychological impact. Berlin is thousands of miles away, in a very complicated situation. People have trouble sometimes remembering, in the United States, that Berlin is in the middle of the GDR. Sometimes it's seen as somewhere along the inner-German border.

In any case, Wall or no Wall, soccer or no soccer, Volker Rühe and his East German contemporaries were well aware even before 1961 that they had grown up in two different states, under very different social and political systems. For Germans of that generation, as for other Europeans, the division has been a fact of life, a "normal" state of affairs at least in the sense of something one is used to, even if one knows that it has been brought about and maintained by force, even if one believes it to be in principle unacceptable and hopes that it will someday be reversed. For us to imagine Europe without it is quite difficult.

Most of us must also have been aware, from quite an early age, that there were only two powers that really counted in the world: Russia and the United States—though there was some confusion about the precise status of "Great" Britain, and perhaps even about France. Mine must have been the very last generation of British schoolboys to look at the globe and take an innocent pride in the amount of it that was painted red, denoting British rule or—as we still thought of it—"possession." Schoolboys of my age in North Germany knew that they were in the British zone, conquered and occupied by British—rather than Russian or American—troops, while some of those in South Germany must have been equally conscious of being in the French zone.

Sergei Plekhanov, a Russian born in 1946 who was to make his career studying the United States (he is now head of political and social studies at the U.S.A.-Canada Institute and speaks English with an uncannily perfect American accent), describes his impressions of the world powers while he was growing up in Moscow.

PLEKHANOV: I didn't think about our country as a superpower or one of the two greater powers. In fact, we didn't have a bilateral view of the world. The Americans were perceived in a negative light because of the war in Korea, because of their pressures on China—I remember cartoons depicting Chiang Kai-shek* threatening the mainland and, you know, having American backing. The nuclear danger, the arms race, and the international tension were there, but somehow it didn't come across as a bilateral situation, as two superpowers fighting for control of the world. It was a different picture.

The only East-West "summit" in the 1950s was still a four-power affair—at Geneva in 1955 between Eisenhower, Bulganin, Sir Anthony Eden, and the French prime minister of the moment, Edgar Faure. Even as late as 1960 Charles de Gaulle was able to host a four-power summit in Paris. But it was aborted by the shooting down of an American U-2 spy plane over Soviet territory—an indirect confirmation that it was now the U.S.-Soviet relationship that really mattered. With the advent of the Kennedy administration in 1961 any attempt to pretend otherwise was abandoned. With or without nuclear weapons, Britain and France had become second-order powers—as the Suez crisis of 1956 had made dramatically clear.†

For us in Britain, Suez was an unforgettable episode. Neil Kinnock, at the mere mention of the word, launches into a strangely literary, almost archaic, snatch of autobiography.

KINNOCK: Oh, that was stark remembrance . . . partly because I had the great good fortune to be a constituent of Aneurin Bevan,‡ whose speeches (entitled "Law Not War") really did make a difference to the conduct of the debate for the whole country, and for no one more than a fourteen-year-old who was just starting to get engaged in politics. And the issue really translated itself to me as in some sense a final vain shake of the conduct of imperial policy and world relationships.

MORTIMER: Were you struck at all by the American role?

KINNOCK: Yes, because . . . at the time I recall thinking, they've moved in to save us, in some ways—to save an immense embarrassment and an embroilment that was intractable, because we'd have been stuck —and at the same time they may be moving in to do something for themselves: in chaos there's profit. And I think that it would be possible

*Head of the Chinese Nationalist government, based in Taiwan after the Communist victory on the mainland in 1949.

†Britain and France invaded Egypt, ostensibly to "separate the combatants" in an Arab-Israeli war but in fact to secure the Suez Canal and in the hope of toppling the Egyptian leader Gamal Abdel Nasser, who had nationalized it. (The Israeli attack had been planned in secret collusion with the British and French.) They were forced to withdraw under pressure from President Eisenhower.

‡Leader of the left wing of the Labour party in the 1940s and 1950s. Widely regarded as Britain's best political orator after Churchill. A Welshman like Kinnock, and something of a role model for him.

to look at Suez and not just see the insistence on new answers from Britain, but the emergence of a new role of power—not a new power but a new role of power—in the Middle East and in the arbitration of world affairs from the United States of America.

Chris Patten, the immensely likable Tory "wet" (i.e., moderate) who is now minister for overseas development in Mrs. Thatcher's government, is two years younger than Neil Kinnock. He remembers his family's reaction to the Suez crisis.

PATTEN: I think it was the only occasion at that sort of age when I had a serious discussion with my father. On the whole my parents, like many others, took the view that politics and religion were not things that you talked about at home, or even talked to the neighbors about, in order to ensure that life went on on an even keel. But I remember my father, when I was . . . I suppose I'd have been about twelve, taking me into the front room. I assumed, given I was that sort of age, that it was another installment in my sex education and I wasn't quite sure what it was that I didn't know. It turned out that he wanted to say to me that he was very concerned about Suez, which I'd read about on the front page of the *Daily Express:* that he thought it might lead to another war and that I might have to grow up rather more rapidly than he and my mother had been anticipating. The prospect of another war hadn't really been something one was directly aware of except that I had an aunt in Bristol who ever since the end of the Second World War had kept her larder full of tins just in case international peace and order broke down again. I must say it was rather a shock. . . .

I think it was a particular turning point in our social and political history. Most of my other recollections before that . . . had been of events which in a way suggested that everything was going to go on the same for Britain, that we hadn't been greatly changed by the experiences of two world wars and that we were still a top dog, and that things were going to go on getting better and better—I'm thinking of going next door for the Coronation on the television in 1952,* the 1953 Cup Final, and all those events which have a tremendously dated feel about them now, and betrayed a view of an England that I think was ceasing to exist. I think Suez was in a rather dramatic sense a sign that Britain was no longer a top dog.

*Queen Elizabeth II, who came to the throne in 1952, was actually crowned on June 2, 1953. Television was still a novelty, and a relative rarity, in Britain at the time.

For me, just a few months older than Chris Patten and in my first term at public school, Suez was certainly an intensely politicizing experience, but I think it affected my attitude to domestic politics more than to the international scene. I remember feeling passionately convinced that the British government was wrong, but more through fear of war and its consequences than through any deep understanding of, or sympathy for, the Egyptian position. My elder brother was in the army doing his National Service, and his unit was put on forty-eight hours' notice to go to the Middle East. I simply could not see that there was anything at stake there that was worth the risk of his life and the lives of thousands of other young men. Not long afterward National Service was abolished in Britain. Although I was personally relieved by this, having not the slightest personal inclination to sample army life, I had—and still have—grave misgivings about it. It seemed to me that my own reaction to the prospect of my brother being sent to Suez was a healthy one; that war was a serious matter, about which governments should think twice or three times before committing themselves, and that they were more likely to do so if the army that would have to fight was drawn from the population at large rather than composed of volunteer professionals for whom death in action could be regarded simply as an occupational risk. Later I discovered that on the Continent, and in France especially, it had historically been the left that championed a "citizen army," composed of conscripts, as opposed to a professional army that was suspected of reactionary sympathies and putschist inclinations. I often wondered why the left in Britain did not follow that reasoning and advocate the reintroduction of National Service.

My misgivings about its abolition were sharpened by the fact that the defense minister of the time, in explaining the decision, said that Britain would henceforth rely on the nuclear deterrent as its ultimate national defense—implying that Britain, if attacked by conventional forces, would have to be ready to initiate a nuclear war. (This, of course, is also true of NATO as a whole—a fact that I still find deeply troubling.) My generation was the first to grow up in the nuclear age, and as a child I was almost obsessed by the fear of nuclear war—an idea conflated in my mind, perhaps not unreasonably, with the end of the world.* Like Chris Patten's father, I feared that the Suez expedi-

*Perhaps I should have taken it less seriously had I been subjected to weekly preparations for it at school, as my American contemporaries were. Kenneth Adelman, director of the Arms Control and Disarmament Agency in the Reagan administration, recalls: "I remember very well in grammar school, at eleven o'clock every Wednesday, having an air-raid siren go off, and we were expected to march to our little lockers, to get down on our knees, to put our heads in our

tion would lead to a general war—I suppose because of the threatening speech made at the time by Khrushchev, the Soviet leader. Perhaps this was not, in fact, very likely, but to me it certainly appeared that Eden's government was running an insane risk, while Gaitskell, the leader of the Labour opposition, appeared the voice of sanity. I was astonished by the passionate hostility that his reasoned criticism aroused in the British establishment—one heard, for instance, of housemasters banning the *Observer* from their houses because it supported him, although I don't think this actually happened in my school. I became suddenly aware almost overnight that I was not, and could not be, a Conservative.

The other thing I remember is that the government caved in very quickly in face of the international outcry and was left looking extremely foolish—though I don't think I was fully aware at the time of the specific role played by the United States. The Conservatives were revealed as people who had naively believed Britain was still an imperial power. Again, I doubt if I understood that clearly straightaway, but certainly it became a commonplace of political conversations in the years that followed. And it was a lesson not lost on my contemporaries in other countries, including the United States itself, such as Joe Biden, now a senator from Delaware.

> BIDEN: I've always been an Anglophile and my interest from preschool, the grade schools, and through high school and college and graduate school has always been history in Europe and particularly Britain . . . and I can remember wondering—I remember incidents like Suez—and thinking that Britain was not what she had been and what I had read about prior to World War II. And so there was a mixture of feelings, but clearly there was the perception, held by, I think, everyone of my generation—and my father's generation after World War II—that the United States was the dominant force in the world. And in fact she was. . . .
>
> The only thing that put a crimp in that whole notion of the United States superiority was Sputnik—when the Soviets put up the Sputnik.

Richard Burt has especially vivid memories of that event, which took place in October 1957.

little lockers, and to wait there for a few minutes because that's the position we would be in during a nuclear war. I always remember thinking, 'My head is fine because it's in the locker, but my fanny is in the hall still'—and what would I look like after this nuclear exchange without a fanny?"

BURT: I think the earliest international event I can remember was the launching of the Soviet Sputnik. . . . I was living in a small town outside Boston. My father was teaching at the Massachusetts Institute of Technology, and maybe because the Sputnik launch had such a traumatic impact on the American educational establishment, particularly the technical establishment, I remember that very vividly. It caused a great crisis, you'll recall, in the United States. It caused everyone to wonder whether there was a problem in American society. They asked themselves, how could this backward Soviet state have launched a satellite before the United States?

I think that I was a typical product of the Cold War period in the sense that I remember, even for someone who's not even a teenager, the sense of competition that we had with the Soviet Union. I remember reading a long article in *Life* magazine which told about the missiles and bombers that the United States and the Soviet Union possessed. On the one hand there was a sense of fear about nuclear war—in those days we had air-raid drills to protect us from nuclear attack—and on the other hand a sense of old-fashioned competition: that we needed to be number one, that we couldn't permit the Soviet Union to beat us in any important field. So I followed athletic contests, Olympic Games, science, the arms race, as a young person, in purely competitive terms: I wanted the United States to be first. . . .

I remember that there was an almost immediate impact in school: suddenly we were taking more science courses; there was talk about going to engineering school.

Needless to say there was a corresponding reaction among Soviet schoolchildren.

PLEKHANOV: When the first Sputnik went up in 1957 we were all very proud that we were the first in space, and that reflected and sort of built upon the pride that we had on the basis of our victory in the war and our ability to reconstruct the country. As to the American side of the equation, I remember reports about American satellites somehow not going up: they had a whole series of disasters at the time—I think in 1957 and 1958 there were about a dozen launchings which didn't produce a satellite flight. So there was a clear perception that in this particular area we were a hit and the Americans were behind.

But for Andrey Kokoshin, born in 1945—now deputy director of the Moscow Institute of U.S. and Canadian Studies, and in that capacity an adviser to Foreign Minister Edward Shevardnadze— an even bigger event was the first *manned* space flight, in April 1961:

KOKOSHIN: For me it was one of the greatest events of my life. . . . We regard it as an achievement of mankind, and we were, of course, very proud that Yuri Gagarin, the first man on the earth who entered the outer space, was Soviet Russian.

And Viktor Mironenko, first secretary of the Young Communist League (Komsomol) of the Soviet Union, who was born in 1953, notes this as the very first international event he can remember, and also one of those that made the strongest impression on him:

MIRONENKO: Nineteen sixty-one, the spring—April: the first space flight of man. I was then in the second grade. . . . Mankind conquered gravity and entered space, and that fact alone had to change the consciousness of mankind, its view of the earth: seeing it from above, how beautiful it was, how small. Much had to change.

One other potential superpower loomed on the distant horizon: the "Yellow Peril." "Optimists learn Russian; pessimists learn Chinese," I remember as a half-joke of my schooldays. But that was for the future. China's hour, we knew, had not yet come. Japan was not even mentioned in such a context. It was America and Russia that held our fate in their hands. And if Russia was the threat, America was the protector. For some Europeans of my generation, like Jacques Toubon, now general secretary of France's main governing party, the Gaullist *Rassemblement pour la République,* the memory goes all the way back to 1945, when he remembers as a four-year-old boy being given chewing gum and a can of condensed milk by American soldiers* in his hometown of Nice, on the French Riviera—a memory that left him, he says, with "a very nice feeling of, I think, love—with people who were at the moment liberating Europe, and France specially." It is therefore perhaps not surprising that years later, in the time of President Kennedy, the twenty-year-old Toubon would instinctively identify with America as against Russia.

TOUBON: It was the competition between the United States and the Soviet Union and we were in favor, in this competition, of the United States—like people who arc attending a basketball game: you know, we were in favor of our champion, and our champion was the United States. I think it's so simple as that.

*David Owen also remembers "as a small boy, calling out from the streets as they drove by in their lorries, 'Got any gum, chum?'—and then they would throw out pieces of chewing gum and we would scatter round and pick them up. That was in Wales, during the war."

But young West Germans, too, soon learned to have similar feelings about the United States. Irmgard Adam-Schwaetzer, now West German minister of state for foreign affairs, recalls growing up in the 1950s with a view of Russia as a threat.

ADAM-SCHWAETZER: [We saw Russia as a] continuous threat to Germany, and this meant also that the picture of the United States consequently—because every one of us conceived Russia and the United States as the big antagonists—so the picture of the United States was really as a patron for Germany, and it was a fairly widespread feeling that this was the patron we had to associate with.

For Matthias Wissmann, now economic affairs spokesman of the majority Christian Democratic Union, it was even more than that.

WISSMANN: For us as children America in the sixties and the fifties had been a world which was fantastic for us. I think the normal child in Germany, and growing later on as a teenager, thought that America is the country of hopes and dreams. . . . Germany's a small country, and the dream was such a big country. Do you know, it's clear that even John Wayne influenced this picture—wide and big, fascinating nature, riding horses. . . .

I had friends in my childhood, children of the American garrison in Ludwigsburg, so we had been playing together and I could talk with them and understand how they live.

Newt Gingrich, now a Republican congressman from Georgia, and a colorful, outspoken right-winger, could easily have been one of those garrison children, though as it happens his father's regiment was stationed in France, not Germany.

GINGRICH: One of the great training grounds of my life was as an eighth-grader and then a freshman in high school, living in Orléans, France: because in the late fifties there was still the bomb damage from World War II. . . .

My dad was a career soldier. . . . I think that he saw his career almost in the sense of a thin red line in northwest India, the sense that he was part of a green line of American troops that, in Korea and in Germany, mark the boundary of civilization and tyranny. . . .

My father's generation spent a lot of time in the fifties talking around the kitchen table with each other, and trying to think this through on the human level: "What am I doing with my life? Why is my family moving every two or three years? Why are we here?" And they really came to a sort of general sense: that was a period when Europe was rebuilding, Japan was rebuilding, and it really was an American peace. And I think frankly we kept it better in retrospect than at the time people felt we were doing—and if you look at it in the scale of world history, the [American] army in Germany has been the most successful army in history: forty years we've had no battles —and we've won. We've had a peaceful, free Western Europe, and that was our goal.

Most Americans, Gingrich feels, "have a terrific affection for Europe." And Joe Biden, the Democrat from Delaware, remembers, in the 1950s, his feelings about the people in postwar Europe.

BIDEN: [We almost felt] a little sorry for the West Europeans, in the sense that you'd gone through so much, your cities had been bombed, you had lost so many people in the war, and because around my home, growing up as a child, in grades one through seven or eight or nine, we had to do things for the Europeans. I mean, you know . . . care packages weren't packages that just went to some Third World country, they were—how did you help the poor people in Germany, who now were our allies, or those poor folks in Italy?—and could we do anything about those poor Hungarians who had been crushed again by the Soviets? And so on.

Among the recipients of those "care packages" were the families of David Owen, in Wales, and Ingrid Matthäus-Maier, now a Social Democratic member of parliament, in Germany.

OWEN: I remember during the war my uncle was a pediatrician in Cardiff, and a friend of his who was an American pediatrician always sent a food parcel for Christmas. And we would settle around this food parcel and absolutely . . . you know, things we'd never seen before: there was always a lovely smoked ham, sweets, and chewing gum, and lollipops—oh, the whole sort of American thing which we as kids never normally saw.

MATTHÄUS-MAIER: My uncle is American—he emigrated during the twenties, he went to America and he worked up from being nothing —and he sent, in 1945, 1946, 1947, the so-called "care packages" to my parents; and the first things I learned about Americans is that we got nutrition and all sorts of clothes from the Americans; and therefore "Americans" was for me always something very positive.

INTENTIONS

Though all that would seem normal and inevitable to us as adolescents in the 1950s, almost none of it would have been easily predictable at the time when I was born. A very different world is depicted, for instance, in the issue of the London *Times* of December 28, 1943, on the front page of which my parents—following the well-worn convention of the English upper-middle class—inserted an announcement of my birth. On that same front page another small advertisement declares:

> HALF OF RUSSIA'S WOUNDED HORSES CAN BE SAVED, if only you will help the RSPCA* send surgical dressings. . . . Russia's horses, repelling panzers, are suffering terrible hardships.

The lead news item (printed in those days inside the paper, on the left-center page opposite the editorials) is headed GERMAN ROUT IN KIEV SALIENT. And on page three, devoted to "Imperial and Foreign" news, appears an extensive report of President Roosevelt's Christmas Eve broadcast, most of it devoted to the Cairo and Teheran conferences, from which the president had recently returned:

> " . . . Mr. Churchill and I have happily met many times before. . . . The Cairo and Teheran conferences, however, gave me my first opportunity to meet the Generalissimo, Chiang Kai-shek, and Marshal Stalin, and to sit down at the table with these unconquerable men and talk with them face to face. . . .
>
> "We did discuss international relationships from the point of view of big, broad objectives rather than details. But on the basis of what we did discuss, I can say even today that I do not think any insoluble differences will arise among Russia, Great Britain and the United States.
>
> "To use an American and ungrammatical colloquialism, I may say that I 'got along fine' with Marshal Stalin. He is a man who combines a tremendous, relentless determination with a stalwart good humour. I believe he is truly representative of the heart and soul of Russia; and I believe that we are going to get along with him and the Russian people—very well indeed."

Valentin Berezhkov, now a handsome and still-vigorous septuagenarian, was actually Stalin's interpreter at that first meeting in Teheran.

*Royal Society for the Prevention of Cruelty to Animals.

BEREZHKOV: The relationship between Stalin and Roosevelt was really a very special relationship. . . . When they met, you know, it looked like they have known each other for a very long time. There was no formality. You know that Roosevelt stayed at our embassy because of security reasons, and the conference itself was also in the Soviet embassy in Teheran—and they met before the conference started . . . and they met without Churchill. So what was interesting in this meeting, first of all it was very informal—you know, it was like really they knew each other. I think that because they had a very intensive correspondence—since 1941 they wrote to each other, sometimes twice a week, about some supplies, about victories, about taking or losing a city, about the situation in the Pacific, everything: sometimes just congratulations for some victories, or sending each other photographs, pictures, or portraits of their own with some signatures, "To my friend Stalin" or "To my friend Roosevelt," something like that—so this created, you know, a very informal relationship, and they met also like old friends or at any rate people who knew each other for a long time.

Just over a year later—and only two months before his own death—Roosevelt would meet again with Stalin and Churchill, at Yalta in the Crimea, in February 1945. Once again, Roosevelt and Stalin "got along fine." The atmosphere was, according to Alger Hiss, a member of the U.S. delegation, highly convivial. Hiss's career was to be ruined after the war when he was accused of having passed classified information to Soviet agents during the 1930s, denied this under oath before a congressional committee, and was then convicted of perjury and sent to prison. He has fought ever since to clear his name. By the time I met him in 1986 he was a frail old man of eighty-two, speaking with difficulty owing to a throat complaint, yet coming alive with passion as he recalled the hopeful atmosphere of early 1945, when he was an up-and-coming figure in the State Department, a fervent New Dealer and admirer of FDR, with whom he had worked directly on the plans for the new United Nations Organization. This is how he recalled the Crimean conference.

HISS: We were in a beautiful summer spa, in the middle of winter. We were housed in *dachas,* or country houses. Each delegation had its own country house with its own staff of cooks and waiters. The Russians had commandeered three hotels and brought all their personnel . . . and all the napery, chinaware, everything that was needed, and the food was quite good. So we could invite our counterparts to a meal if we chose, and vice versa. Also three young women added to the lightness of tone: Churchill's daughter was there, Sarah Oliver; Anna Boettiger, Roosevelt's daughter; and Kathleen Harriman, Averell Harriman's daughter.* So that often the atmosphere was that of a country house party, and Roosevelt's good humor and really irrepressible jollity—even though he had been tired when he arrived his spirits had revived, and he was really like the father figure at a country house party.

That I'm sure had a lot to do with the relaxation of the mood but in addition there was the belief that the postwar world had to be different from the world of before, which had been responsible for bringing on the vast carnage and terrifying destruction of the war itself. This was what led to hope, to idealism, to a belief that things not only had to be better but in fact could be better. . . .

There was . . . something which came to be known as the "spirit of Yalta," which . . . looked to the future, not with negativism, not with foreboding, but with a belief that somehow the three great powers could preserve a semblance of unity. In the speeches by Churchill, Stalin, and Roosevelt, particularly Stalin and Churchill, the phrases "unity of the great powers," "the need to preserve unity," were a constant refrain, and it certainly played a part in the belief of those of us who left Yalta with spirits of . . . of jubilation really, that we had accomplished a nearly impossible task in bringing about cooperation, accommodation for the future.

So ardent, indeed, was Roosevelt's courtship of Stalin that it seemed sometimes to be carried on at Britain's expense. Berezhkov recalls their first meeting in Teheran.

BEREZHKOV: Because this meeting was in the absence of Churchill, I think that Roosevelt on purpose wanted to create an impression that he would like to have an intimate relationship with Stalin; and in this very first meeting that they had, among many other things that they discussed—about the situation at the fronts, about the agenda of the conference, all kinds of things—Roosevelt raised also the question of colonial empires after the war: what will happen with colonial empires. And he immediately said, you know, "I raise this question with you in the absence of our good friend Churchill, because he doesn't like such kind of talk. . . ."

Stalin was very cautious, you know. He didn't want to be involved in this kind of situation, especially because when Molotov† went to

*Harriman was U.S. ambassador to Moscow at the time.
†Vyacheslav Molotov, Soviet foreign minister.

Berlin in November 1940, the first thing that Hitler told him was that "the British empire is doomed" and that "we have now to discuss what will be the fate of the British empire after the war"—and here some two years pass and now Roosevelt approaches Stalin and asks what is going to happen to the British empire and whether we should discuss it in the absence of Churchill. So Stalin was really rather cautious. He said—well, he agreed that for people who are not involved in these colonies it may be easier to discuss it than for people who want to preserve these empires, but he didn't go into the discussion of this whole thing, because, I think, he was very much interested in preserving this coalition and didn't want to have troubles and problems with Churchill.

Frank Roberts, a British Foreign Office official specializing in the problems of Central and Eastern Europe, was not at Teheran but did attend the Yalta conference. Immediately afterward he took up his post as British minister in Moscow. Later in his career he was to be ambassador successively in Yugoslavia, the Soviet Union, and West Germany. Now in his eighties, he is a very small man physically but still endowed with astonishing energy and a crystal-clear memory. He is eager to defend the Yalta conference, and especially the British role in it.

ROBERTS: Roosevelt was so anxious to get Stalin into his thinking on the United Nations, and above all to get Stalin to promise to come into the war against Japan, that he wanted to remove any idea that there was a special Anglo-American agreement and a special Roosevelt-Churchill relationship from which he was excluded. And in order to put this across he did go rather out of his way to—I won't quite say "insult" —but to rather play down Churchill; and there were occasions when, with Stalin there, he would say, "Well, you know, Mr. Stalin, we don't need to pay too much attention to this great imperialist here, we don't quite go along with his ideas. . . ."

And once he went so far in this direction that Churchill got very angry, because he thought first of all it was insulting, and secondly he thought it was bad tactics vis-à-vis Stalin. And he got up in real indignation and was walking out of the room. And it wasn't Roosevelt who brought him back: it was Stalin who brought him back and said, "No, no, Mr. Churchill, we admire you greatly as a war leader—I am sure the president was only joking!"

Certainly, then, there was nothing premeditated, at any rate on the American side, about the bitter East-West conflict that was to develop after Germany and Japan had been defeated. Was there, on the contrary, a Soviet-American concordat to carve up Europe and the world between them? Maurice Couve de Murville, a senior French official at the time, later foreign minister and prime minister under de Gaulle, believes so.

COUVE DE MURVILLE: As regards the United Nations, it was an agreement between the United States and the Soviet Union to share the world. I mean, it was decided that they were the big powers, that they dominated the world . . . and the world was either divided between them or under their common domination.

But this is surely an exaggeration. Sir Frank Roberts recalls the assumptions shared at the time by British and American officials:

ROBERTS: People were not going into the postwar world in 1945 with the plan which eventually emerged, of accepting the division of Europe (which we had to) and building up Western Europe and then getting America back into Europe—that wasn't the plan at that time at all. In fact, at Yalta Roosevelt made it clear to Churchill, and unfortunately also to Stalin, that it was his firm intention that the American troops would leave Europe within a year or two after the end of the war. And it was partly because of that that Churchill insisted so very much on France being given a role in Germany, which neither Stalin nor Roosevelt wanted her to have: because Churchill realized Britain alone—I mean, if the Americans were going to withdraw—in a Europe that was terribly weakened by the war, just wouldn't be able to produce a balance for the Soviet Union.

The idea of a peacetime involvement of America in Europe, Roberts recalls, was in conflict with tradition.

ROBERTS: . . . the whole tradition of the United States ever since its inception. I mean, the founding fathers in the eighteenth century had said that America must never get mixed up with Europeans, she must never have peacetime alliances. The Monroe Doctrine was to keep them away from all that kind of thing.

Ernest Gross, who as an officer in the Pentagon dealt with the economic affairs of liberated Europe and occupied Germany, was later to become a senior official in the Truman administration, winning support for its Cold War policies both in Congress and at the United

Nations. After that he returned to private law practice. He remains a convinced internationalist, but a comfortable, establishment figure, with none of Alger Hiss's deep personal need to condemn the Cold War and defend the "spirit of Yalta." But he confirms that the U.S. intention was to withdraw from Europe as quickly as possible.

GROSS: We assumed that there would be a gradual relinquishment of occupation duties. In terms of local military government missions in cities, towns, villages, the whole project was to reestablish local civilian government as rapidly as possible. General Marshall, who was chief of staff, had one rule, which he gave personally to some of his section chiefs, and that was that the first duty of military government was to get out of business as soon as possible. That was his motto, and that was our objective. So it is rather ironic now to find, after all these years, the 350,000 or so American troops on the Continent.

Did no one then realize that Soviet influence in Eastern Europe might have to be balanced by America exercising a predominant influence in Western Europe? No, says Alger Hiss.

HISS: I would think not. We were all so aware of the strength of the mood for independence and regaining the nation on the part of France and Italy, and the independent strength of Great Britain, that I think it was far from our imagination that Western Europe could be a sphere of influence of the United States.

It was Great Britain, in Roosevelt's mind, that would share with Russia the main responsibility for security in postwar Europe. According to Arthur Schlesinger, Jr., one of today's leading historians of that period who himself served in U.S. military intelligence during the war, the United States "saw itself as one of the three powers, along with Britain and the Soviet Union, and with kind of marginal roles for France and China, which would provide world leadership—leadership in the new realm, the new international organization.

It was understood, however, that the Big Three would not be equally big.

SCHLESINGER: Obviously the United States and the Soviet Union were the emerging two, the two great powers—because of population, because of military strength, because of economic strength. I mean, this was Great Britain's last great fight, but it was not expected to assume the same role in the post–Second World War world that it had played for the century or two preceding.

Churchill himself said that he "realised at Teheran for the first time what a small nation we are. . . . There I sat with the great Russian bear on one side of me, with paws outstretched, and on the other the great American buffalo, and between the two sat the poor little British donkey, who was the only one, the only one of the three, who knew the right way home."[1]

Oliver Franks, during the war a senior official at the British Ministry of Supply, had—indeed still has—an unusually sharp, clear, logical mind. He was in many ways the ideal civil servant, always understanding exactly what was required of him by his political masters and finding a way to achieve it with the minimum of fuss. He was later to play a key role in coordinating the European response to the Marshall Plan. Later still he would be ambassador in Washington, head of two Oxford colleges, chairman of innumerable committees and commissions of inquiry, often on very sensitive subjects. Today, in his early eighties, he remains an authoritative yet modest, even austere, figure. He has written no memoirs but is willing to answer questions about the past with the same care and precision that he applied to them when they were problems of the present and immediate future.

I asked Lord Franks how far he had been aware, at the end of the war, that Britain was a power in decline.

FRANKS: Well, I knew, I think very clearly, that at the end of the war two superpowers had emerged, one the United States and one the Soviet, and that Britain couldn't match either. This had been obvious even in the course of the war when gradually the troops and the navies of the United States far exceeded our own. And further I knew that our economic base had been weakened. We'd lost all sorts of overseas markets. We'd piled up very large debts in sterling to other countries, to India, to Egypt, and so forth. . . . Therefore our problem was, with whom would we be friends? Now for Churchill it was fairly clear. He mistrusted Russia—he didn't know about it. He looked for fraternal association with the United States. It wasn't the same with Attlee and Bevin and the Labour government they formed in 1945. They hoped that there would be friendly relations with both the Soviet Union and the United States, and they weren't sure that there would be friendly relations with either.

MORTIMER: This eclipse of Britain: did you think of it as something permanent, or only temporary?

FRANKS: I didn't use the word "eclipse." Nor would I use it. I would use a different phrase in relation to the United States: "unequal partners." We were unequal. Remember, at the time the United States disposed of 50 percent of the entire productive power of the world. We —nothing like that. But the astonishing thing was that after the war we retained global commitments—we were expected by the Americans to retain them. We played a role in the world. And when I was in Washington, we were unequal *partners*—first to be consulted, and doing things with the Americans in various parts up and down the world.

MORTIMER: How far was the wider British public aware that Britain's period as number one world power had come to an end?

FRANKS: My impression is that the wider British public was not aware of it. I think when the war ended they hoped that things would be broadly as they'd been before: we at the center of a great Commonwealth, with an empire—recovering our markets, holding our place in the world—they hoped that this would be so, and they didn't realize either the extent to which these vast armaments and powers had been created in America and in the Soviet Union, nor the extent to which our resources had been weakened and depleted by the war itself.

MORTIMER: And when did the penny drop?

FRANKS: The penny very slowly dropped, but finally—and with a clang—in 1956: Suez. That was the end.

The decline of Britain and the domination of the world by two superpowers were thus at least partially perceived at the end of the war—though better by the policy-making elite than by the public at large. But the bitter conflict between the superpowers and the division of Europe between the rival camps was not generally expected—especially not by the Americans—still less intended by policy-makers either in London or in Washington. But what about Germany itself? After fighting two world wars within thirty years to defeat German expansionism, did the Allies not quite deliberately partition Germany in order to prevent any further recurrence? The witticism of François Mauriac—"I love Germany so much, I'm delighted there are two of her"—was quoted approvingly in public by the Italian foreign minister as recently as 1985, and surely reflects the private feelings of many other European leaders, particularly those old enough to remember the Nazi occupation of their countries. How much stronger must such feelings have been at the time, among those actively engaged in the war against Hitler. It is hard to believe that the postwar division of Germany was a purely accidental by-product of the unforeseen East-West conflict.

Certainly at the Teheran conference all three Allied leaders—Churchill, Roosevelt, and Stalin—were talking, albeit rather vaguely, in terms of a dismembered Germany. Roosevelt suggested a possible plan involving the division of Germany into five parts, plus two regions placed under international control for the benefit of all Europe. Stalin (according to the British and American, but not the Soviet, record) expressed himself "in favor of dismemberment," but said teasingly that Churchill would object to discussing this since *he* wanted Germany to remain united. Churchill denied this, saying he was interested in detaching Prussia from the rest of Germany, because Prussia and its military class were "the root of the evil." Prussia should be destroyed, he said, while the inhabitants of the rest of Germany should be offered the option of inclusion in a "Danubian Confederation" (which, he explains in his memoirs, he saw as a revival of the old Austro-Hungarian empire). Stalin opposed this, saying that if Germany was going to be dismembered, they had better do a proper job, and he therefore preferred Roosevelt's plan to Churchill's. He agreed with Churchill, however, that this discussion could only be a "preliminary survey" of a vast problem, and no definite conclusion was reached.[2]

The following year Roosevelt's secretary of the treasury, Henry Morgenthau, Jr., produced his famous plan for eliminating the metallurgical, chemical, and electric industries in the Ruhr and the Saar and "converting Germany into a country primarily agricultural and pastoral in its character." Roosevelt and Churchill were both persuaded to put their signatures to this at the Quebec conference of September 1944. (But not, it should be noted, to Morgenthau's accompanying territorial proposals, under which Poland was to receive Upper Silesia and part of East Prussia [the remainder going to the Soviet Union]; France, the Saar and adjacent territories; and Denmark the area north of the Kiel Canal; while the canal itself and the Ruhr were to become an international zone, forbidden to trade with either of the two independent states, north and south, into which the remainder of Germany would be divided.) Both, however, were soon persuaded to withdraw their approval by their respective advisers, who realized that a completely impoverished and largely unemployed German population would cause more problems to the rest of Europe than one capable of earning its own living.[3]

But the idea of dismembering Germany politically remained very much alive. Although both the U.S. State Department and the British Foreign Office were against it—fearing that it would result in the permanent alienation of the German people and thus make it more difficult to wean them away from Nazism and revanchist aspirations —all three Allied leaders at the Yalta conference again declared themselves in favor of it, and it was agreed to amend the terms of surrender to be imposed on Germany so as to state explicitly that the three powers would "take such steps including the complete disarmament, demilitarisation *and the dismemberment* [italics added] of Germany as they deem requisite for future peace and security."[4] The "study of the procedure for the dismemberment of Germany" was referred to a committee comprising the British foreign secretary and the American and Soviet ambassadors in London.

All these proposals seem to have stemmed from a mixture of sheer vindictiveness toward the Germans, genuine desire to prevent the revival of Germany as an expansionist military power, and anxiety (particularly on Churchill's part) to rebut any suggestion or suspicion of pro-German sentiment or softness toward the common enemy emanating from either of the other two leaders. Only the British military Chiefs of Staff, in late 1944, gave as a reason for favoring a divided Germany the argument that it might prove necessary to recruit the western portions of that country into an alliance against Russia.[5] They were well ahead of their time. In the weeks after Yalta, when the American and British armies began breaking through the German lines much faster than foreseen (while at the same time Stalin's aims and methods in Eastern Europe were becoming much clearer), mutual suspicion between the Allies did for the first time become an important determinant of policy for all three of them. But its effect was to make them give *lower* priority to the idea of partitioning Germany, and indeed very soon to abandon it altogether. While Churchill was more doubtful than ever ("I hardly like to consider dismembering Germany until my doubts about Russia's intentions have been cleared away," he wrote in March 1945), Stalin seems suddenly to have conceived either the fear that the British and Americans might steal a march on him by secretly promising the Germans that their country would not after all be partitioned, or the hope that if Germany remained a single unit during the traumatic period of defeat and its immediate aftermath, there was a good chance that all of it would end up under a Communist or pro-Communist government. On March 26, at a meeting of the tripartite European Advisory Commission in London, the Soviet ambassador stated that his government did not regard the Yalta decision on dismemberment of Germany as obligatory, but rather as a possible way of exercising pressure to make Germany harmless if other means proved insufficient. At the same time the tone of the Soviet press and propaganda toward the Germans softened perceptibly, making a much clearer distinction than in the past between the Nazi regime and the German people as such. Finally, on May 9, in his victory proclamation after the German surrender, Stalin said that the Soviet Union "does not intend either to dismember or to destroy Germany"; and neither the British nor the Americans made any attempt to keep dismemberment on the agenda.[6]

In retrospect, both British and American officials involved in wartime planning for the future of Germany insist that they did not take the dismemberment proposals all that seriously. Ernest Gross says that his work was concerned with reconstruction, and brushes aside questions about the Morgenthau Plan.

GROSS: Oh, he was overborne very quickly. I was in the Pentagon at that time, and we were horrified by what we called the Treasury view, which was really Morgenthau's view and certain of his assistants', of what he called pastoralizing Germany: we realized that we were buying another Treaty of Versailles.* I mean it was that obvious to those of us who were planning. The State Department agreed thoroughly, the State and War departments were of one mind on that. Morgenthau never had a chance with Roosevelt on that one.

MORTIMER: And you thought in terms of a united Germany after the war?

GROSS: Entirely, entirely. The division of Germany—indeed, the division of Europe—would have been a horrifying spectacle if it ever had occurred to us as a possibility. That was a postwar development.

Sir Frank Roberts, who was acting head of the Central Department of the British Foreign Office, is equally categorical.

ROBERTS: Of course there were all kinds of odd ideas, in fact at one point you may remember there was the Morgenthau Plan for pastoralizing Germany, and Churchill's idea of breaking it up into about five states, a Danubian federation and all the rest of it. This was never Foreign Office thinking at all, and it wasn't even Churchill's thinking for very long—wasn't really serious.

MORTIMER: How difficult was it to overcome such extreme proposals?

ROBERTS: As I remember it, not very. Morgenthau, of course—first of all, he was a Jew and therefore very strongly anti-Germany, as you

*The settlement after World War I, which had left international economic relations bedeviled by Germany's inability to pay the reparations imposed on her.

can well imagine—and he'd produced this idea of turning Germany entirely into an agricultural state. I mean, all industry was to be destroyed, or given to the Russians, or taken from them, and they were left to do sheep-farming and that. Well, I mean, plainly, this was quite out of the question because after all we had to start building up German industry immediately after the war, or the alternatives were . . . we would have had to feed them. So that didn't really get very far—but at one moment Churchill had been over at some meeting with Roosevelt and was a little bit attracted by it, but it never seemed very serious, and we didn't take it too seriously at the Foreign Office. . . .

But what was a little more serious was, Churchill had this historical imagination: he was saying, "We can't have Prussia again." I think myself he was rather unfair to the Prussians; in fact, they're not the worst Germans by any manner of means—but Prussia as a great part of Germany had to be destroyed. And this meant other things, and he thought, well, you know, the old Austro-Hungarian empire hadn't been so dangerous, and so a Danubian monarchy—and that would deal with Bavaria; and then the Rhineland—you know there had been a sort of Rhenish Confederation under Napoleon, and he was thinking rather in those terms. But they were never the basis of any serious planning, and were never pursued very hard by Churchill himself.

MORTIMER: Was there no undercurrent of feeling among Allied leaders in 1945 that they were pleased at Germany being split?

ROBERTS: Certainly not those with whom I was dealing. . . . After all, the planning was done in the European advisory group during the war, which was Russian-American-British, for the occupation of Germany. And this was the scheme that was approved at Yalta by Churchill and Roosevelt and by Stalin—and there was no question of dividing Germany. It was to be run as a unit from Berlin, but with the various military zones, which were not intended to be a means of dividing the country. In the event they became that, but that was not the intention.

Indeed, as so often in history, the grandiose thoughts of the political leaders about the long-term future came to nothing, while administrative arrangements made by officials for the immediate future proved to be of lasting significance. As the French say, *Il n'y a que le provisoire qui dure.* What was eventually to become the border between East and West Germany—and therefore between the Free World and the Soviet bloc—was first drawn on a map by a group of British officials chaired by Gladwyn Jebb (now Lord Gladwyn), in 1943. Gladwyn, who retired as ambassador to Paris in 1960, subsequently joined the Liberal party in order to campaign for a stronger British commitment to European unity. In his late eighties he was still Liberal spokesman on foreign policy and security matters and a trenchant critic of President Reagan's Strategic Defense Initiative—but equally happy to reminisce about his exploits of the 1940s.

> GLADWYN: I was the chairman of the Post-Hostilities Planning Subcommittee of the Chiefs of Staff. We were supposed to think about the future and all that in a strategic sense and so on, and we were instructed to draw up a plan for the division of the old Reich into three equal parts. I wasn't responsible for that decision—I don't quite know who was—but I know that as chairman I thought that was a sensible thing to do, because nobody knew at the beginning of 1943 whether we would arrive on the Rhine before the Russians or whether the Russians were going to be before us. . . . And that is what we did, and we had various experts there who devised the actual line, in relation to the *Kreise* [districts] and the various divisions of Germany existing at the time. Then I think our plan went to the ministerial committee [a Cabinet committee chaired by the Labour leader Clement Attlee, then deputy prime minister], who blessed it.

In fact the plan put 40 percent of pre-1937 German territory and 36 percent of German population under Soviet control. According to Sir William (later Lord) Strang, who presented the British proposals to the first meeting of the three-power European Advisory Commission in January 1944, the British hoped thereby both to ensure Soviet cooperation and to limit the cost to themselves of the occupation. The Russians quickly accepted the zonal boundaries proposed by the British: this seemed at the time a good deal from the Western point of view, since there were as yet no Anglo-American forces in northern Europe and it appeared unlikely that Western troops would beat the Red Army to the Elbe. But things changed in March–April 1945, when Anglo-American forces advanced with surprising rapidity into the heart of Germany, crossing the Elbe and the Mulde and liberating cities as far east as Wittenberg, Magdeburg, Leipzig, and Erfurt (all of them well inside what is now East Germany).[7] At the same time there was acute concern in both London and Washington about the way that Stalin was implementing (or not implementing) the agreements reached at Yalta on Poland and the other "liberated" countries of Eastern Europe.

> GLADWYN: We could have said if we wanted to, or the government could have said, "You have torn up the declaration on liberated Europe

> and so on: we're going to tear up—not going to abide by—the agreement on the zones. We shall stay where we are." In which case, of course, they would not have been able to have any Deutsche Demokratische Republik, that wouldn't have been possible—too small a part of Germany would have been in Russian hands. (The Russians would, of course, have hung on to East Prussia and Berlin—and we'd never have got them out of Vienna.) Indeed, Churchill considered that—but it was quite impossible politically to do that. The Russians at that time were regarded by the people here—and indeed in America—as the people who'd won the war, and so they had: if it hadn't been for the Russians beating Hitler, we'd all have been in salt mines after all in this country. And so, therefore, the popular view was that the Russians had won, were largely responsible for winning the war, and you couldn't really go back on an agreement for dividing up Germany—more especially as it still was the intention, in spite of what the Russians' behavior had been after Yalta, it still was the intention to work with them and try and get agreement with them on the control of Germany after the war. If you had wished to tear up the zones, it would have been impossible to get it through the House of Commons, or indeed through Congress.

So the division into zones was respected. American and British troops pulled back, in June 1945, to the line drawn by Gladwyn Jebb's subcommittee in early 1943, and were allowed by the Russians to occupy their agreed sectors in Berlin and Vienna. Roosevelt by this time was dead, but his successor, Harry S. Truman, prepared to meet Churchill and Stalin in July, at Potsdam, on the outskirts of Berlin.* Truman was convinced, as his representative told Churchill, "that without continued unity of the Big Three there could be no reasonable prospect of peace."[9]

WHAT WENT WRONG

How, then, did the actual Europe we grew up in turn out so different from the one envisaged and intended by Allied leaders during the war? With hindsight, in the view of the American historian Arthur Schlesinger, it is not so surprising.

*Morgenthau resigned as secretary of the treasury because Truman would not allow him to come to Potsdam. " 'All right,' I replied, 'if that is the way you feel, I'll accept your resignation right now.' And I did. That was the end of the conversation and the end of the Morgenthau Plan." Truman adds simply that "those of us who looked into it did not think much of his plan. I did not like it."[8]

SCHLESINGER: You had the situation where the Second World War left great vacuums of power in the world. The defeat of the Axis powers, the exhaustion of the triumphant West European states, like Britain, France, and so on, the collapse and dissolution of the colonial empires, left great vacuums of power with only two powers that had the military strength, the economic potentiality, and the ideological dynamism to fill the vacuums—and they were the United States and the Soviet Union. In addition to which they were divided very sharply by concepts of personal freedom and concepts of democracy as against dictatorship and the like. So I think really the surprise isn't that there was a Cold War, it would have been if there had been no Cold War, given that combination of geopolitical and ideological conflicts.

From the Soviet perspective, Valentin Berezhkov reaches a somewhat similar conclusion.

BEREZHKOV: As far as we were concerned, we have always been thinking about cooperation on an equal footing—that we should be accepted as an equal partner—and that was very important, especially because in the interim period between the two world wars we were looked upon as some outcast. You know, our new system that emerged after the war was not accepted by many in the West: many have been thinking, "This is some temporary historical mistake, and something will happen and Russia will become again capitalist like everybody else"; and actually also the idea of Hitler and his promise to destroy Bolshevism was looked upon with sympathy by many people in the West . . . and during the war also we had the feeling that we were still looked upon as a partner, as an ally, but not quite an equal ally, and there were different examples. Of course, the most important that I could give is the Second Front, which actually was started only in 1944 after three years of fighting between the Germans and the Russians, while there was no other fighting in Europe and only we carried this burden. . . . The attitude was that the Soviet Union and the Germans should fight each other as long as possible, so that by the end of the war Germany would be destroyed, the Soviet Union would be weakened, and then, of course, the postwar period . . . was certainly visualized by the British and by the Americans in the sense that the Soviet Union would be a weak and half-destroyed country and with enormous losses: so the Americans and the British will arrange the world after the war in a way as they like it, and the Soviet Union should accept it. . . . For us, it was important that we are considered as equal partners, and not some inferior country which at that time was helping to fight the Germans but after the war it would be different.

It was over Eastern Europe that the ideological and political conflicts first came into the open. British officials like Frank Roberts had long been aware of the overriding priority that Stalin gave to asserting exclusive Soviet influence in this area.

ROBERTS: The Russians had been immensely—what shall I say?—all the time they were wanting exactly the same thing. I went to Moscow in 1939 with William Strang on that mission to try and get the Russians to come with us to prevent the war, and those negotiations broke down on two things. The first was Stalin wanting us to agree that he should have—he didn't quite put it this way, but in fact to have—control of the Baltic states, which at that time were independent countries. And I well remember the French ambassador with whom we were negotiating, when we told him that there was no provision for saying anything to the Russians about the Baltic States, he said, "Well, we're wasting our time"—because that had been part of czarist Russia and Stalin wanted it back. Again—rather more reasonably, because we were saying, "We want you, the Russians, to help the Poles to resist a German military attack"—he [Stalin] not unnaturally said, "Well, in that case, obviously my troops have to have the right to move into Poland." Well, the Poles, in view of the history between Poland and Russia, the last thing they wanted was to have any Russian troops in their country. But what Stalin really wanted was to reestablish Russian control. . . of what was then eastern Poland, in other words, the other side of the Curzon Line. He didn't mention to us actually Bessarabia and northern Bukovina,* but he did, of course, when they were talking to Ribbentrop at the same time.

And, of course, once the war had come, what did Stalin get from the Germans? He took them, I mean, but with German agreement he got: the Baltic states, the eastern provinces of Poland, Bessarabia, and Bukovina, and—after the Finnish war—bits of Finland. . . . But then he lost them again, you see, when Hitler invaded Russia.

When I went to Moscow with Anthony Eden [then foreign secretary] in December 1941—the German armies were, I think, at that time fifteen kilometers from the center of Moscow: as we now know, the German attack had, in fact, stopped, but there was no particular reason to assume that at that moment—when we started the talks, we were concerned with what did we do about Turkey and Iran, and how did we get arms to the Russians to go on fighting—I mean, were they going to give up? Well, almost the first thing Stalin asked for, he

*Territories then part of Rumania. Before the First World War Bessarabia had been part of czarist Russia; Bukovina had been in the Hungarian half of the Habsburg empire, but was now claimed by the Soviet Union as being an integral part of the western Ukraine.

said, "Mr. Eden, I want your agreement at the end of the war"—*he* was thinking of the end of the war, we weren't yet thinking of it!—"that Russia should get back the Baltic states and" (the eastern provinces of Poland—he didn't describe them as such) "and Bukovina and Bessarabia." . . . So that when later on we had the problem of having the Poles as our allies and the Russians as our allies, it was fairly clear that we were up against considerable difficulties in getting any agreement. . . .

And sure enough, when the Red Army began to move forward and, as they have said, "liberated"—whereas other people would say "occupied"—Eastern Europe, it was pretty plain that once they had the military strength they were going to take all these areas which they regarded as having been part of the Russian empire.

So we realized all this, but plainly we had to make the best deal we could for Poland. On paper we did make a deal which was perfectly defensible—we, of course, were not by any means sure that it was going to work in practice, but that's all diplomats can do. I mean, we were then operating in a world of armies that were occupying countries. At the time of Yalta the Russian army had gone right through Poland and was well into Germany. And the same thing applies to the other parts of Eastern Europe. . . . I remember Tito telling me—I was ambassador in Yugoslavia from 1954, and in 1956, at the time of the Hungarian uprising, I was talking to Tito. . . . So I said to him rather innocently or naively, why was it that Hungary couldn't be a neutral country leaning toward the East? And Tito said, "But you've lived in Russia, surely you know the Russians will never accept that: you've got to be on their side or not." He said, "You and I wouldn't be talking here today if I hadn't first of all liberated Belgrade myself, and then got the Russians very rapidly out of Yugoslavia and into Hungary. Otherwise I would be caught just like the others."

So we knew it was going to be a sphere of interest, but we did hope, or think, that if Russia could be got to cooperate generally in the economic reconstruction, benefiting from it in the United Nations scheme of things, she would behave better in defending her interests in Eastern Europe. Many of us were skeptical about that, but it was a possibility, or seemed to be.

I asked Alger Hiss, who attended the Yalta conference as a U.S. State Department official working on the plans for the new United Nations Organization, whether it was true that Roosevelt had been prepared to grant Stalin a sphere of influence in Eastern Europe as the price of his cooperation in this project, to which Roosevelt attached such great importance.

HISS: That's a difficult question to ponder and to answer in the precise terms that you have put it. I think those of us working on the United Nations aspects felt that the Russians would insist that the old *cordon sanitaire* [the belt of small Eastern European states supported by France and hostile to Communist Russia] which had been set up at the time of the League of Nations [i.e., after the First World War] would be eliminated. That meant almost certainly that they would insist upon "friendly" regimes in Eastern Europe. Before the Yalta conference Stalin and Churchill had their own separate meeting at which something very like a sphere of influence was granted to Stalin, and Greece to be a sphere of influence for Great Britain.* It was an informal and rather strange arrangement. . . . The State Department and United States in general were opposed to spheres of influence per se, so that we did not at Yalta grant actual spheres of influence. But, as I said, there was a recognition that the ancient *cordon sanitaire,* which had facilitated Hitler's invasion of Russia, since all the Balkan states had become dictatorships under Hitler's aegis—this, we in the United Nations element of the State Department recognized, would have to be eliminated. . . .

The seeming acceptance of the insistence by the Russians on "friendly" states [in Eastern Europe] in a sense meant states they had as much influence over as we have had in the past under the Monroe Doctrine over Latin American states. Secretary of War Stimson,† who was one of the wisest, most levelheaded men in the Roosevelt cabinet, said that he saw no objection to the Yalta settlement and compared it to the Monroe Doctrine. He thought the Russians would wish to have some buffer to protect them from invasion. After all, Napoleon had invaded them, the Germans in World War I, and then Hitler through this same corridor in World War II.

But it was difficult for the British to take quite such a sympathetic view of the Soviet position, at any rate on Poland, as Sir Frank Roberts explains.

*This was the famous "percentage agreement" of October 1944. Churchill proposed, and Stalin accepted, that Russia should have "ninety percent predominance" in Rumania and 75 percent in Bulgaria, while Britain ("in accord with USA") got 90 percent in Greece and they went "fifty-fifty" in Yugoslavia and Hungary.[10] Churchill was thus prepared to legitimize Stalin's control of the Balkans (though not of Poland) in order to secure a free hand for himself in Greece. Berezhkov's account of what happened there is not much exaggerated: "When the British landed there at the end of 1944 actually the whole country was liberated by the resistance movement, and in the resistance movement the most active fighters were the Communists; and when the British came they have arrested many of the Communists and sent them to the former German concentration camps on the Greek islands; and they brought the king, and actually forced him on Greece—and this was considered lawful!"

†Colonel Henry L. Stimson, secretary of war under Roosevelt, and under Truman until September 1945.

ROBERTS: As the war went on we had to think about Poland and Eastern Europe, because, when all was said and done, we'd gone into the war as allies to Poland. We did not commit ourselves to restore Poland within the boundaries that it had before the war, because we in 1920 had thought that she should have the Curzon Line* boundaries, which, of course, put us in a rather difficult position when the Russians were brought into the war and we had these two very difficult allies. But we were trying very hard to get a Russo-Polish settlement while the Russians were still on the defensive—before, as it were, they were reoccupying Poland—difficult though it obviously always was going to be. . . .

Now there were disappointments. I mean, Churchill, of course, was very disappointed over Poland. . . . First of all it was Katyn† and the [Soviet] break of relations with Sikorski's‡ government, but I think most of all in 1944 when the Russians reached Warsaw and stopped on the other bank [of the Vistula], having encouraged the Poles to rise in Warsaw: they now say that they were exhausted and couldn't move any farther forward, but anyway they left the Poles to be massacred by the Germans.

Not surprisingly, Poland proved one of the most difficult issues between the Allies at both Teheran and Yalta. Both Churchill and Roosevelt would have liked to obtain Soviet recognition of the Polish government-in-exile in London in return for acceptance of the Curzon Line as the Polish-Soviet frontier (with territorial compensation for Poland in the west at Germany's expense). But Roosevelt told Stalin, in a private conversation during the Teheran conference, that he could not "participate in any decision" on these matters, or "take part publicly" in any arrangement, until after the 1944 presidential election, for fear of alienating the six or seven million American voters

*This was the line proposed by Lord Curzon, British foreign secretary, during the Russo-Polish war of 1920 as the basis for an armistice, at a moment when Russia appeared to be winning. The Poles never accepted it, and were able to obtain a frontier much farther east when the tide of battle turned in their favor.

†"On 5 April 1943 the Germans announced that they had found the bodies of over 10,000 Polish officers who had been taken prisoner by the Russians in 1939 and cold-bloodedly murdered. The bodies had been discovered buried in a wood at Katyn, not far from Smolensk. Since the Poles themselves had long been trying to trace several thousand of their officers who had disappeared in Russia in the spring of 1940, the German claim that the massacre had been committed by the Russians seemed plausible. The Poles demanded an independent Red Cross inquiry. The Soviet Government alleged that the massacres had, in fact, been carried out by the Germans. There seems little doubt that the murders were, in fact, the work of the Russian security forces. When, in 1945, Goering and other war criminals were indicted at Nuremberg as being responsible for the Katyn murders, they were acquitted of these particular charges, and the accusation was quietly dropped."[11]

‡Wladyslaw Sikorski, Polish prime minister in exile.

of Polish origin. This, combined with the fact that the Polish government itself firmly refused to accept the Curzon Line frontier, enabled Stalin to avoid any commitment to resume relations with it.[12] By the time of Yalta, with his troops already occupying Poland and a Communist Provisional Government installed there, he was in a much stronger position. After long and difficult negotiations a Declaration on Poland was agreed upon, which gave him satisfaction on the frontier issue without mentioning the government-in-exile. It did, however, call for the Provisional Government to be "reorganized on a broader democratic basis with the inclusion of democratic leaders from Poland itself and from Poles abroad." This "reorganization" was supposedly to be the fruit of consultations conducted by a commission composed of Molotov and the American and British ambassadors in Moscow. The enlarged government would be "pledged to the holding of free and unfettered elections as soon as possible on the basis of universal suffrage and secret ballot. In these elections all democratic and anti-Nazi parties shall have the right to take part and to put forward candidates."

Churchill, on his return to London, put a hopeful construction on this agreement. It provided, in his view, "for consultations with a view to the establishment in Poland of a *new* Polish Provisional Government of National Unity," and he pledged that "His Majesty's Government intend to do all in their power to ensure that . . . representative Poles of all democratic parties are given full freedom to come and make their views known."[13] Frank Roberts's view that the deal was "on paper . . . perfectly defensible" has already been quoted. But Alger Hiss, who was less directly involved with Polish issues, takes a more detached, if not cynical, view of it.

HISS: Since at Yalta the Polish issue had been the most difficult issue to resolve, I was not as surprised as some others by the fact that the plans for the new government went awry and the Russians were insisting on their domination. It was, however, one of the points that definitely caused the Cold War to intensify. . . . We thought we'd done a pretty good job in arranging for the Polish borders, which after all went back to the Curzon Line which a British official had himself proposed earlier on, [but] the agreement as to the personnel of the government, which was reached only after the conference nearly foundered, was—it seemed to me—a makeshift arrangement. I've always felt that the terms of the Polish settlement were written in words of rubber, stretchable —that they had a different meaning for the Russians than for us. Take a phrase like "democratic elections": that depends who's running them.

We've witnessed in recent years some elections in Central America which didn't please the United States government, and yet others thought of them as perfectly democratic. So the Russians regarded democratic elections as a totally different concept, perhaps a cynical one, from ours; and much of the agreement, which began to come unstuck while we were at San Francisco,* was of that nature.

At Yalta, it's important to understand, the necessity of the military situation was all-pervasive. The three powers *could not* leave in disagreement. The Battle of the Bulge had occurred in December and early January, showing that the German army still had great power. The war against Japan was still seemingly far from settled. . . . The Joint Chiefs of Staff had for months been insisting that unless the Russians agreed to come into the war against Japan on a specific date we, the United States alone, would suffer a million casualties in the war against Japan, and that the war would be continued certainly late into 1946. If one could use the word "appeasement" [about U.S.-Soviet relations, it would apply to the attitude of] the Joint Chiefs of Staff [at that time: they] were anxious that the State Department do nothing that irritated the Russians—so we came to Yalta as supplicants, we came asking the Russians to enter the war against Japan and name a particular date. They had indicated at Teheran that they would do so, but that had been left indefinite—and at Yalta, as far as I know, it was the only full-scale [U.S.-Soviet] military collaboration. Some seventy-five American and British members of the Joint Chiefs of Staff, military men, flew to Yalta—the contingent vastly outnumbering the diplomatic contingent—and they worked with their Russian counterparts apparently amicably throughout the eight days of the conference. . . . So it was, I think it's fair to say, unthinkable that accommodation on political matters could not be reached. It had to be reached. It was a necessity.

Ernest Gross concurs in stressing the *realpolitik* element in the agreement, and the overriding need to bring the Russians into the war against Japan.

GROSS: I think that Roosevelt was deceived at Yalta, but not naively. I think that Stalin betrayed his promises. I think that Roosevelt accepted Stalin's promises, believing them—maybe he was naive in that respect—but that didn't matter, whether he believed them or not, deep down in his mind, because it was better to have Stalin's promises *even if he was going to violate them* than not have his promises at all. Well—that's a way

*The founding conference of the United Nations Organization, held at San Francisco from April 23 to June 26, 1945.

of looking at it, perhaps: some people would regard that as a rationalization. Certainly the Joint Chiefs [of Staff] at the Yalta conference were very, very strongly of the view that the Soviet Union simply had to come into the war against Japan in some timely fashion. And *they* weren't prepared to recommend to the president a break, even if the president had had that in mind, which he did not.

This military dimension of Yalta seems rather to have been lost sight of in the folk memory of a later generation of American officials, such as Richard Perle, the ultrahawk or "Prince of Darkness" in the Reagan administration. He is ready enough to accuse his elders of having underestimated the importance of military strength in the power politics of the 1950s and 1960s. But when I asked him how he felt the United States *should* have responded to the attempts by Eastern European peoples to challenge Soviet domination in that period, his response was to shift the blame further back.

PERLE: I didn't mean to suggest, in saying that we were ineffective then, that there were easy options for us to pursue. . . . The mistakes were made earlier on, it seems to me, at Yalta and in the immediate postwar relationship with the Soviet Union. It took us rather longer than it should have to understand that our wartime ally would, if left to his own devices, dominate as much territory as we would permit him to establish control over.

MORTIMER: What do you think *should* have been done at Yalta?

PERLE: I think we ought to have insisted upon the immediate self-determination and democratization of all of the territories occupied during the war.

MORTIMER: What about the argument that the U.S. and Britain weren't in a position to do that?

PERLE: We lacked the will to insist. I think we probably had the means. . . .

MORTIMER: What about the argument that you wanted to get Stalin's agreement to enter the war against Japan?

PERLE: It was bloody useless: they entered the war nominally, a week before it was over, and made virtually no contribution to the war, except they grabbed some islands from the Japanese that they continue to occupy to this day. It was just a diplomatic blunder.

That judgment assumes, of course, that it was possible for Roosevelt and his military advisers to know for certain, in early February, that the atomic weapon would be available and would enable them to win the war against Japan by August—which was not the case. It is also highly questionable, to say the least, whether the United States "had the means" to oblige Stalin to accept "the immediate self-determination and democratization of all of the territories occupied during the war," even if that *had* been the top priority for Roosevelt and his advisers in February 1945.

Better-informed critics of the Yalta accords accept that Eastern Europe was by then under Stalin's physical control and that nothing the Western leaders said or did could have prevented him from imposing his domination upon it, but assert that the accords conferred on this domination an international legitimacy or respectability that could have been withheld. De Gaulle, for instance, who bitterly resented the fact that he was not invited to Yalta even though France had by then been liberated and he was the head of its provisional government, always spoke of Yalta as the origin of "the policy of blocs," by which Europe was divided into spheres of influence dominated by rival superpowers. Maurice Couve de Murville, whose government expressed this view of de Gaulle's in an official reaction to the Soviet invasion of Czechoslovakia in August 1968, today gives a slightly subtler interpretation.

COUVE DE MURVILLE: First of all, I would say that the division of Europe is not the result of Yalta. Yalta is a sort of symbol of the division, but the division is just the result of the war—simply because one part of Europe, that is, the east, was occupied by the Russian army and the other part by the American army. If de Gaulle had been at Yalta and Potsdam, it would have made a great difference for France in its way to international recovery—I mean, we would have been accepted as equal partners, two years before it really happened. [But] it wouldn't have changed the fact that Europe was occupied in the east and in the west. . . . The result probably would have been about the same, with this difference, that maybe it would not have been considered as a willingly accepted fact.

MORTIMER: Do you then agree with those in the United States who say that Roosevelt gave away Eastern Europe to Stalin, or at least legitimized Soviet rule over Eastern Europe?

COUVE DE MURVILLE: I think it's true in a way, yes. He couldn't help it because it was a military situation. But he accepted it not only as a *fait accompli,* but as something that was legitimate, and that was surely wrong. It's why I said that if de Gaulle had been there, it might have been a little different in the spirit.

Was Roosevelt then duped by Stalin, or did he—as Alger Hiss and Ernest Gross both seem to hint—deliberately go through the motions of being duped because he knew that he was, in fact, powerless to save Eastern Europe, whereas he believed it both necessary and possible to secure Soviet cooperation in the war against Japan and in the construction of the United Nations Organization? The answer is, probably, a bit of both. No one disputes the fact that bringing the war in both theaters to a successful conclusion and building an international organization strong enough to prevent its recurrence were his two overriding priorities, while he looked on Eastern Europe as an area that was not primarily an American responsibility, even if he recognized that important principles were at stake there. He may also reasonably have thought, as Arthur Schlesinger suggests, that if there was any hope at all of changing the Soviet system for the better, it lay in working with Stalin rather than against him.

SCHLESINGER: The only possible change in Soviet ideology could be made by Stalin himself, who by this time regarded himself as co-equal with Marx and Lenin in the formulation of ideology, and I think Roosevelt was quite right in believing that Stalin was the only means of getting any change in this otherwise rather bleak view of postwar cooperation.

Stalin's personality was indeed complex and enigmatic, and exercised considerable fascination over those who had the chance to observe him at close quarters—like Frank Roberts, who after Yalta spent two years as British minister in Moscow: two years during which the wartime alliance rapidly gave way to the Cold War.

ROBERTS: Stalin was an entirely different type of dictator from, say, Hitler or Mussolini. The Russians always present him as a great big man, in their pictures and so on. He was actually tiny: he was five foot three or four or something like that. Rather, not only [that] but small in every way: he had a bad arm, you know, so he didn't gesture or anything. Very soft voice—not at all, you know, the great dictator he was always presented as being. The other thing about Stalin was that as long as the negotiations were difficult, that was left to Molotov, or even to Vishinsky.* They could keep on saying *"Nyet, nyet"* and be extremely difficult, while Stalin stayed in the background. When the moment was coming for an agreement, then Stalin would come along

*Andrei Vishinsky, Soviet assistant commissar for foreign affairs, previously chief prosecutor at the Moscow trials of 1937–38. Regarded as a particularly difficult and unpleasant negotiator by his Western interlocutors. Among other exploits, he organized the enforced appointment of a Communist government by King Michael of Rumania, in a Bucharest ringed by Soviet tanks, at a moment when the ink on the Yalta "Declaration on Liberated Europe" was scarcely dry.

—and obviously in a very good humor, because one had reached a stage of agreement. So you had to be awfully careful . . . to realize that this man you were dealing with—soft-spoken, highly intelligent, apparently amiable—was the man who had bumped off nearly all his colleagues in the Politburo, killed I think two-thirds of the members of the Central Committee of the party, and I don't know how many million Russians, in other words a highly dangerous and evil character. But he didn't so appear. And I think this is why he created, even with Churchill and Roosevelt, this idea of being a potentially avuncular "Uncle Joe." He wasn't. . . .

But they did feel this more and more, as the war went on and as we three were running the war together. They had—what I think even then I thought was a bit unrealistic, but I certainly do today—the idea that if you treated Stalin as a member of this Western club, he would eventually behave like a member of the club—completely forgetting that, of course, he had a Communist club of his own, of which he was the boss, and he didn't particularly want to be a country member of our club. But this was their idea, and they kept it quite a long time.

Valentin Berezhkov gives an interesting account of the same relationship, seen from the other side.

BEREZHKOV: He [Stalin] always had everything from his head. The only [adviser] who was present was Molotov. There were no other assistants, and nobody who would pass him a note or give him some figures or something like that—nothing at all. Molotov usually was not speaking—very, very few, a couple of sentences—so all the conversation was made by Stalin, never checking or consulting any paper. He probably was making his homework before, preparing—for he knew what the talk would be about, more or less—but even if some questions came up which he didn't expect, he immediately said whatever answer it was, or he would say, "I have to think about that," or "[I have] to consult my colleagues; I will tell you next day"—something like that. Very efficient, I would say, very businesslike. He was a good negotiator. . . . Somehow he knew how to deal with these people. You know that even Truman has had very positive paragraphs [in his memoirs] about his impression of Stalin, and certainly Roosevelt and Churchill, too.

Churchill, by the way . . . when they met several times after the dinner, late dinner party, when they went to drink coffee and some brandy—although Stalin never drank, only maybe some dry wine or something like that, but Churchill certainly drank—and then he would

[ask] sometimes, repeating the same thing, the same sentence, whether Stalin is prepared to excuse him or to pardon him for his attitude toward the October Revolution and intervention—that he was involved in intervention and tried to kill the infant (so to say), the socialist infant —and whether Stalin would now pardon him for what he did. But Stalin was never serious about that, and he said, "Well, if you believe in God, maybe God will pardon, but don't ask me about that," or something like that. . . . Informal talks sometimes went on late at night during this kind of visits.

MORTIMER: Do you think Stalin liked dealing with foreigners?

BEREZHKOV: Well, he probably understood that this is necessary, and he probably understood that it is important. I don't think he especially liked it. It was certainly a thing that he had to do. But, you see, he knew also how to deal with them in the psychological sense. . . . I remember, for example, his first talk . . . when Beaverbrook and Harriman came.* It was a time when the Germans moved toward Moscow and really a terrible, terrible situation for us. And Harriman was advised by his military attaché that he should wind up the talks as quickly as possible, because any moment the German parachutists may be dropped on Moscow and he will be taken prisoner by the Germans, so he must quickly leave Moscow and go away; and when he came to Stalin he was certainly under this impression, that Moscow was under siege, that any moment the Germans may be here. And Stalin, in his talks, behaved like he has a normal amount of time. He was never in a hurry. He was very relaxed, very quiet, you know—out of place, sort of thing, because really around Moscow was a terrible battle. And the other thing that impressed them was that he, for example, asked not only for ammunition, for tanks or lorries, but he asked for factories. He needed factories for making gas, or aluminium, or for making some special equipment, for making some special sorts of steel. And they immediately have been thinking, "What is he talking about? The Germans are here at the gates of Moscow, he wants factories! The factories will be delivered or installed in two or three years, so what is he speaking about?" But at the same time this kind of talk, you know, created in them a feeling that maybe something is wrong with this advice [of their] military experts—that Russia will *not* collapse, that Russia will stay, and that Stalin *is* expecting to get his factories, to start them producing, and . . . they went out from his study in quite a different mood, you see. So in this terrible situation that we were in,

*Max Aitken, Lord Beaverbrook, newspaper publisher and minister of supply in Churchill's government, was sent with Roosevelt's envoy Averell Harriman to offer aid to Russia, after the Atlantic conference of August 1941. The United States was not yet a belligerent.

to have such a self-assurance, and to inflict it upon people who came with the idea that the Soviets will collapse in four or five weeks, and all of a sudden they came out, and the report Harriman [made] to Roosevelt [was] that the Russians will repel the Germans and they will win this war. And this played a tremendous role in the political thinking in America and even in Britain, I think.

A relationship of genuine trust and cooperation with Stalin was something so desirable, if it could have been achieved, that one should not be too surprised at Roosevelt's readiness to believe in it. For there is no doubt that he did hope for such a relationship, nor that Stalin's high-handed interpretation (or flagrant disregard, depending on your view) of the Yalta accords, together with his brusque and discourteous refusal to accept assurances that the Western allies were not negotiating a separate peace with Germany,[14] cast a shadow over the last weeks of Roosevelt's life.* Ernest Gross goes even further.

GROSS: Stalin's betrayal of his promise with respect to free elections and a freely selected government of Poland was *the* great postwar betrayal in the minds of our most elevated officers. . . . Of course, Roosevelt never lived to see the full fruits of Stalin's betrayal. There is an interesting sidelight on that, and that came out later. I'd heard at the time, shortly after Roosevelt's death, one of his principal confidants was Judge Samuel Rosenman, who was one of the primary speechwriters and advisers to Roosevelt. And he wrote, when he wrote his memoirs some years later, he repeated something that he had said at the time, shortly after Roosevelt's death—and I think I can almost quote the words: he said, "I am sure that Stalin's betrayal of Roosevelt at Yalta hastened the president's death." I mean, that's strongly put, by one of his principal advisers.

But Stalin seems to have feared it was Roosevelt who was about to betray *him.*

BEREZHKOV: It developed at the end of Roosevelt's presidency. It was, I think, in February or March, when there were these separate talks in Italy between the Germans and the American and British command in Italy, where our representatives were not permitted. We have considered it as a violation of Allied relationships. We didn't want to influence something, but we wanted to have our observer who should

*Roosevelt died unexpectedly on April 12, 1945.

at any rate know what they are talking about, because we had a provision that nobody of the participants in the anti-Hitler coalition should have separate talks or separate agreements with the Germans, and especially because at that particular moment, when these talks were going on, the Germans were bringing over many of their divisions from Italy to the Soviet front. So it was an indication that maybe there is some promise on the part of the Allies which gave the German command the possibility to send fresh troops to our front, and this was a very dangerous thing, very dangerous for the alliance, and there was a lot of correspondence between Roosevelt and Stalin to this effect.*

Arthur Schlesinger points out that events might have been different if Roosevelt had not died.

SCHLESINGER: [It might] very well have been, had Roosevelt survived, that the U.S. policy would have hardened more quickly toward the Soviet Union. If you read the dispatches from the British embassy in Washington to the Foreign Office for the period 1945–47, one finds, among the major themes in them, Truman's alleged irresolution, the fear that Truman will see himself as a mediator between Britain and Russia, the doubt that the United States will commit itself to any kind of long-term containment of the Soviet Union, and so on. I mean, the British in that period were the forward players in the Cold War, in the resistance to possible Soviet expansion, and they regarded the Truman administration, up really until 1947–48, as a doubtful partner in this enterprise.

That may be true of some British officials, and of Churchill, but according to Lord Franks it is not true of the Labour government that took office in July 1945.

FRANKS: They were working for happy, constructive relations, both with the United States and with the Soviet Union. Bevin himself, the

*"Harriman had advised the State Department that he saw no warrant for the Soviet request, since the Germans were merely proposing to surrender military forces on an Anglo-American front. He did not think that the Soviets would allow American officers to participate in a parallel action on the Eastern Front, and indeed he doubted whether they would even have let us know of soundings for such a surrender. In his opinion, no advantage of any sort would be gained by acceding to the Soviet wish; on the contrary, the Russians would take it as a sign of yielding and make even more unreasonable demands in the future. . . . The Combined Chiefs of Staff had reached the same conclusion. They did not want Soviet officers to figure in these preliminary talks in Switzerland. But in recognition of Soviet interest in the way any surrender would be set and carried out, they were willing to have them present at any substantive talks that might follow in Italy."[15]

foreign secretary, was very slow to give up the notion that you could live with the Soviet Union. In my opinion he didn't give it up until the end of April 1947, and all the way through you can find him coming back to "I can find a way—Stalin is somebody that you can negotiate with." It's quite untrue that in the early years—1945–46—everybody was accepting what we now with hindsight see was coming about in '47, '48, '49.

The end of the European war brought the first direct contact between American and Soviet troops in Germany. For some American officials, who were later to play a role in shaping the new administration's policies, this was an eye-opening experience.

Paul Nitze visited Germany in 1945 as vice-chairman of the U.S. Strategic Bombing Survey—a unit set up to quantify the damage done to the enemy by Allied bombers. He was later to hold high office in the Truman, Kennedy, and Johnson administrations, later still to be recalled by Reagan and play a key role in the arms control negotiations of the 1980s. He was in the thick of these when I met him in his office in the State Department in 1986, yet turned his seventy-nine-year-old brain with perfect ease and grace to recalling the events and arguments of forty years earlier. Immaculately dressed and still strikingly good-looking, with every white hair exactly in place, he seemed the perfect embodiment of the American tradition of committed but nonpartisan public service.

NITZE: I was shocked by being reprimanded at the end of the war by a U.S. Army colonel for giving candy to a German child—this seemed to me to be just totally inhuman. And then I got to Berlin and there the Russians had put enormous signs in white, with blue printing on them, saying, "We have no quarrel with the German people. Our quarrel is with Hitler and his associates." And I thought, "Here—the Russians are the ones who really understand this thing correctly, and we have been totally ununderstanding what is up and what is down in this issue." But then later I saw what, in fact, was happening in Berlin: I saw these Russians tearing up the rail lines that were essential to getting supplies into Berlin, taking everything out of Berlin, acting in the most unspeakable way, while our people were really trying to help. So that, you know, scales came off one's eyes, that there really was a difference in the approach of one system and of the other system.

Ernest Gross has very similar recollections.

GROSS: When we arrived in Berlin in late June of 1945 the city was still smoldering. The streets and buildings were indistinguishable . . . and the Russian troops were looting the city. And this was obvious —there was no pretense otherwise. Truckloads of looted—I suppose the Russians would say "liberated"—goods were being moved, the small articles in wastebaskets—wastebaskets became a very rare commodity in Berlin at that time—to the canal. And that was some tragic illusion there, in a sense, because they really visualized that all those articles, household articles mostly, were going to be moved on the barges on the Sprey River and the canals, by inland waterways to the Soviet Union. Very few ever got away from the piers there in the Berlin area. But I never thought that in my lifetime I would see a city being sacked and vandalized—it seemed to me that that was something one read about a millennium ago.

Then our party was allowed to visit East Berlin under Soviet occupation, and among other sights—spectacles—we visited Hitler's bunker, where he had committed suicide, and the Reichschancellery, which was a complete wreck. We were allowed to wander about a bit, but always with young Russian troops, machine guns at port, and they were all—without exception, I would say—eighteen-, nineteen-year-olds, obviously from very, very uneducated, illiterate stock. I don't think that the Russians wanted to expose to the Germans, or in the West generally, soldiers that might be intelligent enough or educated enough possibly to become subverted. I felt that these were a very, very ignorant lot. When we tried to size them up and talk with them, we found that they were really not very literate, to say the least. There was a portrait there of an almost barbaric regime—I'll strike out "almost." That was my first impression.

Truman himself came to Berlin in July 1945 for the Potsdam conference with Churchill and Stalin. At first he seems almost to have regarded himself as a kind of impartial, honest broker between the other two. As he recounts in his memoirs:

After that first meeting with Mr. Churchill and Stalin, I returned to my temporary home at Babelsberg with some confidence. I hoped that Stalin was a man who would keep his agreements. We had much to learn on this subjcct. Because the Russians had made immense sacrifices in men and materials—over five million men killed in action, more millions slain and starved wantonly by Hitler in his invasion of the Ukraine—we hoped that Russia would join wholeheartedly in a plan for world peace.

> . . . I realised that, as chairman, I would be faced with many problems arising out of the conflict of interests. I knew that Stalin and Churchill each would have special interests that might clash and distract us.[16]

But as the conference wore on, he became increasingly disillusioned with the Soviet approach. Within two weeks he was writing to his mother and sister, "You never saw such pig-headed people as the Russians. I hope I never have to hold another conference with them —but, of course, I will."[17] And his conclusion at the end of the conference was

> that the Russians were not in earnest about peace. It was clear that the Russian foreign policy was based on the conclusion that we were heading for a major depression, and they were already planning to take advantage of our setback.
>
> Anxious as we were to have Russia in the war against Japan, the experience at Potsdam now made me determined that I would not allow the Russians any part in the control of Japan. Our experience with them in Germany and in Bulgaria, Rumania, Hungary and Poland was such that I decided to take no chances in a joint setup with the Russians. . . .
>
> Force is the only thing the Russians understand. . . . The persistent way in which Stalin blocked one of the war preventative measures I had proposed showed how his mind worked and what he was after. I had proposed the internationalisation of all the principal waterways. Stalin did not want this. What Stalin wanted was control of the Black Sea Straits and the Danube. The Russians were planning world conquest.[18]

Ernest Gross provides evidence that this was indeed Truman's state of mind and that of his advisers at the time, and not an ex post facto rationalization when he came to write his memoirs.

> GROSS: In Paris . . . I met my chief, General John Hilldring, who was chief of the Civil Affairs Division, on his way back from the Potsdam conference . . . to discuss what implications the conference might have had with respect to our planning for the postwar occupation regime. And I remember a phrase, that General Hilldring looked at us —he said, "There's just one way I could describe to you gentlemen what happened at Potsdam." So he said, referring to Truman, "The old man was badly shaken." . . . And I believe that after that Potsdam conference, even without the background of the Yalta deception, that there was no way that the United States government, from top to bottom, from stem to stern, could consider the Soviet Union as any-

thing but a threat, and that the wartime alliance was just over. There was no question about that in people's minds. The question was how you dealt with it.

In Stalin's eyes, of course, it was the United States that was threatening the Soviet Union.

BEREZHKOV: There was this order of Truman to stop the Lend-Lease [after the German surrender], very abruptly, without even telling us something: even the boats that were somewhere in the Black Sea were immediately turned back [without being] unloaded: it was just like a demonstration. Truman said he didn't know about that, but now we know he knew about it from documents and talks that he had with his subordinates.* And then finally the Potsdam conference, where, after the atomic bomb was tested in New Mexico, Truman, in a very general way, told Stalin that "we have developed a new, very destructive weapon," but at the same time he wanted to revise the agreements which were made on the Polish provisional government and also on the territorial problem about Polish borders—he wanted to push them back from their former German territories, so that the agreements that were made in Yalta about the new Polish territories were actually questioned by Truman, and actually accompanied by the statement that "I have got a new weapon," and Stalin certainly immediately understood that this was an atomic weapon. He ordered even by a telephone call from Potsdam to accelerate our work to develop our bomb, and it took us only four years after that to develop our bomb. . . .

At the London conference [of foreign ministers] in September 1945, James Byrnes was already secretary of state, and he said to Molotov at that time that "if you don't behave then you know I am a southerner, and we always keep our gun in our pocket, and if you don't behave we will take out our atomic gun and show you. . . ." If one foreign minister talks to another foreign minister like that, what conclusions can you make out of it? It is not a very diplomatic talk, I would say. But it is clear that we were in danger, certainly, and that's why we have to take measures to secure our independence and our system and our security, and that's actually what happened after the war.

*Truman "barely glanced at the vaguely worded termination order which Harriman and others had approved." The turning around of ships already en route for Soviet ports was, apparently, the result of excessive bureaucratic zeal. [See Walter Isaacson and Evan Thomas, *The Wise Men* (New York: Simon & Schuster, 1986), pp. 278–79.]

Was the division of Germany then already sealed at the Potsdam conference? Yes and no, according to Lord Franks.

FRANKS: The communiqué issued after it was ambiguous. It talked about Germany as a unity, administrative and economic, and, of course, run by the Control Commission, the generals of the occupying forces —the Four.* But it also made arrangements about reparations which presupposed a divided Germany. The Russians were taking all they wanted out of eastern Germany, both capital goods and also goods for consumption. What was agreed on our side was that after keeping enough [industrial plant] for a tolerable level of living in the western zones, the Russians should have a free percentage—10 percent—and 15 percent more in return for minerals, coal, and food from eastern Germany passing back to the western zones, where there were more millions of people than could be fed. Now this presupposed separate treatment for western Germany and eastern Germany, and that was the effective thing: it lived on. Everybody proclaimed in 1946–47 that what they wanted was economic unity, [but] nobody could give away enough for it to be possible. The Russians wanted their form of economic unity, we wanted our form of economic unity. Therefore what prevailed was the division. And it was General Marshall,† in Moscow in April 1947, who said, "We can no longer paper over with talk about economic unity."

MORTIMER: But in 1945 what was said about maintaining German unity was sincerely meant?

FRANKS: Yes.

MORTIMER: There was no secret feeling that actually it would be safer for everyone if Germany were divided?

FRANKS: I'm not prepared to say there was no thinking of that sort around. I am prepared to say that as far as the policy of the British government went, or of the American government, that was not part of their policy in 1945 or the first half of 1946.

MORTIMER: Then had they not thought through the implications of the arrangements they agreed to at Potsdam about reparations?

FRANKS: No, it wasn't that. It was that they hadn't seen at that stage reason to be worried about the expansive tendencies of Russia, the possibilities of aggrandizement. That began with the difficulties about Eastern Europe, but it reached the turning point about Iran in Decem-

*At Yalta Churchill had won agreement that France should have an occupation zone in Germany (carved out of those originally allocated to Britain and the United States) and a seat on the Allied Control Commission.

†U.S. secretary of state, 1947–49.

ber 1945 and the early months of 1946. That was the real turning point in opinion and policy about the Soviet Union.

MORTIMER: Iran, not anything that happened in Europe?

FRANKS: No, most certainly: the southern frontiers of Russia.

MORTIMER: Yet Stalin withdrew from Iran without a military confrontation.

FRANKS: Yes, but consider what happened to produce that answer. First of all the Russians had set up their own Communist government in Azerbaijan, the northwestern province [of Iran]. They'd agreed to take their troops out by March 2. We, the British, and they had troops there [in Iran]. We took ours out, they did not take theirs out. In March they had the Iranian prime minister in Moscow. They said they would take their troops out according to the agreement from other parts, but not Azerbaijan, and they further said that Azerbaijan must be recognized as an autonomous republic. It was at that stage that Jimmy Byrnes, the American secretary of state, sent one of the stiffest notes I've ever seen to Russia, and what's more arranged for the battleship *Missouri* to be sailed to the Dardanelles. He then sent another cable, equally firm, saying that he had heard from the consul in Tabriz [capital of Azerbaijan] that the Russians were moving tanks into the area. Were they? And would they get them out at once? It was after that that the Russians withdrew, in May. It was a major confrontation, which ended diplomatically.

Thus in Lord Franks's view it was attempts at Soviet expansion southward, rather than westward, that directly aroused American fears and prompted the United States to overcome its traditional antipathy to long-term entanglements outside the Western Hemisphere. Certainly Soviet behavior in Iran figures prominently in the written rebuke administered by Truman to his secretary of state, James F. Byrnes, on January 5, 1946, with its famous conclusion, "I'm tired of babying the Soviets." Truman made it clear that he saw "the Russian program in Iran" as an extension of the policies already adopted in Eastern Europe, and asserted, "There isn't a doubt in my mind that Russia intends an invasion of Turkey and the seizure of the Black Sea Straits to the Mediterranean. Unless Russia is faced with an iron fist and strong language another war is in the making."*[19] Sure enough, after Iran came Turkey, as Lord Franks recalls.

*It was after this, in February, that George Kennan, then U.S. chargé d'affaires in Moscow, sent his famous "long telegram" analyzing Soviet policy, warning that Stalin would use every means to infiltrate, divide, and weaken the West and that a *modus vivendi* with him would prove impossible; and in March that Churchill delivered his "Iron Curtain" speech at Fulton, Missouri.

FRANKS: [There was] the case of Turkey, in August 1946, when Russia demanded that only the Black Sea powers should control the Dardanelles, and to share the defense of the Dardanelles with Turkey. The Turks resisted: the Americans supported them. Truman insisted that they should support them. General Eisenhower, chief of army staff at that time, said, "Do you realize, Mr. President, this may mean war?" "Yes, I do," said the president, and gave a lecture on the strategic importance of Greece and Turkey in the Mediterranean and the Middle East. And he ordered the *Franklin D. Roosevelt*—the biggest aircraft carrier, with supporting cruisers and destroyers—into the Dardanelles.

Then again there was the case in February 1947 when the British government had to tell the American government it could no longer pay for its troops in Greece or pay for food for the Greeks, and at the same time it couldn't continue aid to Turkey. The Americans felt compelled, for strategic reasons, to pick up the bill. The result was the "Truman Doctrine"—the proclamation of the willingness of the Americans to uphold and maintain free peoples everywhere. And this was the third element where they feared Communist expansion to the south—where they feared they saw aggrandizement—and why they became determined to resist.

In the case of Western Europe, the prevalent fear in the immediate postwar years was not a Soviet invasion, but a political victory for local Communists enjoying Soviet support and exploiting the acute economic crisis that followed the disruption caused by the war and the collapse of the Reich.

NITZE: I can remember a labor conference, of the World Federation of Trade Unions, in London in 1945, at which the delegates were arguing the time periods when various countries in Europe would be taken over by the Communists. The shortest time period was with respect to Italy, where it was expected that they would take power within six months. . . . In France it might be a year, in Germany a year and a half, five years in England.

GLADWYN: The Russians thought, not unnaturally, that Europe being in this terrible state there might be some kind of revolutionary situation, and in any case that the Communist parties, notably in France and Italy, would probably take over. . . . They didn't want to come and occupy the damn place—that would have been against their interest, presumably. The idea that the Russian army would sweep over Europe was always rather an illusion. . . . But that they might get Russophile governments, acceptable to the Soviet Union, in France and Italy would not be surprising at all in those circumstances. And if it hadn't been for Marshall Aid, that might well have happened. It's quite possible. And then, of course, there might well have been some kind of left-wing, pro-Soviet feeling in western Germany, and you might well have got the famous "Finlandization" of Europe long before it was even talked about.

All sources agree that anxiety to prevent such developments was a primary motive behind the massive American assistance program known as the Marshall Plan, after the new secretary of state, General George C. Marshall, who announced it in a speech at Harvard University on June 5, 1947, calling on the Europeans to agree on a joint recovery program to ensure that American aid was not wasted. A few weeks before, Marshall had returned from a grueling four-power conference in Moscow at which no significant progress had been made on any of the issues dividing the former allies. He was clearly shaken by what he saw of the state of Europe on his way to and from Moscow. "The recovery of Europe has been far slower than had been expected," he said in a radio broadcast. "Disintegrating forces are becoming evident. The patient is sinking while the doctors deliberate. . . . Action cannot await compromise through exhaustion."[20]

In the view of Lord Franks, who chaired the conference in Paris that drew up Europe's response to the American offer, the Marshall Plan marked the decisive moment when America made her commitment to Europe.

FRANKS: What grew out of all that was a judgment by the Americans that Western Europe was of prime strategic importance to them; that they could not afford that these 250 million people—busy, active, intelligent people—should "disintegrate," as General Marshall feared when he spoke on wireless after getting home at the end of April. . . . He was afraid that in that social and political and economic disintegration, the strong Communist parties of France and Italy might take over. He wanted to prevent that. He wanted to be sure that western Germany and Western Europe—the one couldn't recover without the other—did recover. And this required the infusion of goods—food, steel, machine tools—which only American dollars could buy. The Marshall Plan was about putting American dollars in the hands of Europeans to buy the tools of recovery.

I think the Americans did this quite largely from humanitarian reasons. General Marshall was deeply moved by the millions of people from eastern Germany sculling about in western Germany without the means of subsistence, supported by food brought in at the cost of dollars by Britain and America; deeply scared about the plight of people in Western Europe. By the spring of 1947 the French farmers, the Italian farmers, were hoarding their grain, not sending it to the cities, using it to feed their cattle, because they thought it wouldn't be there. Remember, food grains ran out in Italy by November 1947. They ran out in France in March–April 1948. There was a crisis. It was this that America stepped into. And it stepped into it both to save the people of Europe, and to preserve Western Europe as a land of democratic, freedom-loving people, and prosperous, *on the side of the United States.* That is when the American commitment to Western Europe was made, in my view.

"Our policy," Marshall said in his Harvard speech, "is directed not against any country or doctrine but against hunger, poverty, desperation, and chaos." Neither the Soviet Union nor Communism were mentioned by name:

> Any government [Marshall said] that is willing to assist in the task of recovery will find full cooperation, I am sure, on the part of the United States Government. Any government which maneuvers to block the recovery of other countries cannot expect help from us. Furthermore, governments, political parties, or groups which seek to perpetuate human misery in order to profit therefrom politically or otherwise will encounter the opposition of the United States.

Formally, therefore, the offer was open to the whole of Europe, including the Soviet Union if it had been willing to mend its ways and agree with the Western European countries on a coherent and convincing recovery program. But, as Marshall's under secretary, Dean Acheson, dryly comments:

> If General Marshall believed, which I am sure he did not, that the American people would be moved to so great an effort as he contemplated by as Platonic a purpose as combating "hunger, poverty, desperation and chaos," he was mistaken. But he was wholly right in stating this as the American *governmental* purpose. I have probably made as many speeches and answered as many questions about the Marshall Plan as any man alive . . . and what citizens and the representatives in Congress alike always wanted to learn in the last analysis was how

Marshall aid operated to block the extension of Soviet power and the acceptance of Communist economic and political organization and alignment.[21]

Some officials, still hankering for the old wartime spirit of U.S.-Soviet cooperation, felt the administration was overreacting to events in Europe.

HISS: I think part of the American change of policy came about through a fear of socialism, not of Stalin marching his armies into Europe. I don't think anyone at the State Department believed there was a danger of Soviet invasion of Europe: they'd suffered twenty million casualties, civilian and military; their whole economy was in disruption and devastation from what the Germans had done to them. There did seem a likelihood that Communist and strong Socialist parties in Italy, in France, Belgium, Holland—the resistance personnel—would form semi-Communist or socialist regimes in Western Europe. This definitely upset a large segment of American leaders. For example, at one point I spoke to Dean Acheson and said that I thought we were allowing the impression to go abroad that there was a danger of Soviet invasion in Europe, and this fear was infecting the public, and the Congress itself was misunderstanding the situation. . . . Acheson said, "If we don't scare Congress, they will go fishing," and I said, "But if you do scare them they'll go crazy!" I thought this was a wisecrack Dean would appreciate—he usually liked that kind of thing. But he was not impressed.

There was, in fact, a contradiction between the diplomatic requirement that Marshall's offer should be seen to be open to all, and the domestic political requirement that it be presented as an effective antidote to Communism. Gladwyn Jebb (now Lord Gladwyn) was a leading adviser at the time to the British foreign secretary, Ernest Bevin.

GLADWYN: I always thought that if maybe the Russians and Molotov had accepted, that an impossible situation would have arisen. I don't know what the Americans would have done. They might have spent even more money and got the thing going in all the countries, but it would have been difficult to get the money out of Congress. If a lot of it had gone to the Soviet Union, then it mightn't have had the effect intended in Western Europe. It would be a very dangerous situation.

Thank goodness—you ought to put up a monument to Molotov for that reason!

Molotov did, in fact, come to Paris on June 27 for discussions with Bevin and his French colleague, Georges Bidault, but after four days he withdrew, rejecting the proposed joint recovery program as a "violation of national sovereignty." Moscow then proceeded to veto the participation of the Eastern European countries—Czechoslovakia, as yet only partially Communist-controlled, being forced by crude and open Soviet pressure to rescind its initial acceptance of the invitation.[22] As Lord Gladwyn explains, Stalin "just thought that if they were going to come, they would be under an obligation to the Americans, the Americans would insist on administering it to some extent, and they weren't prepared to accept any kind of American influence on their internal affairs."

Berezhkov confirms this.

BEREZHKOV: There was a lot of political interference connected with the Marshall Plan, which we also considered to be unacceptable, and that the countries which received the help were to some extent put into an inferior situation towards the country that gave that. . . . And when they were working out the conditions of the Marshall Plan they were doing everything they could in order to make it unacceptable for us, and during this couple of days that we didn't give the answer they were so nervous in Washington, in case we decided we accept and then all their plans will be ruined.

According to Frank Roberts, who in 1947 became Bevin's principal private secretary, the Russian decision was disappointing.

ROBERTS: It was a terrible disappointment actually to Bevin, who was thinking very much in terms of economic reconstruction, when the Russians decided no, they didn't want to get involved in what they regarded, of course, as an American-dominated enterprise, even though it was going to bring them a lot of economic aid. And they pulled the Czechs and the Poles out, so that we were left with a Marshall Plan for Western Europe, embodied in the OEEC [Organization for European Economic Cooperation, later OECD—Organization for Economic Cooperation and Development], which did, in fact, restore the economies of Western Europe. . . . But this was the first thing that, I think, convinced Bevin that you couldn't work with Stalin.

Both sides now rallied their forces for the Cold War. In September, at Szklarska Poreba in Poland, was held the founding meeting of the Cominform (Communist Information Bureau)—a slimmed-down, all-European version of the old Communist International (Comintern), which Stalin had disbanded, as a gesture to his wartime allies, in 1943. The French and Italian Communist leaders were given a severe dressing-down by Andrei Alexandrovich Zhdanov, a member of the Soviet Politburo, for meekly allowing themselves to be ejected from their countries' governments in the spring and failing to understand the "imperialist" character of American policies, specifically the Marshall Plan (which the French leader, Maurice Thorez, had said publicly that France should accept, even after Russia and her satellites had rejected it). Duly chastened, they returned home to make as much trouble as possible during the winter through violent strikes and other disturbances.[23]

Ernest Bevin became convinced that the Marshall Plan would not in itself be enough to bolster Western European resistance to the Soviet threat.

ROBERTS: It all started with a dinner party in London at the end of 1947, at the end of the four-power meeting with the Russians, which had produced nothing. Bevin had a small party for Attlee and the leading Americans, to say, "Well, you know, our attempts to get on with the Russians are useless. The Russians are becoming rather dangerous. We must move . . ." in the direction which led eventually to the Alliance. And the Americans told him—he didn't have to be told —the difficulty they would have in selling this to Congress and internally in the United States. And that was why he had to do what he could, as it were, with the weak Europe as it then was.

On January 22, 1948, in a speech in the House of Commons, Bevin called on the states of Western Europe to unite for their own protection. The result was the Brussels Pact, signed on March 17 by Britain, France, and the three Benelux countries, and providing for collective self-defense as well as closer collaboration in economic, social, and cultural matters.[24]

FRANKS: When Mr. Bevin went to Brussels to sign that treaty . . . he found the state of mind there profoundly depressed. There'd been the coup in Czechoslovakia.* This had made people wonder how

*February 25, 1948.

far the Russians would go. A government which was democratic had been overthrown and a Communist government had been put in its place.* All the governments were now Communist or Communist-led in Eastern Europe. Mr. Bevin found that at least one of the ministers signatory to the treaty expected the Russians to be in Paris by August —and the French chief of general staff said he did not dissent. This meant there was widespread despondency. It was perceived . . . that the Russians were in some way menacing. Mr. Bevin still didn't think that the tanks would roll. But he was quite clear that economic recovery in Europe had to be accompanied by reassurance, and therefore [he] took the initiative all through the early months of 1948, trying to persuade the United States that it was necessary to have some sort of agreement across the Atlantic—a military agreement, an alliance, which would give reassurance to the Europeans in a military way as well as giving them economic aid and succor.

ROBERTS: It was one thing, the economic help, because that was America being generous with economic aid. But it was quite different taking on military commitments, and in the State Department there were two people, sort of third rank down—[Theodore] Achilles and [John D.] Hickerson, I think it was—who were fighting this battle. But, as they themselves have said since, they had to first of all get over a lot of opposition from the senior American State Department people—people who were as well known as Chip Bohlen and George Kennan,† who were each of them against it for different reasons. . . .

So they had to be got round, and I think myself, looking back on it all, the only reason that this policy was in fact agreed on in the United States was because there was a great example of bipartisanship. There was a Republican majority in the Senate. So a great deal depended on the senior Republican in the foreign affairs committee, Senator [Arthur H.] Vandenberg, and it's he who was persuaded that this was necessary, and it's he who sold it to the Senate and eventually to the American people. . . . It's fair to say now that it was sold with the understanding that the American troops would come back [to Europe] but not for long. But, of course, they've stayed for the last forty years.

*The government was already Communist-led, since the Communists had emerged from the free elections of 1946 as the largest single party. But in February 1948 the pro-Western ministers were forced out. A wave of arrests and executions followed, and the foreign minister, Jan Masaryk, fell or was pushed from his office window on March 10. A full-dress Communist regime emerged, and thereafter no opposition was tolerated.

†The department's two most influential experts on Soviet affairs at that time.

On the same day that the Brussels Pact was signed, President Truman reintroduced compulsory military service, telling Congress: "I am sure that the determination of the free countries of Europe to protect themselves will be matched by an equal determination on our part to help them to protect themselves." Six weeks later, on April 28, 1948, the Canadian prime minister, Louis Saint-Laurent, became the first national leader to advocate publicly a single defense system linking the two sides of the Atlantic. On May 12 Vandenberg introduced in the U.S. Senate his resolution recommending "the association of the United States by constitutional process, with such regional and other collective arrangements as are based on continuous and effective self-help and mutual aid, and as affect its national security." This was adopted on June 11 by 64 votes to 4.[25]

Meanwhile a crisis was rapidly developing in Germany, where the Western allies had despaired of reaching agreement with the Russians on an overall peace settlement and were gradually organizing West Germany as a separate economic and political entity.

> BEREZHKOV: The decisions from the Potsdam conference were treating Germany as a unity . . . but, as you know, afterwards the Western powers decided to use their occupation zones to create some kind of an entity which would be directed against the Soviet Union and against the eastern parts of Germany which were at that time under Soviet occupation. And there was a separate currency introduced by the Western powers,* to which we objected. We said that this is the first step towards division of Germany. . . . So this was, I think, considered as a test towards us, whether we will capitulate . . . whether we would really, with the existence of the bomb . . . be prepared to say, "Okay, now whatever you want from us." And this was really a very dramatic situation, and I think that maybe there were also other reasons, but one of the reasons may be that we wanted to show that we stand firm, that we are not going to capitulate, that in spite of the fact that we don't have the bomb we really had a very strong army at that time, we had a very big military potential, and we are not going to capitulate—that when the Western powers make trouble for us we are prepared also to make trouble for them.

On June 24 Stalin responded with a blockade of all land and water traffic in and out of West Berlin, which was to last for nearly a year and which, in Frank Roberts's words, "was very nearly a military act:

*June 18, 1948.

I mean, we had to put the whole of the air forces of America and Britain into the thing to beat it."

Against this background, Truman directed on July 2 that the Vandenberg Resolution be implemented "to the fullest extent possible" and at once. Negotiations began between the U.S., Canada, and the parties to the Brussels Pact on July 6, and were later expanded to include Norway, Denmark, Iceland, and Portugal. The negotiations lasted through the winter—the most difficult point being the inability of the United States to commit itself to go to war if one of its allies were attacked, the power to declare war being reserved to Congress by the Constitution. This was eventually solved by the parties agreeing "that an armed attack against one or more of them in Europe or North America shall be considered an attack against them all," and that each of them in that event would take "forthwith, individually and in concert with the other Powers, such action as it deems necessary, including the use of armed force, to restore and maintain the security of the North Atlantic area."

The treaty, which Truman called "the first peacetime military alliance concluded by the United States since the adoption of the Constitution,"[26] was signed in Washington on April 4, 1949, but still had to be ratified by the Senate.

> GROSS: For a while, when Acheson was secretary of state [i.e., after January 1949], I was assistant secretary for congressional relations, and one of my tasks was to help the secretary steer the North Atlantic Treaty through the Senate. Acheson . . . was a principal architect of NATO, as you know. Kennan, who was director of the Policy Planning Staff of the State Department, was against the North Atlantic Treaty. He did not consider it to be wise for the United States to commit itself to a military alliance. He thought that the Western European countries should follow through on that so-called Western European Union initiative [i.e., the Brussels Pact]. And I found many times, in my wanderings about on the Hill in consultations with the Senate leadership, that this difference between Acheson and Kennan was quite well known up there. To say the least, regardless of who was right or wrong, it didn't help us navigate the treaty through the Senate.

Nonetheless, the treaty was ratified on July 21, by 82 votes to 13, and went into effect on August 24, 1949. But at this stage it was, in the words of Paul Nitze, who succeeded Kennan as head of the Policy Planning Staff at the beginning of 1950, "essentially a political commitment, by the United States and Canada, to come to the support of

Western Europe if it were attacked." This was appropriate so long as its main task was seen as being reassurance to Western European countries demoralized by the postwar crisis, and the main threat was seen as being Communist subversion. But something more was needed once it was believed there was a danger of actual Soviet military invasion. I asked Ernest Gross when that was.

> GROSS: When it became increasingly clear that, with the strengthening of Western Europe, subversion was not productive for the Russians, despite the fact that they maintained a steady pressure in Berlin, in Czechoslovakia, in Hungary—a steady pressure which threatened military action implicitly. Because I think that they had expanded politically and by subversion as far west as they could go without risking war, which they were not prepared to do at that time. . . . When they found they could not get their control by subversion, we thought that they might have recourse to military action. This is when we wanted to have an American force there *coûte que coûte*—no matter what it cost.

But it was only the outbreak of the Korean War in June 1950 that decided the argument on this point within the American political and military establishment, as Arthur Schlesinger explains.

> SCHLESINGER: Reaction to the Korean War was a culmination of the growing view that the Soviet Union was bent upon aggression through military means, and therefore this required a military reaction. The American defense budget had been held under the Truman administration to $10 billion a year. The U.S. army consisted of ten and a half divisions in June 1950, when North Korea invaded South Korea. So immediately it set in motion a process of American rearmament. . . . A paper arguing the need for such rearmament languished in Truman's office for some time: that was National Security Council paper number 68, in which the hawks, so to speak, of the administration had been for some time contending for intensified military buildup. Truman had not rejected the paper, but he had deferred consideration of it. As a result of the Korean War, NSC 68 was adopted as national policy.

Paul Nitze, now regarded as a "dove" in the Reagan administration, was one of the "hawks" to whom Schlesinger refers, and the main author of "NSC 68." He confirms the crucial impact of Korea on defense thinking in and about Europe.

NITZE: After the surprise attack by North Korea into South Korea —that demonstrated that there was a military component to the Soviet grand strategy: granted, at that time through a satellite, but still there was a military component to what they not only planned to do but had demonstrated they were capable of doing—at that time the Europeans became very much concerned that they might be the next to be attacked, and therefore they saw the threat to Europe in military terms as much greater and more imminent than they'd seen it before. So they were the ones who urged us, at that time, to address ourselves to a military defense of Europe and, in the first instance, we increased the military assistance program. I think we went up to $4 billion in 1951, with respect to Europe, which was much greater than anything we'd done before. And then it was later than that that it was decided to try to create an organization, a military command structure . . . the things which were involved in creating the North Atlantic Treaty *Organization* as opposed to the North Atlantic Treaty.

Ernest Gross also witnessed these events from a crucial vantage point, as deputy head of the U.S. mission to the United Nations.

GROSS: Time and time again I was told, when I was at the U.S. mission, that the position of the White House and the Department of State was that the Korean aggression was Soviet-mounted and in all likelihood was a first step in a major worldwide aggressive move on the part of the Soviet Union. There was no question, in the minds of many of our military leaders as well, that the invasion of the Republic of Korea below the thirty-eighth parallel on June 25 was not an action isolated and without some sort of a master plan. Historians can debate that one as a matter of hindsight, but the record will show—particularly the secret record will show—that that was a widely held view. And from that point on, therefore, the defense of Europe became even more acutely of interest to the United States. From June 1950 on there was no way in which the United States would withdraw its forces from Western Europe, whatever the Western European countries did by way of conventional defenses.

In December 1950 the North Atlantic Council agreed to set up an integrated military force under an American general, and in January 1951 General Eisenhower set up his headquarters outside Paris. But Gross also gives another reason why the American military presence in Europe was gradually strengthened and made more permanent.

GROSS: As it became clearer and clearer that the European governments generally speaking, for budgetary and other reasons, had higher priorities than strengthening their conventional defenses, the more that happened—or didn't happen—that is, that the Western conventional defenses were *not* strengthened, the more pressure there was upon the American strategic nuclear weapon, and the more of an implicit commitment was developing that the Americans would respond to conventional Soviet aggression in Europe by nuclear retaliation. And this became very dangerous to the United States, and I think that that as much as anything else induced a very reluctant Congress to appropriate unexpectedly large funds for the maintenance of a large American military force in Europe. . . .

The situation then—and by then I mean 1950, '51, '52—was that the United States had detected the first Soviet atomic explosion in the fall of 1949. So we knew they had the Bomb. Secondly, that, as I said before, although we had the nuclear weapon, we didn't want to engage it as a response to that. . . . Acheson's secret sessions of the North Atlantic Defense Council, from the very first day (which was December 1949), urged the building of conventional defenses. We promised the Congress that this was going to be our first priority, and we wanted it that way. The Europeans promised to attain certain force goals. In 1952 they set them. They've never been accomplished. Now at that time, given the fears of the Soviet Union, given the fears that Western Europe could go Communist in elections . . . we were not in a position to do any bargaining, or we didn't wish to do any bargaining, say, "We will pull our forces out unless you strengthen conventional forces." To do that effectively you'd have to give a deadline and effect an ultimatum. We weren't about to do that. And in order to defend against conventional Soviet attack we wanted to have a stronger conventional force in Europe than the Europeans were in a position to—or willing to—provide.

From September 1950 onward much of America's diplomatic talent and energy were directed at strengthening NATO, and the conventional defense of Western Europe, by finding a formula that would enable West Germany—officially proclaimed as the Federal Republic in May 1949—to play a part corresponding to her strategic position in the front line of the Cold War, and to her demographic and economic potential as one of Europe's leading nations. Americans and even British were able to adapt surprisingly quickly from thinking of Germany as a deadly enemy to thinking of her (or half of her, anyway) as an essential ally in the struggle against Communism. To the French, who had suffered three German invasions in the past century, it came much less easily. Initially it seemed that their anxieties could be more easily overcome if Germans were re-armed not as a separate German army but as part of an integrated European Defense Community. An agreement to create this body was signed in Paris in May 1952 by France, West Germany, Italy, and the three Benelux countries (with Britain and the United States supporting it from the outside)—but never ratified by the French parliament. By 1954 the French had discovered that they were less appalled by the thought of having West Germany as an ally within NATO than by that of having to merge their own armed forces with hers. On May 9, 1955, the Federal Republic was admitted to both NATO and the Brussels Pact (renamed the Western European Union). For Matthias Wissmann, and no doubt for many other Germans of his age, that was the most memorable event of his early childhood.

> WISSMANN: The first thing I can remember, that must have been at the time when I was six years old—1955—was the situation where I was driving with my father in our car, and suddenly we heard a radio speech of Chancellor Adenauer, and the message which I got was—and perhaps my father explains it, I don't know exactly—"Germany is a sovereign country again." That must have been at the time when a treaty has been made, of Germany as a full partner in NATO, and . . . later again I understood that Germany is split, and I started to understand what the reason for it was.

These two aspects of postwar German history—the split, and the sovereignty of the Federal Republic—are indeed closely connected, for the Russians have been careful to see that their zone of Germany keeps pace with each step organized or permitted by the Western powers in theirs. The creation of the Federal Republic in May 1949 was followed by the proclamation of the German Democratic Republic in October; and the admission of the former to NATO on May 9, 1955, was matched a mere five days later by the creation of the Warsaw Pact with the GDR as a full member. The following day, in a contrasting but complementary development, the Soviet, British, American, and French foreign ministers signed a treaty with Austria providing for the withdrawal of all occupation forces by the end of the year. Austria espoused permanent neutrality and wrote it into her constitution. Only Berlin was left as an untidy sequel of World War II, a kind of leaking valve between the two halves of divided Europe. That leak was to be plugged in 1961, when Khrushchev had finally despaired of dislodging the Western powers from their half of the city. The process that Gladwyn Jebb had unwittingly begun when he drew his line on the map in 1943 was at last complete.

CHAPTER 2

Legacy of Bretton Woods: The Empire of the Dollar

MEMORIES

ABRAMS: There is a sense . . . you know, part of it relates to the dollar, a sense that it is normal that everything in the world can be denominated in dollars—"How much is that in dollars?"—and there is the sense that America was everywhere, and that it was appropriate for Americans to travel everywhere and be everywhere, and that English was becoming the dominant international language and the dollar the dominant international currency, and somehow you pick up the notion that the United States is supposed to be—to borrow a phrase—the top country.

That is how Elliott Abrams, one of the standard-bearers of American neoconservative thought on human rights and Third World issues, now under secretary of state for inter-American affairs in the Reagan administration, recalls learning about the relationship between his country and the rest of the world as a child in the 1950s. C. Fred Bergsten, head of the Institute for International Economics, can pinpoint the same experience more precisely.

BERGSTEN: I think my first real impression of world affairs—and it had an important impact on my future career decisions—was spending the summer in England in 1950. I went with my family and there were still queues for food, much of London was still bombed out, and my initial image was of a Europe, and its leading country at the time, England, which was decidedly less well off than my own. My next major experience was in 1960, when I traveled to Berlin—and Germany, more broadly—but visited both West and East Berlin and saw, in East Berlin in particular, a vast difference from the West as I knew it, including in Western Europe; and those differences left very strong impressions, particularly of—at least at that time—the United States as by far the wealthiest, most prosperous country in the world economy.

Newt Gingrich, growing up on a U.S. army base in France, had plenty of opportunities to make the same observation.

GINGRICH: I think first of all in the fifties you had an enormous sense of superiority. I mean you—we—had money at that time sufficiently powerful that we were paid in scrip—because if we'd been paid in greenbacks in France or Germany it would have led to mass inflation, as everybody bought it in the black market. So you grew up with a sense that you came out of a special nation—that we'd won.

They had, indeed, won. Joe Biden, Democratic senator from Delaware, also grew up with the knowledge that "the only nation that was left basically unscathed in a major sense by the war was the United States" and that this had left his country with an overwhelming economic superiority.

BIDEN: When I was growing up, if it didn't have a stamp "Made in America" on it, it was automatically assumed it was inferior. It didn't matter—it could be German, it could be French, it could be British, it could be Japanese, if it didn't have an American label on it, it was inferior.

"After World War II, let's face it," says Pat Schroeder, Democratic congresswoman from Colorado, "we were like a cornucopia, the fruits just flowed out—we were the only industrialized nation that hadn't been reduced to rubble."

The Republican Larry Pressler grew up in South Dakota, which he now represents in the Senate, and which is about as far from the outside world as an American can hope to live. But he, too, remembers being told of America's economic superiority to the rest of the world:

PRESSLER: I was very active in the 4-H Club—that's a rural youth group, it's something like the Boy Scouts would be, among farm kids. We always used to hear that "American know-how" builds the greatest things in the world, we're the greatest country, most powerful nation on the face of the earth. . . . We know how to get something done. . . . If you were sent abroad on a 4-H trip, you were going to tell the other people about American know-how.

And George Will, the influential conservative commentator, recalls his sense of "new material wonders."

WILL: All of a sudden people stopped traveling to the West Coast by train, they went by plane. In the space of about five years we became a wired nation: television—a fantastic product, boom, like that! It was a big deal in the United States when I was thirteen or fourteen years old, to get on your bike and ride round to the new automobile dealerships every fall to see the new automobiles. Everyone was buying their second car, and it was a tremendous sense of sheer material excess. It was great fun.

For us in Europe, of course, America was the land of boundless plenty, from which came everything big and grand and expensive. We knew we were poor relations. But we also knew we were members of the family. We shared in the general feeling that, materially at least, things were getting better and would—by some unwritten law of nature—continue to do so. It was the age of "economic miracles," when Europe was rapidly recovering from the war and following the American path to prosperity. For young Germans, of course, this process was particularly striking—the unforgettable backdrop against which their whole childhood was lived.

JOFFE: What you were conscious of in the fifties is that a country that was literally in ruins was literally being reconstructed. As a very young kid I roamed the ruins of Berlin. Berlin was about 60 percent destroyed and this was a great adventurous time for a little kid—he could build all kinds of things and go through all kinds of adventures. And we lived through a process of rebuilding, which was as simple as visually rebuilding the cities in which we lived. It was also a process of steady and pronounced economic growth. . . . At the beginning of the fifties there were maybe only two cars in our street; by the end of the fifties you couldn't find a parking space. Same thing with telephones, with the successive waves of consumption—furniture, gadgets, travel, food.

ADAM-SCHWAETZER: This was quite normal for every one of us, that the gross national product every year was growing, and that the unemployment we had started with at the beginning of the fifties was decreasing, and we have been enormously successful economically—that the name "Made in West Germany" was a figure on world markets. We have been proud—as youngsters we have been proud of that also. . . . It was the image of a nation beginning to be saturated economically, and being proud of it: being proud of the success we had had, as we felt it, by our own forces.

WISSMANN: When I was first driving—some parts by bicycle, others by car—through Great Britain . . . I could see that there seems to be a difference as far as wealth of people and material background, housing, is concerned. Honestly spoken, I understood more at this time—when I was nineteen or eighteen—than before, how big the step has been which in Germany was done between 1945 and 1968. I don't want to exaggerate, but it's in some aspects true that we have lost the war, but won the peace.

That last remark was, by the late sixties, something of a cliché in British discussion of Germany. Certainly by the time of the devaluation of the pound sterling in 1967 awareness of Britain's *relative* decline, vis-à-vis her European neighbors, had forced itself upon the British public. Until then we were much more conscious of being, in absolute terms, better off than most of them. I can remember feeling quite snooty about the litter in the Paris streets on my first trip abroad, at the age of twelve, in 1956, and I retained a low opinion of French public hygiene after a camping holiday in Provence in 1961. The following year, when I worked as a volunteer teacher at Saint-Louis in Senegal, a newly independent French African colony, I used to enjoy provoking French expatriates who asked how I liked the town by opening my reply with the statement, in carefully practiced French: "Like all French cities, it's a bit dirty, but . . ."

But France, too, was going through her economic miracle, for which Jacques Toubon, as a good Gaullist, gives the credit to General de Gaulle (though economic historians find evidence for it's starting well before he returned to power in 1958).

TOUBON: I think that in 1950 or 1955 France was, in comparison with some other countries, much more a nineteenth-century country. And I think that General de Gaulle got France into the twentieth century. I think so.

MORTIMER: What could you see that made you aware of that, in the France of the early sixties?

TOUBON: Things like refrigerators in houses, and cars—you know, French little cars—the Quatre Chevaux or Dauphine. I think the Dauphine was a symbol of the renewal of the French economy.

By the late sixties, when I lived in Paris, France and Britain were materially on more or less equal terms, and in the seventies each time I returned from a visit to France it was the squalor and untidiness of British towns that struck me by comparison. But in the fifties, as Conservative politician Chris Patten also recalls, it was the absolute improvement we were conscious of, not the relative decline:

PATTEN: The fifties and sixties were a period in which everything seemed to be getting better. People in the 1950s were buying a car for the first time, buying a television, buying white goods for the kitchen, taking the family abroad for the first time. I can remember all those things—I was a product of that generation.

It is true that in my early childhood there was a familiar grown-up litany, in the upper-middle-class milieu to which my parents belonged, about this or that having been better or more easily obtainable "before the war." But it faded fairly quickly as it became apparent that most of the things of which it was still true had been rendered scarce by the rising prosperity of the majority of the population—the most obvious examples being domestic servants, and roads uncluttered by other people's cars. When I was fifteen, in 1959, Harold Macmillan secured the third consecutive Tory election victory by using the slogan, "You've never had it so good!" I remember objecting to this on the grounds that it encouraged people to be selfish, to ignore the plight of others worse off than themselves. What no one disputed was that, for the great majority of British people, it was true. And though Labour did return to power five years later, under Harold Wilson, that was because many of my elders (you had to be twenty-one to vote in those days) by then shared my view that prosperity could be more fairly distributed and more competently administered, not because they denied its existence.

PATTEN: The sixties were an attempt, I think—not a very good one because it lacked any social-democratic coherence—but an attempt by Wilson, I think, to turn those individual gains into collective gains—and I think there was a certain amount of excitement about Wilson early on.

Chris Patten is now a Tory minister. I remember him as, for the time, an unusually nonpolitical Oxford undergraduate. But I dare swear that, like me, he would have voted Labour in 1964 if we had had the vote.

In fact it did not make that much difference which party was in power. The sixties were a decade of rapidly rising public expenditure. New universities, theaters, hospitals, seemed to be springing up everywhere. Unemployment may have been occasionally mentioned by politicians, but it was a marginal phenomenon, statistically insignificant by today's standards, and not something that one worried about personally—especially if one was young. There was a cult of youth—associated in Britain with the Beatles, and Carnaby Street, and "swinging London"—which even at the time seemed rather excessive, and in retrospect seems thoroughly indecent. I myself became a foreign correspondent on the London *Times* at the age of twenty-three. Formerly (and since) this honor would have been reserved for a journalist of several years' professional experience. I had none, and I suspect my lack of it counted in my favor. At the same period the paper was seeking to attract new readers with an advertisement giving photographs and short biographies of three of its specialist writers, with the punchline: "We just had to get the best people in the field—we can't help it that they're so young!"

It was, when all is said and done, a remarkably cheerful world to grow up in on either side of the Atlantic. Stability, comfort, full employment, economic growth, steadily rising standards of living: all this we took pretty well for granted, even if those growing up in countries that had been defeated or occupied during the war had a clearer notion than their British—and *a fortiori* their American—contemporaries what a remarkable piece of good luck for our generation this was. Our parents, at the same age, had lived through the slump, the Depression, and then the war. It seems surprising in retrospect that we were not more curious to know what had brought about this remarkable change in the world's economic fortunes at the end of the war.

HOW IT WAS DONE

BERNSTEIN: We had a world in which centers of deflation were created, and they came to a head in an enormous amount of unemployment, of hardship—a great fall in output in the United States, for example: our unemployment rate was 25 percent of the labor force; our

> output—gross national product—fell by about 30 percent; and world trade fell by more than half in volume. This was not a world in which people could find a decent standard of living, find work, or for that matter have any great outlook, any hope for the future. This was what we were trying to remedy. Now we thought in the United States that the problem was a consequence of mistakes. It wasn't inherent in the world to be poor or to become poor. We made it that way, and we thought that perhaps we could find a way to avoid it in the future.

That is how Edward Bernstein, one of the top economists at the U.S. Treasury during the war, remembers the spirit in which international economic problems were approached. It was generally agreed that in the interwar period they had been disastrously mismanaged, and that this had both directly and indirectly contributed to the breakdown of peace. The dispute between Japan and the United States, which led to Pearl Harbor, was largely about markets and access to markets. The dispute between Hitler and his enemies in Europe was more crudely about territory. But economic causes had clearly contributed to the rise of the Nazi regime.

> BERNSTEIN: The Germans had the most severe Depression next to the United States—the unemployment rate in Germany may have been of the order of 20 percent—and they felt imposed upon because in spite of the Depression they were expected to pay reparations. And that made it very easy for Hitler to rouse his countrymen—they'd been treated unjustly, harshly—there'd never been such a vindictive peace treaty, and he was obviously the man who was going to destroy it, and not only destroy it but get back for Germany everything it had lost. . . . I think that did help a good deal. And I think the fact that Britain and the United States and France, especially France, were having great difficulty in dealing with their economic problems made them passive as Germany took each extra step. I think we can explain . . . this eagerness of Britain and France to conciliate Hitler at least in part by their feeling that their countries weren't really ready because of the Great Depression.

Hitler's arrival in power in 1933 coincided with Germany's economic revival. His dirigiste and nationalist economic policies had been apparently highly successful in the 1930s by comparison with those of more liberal governments in other countries, and after his victory over France in 1940 his economic affairs minister (and president of the Reichsbank), Walther Funk, announced plans to extend these policies to Europe as a whole. "We will not," he said, "allow the unregulated play of economic power, which caused such grave difficulties to the German economy, to become active again."[1]

The fall in world output during the 1930s was accompanied by, and closely related to, a collapse of international trade. British economist Sir Alec Cairncross recalls these years.

> CAIRNCROSS: It wasn't just that trade ceased to expand in 1929. It really plunged downwards, and when it plunged downwards it began to be regulated and become governed by political forces, where your sheer competitive power was largely irrelevant. You couldn't be in markets easily merely by offering the right goods: people would not be able to afford them. They would enter into trading agreements with you, which allowed for so much of a swap, but not free trade. So I think there was a disposition to say, "We must have freer trade in the postwar period. . . ." And the Americans, of course, were very strong on this. They were not a trading nation of the kind that we were, but they were very anxious to make way for American exports, and they were often rather puzzled why things should have been done after the war that appeared to limit the demand for their exports, when they were being so generous to the world. But, of course, what could be bought in the way of American exports depended on whether people had the dollars to pay for them, and if everybody was in debt to America, and everybody was in deficit in their payments to America, you couldn't buy any more.

The problem as seen from the United States, and especially by the secretary of state during Roosevelt's first three presidential terms, Cordell Hull, was the lack of free trade. The problem as seen in varying degrees by almost everyone else was the overwhelming competitive strength of the United States, which in conditions of unrestricted free trade led to the concentration of the world's gold reserves in that country and the inability of other countries to pay for their imports. In the words of the British economist John Maynard Keynes—the leading economic thinker of the day—the United States as a creditor nation with a large export surplus, refusing to take full payment in goods and instead accumulating gold, had "made any general international system unworkable."[2]

> CAIRNCROSS: It was arguable, and Keynes himself for quite a time in the war argued, that we [the British] would have to be very restrictive in our use of what foreign exchange we had. We couldn't afford

> to admit goods freely. We would have to ration ourselves for imports —and these restrictions were simply necessary because we lacked the funds. Now that was one point of view. But there were others who thought that we really must aim, eventually at least, after a period of transition, to establish much freer trade, so that there were not the squabbles between countries, and so also that we got the economic benefits of cheaper imports made by people who specialized in the things we were buying.

As country after country got into balance-of-payments difficulties, three main types of defense were in vogue. One was deflation—deliberate reduction of domestic demand, by increasing taxes and/or tightening credit, so as to reduce imports and redirect domestic production into exports. The second was to devalue or depreciate your own currency, so as to make your exports cheaper in foreign markets while making imports more expensive than home products for your domestic consumers. This could work quite well for a time as long as you were the only country doing it, but inevitably more than one country resorted to it, each trying to defend its own competitive position—what became known as beggar-my-neighbor policies. The third was protection, either by straightforward across-the-board tariffs on imports or by discriminating in favor of imports from countries that were willing to buy your exports in return: this could be done by discriminatory tariffs or by paying for imports in your own currency and then restricting the conversion of that currency into other currencies or gold, so that the supplier who received it was obliged to spend it in the country he got it from.

All these devices, while they might benefit one country or group of countries in the short term, had the effect of restricting international trade and thereby ultimately impoverishing the world as a whole, or at least reducing its potential prosperity. The Americans disliked all of them, but they particularly disliked the discriminatory building of trade and currency blocs to which Japan (the Asian Coprosperity Sphere), Germany (the New European Order), and Britain (imperial preferences and the sterling area) all resorted. The Most Favored Nation principle—according to which privileges granted to one trading partner should automatically be extended to all the others —was a hallowed tradition of American foreign policy extending back to George Washington, and for Cordell Hull it was something like a religion.

Therefore when Britain in 1940–41, left alone to face Hitler and with virtually exhausted financial reserves, looked to America to supply the necessary war matériel on credit, the Americans not unnaturally sought a *quid pro quo* in the form of an undertaking from the British not to discriminate against American imports after the war. Keynes, who had been sent to help negotiate the American credits, was strongly against this. He believed that if Britain were obliged to allow free access to American goods, she would have to return to the gold standard (which she had abandoned in 1931) and to disastrous deflationary policies.

"My so strong reaction against the word 'discrimination,' " he wrote to Dean Acheson, then assistant secretary of state for economic affairs, "is the result of my feeling so passionately that our hands must be free to make something new and better of the postwar world."[3] This feeling led him to formulate his famous proposal for an international "clearing union," in which surpluses of foreign currency built up by one country would automatically be available (like the deposits in a clearing bank) for lending to other countries to finance international trade. The clearing union would have its own unit of account with a fixed gold value, and member countries would fix the value of their currencies in terms of that unit. All foreign exchange would be centralized in the hands of the central bank of each country, and all international payments would be cleared between those central banks through the clearing union. A country whose account was in debit by a certain amount would be allowed to depreciate its currency, by not more than 5 percent in any one year. Each country would be entitled to borrow from the clearing union up to a certain quota, but if the borrowing exceeded half the quota, it could be *required* to depreciate so as to correct the imbalance. Correspondingly, a country in credit might be required to *appreciate* (revalue its currency upward). Any credit balance it built up in excess of its quota would be transferred to the clearing union's reserve fund. The credit balances would be used to finance a supranational policing body, charged with the preservation of world peace, and an international organization to provide funds for postwar relief and reconstruction.[4]

These proposals were much too ambitious and interventionist for the Americans. But the view that the postwar world economy would have to be better organized than the prewar economy, in order to permit an orderly expansion of world trade, took hold in Washington, too. In particular it was felt that a more stable currency system was badly needed, but that this could not simply take the form of a return to the gold standard, as after World War I.

In December 1941, just after Pearl Harbor, the U.S. secretary of the treasury, Henry Morgenthau, asked his assistant, Harry Dexter

White, "to think about and prepare a memorandum and plan for setting up an Inter-Allied Stabilization Fund . . . to be used during the war to give monetary aid to actual and potential allies and to hamper the enemy; to provide the basis for post-war international monetary stabilization arrangements; and to provide a post-war 'international currency.' "[5] The result was the proposal for what was eventually to become the International Monetary Fund. Instead of the international clearing bank proposed by Keynes, multilaterally controlled and with lenders and borrowers effectively on an equal footing, this was to be a specific pool of money contributed by each participating country, partly in gold, partly in its own currency and government securities, according to national quotas "based on pertinent considerations including national income, gold holdings, population, foreign debt," and controlled by representatives whose voting strength would reflect the value of their country's contribution. "In view of both the size and quality of the U.S. contribution (there being *no question about a possible inability to exchange dollars for gold* [italics added] for purposes of settling international balances) the U.S. should have enough votes to block any decision, i.e. more than 20 per cent."[6]

In his memorandum presenting the plan to Morgenthau, White stressed the underlying urgency of the problem:

> A breach must be made and widened in the outmoded and disastrous economic policy of each-country-for-itself-and-the-devil-take-the-weakest. Just as the failure to develop an effective League of Nations has made possible two devastating wars within one generation, so the absence of a high degree of economic collaboration among the leading nations will, during the coming decade, inevitably result in economic warfare that will be but the prelude and instigator of military warfare on an even vaster scale.[7]

The scheme was thus a classic emanation of the Rooseveltian internationalist philosophy. American national interests and those of the wider international community were assumed to coincide. American strength was to be placed at the service of the world, and America would therefore naturally take the leading role in the new international system. As White explained it when he first made the proposal public, early in 1943:

> The dollar is the one great currency in whose strength there is universal confidence. It will probably become the cornerstone of the postwar structure of stable currencies. The United States holds the greater part of the world's resources of gold and foreign exchange. These resources

must be available to give assurance of universal strength and confidence in the stability of currencies. . . . Stable currencies are an important element in the healthy environment which is indispensable to the attainment of . . . full employment and [a] rising standard of living everywhere.[8]

These ideas were to form the basis of the agreements eventually reached at the Bretton Woods conference of July 1944, setting up the International Monetary Fund and the International Bank for Reconstruction and Development (later known as the World Bank).

In 1986 the octogenarian Edward Bernstein still chuckled with enjoyment as he recalled the atmosphere of that historic meeting in the mountains of New Hampshire.

BERNSTEIN: The conference was held in the country . . . very far out from any city. It was held there because we wanted the delegates to be isolated. If they were in New York, they would be running off to see what the city offered. There was nothing they could do at Bretton Woods but work! They could look at the mountains, but they couldn't even take a ride because there wasn't any gasoline available for the delegates.

So they were in a sense dedicated to work—but it was work which also had some social life to it. . . . It came at a time when the turn of events in the war made everybody feel more optimistic for the Allied powers—though there was a good deal of difficulty still. In London, for example, the buzz bombs—the V-bombs—had begun to fall even while the delegation from the United Kingdom was coming to the United States. [But] at Bretton Woods itself we had a very elated feeling. The national holidays for the United States and France were celebrated with a great deal more patriotic enthusiasm than you would normally expect for sophisticated people. And, of course, when the attempt on Hitler's life was announced we all felt we were getting near the end. . . .

There were forty-four countries there. Many of them had ideas of what they wanted in the "final act," that is to say in the agreement for the International Monetary Fund and for the World Bank, and it was the job of the United States—and, I'm sure, of the United Kingdom—to see that while we'd agreed on principles, everybody had an opportunity to express views of consequence to his or her country.

The conference ran very smoothly, but there was a lot of work to be done. For the United States, for example, we had to see everybody who had anything to say, and we couldn't possibly see all forty-four countries on all issues. I'm sure the United Kingdom had a similar problem because the delegates from the occupied countries in Europe, that's the governments exiled in London, all came by battle cruiser with the British delegation and they had plenty of time there to talk, but they also at Bretton Woods had their own views and were free to express them. The United States as the host country, and, of course, showing its interest—it was going to finance everything in any case—was regarded by everybody as the one they must persuade on any issue.

MORTIMER: Wasn't it also a matter of American self-interest? You were much the strongest commercial economy, and you wanted to make sure that markets everywhere were open to your goods?

BERNSTEIN: It was very important. After all, I think we must start with the proposition that the Americans were mainly interested in themselves. I don't mean that we didn't care about what would happen to Britain and to Europe in general—we did. But our first concern was to protect the interests of the United States. And we felt that the International Monetary Fund—with the regulation of exchange rates and international responsibility, with the requirement that currencies be convertible (which means that if anybody earned—say the Canadians earned—money by exporting to Britain, they could spend the money in the United States)—we regarded this as very important. And, incidentally, so did the Canadians: in fact, the main thing the Canadians wanted in the International Monetary Fund was a provision that said a country that earned money in one country could spend it in another. Convertibility, multilateral settlements: these were the technical terms they used. Yes, we were looking out for it.

We were confident, too. We were confident that this would be in the general interest. . . . In fact, Keynes had a little trouble with it in Britain, because there were still people in Britain who thought that imperial preference [was better]—"Go it alone, and don't depend on that uncertain country, the United States!" (I mean, uncertain for economic policy.)

Both the American and the British governments had some difficulty in defending the agreement to their respective parliaments and publics. American conservatives were deeply suspicious of Morgenthau and White, both of whom were known as enthusiastic New Dealers —protagonists of the interventionist and socially redistributive policies introduced by Roosevelt to cure the Depression in the 1930s. The Bretton Woods agreement was represented as an international version of the New Deal, through which hard-earned American dollars would be handed over to feckless foreigners to spend as they liked. However, in 1944–45 the notion of international cooperation to secure a better and more orderly world was still popular with the public at large. Randolph Feltus, the professional public relations expert hired by Morgenthau to "sell" the agreement, decided:

> Bretton Woods will be hitched to the star of Yalta. It will be fitted into the San Francisco conference picture. It will not stand alone but will be pictured as the first step in the implementation of the Yalta agreements.[9]

Edward Brown, president of a large Chicago bank, "a large, industrious, outspoken man who represented the tractable element of the banking community" and in that capacity had served on the U.S. delegation at Bretton Woods, told the House of Representatives Committee on Banking and Currency that "if a fund and bank had been in operation in the early twenties, the present war would probably not have occurred. . . . It would have prevented the breakdown of currency systems" and "the lending of money for unproductive purposes, of great sums of American money, which enabled Germany to build up its armament industries."[10]

This line of argument worked. In the House debate on ratification one speaker described Bretton Woods as

> a reasonably workable plan and agreement among the several nations to stop once and for all this traditional and staged rise and fall of the different moneys of the world. . . . With world money markets and standards the subject of economic warfare, anyone trading on the world market never could tell, from one moment to the next, where his business was. The only profits made in this type of financial piracy were made by the small handful of economic freebooters who unscrupulously manipulated the rates of exchange, sending the value of all moneys affected up and down in a sea of chaos and money madness. Is it any wonder war followed? Small wonder, indeed.[11]

The agreement passed the House by 345 votes to 18 on June 7, and the Senate by 61 to 16 on July 19, 1945—just two weeks after Morgenthau's resignation.

In Britain, Bretton Woods aroused hostility for the opposite reason. It was seen as a covert way of forcing the country back onto the gold standard and depriving her of the right to control her own economic policy, whether through imperial preferences (enshrined in the Ottawa Agreements), through devaluing the pound, or through temporarily or partially suspending its convertibility. Lord Franks, who was then at the Ministry of Supply, recalls the differences between the British and American outlooks at the time.

FRANKS: What the Americans wanted was a wide-open world, wide open to commerce, wide open for free and democratic governments—and the British hesitated. They knew they were weakened. They wanted to keep their defenses. They wanted to keep the sterling area. They wanted to keep the Ottawa Agreements. And the Americans attacked this. At the time of the British loan, at the end of 1945, they could force us to give way. They could make us promise, about the British loan, that within a year we would make sterling convertible, and they made us make concessions about the Ottawa Agreements. They were sufficiently powerful to bend our wishes to their will, in part—so that it's not true that at the beginning, in 1945, Britain and the United States were seeing eye to eye.

Britain was, indeed, in a very weak position after the abrupt termination of the American Lend-Lease facility on the cessation of hostilities in August 1945. When her representatives, including Keynes, came to Washington to negotiate a new peacetime loan, they were shaken by the toughness of the American attitude. Ratification of Bretton Woods became one of the conditions of the American loan, and thus went through the British Parliament virtually under duress.[12]

It was, very clearly, an American-dominated system. Harry White had slipped into the text—unknown to Keynes until too late—wording that gave the dollar a special status as effectively equivalent to gold.[13] This made little practical difference at the time, when the United States controlled three-quarters of the world's gold reserves and was clearly the only country whose ability to redeem its own currency for gold at the announced parity, if called upon to do so, was not in doubt. But it was symbolic, and important for the future. Moreover, the head offices of both the Bank and the Fund were to be in Washington, under the eye of the U.S. government, whose quotas gave it a dominant position in both of them. I asked Edward Bernstein why the Americans had insisted on having the system so clearly under their control.

BERNSTEIN: I think in part it came to the question: "We're putting up the money, and Congress is going to ask us, 'Who's going to run this?'; and we want to say, 'It's run by the United States.' " . . . Now Keynes didn't want it in Washington because he felt it would be under the dominance of the [U.S.] government, and political considerations would enter. . . . And that was the question: "Who is going to run it?"

The question was answered fairly brutally at the inaugural meeting of the boards of governors of the Fund and the Bank, held at Savannah, Georgia, in March 1946. The new U.S. secretary of the treasury, Fred Vinson (later chief justice of the United States), used "bulldozer" tactics to get his way on every question, particularly the location of the headquarters of both bodies (in Washington rather than New York) and on the salaries of the executive directors of the Fund, whom the Americans wanted to be highly paid full-time officials with "a strong international viewpoint," while the British would have preferred them to be part-time, representing primarily the views of the national governments that appointed them and leaving the day-to-day running of the Fund to the managing director (who, Keynes had hoped and expected, would be Harry White himself—the man whose brainchild the Fund was). As Keynes's disciple Paul Bareau later said,

> It was a harsh fight in which Keynes, for the first time in his dealings with Americans, found himself faced not by arguments but by the big battalions of voting blocks. . . . We lost on every issue, not by the process of rational argument in debate but by the solid massing of the cohorts which voted automatically with America, mainly South American states, whose representatives could be depended on to read, sometimes with considerable difficulty, the speeches prepared for them by the secretariat of the United States delegation. . . . The lobbying for votes, the mobilisation of supporters, the politics of the lunch and dinner table, were not arts in which Keynes excelled or indeed which he attempted to cultivate. All the more reason for his bitter disappointment at the manner in which a trip he had anticipated as a pleasant interlude, a voyage to Savannah when the camelias were in bloom, an opportunity of meeting so many of his friends, should have turned out as it did. "I went to Savannah to meet the world," he said, "and all I met was a tyrant."[14]

Keynes died shortly after his return to England. White, to almost everyone's astonishment, was not proposed by the U.S. government as the first managing director of the IMF: the post went instead to a Belgian politician, Camille Gutt. The reason emerged only later. In the rapidly developing Cold War climate, White, like many other New Dealers, had fallen under suspicion of being pro-Soviet and, it was alleged, "furnishing data and information to persons outside the Federal Government, who are in turn transmitting this information to espionage agents of the Soviet Government." No charges were ever brought against him, but in 1948 he was investigated by the House Un-American Activities Committee, where he appeared by his own request and made a robust statement of his liberal beliefs without denying that people now named as Communist spies had been among his friends and subordinates. Three days later he died of a heart attack at his home in New Hampshire.[15] It was a sad irony that the man who had done more than anyone to ensure that the postwar world economy would be run on American principles, in conformity with American interests and under American control, should have fallen under suspicion of disloyalty to his country.

A further irony is that, although during and after Bretton Woods the Americans firmly resisted Keynes's arguments, they subsequently behaved—and allowed others to behave—very much as his proposals would have required. Had the Bretton Woods agreement been applied to the letter—that is to say, had Britain and other European countries accepted full convertibility within a year,* and had the Americans accepted no obligation to recycle their massive surplus to finance trade by other countries—there would almost certainly have been the severe postwar depression that Keynes feared.

> CAIRNCROSS: The world economy, at the end of the war, looked as if it would take a long time to recover. The main countries in the world were virtually all in deficit. They could not procure the imports that they needed and pay for them at the same time. The United States was virtually the only country that had a surplus. And throughout Europe you had countries whose communications systems were in ruins, who had suffered enormous damage to their housing, their factories, everything that went to yield the product that was necessary to pay for what they required—and that looked as if it would involve a very long period of reconstruction, longer than at the end of the First World War because so much more damage had been done and the war had been so much longer and fiercer. . . .
>
> There had been an agreement which we entered into with the Americans, both under Bretton Woods and under the Loan Agreement, that we would observe no discrimination initially, that we would be good boys in international trade and not have high tariffs and behave unnecessarily partially. Now all that came unstuck in 1947, because the effort to establish a free-trade free-payments system failed in the early postwar period for lack of the means of payment.

European governments facing bankruptcy would have had to adopt very severe deflationary policies, many people in Europe might literally have starved to death, and the contraction of the overseas market combined with the winding down of war production would have

*"Britain, under intense American pressure, tried to restore the pound's convertibility in 1946. Within a few weeks, sales of pounds for dollars were so heavy that Britain ran through most of its reserves of foreign exchange, including a large loan from the United States. Thereafter Britain, like all the other European states, maintained exchange controls."[16]

produced a severe recession in America, too. Within a year of Keynes's death these dangers were glaringly apparent, and this—besides the fear of Communism—was crucial in persuading the United States to undertake the Marshall Plan, as Paul Nitze recalls.

> NITZE: The economic problem became very clear indeed by 1947 because by that time it was clear that the United States was running a balance-of-payments surplus of some five to seven billion dollars a year—which was, in those dollars, a very large sum indeed. It would seem small today, but everybody else was running a deficit and we were gradually absorbing all the gold and hard currency—foreign exchange resources—of the world; and this was driving one country after another into balance-of-payments problems where they couldn't pay their bills for the necessary imports. And then something had to be done about it: we would have had a general progressive economic breakdown in the world. And so we did do something about it: we took the action in good time so that the Marshall Plan was an enormous success—but thank goodness we did it when we did.

Oliver Franks, as chairman of the Paris conference that drew up the European response to Marshall's offer, was sent over to America with his executive committee in the autumn of 1947 to explain this point to the American people.

> FRANKS: First of all to explain to the American administration what we'd been doing in Paris, but after that, for a month, I was sent out all over the United States explaining. I talked on the radio. I talked to schoolteachers. I talked to committees of young businessmen. . . . I had a generally friendly reception, but a great many people simply didn't understand what it was about. I spent a lot of time in that vast Middle West area between the Rockies and the Alleghenies, all the way from the Great Lakes down to the Texas Gulf and New Orleans, explaining to wheat farmers, for example, in Kansas that a Frenchman who wants a loaf of bread has to buy flour: "It's no good his approaching a man in Kansas City with French francs—what will he use it for in the shop? He wants a dollar bill. There's a problem about the exchange: the mere fact that he has the wheat and the Frenchman needs it doesn't solve it. That is what the Marshall Plan is about: it's putting dollars in the hands of the Europeans so that they can buy your wheat and you can sell it."

But it was not only about that. Part of the European recovery program drawn up by the Paris conference—and accepted by the Americans—was the creation of the European Payments Union

(EPU). Under this, when European countries exported to each other (even though it was often by using Marshall Aid dollars to buy American capital equipment that they were able to produce the goods in question), the currency they earned was convertible only within Europe, not into dollars or gold: it could be used to purchase other European goods but not for additional purchases from the United States. This was exactly the sort of discriminatory currency bloc that the Americans had always criticized, and that Bretton Woods was supposed to have outlawed. But they tolerated, even encouraged, it because they saw that the revival of Western Europe as a viable industrial economy and therefore a continuously expanding market was essential to their own interests. It was not until 1958 that the EPU was dissolved and the main European countries accepted the full external convertibility of their currencies* to which they had pledged themselves in 1945.

Thus when people speak of the phenomenal success of the Bretton Woods system it would be more correct to understand it as "Bretton Woods plus Marshall Plan." But if one takes "Bretton Woods" as shorthand for the overall postwar economic order as it eventually emerged—just as "Yalta" is often used as shorthand for the overall postwar political order in Europe—then it must be adjudged a phenomenal success indeed, as those who took part in its creation recall with legitimate pride.

> BERNSTEIN: What has happened is that the world has had the greatest expansion, the greatest growth of output, in history. It's impossible to find a comparable period in the past. Every country doubled, trebled, or quadrupled since the end of World War II.

Such was the postwar economic order in which the political leaders of tomorrow—my contemporaries—grew up. What is striking is how few of them seem to be clearly aware that it did not just happen—that it was the product of political decisions taken by leaders who were all too well aware what the consequences of inaction could be. Those decisions were, first, to create a set of rules and institutions ensuring reasonably stable exchange rates so that people could sell goods for foreign currencies with some confidence in the value of the payments they were receiving; and, secondly, a decision—taken belatedly and

*In other words, a foreign holder of any of these currencies could convert it into dollars by presenting it to the central bank of the country that issued it. This did not automatically imply "internal convertibility," which is the freedom for residents of the country in question to acquire foreign currency without restriction.

in the nick of time but with great boldness once it came—to use political power to make money available where it was most needed. (But political power, it should be noted, did not intervene directly in the production or distribution of the goods on which the money was spent: that was left to the private sector.) Though Keynes did not live to see the Marshall Plan, it can be regarded as his most fitting memorial—the largest-scale and most unquestionably successful application in practice of his economic philosophy. While American conservatives of today like George Will are willing to acknowledge "the building of NATO and the structure both moral as well as institutional of the North Atlantic community" as "a period of just breathtaking creativity" and can also wax lyrical in describing the expanding prosperity of the America they grew up in, they tend to be more reticent about the creativity, wisdom, and courage of the interventionist economic policies involved. Of the political leaders interviewed for this book only Chris Patten—a British Conservative of the "wet" school—clearly acknowledged the connection, though even he admitted it had not been immediately obvious to him in the early seventies, when the Bretton Woods system was breaking down.

PATTEN: I think we all underestimated the importance of Bretton Woods to economic progress and economic stability, and we overestimated our ability to put something else in its place, and that was, I think, a ludicrous overconfidence in market forces, in leaving everything to the international banking system, or to the nose for an interest rate of bankers.

CHAPTER 3

Legacy of Dumbarton Oaks: The Generous Vision

MEMORIES: "AN OPTIMISTIC GENERATION"

GINGRICH: It really was an American peace. . . . But we're very uncomfortable with that. The American dream is not of an American peace. The American dream, I honestly think, is of a human peace, of living in a neighborhood where we're all good neighbors. . . . I think that I grew up with a sense . . . that we do have a destiny on this planet and we do have a unique sense of mission. And it does relate to the rule of law, and free elections, and this almost outlandish sense of the assertion of the right to be free.

Newt Gingrich, commenting above, is the maverick right-wing congressman from Georgia (but born in Pennsylvania), whose father fought in Korea and helped to keep the "American peace" in France in the days before de Gaulle withdrew that country from the military structure of NATO. In the previous two chapters we have seen how a generation of Americans grew up in the 1950s with a sense of responsibility, and affection, for Western Europe, and with a strong awareness of being the dominant power in the world economy. But that belief in their own leadership, that overflowing goodwill toward men, extended to the rest of the world, too, with the sole exception of those "governments, political parties, or groups which seek to perpetuate human misery in order to profit therefrom," to which Marshall had referred in his Harvard speech. For many, the sense of obligation was particularly strong toward the emerging colonial peoples.

GINGRICH: I was very worried, when I was a high school student: I organized the book program for Ghana, which gathered up used books and sent them to Ghana. It was that we had an obligation to try and help people improve themselves in Africa.

Larry Pressler remembers similar attitudes during his childhood in the wheat-growing state of South Dakota.

PRESSLER: I had a great hope that we could feed the world. I used to listen to George McGovern and Karl Mundt, two of our senators, talk about food for peace, and how we could help the Third World develop agriculturally, and how we should give away food and not money—and I really believed that we could, that the time would come when there wouldn't be hungry people, in our country or abroad.

Joe Biden, now a Democratic senator from Delaware, identified strongly with the colonized peoples in their struggle for independence.

BIDEN: The feeling was that you all [Europeans] owned them, and it wasn't right. The feeling was growing up—and in fact was true—that immediately after World War II, in the decade of the fifties, which were my formative years in memory, you [British] and the French and the Germans—who had lost them in the war*—basically had colonized the rest of the world. And so when you thought of Africa you thought in terms of—well, I as a young person thought in terms of: "Why don't the French and the British go home? I mean, why are they doing that?" There was this sort of nobleness about—you know how young children think, I mean they basically have a sense of equity about it, and it just didn't seem right. . . .

I can remember memories of the British disengaging, and at least—unlike other colonial powers—trying to disengage with some sense of order and some sense of responsibility; and that was a clear memory that I had as distinguished from my view of how the French disengaged or other European powers were disengaged—so that there was a feeling that the Third World, but for Latin America, was really the enclave of Europe, and a general feeling that we had an obligation to deal with the concerns of the people in the Third World.

*Germany lost her colonial possessions in World War I.

Sam Gejdenson, a fellow Democrat (from Connecticut), recalls feeling that his own country, too, had something to answer for in its relations with the Third World.

GEJDENSON: I think there's a great feeling that it had been exploited by all of us: first by the European colonial powers in a very direct sense, as they governed those countries, and then in an economic sense by the American corporations—the United Fruit Company in Central America—and here American policy often seemed to be formed by what was in the best interests of our major corporations and not necessarily in the interests of the people of those countries.

Certainly, the notion of the United States as an imperialist power would have been more familiar in Latin America in the 1950s than elsewhere in what was to become known as "the Third World." Jorge G. Castañeda, a politically minded Mexican journalist and academic, son of a former foreign minister, recalls that, among the intellectual middle class, "most Latin Americans through the first half of this century already had a very strong American culture." Writers now in their fifties and sixties, like Gabriel García Márquez and Carlos Fuentes, "have had a very strong American literary and cultural influence on them. The very European-oriented Latin American intellectual elite I wouldn't say is something of the nineteenth century, but it is certainly not something which is still with us in mid-century. . . . The most important cultural influence begins to be the United States, even since then."

MORTIMER: And do you think that's made you more or less hostile to the United States?

CASTAÑEDA: It's difficult to say. I think it has, in a sense, made most Mexicans and Latin Americans in this situation on the one hand more receptive to that which is good in the United States—be it the American movies, American literature, American technology, know-how, getting-things-done spirit and drive—and there is a lot of sympathy for all of this, even among left-wing Latin American intellectuals today. There is a lot, a lot more receptivity than one may think at first glance. But on the other hand, all of what is negative in the United States, and which has created serious problems for Latin America, or for the rest of the world with which Latin American intellectuals or politicians identify—not the masses, but the elite identify—has provoked greater hostility. I think because there is more to gripe about, so this greater influence, this greater cultural presence—television—I think has also in that sense made Latin American elites perhaps more nationalistic, more anti-American as you put it.

But in Africa such ambivalent or hostile feelings about the United States were to come much later. I asked the Nigerian Olu Adeniji, widely regarded as one of Africa's outstanding younger diplomats and a possible future United Nations secretary-general, whether at the time of Nigeria's independence in 1960 he remembered thinking of America as part of the same white, northern world from which colonialism came.

ADENIJI: Amazingly enough, I saw the United States at that time as in a slightly different category because, you know, it was not tainted with colonialism in Africa, and one considered it as this huge republic, which virtually first showed the way for taking the step of detaching itself from the mother country—from England, which also was Nigeria's own colonial master, of course, and therefore, coming at that time with the Kennedy administration, there was a vision that the United States was going to assume a role whereby it will encourage the newly emerging countries of Africa to look forward to it by way of assistance in their economic programs—that the idea of democracy which the United States represented was one that the African countries could emulate, and that this would be done, of course, with concrete support from the United States. Again, because the United States has this large number of people of African descent, there was that draw, that pull, as it were, that the independence of Africa was going to have a solidary influence on the United States in the way it handled its own black population, and so there was that hope: that these cross-exchanges between the United States and Africa were going to be mutually beneficial, to both parties.

Fouad Ajami, now an American citizen and a professor at Johns Hopkins University, was born in 1945 into the underdog Shiite community of South Lebanon. A mercurial figure, he is one of those non-native English-speakers with an ultrasensitive ear for the language, bringing to life some words—"wrath," for instance—that have passed out of current usage. Restless and something of a loner, Ajami is clearly alienated both from the facile nationalism of the Arab world he has left behind, and from the glib, patronizing attitude to it of the contemporary American establishment. He recalls, however, that in the early postwar years many young Arabs, like their African and Latin American counterparts, had very positive feelings about the United States.

AJAMI: There was a tremendous cultural vulnerability to America, and a great affection in many ways, and a great sense that here is this power *outside,* to which you could come for a hearing: you see, because the Arab world had always lived under some kind of universal umbrella —first the Ottoman empire for many centuries, then Pax Britannica, then Pax Americana. I mean, there was this tremendous sense that the Americans were *untried.* . . . A whole generation used to think of the British and the French as being very duplicitous people—you know, the British with their many promises in Palestine, their many white papers canceling out other white papers. Well, the image of America was that here was a power that does not lie, a straight power, a very new power . . . and a sense that this is from a New World, and it is very different from the Old World. Europe was tarnished, and Europe was dirty, and Europe was—you know, the Sykes-Picot deal* and all the bargains and all the pledges and the broken promises—while America was untried, and America was straight.

Ajami even claims that the thing he remembers most about 1958, when U.S. Marines landed in his own country, Lebanon,† is the introduction of American canned food.

AJAMI: I developed a great romance and a great affection for American canned food. . . . All over Beirut there are enormous amounts of canned American food. I mean, this is the image I remember most vividly, and the great affection you develop for this great new product. . . . Here is the world of your elders, the world of your aunts and your mother, where cooking goes on for hours and hours, and here is this great new American invention, that you can actually tap into a can and you can get out of this can a full meal. I suppose, in retrospect, and in terms of what America came to mean in the region . . . much may be read into the canned-food episode!

MORTIMER: It was more important than the fact that these Marines were landing in your country?

AJAMI: Right. I mean, I don't think there was a great deal of intensity about the landing of the Marines. . . . Yes, it was a political episode,

*A secret treaty between France and Britain during the First World War, subsequently made public by the Bolsheviks after the Russian Revolution. It provided for the partition of the Middle East between the two European powers, in contradiction to promises of an independent Arab kingdom made at the same time to the Arabs to get them to revolt against the Ottoman empire.

†A crisis developed in Lebanon in 1958 between the pro-Western president Camille Chamoun, who wished to amend the constitution to allow himself a second consecutive term of office, and the Arab nationalist opposition, supported by the newly formed United Arab Republic (Egypt and Syria) of Gamal Abdel Nasser. A revolution occurred in Iraq at the same time, and it was feared in London and Washington that the whole Middle East was about to be engulfed by a wave of anti-Western radicalism. UN troops, as well as U.S. Marines, were landed in Lebanon to help restore order, after which Chamoun agreed to retire and a compromise candidate, Fouad Chehab, was elected president.

the Marines had landed, but I think the spectacle was even more interesting—you know, the coming of a great power, the coming of these strange people into Lebanon, and the fact that Lebanon had become big news.

So young Africans and Arabs, whose countries were breaking free of the European colonial yoke, looked to the United States for a sympathy and a support that, it seems, young Americans were willing enough to give. And these attitudes, too, were firmly founded in the Rooseveltian vision of 1945.

WHERE IT CAME FROM: FDR'S WORLD ORDER

No one seems to have doubted, in 1945, that the postwar world would have to be *organized,* politically as well as economically—and better organized than it had been in 1919. One who certainly had no doubt was Brian Urquhart, one of the youngest British soldiers to have served right through the war from September 1939 to VE Day. Too young to be demobbed, but with too long a service record to be posted to the Pacific theater, he was recruited by Arnold Toynbee into the Foreign Office Research Department (which Toynbee was then running) and then, in the summer of 1945, became private secretary to Gladwyn Jebb, who was executive secretary of the preparatory commission set up by the San Francisco conference to get the new United Nations Organization started. Urquhart was to remain with the UN throughout his career—retiring as undersecretary general in January 1986, described by an astonishingly broad spectrum of world leaders as an outstanding international civil servant. Clearly a man of such talents could have made a brilliant career in British government service, and Britain was, in 1945, one of the Big Three powers that held the world's destiny in their hands. I asked Urquhart what it was that had made him prefer to work for a new and untried international body.

URQUHART: Well, I was brought up to believe that the League of Nations, even if it didn't succeed, was a very important precedent that had to be built on; and then I was in the army for six years in the war, which certainly reinforced my feeling that it might be a good idea to organize the world a little better—so that I didn't have any difficulty in deciding that I wanted to work for the UN, and I thought myself very lucky to be allowed to do so. . . . Of course, it's very hard now to throw oneself back into the state of mind of people in 1945. The [UN]

Charter itself was written before the war had actually finished, and I think at the insistence of the United States, in order not to lose the kind of momentum which they felt had been lost in the setting up of the League of Nations in 1919. And we had all been through, one way or another, an extraordinarily disagreeable six years, and there was a great sense of survival, and a great sense of determination that that should never happen again. And I think that went right up to the top, so there's no question that if you read the speeches of Stalin or Churchill or Roosevelt, you will see the same spirit. . . . I don't think there was anything particularly silly about the idea that, just as in a national state when you've got to a particular phase of development—and also a particular phase of mayhem—you were going to have to have a much more articulate central system to preserve justice, order, and some reasonable form of life, so we'd reached that phase, after two world wars, on the international scene. And I still think that it was right.

No one was more passionately attached to that idea than Franklin D. Roosevelt himself, as Alger Hiss—one of the group of State Department officials who drew up the plans for the new world organization—recalls.

HISS: I think the best way to describe the whole background out of which the United Nations developed, and our aims for the peace, was almost a heavy idealism. President Roosevelt himself had taken a great personal interest in the United Nations. He had served as assistant secretary of the navy under President Wilson during World War I, and at that time had been a strong supporter of the League of Nations, and he'd been greatly disappointed at the political imbroglio in the Senate which prevented the United States from joining the League of Nations.* He wanted to be sure no such thing occurred in the case of the United Nations, and took a direct personal interest continually, so that after each session, each daily session, of the meetings at Dumbarton Oaks† a report was made directly to the president.

The sense of guilt and frustration at America's failure to join the League of Nations, which had been President Woodrow Wilson's brainchild, and the belief that this untimely relapse of the United

*Roosevelt was also personally a victim of the Republican backlash against the League, as vice-presidential candidate on the losing Democratic ticket in the 1920 presidential election.

†The conference at which the UN Charter was drafted, from August 21 to October 7, 1944—initially by U.S., British, and Russian delegates and subsequently by U.S., British, and Chinese. (The Russians did not regard themselves as allies of China, having signed a treaty of neutrality and nonaggression with Japan in 1941.)

States into isolationism had been, at least in part, responsible for the League's failure and so for the chain of events leading to World War II, were clearly very widespread at the time.

HISS: The belief in the League of Nations was by no means Roosevelt's unique wish. Wilson, as we know, ate his heart out in his grief over the League of Nations. At the time it was also the hope of Europe —all the European leaders and thinkers cared very much for the League. It almost went without saying that people of goodwill, people of intelligence, thoughtful people, in this country* and all over Europe, regarded the League as an ideal which had their warm support, so that Roosevelt was really just being a man of his time. I, as a young student, had the same feeling about the beauties of, the hope for, the League of Nations, and was disappointed—as were most of my associates—that what we considered a small band of embittered, unthinking senators blocked access to it by the United States. . . .

I've spoken of the group working on the United Nations as idealistic, but we thought of ourselves also as practical. For example, we studied the League of Nations—how it had made mistakes, where it had gone wrong—and we tried to take care of those situations in the drafts we prepared for the Charter.

Lord Gladwyn, who as Gladwyn Jebb was the British official most intimately involved in planning and setting up the UN, remembers this as one of the reasons why both Dumbarton Oaks and the founding conference at San Francisco the following year were held in the United States rather than anywhere else.

GLADWYN: We always had at the back of our minds the possibility, or danger, that as it happened after the First World War the Americans might go home to America, and we wanted to make it absolutely essential that they should come and play their part as a full partner in any international organization there was.

Consequently the Americans played the leading role in planning and setting up the UN, both by their own desire and by that of their allies.

HISS: Since we had greater manpower resources, most of the studies for the United Nations were actually done by the State Department,

*The United States.

by our group. The British were hard-pressed for manpower, and obviously the Russians, too, with their great losses and huge armaments, so that in one sense the structure of the United Nations was largely an American product—to which the British and the Russians offered changes and amendments, but in large part we tried to take their interests into account. In large part it was an American product.

URQUHART: Of course, the Americans in 1945 were so overwhelmingly the leader of the alliance, the great benevolent power, the country which was not only leading the formation of the new international organization but was also, through the Relief and Reconstruction Administration, conducting this immense rehabilitation program all over the world—including in the Soviet Union and China—to the tune of billions and billions of dollars. They were in an absolutely exceptional position—and also they were the only functioning nuclear power. They had great expertise in the whole matter of international organization. They had a very impressive delegation, both of politicians and of experts: they had on that delegation most of the people who had actually written the Charter. . . . And they were very much the leader.

I think in retrospect that the U.S. perhaps overcompensated for its absence from the League of Nations by going overboard on the UN, and I think certainly in the U.S. itself the prospect of the UN as producing a completely new period in human civilization was grossly overdone: it was oversold, with the resulting excessive disillusionment later on. But, nonetheless, this was the case.

At the beginning it was assumed that the Soviet Union (which had also been outside the League of Nations until 1934) would be an indispensable partner in world leadership. Valentin Berezhkov, Stalin's interpreter, remembers that from the Soviet point of view unanimity of the big powers was the important thing.

BEREZHKOV: And that's why the idea came up of permanent members of the Security Council, certainly when the discussion took place in Dumbarton Oaks in the summer of 1944. I was also there in our delegation, and Gromyko* was ambassador at that time: he was heading the delegation. The discussion was just about the organization of this international body, and the problem was the unanimity and the vote in the Security Council; and that is where we saw that only if in this organization there would be unity of the permanent members,

*Andrei Gromyko, Soviet ambassador in Washington, 1943–45; permanent representative at the UN, 1946–49; foreign minister, 1957–85; head of state since 1985.

which were Soviet Union, the United States, Great Britain, China, and France (although France at that time was still actually only being started to be liberated) . . . [would it work].

But this was the main controversy in the Dumbarton Oaks conference, and then afterward also at the Yalta conference, because the idea of the Western powers was that if there is a debate of some kind, a conflict, which touched upon the interests of one of the permanent members, this permanent member should not vote. Of course they were prepared to accept the same provision for themselves, but at that time, of course, they understood that the vast majority of the organization will be capitalist, not socialist, and Soviet Union was the only socialist country; and so they were sure that in case of really important controversy America, or Britain, or even France, will never be defeated, because they'll have a majority in the General Assembly—and we couldn't have it. So we said, certainly, that we must preserve, in every important case, at any rate, the provision for unanimity—and this was what then was labeled, you know, "veto power."

But actually, now we see that in many cases the United States is now using this veto, because the majority of the General Assembly is sometimes voting against the Americans. . . . So now we see that really this provision was important, that you can never force upon one of the big powers some kind of decision which is unacceptable for this power.

The name "United Nations" had been coined by Roosevelt to designate the alliance of powers fighting against Nazism and fascism, and the new world organization was intended quite explicitly as a continuation of that alliance into the postwar world. The original "Declaration by the United Nations," issued on New Year's Day, 1942, committed its signatories to employ their full resources—military or economic—against the Axis powers, and not to make any separate armistice or peace with them;[1] and only nations that signed this Declaration (thereby declaring war on Germany) before March 1, 1945, were invited to the San Francisco conference.[2] But in practice, of course, the alliance soon broke down.

URQUHART: The idea that the victorious alliance would remain in being to supervise and if necessary enforce the peace, in the form of the five permanent members of the Security Council—that very soon turned out to be a false assumption. But this was the basic assumption of the primary part of the Charter, which is the part about international peace and security.

GROSS: I would sum up the visionary aspect of it by referring to the provision in the Charter for the provision of armed forces to the Security Council, at its call, to enforce the peace. I think that was a visionary proposal. I was involved later in the negotiations on giving effect to that article of the Charter, article 43; and it was obvious from the very first that the Soviet-U.S. differences were what I thought later was the opening, the signal of the opening, of the Cold War: because that tested the ultimate realities and purposes of the Soviet Union, in the sense that they were afraid—literally afraid—to agree to any arrangement of contributions by the members of the UN that did not provide for exactly equally, identically composed armed forces. To them the idea of any one nation having more aircraft there—or more submarines, if they were ever to be made available to the UN; that was never discussed specifically—would be at least a symbol of inferiority, or difference, which they weren't prepared to accept.

MORTIMER: Then how important was cooperation with the Soviet Union in the American vision of the postwar world order?

GROSS: Crucial, crucial. I think that was one of the assumptions which drove Truman toward, or impelled—because I think it was natural with him, intuitive—impelled Truman toward support of the United Nations, if anything even more strongly than Roosevelt had time to generate—and his demise, two weeks before the San Francisco conference, was a great tragedy in itself, in the timing.

MORTIMER: It was assumed that the UN would only work if the U.S. and the Soviet Union could work together?

GROSS: It would only work *well.* Mind you, one has to draw a distinction, which I think we drew and I believe that Truman drew—I never heard him specifically address that subject, but there was a responsible weight of opinion of those involved with the UN—that it was *more* necessary rather than less to have a functioning United Nations, in direct proportion to the increased animosity between the Soviet Union and the United States. I would draw a line between the premise that the United Nations could only work well in a world in which the United States and the Soviets cooperated, on the one hand, and on the other hand, the premise that I consider correct—and others did, including Senator Vandenberg; and other leaders of the Senate whom I talked to at the time believed that—they were convinced, the greater the friction between the two superpowers, the more important it was to have a functioning international organization—and I think one can demonstrate the validity of that point of view by subsequent history.

Brian Urquhart discusses the unique value of the UN historically.

> URQUHART: The UN is of unique value to the nuclear powers when they get into a confrontation, and has been used over and over again as the mechanism to get them out with dignity. It has been done over and over again: in Suez, in the Congo, in Lebanon in 1958, in the Indo-Pakistan war of 1965—which was a very serious crisis—and most recently in 1973, when you suddenly had—and out of a clear blue sky —a very dangerous confrontation indeed between the Soviet Union and the U.S. over the October War between Israel and Egypt.

To this catalogue should be added the Berlin blockade of 1948–49, which, as Alger Hiss recalls, "was finally settled by negotiations that were conducted in the Delegates' Lounge of the UN." No doubt the earliest instance was the crisis over Iran in 1946. Soviet troops were withdrawn from Iran in May of that year under very strong American pressure,* but Lord Gladwyn cites this as a success for the United Nations: "Remember, the Russians caved in after the vote in the Security Council." (A third, Iranian, version attributes the withdrawal to the political and diplomatic skills of the Iranian prime minister, Ahmad Qavam al-Saltaneh, who offered the Russians an oil concession but said he would propose it to an Iranian parliament, which could only be elected once all foreign troops had been withdrawn from the country—and which, when the time came, rejected it.[3] It seems quite possible that, in fact, all three—the American stick, the Iranian carrot, and the UN as "the mechanism to get them out with dignity"—were necessary conditions, while no two of them might have been sufficient without the third.)

Moreover, Brian Urquhart points out that, in spite of the Cold War, there have been many occasions when the five permanent members have voted together, some of the most significant being in the context of the Arab-Israeli conflict. "Israel was created in the UN," he asserts —which is true in the sense that the Partition Resolution of November 29, 1947, dividing Palestine into a Jewish and an Arab state (passed by the UN General Assembly with the support of both superpowers, though Britain abstained), provides the only generally accepted legal basis for Israel's existence.

> URQUHART: It was protected by the UN in the beginning: in fact it was the Security Council order for a cease-fire in July 1948 that stopped

*As recounted by Lord Franks in chapter 1 of this book.

the first Arab-Israeli war at a time when Israel was on the ropes militarily. . . . It was very effective: the fighting stopped.*

Even when voting together, the five permanent members have never been able to go to the point of actually enforcing their decisions, and this, I think, has been a great disillusionment—especially in the West. . . .

I think one has to remember that in 1945 it was widely believed that the Charter would work as written, that is to say that you would go through the effort to settle disputes peacefully, and if that didn't work, you would go on to chapter 7, which is the "enforcement" chapter, and the Security Council could vote the membership into, not only sanctions and that kind of thing, but eventually into providing forces for an enforcement action. . . .

Well, we set the Secretariat up as if it was going to work. I mean, for example, we had an Enforcement Division in the Secretariat—the head of it was Bill Williams, who had been Montgomery's chief intelligence officer—and we had a whole lot of extremely bright, youngish people who were supposed to make the thing work. But it very soon became clear that both the will and the unanimity to make that happen didn't exist—and also the situations in which you could use forceful measures really didn't exist either. I mean, there was a lot of talk, for example, during the Palestine crises of 1948, about the Security Council using force to stop the war in Palestine. But the moment you began to study how it was going to do that, it was obviously completely impossible. Who was going to command the troops? Wherever were they going to come from? Who were they going to shoot at? Who was right and who was wrong? How was anybody ever going to agree, in the extremely complicated circumstances in Palestine, about what to do? It simply wouldn't work. I mean, it wasn't like resisting Hitler going into the Rhineland or something like that: it was a completely different form of problem. And I don't think that was clear in 1945. I don't think people thought about it in that way.

Yet there was one case in the UN's early history when "enforcement" *was* carried out by it—or at least in its name and under its flag—on a massive scale: the Korean War of 1950–53.

*This may have been forgotten in America, but in the Arab world it certainly has not. I asked Prince Abdullah Bin Faisal Bin Turki, a member of the Saudi royal family who was not yet born in 1948, whether he felt the UN was taken seriously today as a force in world affairs by Arab leaders and peoples, or regarded merely as a forum for ventilating the Palestine question. He replied, "Well, we need any forum we can get, believe me. On the contrary, it was in the United Nations that the Soviets and the Americans and the British and others sided with the Jews who were coming from Europe, and helped them establish a state on Palestinian soil."

> Here for the first and only time in its history the Security Council called on its members to go to the defence of a state [South Korea] under armed attack. Here, in consequence, the forces of a number of countries fought under the UN flag to defend the principle that aggression should not be allowed to succeed. Through these efforts a small state that would otherwise certainly have been defeated and annexed by its northern neighbour was enabled to defend its borders and maintain its independence. This, in the eyes of many, was what above all else the UN was created to achieve.[4]

I asked Arthur Schlesinger, the American historian, whether he felt this use of the UN corresponded to Roosevelt's original vision of it.

> SCHLESINGER: It did correspond to that vision, because I think Roosevelt did believe that the United Nations could play an active role in peace-keeping. The fact that it corresponded to that belief, however, is quite accidental—and indeed the peace-keeping role of the UN, even as Roosevelt conceived it, could only work in cases where great powers were not in conflict, because the great powers could otherwise veto the use of UN forces for peace-keeping purposes. It happened in 1950 that the Russians were boycotting the Security Council—they were irritated by the fact that the Chinese Communist regime had been denied admission to the UN—so that they were not in a position to exert the veto, and the UN therefore did play a role in the Korean War.* Moreover, in that period the Western democracies had a working majority in the General Assembly—which with the proliferation of Asian and African micro-states in recent years has long ceased to be the case—so it's quite accidental that in 1950 the United Nations was able to play that role.

The episode does, however, serve as a reminder that for a long time after 1945—and long after the outbreak of the Cold War—the United States took a paternal pride in the UN, found it natural to pursue its main foreign policy objectives through the UN machinery, and saw no contradiction at all between the defense of national or Western interests and the exaltation of the UN both as an ideal and as an institution. That is particularly true of President Truman, one of

*BEREZHKOV: Somehow it happened that our representative was not there . . . and that gave them the possibility to cooperate with the flag of the United Nations and create an impression that it was a United Nations action against North Korea. If our representative would be there at any rate this part of the story would maybe not happen, because he would then work against it and then they couldn't say that there is a decision of the United Nations . . . and that is another example of how important it is that we have unanimity and that veto power is really used in such cases.

whose great strengths, in Ernest Gross's view, "was his—not only appreciation, but leadership toward the public understanding and acceptance, of the basic human rights provisions [of the UN Charter] and their value."

In one case at least Gross himself, though very much a "UN man," feels that Truman showed excessive respect for the organization.

> GROSS: Truman made a mistake, in my respectful judgment, in taking the United States International Control Plan [for atomic energy] into the United Nations in 1946, with the eloquent Mr. Bernard Baruch presenting it, without any advance discussions with the Soviet Union; without attention to the almost inevitable probability—certainty—that the Soviets would refuse to accept it and that international control and ownership of resources, facilities—particularly atomic—in the Soviet Union was completely unacceptable to them. . . . We nonetheless brought it in with great gusto, and I think that was a mistake. But it was a mistake, in my view, that Truman made honestly; and I think that might have been attributed to the fact that he really was convinced that the United Nations system was the repository of world peace, and that unless the international control of atomic energy was put before them, almost regardless of the consequences, that they would cripple the United Nations at the start—if the greatest problem of security could not be put before the organization that was set up for postwar security.

Yet to see U.S. foreign policy as essentially bound up with the UN Charter was no personal idiosyncrasy of the president's. It was strongly shared in Congress as well.

> GROSS: I remember one day we were drafting, with the chief of staff of the Senate Foreign Relations Committee, their report on the military assistance program; and one of the key senators insisted on putting into the report recommending Senate approval of the program that these activities were all parts of a single program, and that that single program included the United Nations Charter, and that none of these programs was in any way to be regarded as a derogation of the United Nations Charter, but in support of it, and that they were all necessary because the Charter was being subverted by the Soviet Union. Well, when that senator made that suggestion, at the private executive session of the committee, I was afraid of it. So I asked permission to get instructions on that, and I talked with the secretary [of state—presumably Acheson] about it later that same day. He was not happy about tying in the various programs—NATO, the Greek-Turkish program,

the foreign assistance military program—with the United Nations Charter. But in the end the Senate did that, and you will find that in the Senate report today.

Even among the broader American public, the proceedings of the UN still aroused intense interest at the time of the Korean War, as Lord Gladwyn, who was then Britain's permanent representative there, has good cause to remember.

GLADWYN: I was the chap representing our case in the Security Council, having these great arguments with Malik [the Soviet representative]. . . . Well, I had an enormous success, because I stood up to Malik—on philosophical grounds and others—and it was the first time when TV was extending to the whole of the United States: it was the first time really you could see in San Francisco what was happening in New York. . . . I became, rightly or wrongly—I'm afraid it's not a thing to be proud of—a sort of national hero. I was a sort of TV personality, and got thousands of letters, mostly from women. My popular rating was just after Bob Hope, and in front of the wrestlers! . . . Everybody looked on the Security Council then as a sort of novelty, as if it was a sort of *Forsyte Saga.* With these long and perhaps potentially rather dreary speeches, which they had to translate into every language, it nevertheless was an enormous success, and everybody looked in at it.

But Arthur Schlesinger adds an important qualification.

SCHLESINGER: I wouldn't overstate the way in which the United States, even in the 1940s, was committed to multilateral institutions. What we had in the 1940s was a rather remarkable group of American statesmen—people like Dean Acheson, Averell Harriman, Robert Lovett, General Marshall and George Kennan, Chip Bohlen, and so on. These were thoughtful, intelligent, able people, and they respected Truman and Truman respected their advice and used them wisely, and I think that produced some impressive results. . . . It wasn't so much a belief in multilateral institutions as it was a belief in alliances, and what these men understood was that the United States could not achieve any objectives in the world by itself, and that therefore working in concert with allies was essential for the interests of the United States, as well as the interests of the allies.

And of course it was not only in Europe that the United States looked for allies, but also among the emerging nations of what was not yet called the Third World. One of the defects of the League of

Nations that Alger Hiss and his group had been careful to avoid in drafting the UN Charter was the fact that "the Far East and Africa had been left out." Great importance was attached to the principle of universal membership, and Roosevelt insisted especially, in the face of skepticism if not hostility from both Stalin and Churchill, on involving China as a participant in the planning of the Charter, a co-sponsor of the founding conference, and one of the five permanent members of the Security Council. He saw China as the natural leader of an Asia shaking off the yoke of European imperialism. It is ironic, therefore, that after 1949 mainland China was to become, on American insistence, the most conspicuous exception to the principle of universal membership—and doubly ironic that this was largely due to the very strength of the ties built up between America and China during the previous period, which gave rise to a powerful "China lobby" pledged to the support of the ousted Nationalist regime of Roosevelt's protégé, Chiang Kai-shek.

But that did not alter America's general commitment to the cause of colonial freedom and full participation of the former colonies in world affairs.

URQUHART: One of the great ironies of the history of the UN is that the U.S., much to the distress of the European colonial powers, were the great animators of the program of decolonization. In fact they had, in 1943, already tried to insist that the liberation of colonial territories be in the Charter, and the British and others had objected.

GLADWYN: A good many [of us] thought that the American administration certainly was too keen on dissolving the British empire, and hadn't really considered what was likely to happen if it were dissolved —I mean, whether the situation was likely to be better or not. . . . There was a certain resentment that the Americans were all out to torpedo the British empire, which was crumbling anyhow.

URQUHART: So we got, instead, to the trusteeship system and the whole mechanism about reports from non-self-governing territories. But they continued to press decolonization as a legitimate extension of the Allied war aims, much to the annoyance of the British, the French, the Belgians, and the Dutch. When I joined the UN in 1945 it was believed that decolonization would take a hundred years, and would be a slow and extremely bloody process. I think perhaps one of the great achievements of the UN has been that it formed a sort of catalyst which made that process, once it started, go through much more peacefully and more quickly than anybody had expected.

PART II

What We Have Lived Through

CHAPTER 4

"All the Stars Were Bright"

I think there is a broad experience that people of my generation have been exposed to [in the early sixties]—given the kind of administration that was in the White House then—you know, the Peace Corps experiment and so on. We were formed at a time when, if you like, all the stars were bright. There was a vision of maybe not a united world, but a world that, you know, felt *human:* where one could bridge the gaps—the image of Mr. Khrushchev weeping as he was signing the condolence book at the death of Kennedy, and yet this was supposed to be two superpowers at each other's throats. So we were formed at a time when it appeared that everything was possible. The world could be reshaped along positive lines—there was a unity of the human spirit.

—BOLAJI AKINYEMI
Minister of External Affairs, Republic of
Nigeria, May 1986

KENNEDY

If one thing surprised me when I was conducting these interviews it was the number of "Roosevelt's children," from a striking variety of countries and present-day political viewpoints, who, when asked to name an international event that had an important and lasting impact on their world outlook, spontaneously mentioned the presidency of John F. Kennedy. I'm not sure why I wasn't expecting this—perhaps simply because it was too obvious. Kennedy's assassination is the one event of my lifetime that *everyone* who is old enough remembers, not just in the sense of knowing that it happened but remembering the precise moment when they heard about it: where they were, what they were doing, their own immediate reaction and that of the people around them. In fact, swapping accounts of this experience became one of the more hackneyed conversational gambits of the later sixties, so that in a sense it is the prototype event for this book: the whole idea is to get politicians to talk about events in general the way ordinary people talk about that event in particular.

So if people had just mentioned, or dwelt mainly on, the shock of the assassination, I should not have been surprised. One or two did, of course. Christine Ockrent, for instance, the French TV commentator, and Norbert Gansel, the Social Democratic deputy from Kiel in North Germany.

OCKRENT: I was finishing school at the Institut d'Etudes Politiques, and I was getting into my car and I switched on the radio, and I stopped in the middle of the street. It's a very strong memory. . . . I think we were all struck by that, even if we have come to realize that probably Kennedy was not as important politically as we thought he was at the time. But I think it had the emotional—the political—the *aesthetics* of a major event, for somebody who was young then.

GANSEL: The first shock I got, actually, was the death of Kennedy —more of a feeling that it appears that America is different—that there is a certain element of the building of power by . . . violence, in its society. Yes, I think that was the first shock I got.

That's certainly the reaction I remember from the American friends —an earnest, mild, liberal, postgraduate married couple—who broke the news to me when I arrived for dinner that evening at their apartment, in a not-too-fashionable part of Oxford. Their national pride, their confidence in their country's progress toward realizing the values they believed in, was badly dented: "We really thought the days of political assassination in the United States were past." I'm ashamed to say I've lost touch with those friends now, but I feel fairly confident that they are still staunch liberals who would not like to be identified with a vigorous Reaganite commentator like George Will. They might, however, endorse this remark of his.

WILL: There is a sense, I think—subconscious, people don't quite articulate it, but—that things began to go very wrong at about noon on November 22, 1963, when he was shot in Dallas: a kind of eruption of randomness, violence, failure, disappointment, tragedy entered

American history in a way that people had just not been used to it. The 1950s were not years of darkness, they were years of great sunnyness in America; and shortly after Kennedy was shot there were the Watts riots [in Los Angeles] the next year—you had five years of domestic disorder, and you had Vietnam, and you had two more assassinations in 1968.

Of course the immediate effect of Kennedy's death was to make him a martyr, to whom many who had been hostile or unenthusiastic in his lifetime felt obliged to pay tribute—even in Moscow, as Sergei Plekhanov, who was at school there at the time, remembers.

PLEKHANOV: You know, when Kennedy was killed, that was widely seen as a result of some kind of a conspiracy of some dark forces. You know: the popular perception was, "Well, you know, they didn't really want him to have a détente with the Soviet Union, and there are those right-wing forces which are now starting this war in Vietnam." Of course that was a very simplified view, but I'm talking about general public opinion.

But that effect long ago wore off. The atmosphere of piety surrounding "Saint Jack" did not last more than a few years—it was certainly well dissipated by the time of Teddy Kennedy's misadventure at Chappaquiddick in 1969. To speak admiringly of John Kennedy has long since ceased to be obligatory—or even, I would have thought, fashionable. But perhaps I am a fashion behind.

WILL: It's easy to make fun of Camelot and all that stuff, but I think we had a period of second thoughts about Kennedy—now's the time for some third thoughts: that some of the second thoughts were too debunking, that Kennedy was good for the country in exactly the way that Ronald Reagan is. Both men understood the first thing an American president has to do—it's not true of a British prime minister, or a president of France, but the first thing that an American president has to do—is make the American people feel confident about their role as a superpower; and both people did.

Precisely what impressed me in these interviews was how many of the subjects claimed—or admitted—to have been inspired and excited by Kennedy *in his lifetime.* I was taken aback, in particular, to discover how many of the luminaries of today's American right—supporters or faithful henchmen of Ronald Reagan—claim, like George Will, to have started their political lives as Kennedy fans, and to see a strong resemblance between their hero of then and their hero of now. "Kennedy's speeches and Reagan's speeches are an awful lot alike," says Elliott Abrams, who was one of the organizers of Democrats for Reagan in the 1980 election and now handles Latin American policy in the State Department. And Richard Perle, still a card-carrying Democrat even when assistant secretary of defense and widely regarded as the Reagan administration's most articulate and influential hawk on East-West issues, recalls, as an early influence on his political outlook, "the Kennedy administration and what appeared to be the promise of that administration, which was a vigorous defense of freedom, an effort to close what was perceived as a possible military imbalance arising out of Soviet technological advances." He remembers Kennedy as "a young and vigorous leader who was going to defend freedom around the world."

Jack Kemp, right-wing Republican congressman from Buffalo and 1988 presidential hopeful, makes no pretense of ever having been a Democrat. But he, too, when asked to name events that helped form his views, talks about Kennedy.

> KEMP: In my former profession as a football player I would say the Kennedy presidency had an impact, not only on me personally but certainly on our country. As I look back—I had recently gotten married, bought a home—there was a general feeling of economic buoyancy in the West and, I think, a sense that we were in control of our own history and our own destiny. That was interrupted, of course, by the Vietnam War.

Of course. One can see that for Americans of that age, irrespective of party affiliation, the early sixties have a strong nostalgic appeal, the appeal of the world *avant le déluge,* almost like the famous "long hot summer of 1914" for Europeans of an earlier generation.

Newt Gingrich is politically close to Kemp but more reflective—being a historian rather than a footballer by profession. As a Republican, he admires Kennedy above all for having known how to contain the American left and keep it within the broad patriotic consensus.

> GINGRICH: I think that the death of John F. Kennedy led to the collapse of the American left having any responsible leader who could articulate why you had to be willing to stand up to evil. . . . Kennedy understood, in the Churchillian tradition, that there is a real difference between tyranny and freedom, between the rule of law and the rule of

> secret police; and Kennedy understood that, at least for the foreseeable future, the country that has to lead is the United States. And Kennedy, as a liberal Democrat, was able to dominate the left wing of his party. . . . When Kennedy was killed, as a Harvard-educated, northeastern liberal Democrat, and replaced by what was seen in the cultural elites on the two coasts as a Texas barbarian, there was nobody to browbeat the Democratic left, which has always had a pacifist strain.

So Kennedy becomes a stick with which to beat the Democrats of today, lumped together as sufferers from "the McGovern-Carter-Mondale psychology." Thus George Will, asked whether Kennedy was an important figure for his generation, replies with what seems slightly malicious pleasure.

> WILL: I think so, but a very ambivalent place he has in people's minds now. If you go back and read his inaugural address, which was a terrific rhetorical moment in postwar history—rhetoric doesn't play a great part in American politics, but that did. . . . Liberals who elected him, claimed him as their own, wince when they read that now because, they say, there were the seeds of Vietnam: "The torch has been passed to a new generation of Americans, born in this century, tempered by war and a hard and bitter peace, and unwilling to witness the slow undoing of human rights to which we are committed at home and round the world." And he said in there, "We're willing to go anywhere, bear any burden, pay any price, to assure the survival of liberty." Well, that's the kind of "globalism," the kind of "overreaching hubris," that liberals say took us to Vietnam. The people today who quote approvingly John Kennedy, and his example as a great American nationalist, are the kind of people who vote most eagerly for Ronald Reagan.

Well, do the liberals wince when they reread Kennedy's inaugural? It's true that none of the Democrats I interviewed could quite match George Will's fluency in reciting chunks of it from memory, but Joe Biden at least tried, and both he and Pat Schroeder cited Kennedy without prompting as an important influence on their political development, showing not the slightest desire to dissociate themselves from his rhetoric. They did, however, have a rather more balanced memory of the content of his message.

> BIDEN: John Kennedy came along and gave the impression that we were not only ready to remain strong, but we were ready to talk: we

were ready to try to work something out. There was the hope, the belief, that somehow things could be made manageable—that the United States didn't have only one of two options. In my grade school years I had the notion that we were going to have to go to war or be overtaken. John Kennedy came along, and I remember his speeches where he said that the eagle, the American symbol, has in its talons—in one hand he clutches arrows, the other an olive branch, and we'll look at them equally. . . . He was the first person that I recall making me think that it's possible for the United States to coexist with the Soviet Union in a way where we protected our interests and at the same time were able to avoid war.

Much of that, when one studies the historical record, seems rather unfair to Eisenhower, Kennedy's predecessor. A good case can be made for thinking that Kennedy was the more reckless of the two in his handling of the Soviet Union, and certainly on two important issues in the 1960 campaign—treatment of Castro's Cuba and the need for increased defense expenditure to close the alleged "missile gap"—he was more hawkish than his Republican opponent, Richard Nixon. It is all the more interesting that he should have come across to the young Biden as more open to dialogue and less likely to threaten world peace—which is also how he came across to me, at the same stage in my education on the other side of the Atlantic, where I can remember the excitement of being invited by my tutor to go to his house in the evenings and watch the televised Kennedy-Nixon debates. I remember Derek Parfit (now a distinguished Oxford philosopher, then my classmate but also my political and cultural mentor) saying that Cuba was the one issue on which Nixon was undoubtedly better than Kennedy. But that was not enough. We eager young English liberals had no doubt which candidate we were rooting for. Eisenhower and Nixon were damned partly by simple association—they were the American equivalent of the despised Tories, partly, I think, by their past (they were dogged by the ghosts of Joe McCarthy and John Foster Dulles), but probably above all by the mere fact that they represented the status quo, which for sixteen- and seventeen-year-olds generally has few charms. Kennedy, of course, was old enough to have been our father, yet we did identify with his "youth" —as, according to George Will, did our American contemporaries.

WILL: This was a young man—he was in his early forties when he was inaugurated, and a lot of us were in college at this time and we were entering our adulthood as he was entering on the center of an American political stage—and a kind of glamour attached to it.

I remember someone commenting approvingly at the time on the fact that, for the first time in living memory, the children in the White House would be the president's own, not his grandchildren. (Kennedy was, of course—and would still be if he were alive—six years younger than Ronald Reagan. But that would have meant little to any of us in 1960.)

Sam Gejdenson of Connecticut perhaps comes a bit nearer to fitting George Will's picture of a wincing liberal. At least, he offered a more detached view of the Kennedy phenomenon, which seems a shrewd enough analysis of his renewed popularity.

GEJDENSON: I think there are a couple of things. One is that he's a fallen hero: someone who was physically attractive and stood for a certain kind of individual strength—caring for the family, the pictures of him with his children, but yet the strong, the hero—the war hero, someone who is out there in the brave cold of winter without a coat on. You know: that kind of strength that Americans like to think of. He's also far enough back in history—it's been over twenty years now—that the blemishes are gone. And so I think what's happened is, the political spectrum have tried to grab this hero. It's good politics: and when it's good politics, politicians like chameleons take on those colors; they take on those attributes. And his tenure in office was short enough so there aren't glaring mistakes—with the exception of the Bay of Pigs* and maybe one or two others—but there was also no definition. He was only there for a handful of years, a couple of years,† and so there isn't this definition of what Kennedy stood for. You know, Ronald Reagan can try to take him as his, and people on the left in the Democratic party can try to take him as theirs.

In fact, of all the people interviewed, the only one who reacted to Kennedy with anything like the embarrassment George Will attributes to liberals were—perhaps significantly—the British Tory and the Social Democrat, Chris Patten and David Owen.

OWEN: I don't think I was really aware of America as a political unit until Kennedy, and I think it would be foolish to deny the influence that he had on my generation, although strangely and somewhat oddly I've never been a great supporter of John F. Kennedy's presidency. I think it was very much more flash and presentation than substance. But that

*Kennedy's ill-fated attempt to overthrow Castro by secretly organizing an expeditionary force of Cuban exiles.

†Kennedy was in office for just under three years, from January 20, 1961, to November 22, 1963.

said, I do give him immense credit for the handling of the Cuban missile crisis.

Patten, indeed, did bring up Kennedy in the context of Vietnam, and also threw in several disdainful references to "Camelot":

PATTEN: It's not a very original observation, but clearly the Vietnam War was partly a consequence of the Kennedy Camelot rhetoric of the early 1960s: the injection of a sort of moral fiber into foreign policy—of a Canningite* view of foreign policy, which I've become increasingly unhappy with. I discovered a couple of years ago, with delight, a remark of Lord Salisbury,† which I think came close to summarizing my own view on foreign affairs, that it was difficult enough going around doing what was right without trying to go round doing what was good—a point of view very much reinforced by reading *Bleak House,* or by any observations of the appalling damage done by the injection of too much moral fervor into foreign policy.

And—as if to confirm George Will's suspicions—Patten later used the same phrases, "Canningite approach to foreign policy" and "moral fervour," to describe the American mood under the Reagan administration. His overall verdict on Kennedy was grudging.

PATTEN: I wasn't very affected by the Kennedy fervor, except in one sense: I think he made politics and public service respectable for young people, and even exciting, in a way that they hadn't been for some time before. John Buchan's remark that politics is "an honourable adventure" might well have been written by one of Kennedy's speechwriters. . . . But I found some of the extravagant claims about what politicians were capable of—I found some of the language of Camelot—vulgar and off-putting. I think that both Eisenhower and [Adlai] Stevenson in the previous generation, and even Johnson afterwards, are far more admirable political figures. . . .

I can remember the night of the assassination: I can remember some left-wing lunatic racing into a party to tell everybody with terrific good cheer that President Kennedy had been assassinated. Because, to be fair to President Kennedy and those around him, he was regarded as, I

*After George Canning, British foreign secretary, 1822–27, who made it government policy to support liberal movements both in Europe and in Latin America. He claimed to have "brought the New World into existence to redress the balance of the Old."

†Conservative statesman; prime minister, 1885–86, 1886–92, 1895–1902.

think, a threat by the more mindless of the left, who thought that their own objectives would only be accomplished both domestically and internationally—it's the same today—by *im*moderate center-right political leadership.* The French have a word for it, don't they?—*"Politique du pire."*†

The feeling that Kennedy offered something new and better in politics, not just in America but in the world at large, which Patten acknowledges rather grudgingly, was felt very strongly in many countries. In Germany, for instance, the Free Democrat Irmgard Adam-Schwaetzer (who, as a recent school-leaver waiting for a university place and meanwhile working in a Berlin pharmacy, actually attended the meeting in 1963 where Kennedy made his famous *"Ich bin ein Berliner"* speech), said she had been impressed by the contrast not so much with his predecessors in America as with her own political leaders at that time in West Germany.

ADAM-SCHWAETZER: I heard him myself speaking on the campus, and we have all been enchanted from the way he was treating politics with ideas, not just the dirty tricks everyone associated with politics, but more moral: so he gave a lot of hope and so consequently we have been all very shocked when he was murdered in 1963. . . . The conservatives at that time, the CDU, really lost contact with the younger generation. There was a feeling that now should come more than just economic success, that there should come also some development in democracy, development in society—and I think also Mr. Kennedy with his visit, and the perception of politics he had given to us, had quite some impact and influenced that development. . . . We had none of that type in Germany.

But what was even more interesting to me was to find that Kennedy had had a similar impact in some Third World countries. When I asked the Nigerian foreign minister, Bolaji Akinyemi—a passionate, often lyrical orator with a reputation as a left-wing nationalist—what international event of his lifetime had made the greatest impact on the way he sees the world, I was sure he would say it was the indepen-

*Most Americans would probably place Kennedy in the "moderate center-left" of the political spectrum. Patten evidently identifies him, not unreasonably, with his own position in British politics, the moderate center-right.

†Policy of the worst. That is, deliberately making things worse in the short run, with an ulterior end (revolution) in view. Talleyrand is credited with the remark *"La politique du pire amène, en général, le pire"*—the policy of the worst can generally be relied on to produce the worst.

dence of his country, which happened when he was eighteen years old (just one month before Kennedy's election). But no.

AKINYEMI: I think it is the presidency of John F. Kennedy, in the sense that I was becoming acutely aware of the world scene during his presidency, and I was fascinated, of course, by how one man presiding over a system can make that much of a difference, and how his message basically reached across the ideological divide, and the economic divide. . . . And it struck me that a leader can overcome, if you like, the locality of his existence. Of course, basically he was an American president, but I think, no, his message was that he could be both an American president and yet be committed to the world, without sacrificing the interests of his nation—and this . . . in my formative years, was a lesson that has been with me all that time. . . . I suppose I have sort of fashioned my own view of the world . . . that one can still be faithful to the world and be faithful to one's background. . . .

Then I was in the United States during the Cuban missile crisis, and the impression again one got was of a leader who matured under fire —I've always admired people who do not panic in the moment of crisis. And yet—and this is something I've always remembered: the mistakes which he made over the Bay of Pigs invasion . . . seeing a president stand up and say, "I'm responsible. . . . We made a mess of it, but I am responsible." He didn't try to explain it away . . . and that didn't seem to have diminished his greatness. . . . I know since then a lot has been written about him, but I think the more serious political historians of the period have chronicled a man who saw opportunities and exploited those opportunities—obviously to the Kennedy advantage, but somehow not at the expense of greater goals and greater visions. . . . I think that the United States has an immense capacity for good as well as an immense capacity for evil, and it simply depends on who is in the White House.

Even more surprisingly, very similar sentiments were expressed by Jorge Castañeda, the brilliant young Mexican political analyst, who also remembers being excited and inspired by Fidel Castro.

CASTAÑEDA: I think the two international events . . . which had the greatest impact, on me at least, were the Cuban revolution and Kennedy's election to the presidency in the United States. They more or less happened at the same time. In Mexico they both clearly had enormous, spectacular importance. They were both media events in addition to being political events. . . . Pictures of the *guerrilleros* entering Havana with their green uniforms and their guns, and Kennedy, this young, boyish-looking fellow with the children and the good-looking wife—they're just blurred images in my mind, but I do associate them very much, and they do seem to have been the two events which, in my childhood at least, were the most important.

MORTIMER: So, if you felt so positive, both about Castro and about Kennedy, how did you react to the conflict between the two?

CASTANEDA: Well, I also remember very clearly—perhaps more clearly than the two previous events, the Bay of Pigs, because in Mexico it was a very important event in the sense that it aroused important domestic political passions in support of Castro and against the United States, against the CIA-sponsored invasion.

MORTIMER: And yet in spite of that you say that when Kennedy came to Mexico people were very enthusiastic.

CASTAÑEDA: Oh, there was an enormous outpouring of welcome, of enthusiasm, when Kennedy went to Mexico. It was absolutely amazing. The welcome he received on his trip from the airport to the national palace was matched only by the welcome that General de Gaulle received at about the same time. The two people captured Mexico City's inhabitants' imagination and enthusiasm like no one ever had before—or, from what I know, has had since. . . . But Kennedy more than de Gaulle. Not necessarily for very clear reasons. I think the fact that the fellow was young, good-looking, and had a good-looking wife was at least as important as the fact that he was the president of the United States and that he represented, if at all, a change in American policy toward Latin America and toward Mexico.

MORTIMER: So people didn't associate him with the Bay of Pigs?

CASTAÑEDA: One thing was Kennedy, the other thing was the United States. It's somewhat absurd, but I really think that that's how it was. The same way, when he was shot there was a great deal of sadness in Mexico: not that there would be a great deal of sadness because the president of the United States was shot—most people would tend to be, if not happy, at least indifferent—but it was Kennedy. . . . It was two different things.

MORTIMER: So Kennedy somehow presented an image of America that Latin Americans could identify with?

CASTAÑEDA: If not identify with, at least look at with a certain amount of enthusiasm and a certain amount of understanding. Here was a fellow with whom it seemed you could talk—you might not agree, but if you didn't agree, you could perhaps convince him, and in any case this was a fellow who projected a very different image from an Eisenhower, or even a Nixon or Truman—the sort of people with traditionally arrogant, old-school—somewhat racist, even, I would say —views of Latin America. Kennedy looked like a guy who actually could like Latin Americans. Nobody really knew if he did or he didn't, but he looked like the kind of guy who could.

Let no one ever say that style and personality are not important in politics! It is fair to say, also, that Kennedy's approach to the Third World is one of the things still remembered and admired by American Democrats.

Pat Schroeder gave a particularly vivid illustration of Castañeda's point about the purpose of the Alliance for Progress, with a story whose grisly detail did, quite literally, make me wince.

SCHROEDER: We had many Colombians at Harvard, and it was in the sixties, when the violence was raging in Colombia. . . . They had taken over the taxis in Bogotá—it was awful. I remember one day going to school, and a friend of mine was reading a letter; and he said, "I can't go back home." And I said "Why?" and he said, "Read the letter!" And it was from a friend of his who was in the ministry, who had been asked to do something by La Violencia, the main terrorist group. He said, "No, it's incorrect. I won't do it." . . . He came to work the next day: they had kidnapped his five-year-old daughter, cut her hands off, and she was sitting outside of his office with a sign pinned to her.

Now that is what we are dealing with. We are dealing with that kind of terrorism, at a gut level—and as a parent I don't know that I could look anyone in the eye and say, "Well, I wouldn't have ever yielded if they did that to me." I don't know what I would do. I mean, that is horrifying, and that's exactly what this man said.

But what do we do? We then had different leadership—we had President Kennedy, who didn't send the Marines into Colombia: we sent the Peace Corps in! We layered them in seven deep, I mean there was hardly an inch of Colombia where we didn't have ten Peace Corps volunteers standing, it was like Hands Across Colombia! And it is hard, because it's mountainous. But, by golly, we stopped it, and we have held that country: it's had a democratic process, elections, and everything else. It is now getting a little touchy again, but for over twenty years . . . Now I think Americans forget the things that were successful and remember the things that weren't, and I hope we remember that model and others that were like it, that did work.

FROM CUBA TO PRAGUE

Apart from his assassination, the other episode of Kennedy's presidency that almost everyone has some memory of is the Cuba missile crisis of October 1962—probably the moment in most of our lives when World War III seemed closest to actually happening, and it hit us at an impressionable age. Chris Patten and I were both in our first term at Oxford—and so, it turns out, was George Will.

> PATTEN: I remember the Cuba missile crisis very clearly because it was my first term at university, and I had a rather squalid little room in Balliol College overlooking the Martyrs' Memorial; and one of the first rallies that was held against the Cuban missile crisis was held at the Martyrs' Memorial. And I remember looking out rather curiously at this group of fifty or sixty people who clearly thought that all the wickedness in the world was caused by the United States, which was about to plunge us into a world war, according to them. It was my first experience of the extraordinarily distorted, slanted view which I think some people have.

> WILL: I'd been at Oxford about three weeks before the Cuban missile crisis occurred, and all kinds of nervous British citizens said, "Oh gosh, there go the Americans taking us to the brink of war." But again that was just the sort of thing that, being an American, you had to learn to live with—special competition between the two great powers, that other powers were affected by and part of, but not central to.

(But Will does also remember "being very stirred" at the time of Kennedy's death, just over a year later, "when I got up on that Saturday in Oxford and saw all the flags of the colleges at half-staff—a great sense of commonality of our two countries, the English-speaking peoples.")

Richard Perle was also studying in England at the time, but at the London School of Economics.

> PERLE: I can recall the emergency debate that the LSE students organized, in the old theater, to debate a resolution that condemned the United States, for having precipitated the crisis that really originated, of course, with the Soviet effort to put missiles in Cuba. . . . I believe I was the only speaker in that debate who held the view, first that there wouldn't be a war, and second that the American administration was doing the right thing in the policy of quarantine—attempting

to stop the further work that would otherwise have led to the installation of those missiles in Cuba.

And I recall the combination of passionate criticism of the United States with real fear that we were on the verge of nuclear war. Bertrand Russell made his way to the Scottish Highlands, CND* fled the major cities in a panic. I remember talking with my parents in Los Angeles, who told me people were buying staples in the supermarkets, in anticipation of a war that never came—and that, it seemed clear to me at the time, wouldn't come, precisely because the United States was sufficiently strong to insist that the Soviets reverse that action and to make that insistence prevail. . . . I think the fear and the panic resulted in part from the mistaken view that one would be cavalier about the use of nuclear weapons, and it was already clear at that point that nuclear weapons have a profoundly sobering effect on the behavior of those who possess them.

A comforting thought if true. I doubt, however, if Perle would follow it to its logical conclusion of distributing nuclear weapons to those Third World governments one would most wish to see sobered, such as that of Colonel Qadhafi.

Richard Burt remembers "going home and watching the president on television with my parents, and we were all wondering whether we were moving to the brink." Meanwhile other schoolboys were going through similar emotions in Moscow.

KOKOSHIN: I remember very well when my father came home one night very late and told my mother, "If this tension will continue the same way one more day I shall send you to my parents"—to the countryside very far from Moscow, about two thousand kilometers. . . . He was military, and he came home to change from regular to field uniform—and it was one of the strongest impressions of the level of tension at that moment.

PLEKHANOV: Of course, we were rooting for the Cubans, and the Cuban missile crisis was viewed in that particular context. Of course, when things really got down to the boiling point, to those few days when the world tottered on the brink of catastrophe, I remember one of those days when we really suddenly realized that we were on the brink. I remember kids talking to each other about it: each one heard something about the danger, and for a day or two we were very, very

*Campaign for Nuclear Disarmament.

much on the edge. The sense of danger was great. Then when it sort of dissipated and the compromise was found, and in the months that followed there were negotiations on nuclear test ban and things began improving in Soviet-American relations, there was, of course, a great sigh of relief.

Neil Kinnock was also at university, and had been a member of CND by then for three years, though he did not personally "flee the major cities in a panic."

KINNOCK: [I recall] an immense reaction all over the country. . . . I realized and had studied all the potentials and a lot of the strategic thinking that had been going on, but here it was, on our doorstep. And all of the discussion, all of the presentation, all of the statements from all of the sides really did look like a film that was happening to another world, until it suddenly clicked with you: this is us. Now I actually didn't think that the total breakdown was going to come—I didn't think there'd be a nuclear exchange. But, of course, you can't afford to act on that basis, and I spent a lot of the time in those days trying to rationalize with others whose response was much more emotional—and anxiety filled people of all ages—trying to set out the reasons why push wouldn't come to shove, and shove wouldn't come to war, and war wouldn't come to nuclear war—and I guess I was more or less absorbed in that, for the period in which it dominated the headlines.

Kinnock concedes that Kennedy's handling of the crisis "in the immediate circumstances . . . became dexterous and effective," but adds that "the same thing could have been said at a day's remove about Nikita Khrushchev"—meaning presumably that Khrushchev was able to climb down without complete loss of dignity once he realized the dangerous situation he had created. But he prefers to concentrate on "the circumstances that permitted it to arise."

KINNOCK: I think that the conduct of international affairs is very much the conduct of crisis prevention—of the anticipation of antagonisms so that they don't get to critical levels and then require great exercises in vanity or concession in order to resolve them, because that makes things much more difficult And in the wake of the immediate outbreak of sweat across the collective brow, the view that I had—and it's a view that remained with me—[is] that if international relations get to such a level of posturing, then they're always liable to break down; and that's the essence of the relationship that prevents people having

> to express themselves, negotiate, and take their contests of ideology or of strategy at the shout and as if they're playing a great game of poker with the world. I think the world's rather too important for that. . . .
>
> It's hardly a novel situation: all the lessons, certainly of the seventeenth, eighteenth, and nineteenth centuries, are there to give us in glorious Technicolor the consequence of the conduct of policies between superpowers when they've decided how the world should be carved up. Now even that's possible, provided that everybody recognizes the degree to which the borders may be crossed or the nature of incursion into one or other's sphere of interest. . . . It really is about the treatment of the world as a chessboard, except that in chess you are allowed at least to take your pieces into the other half of the board.

I don't myself remember having any thoughts quite so high-flown. I was, believe it or not, actually a member at the time of the Oxford University Communist Club—not because I had espoused the doctrines of Marxism-Leninism or had any intention of joining the Party but simply because someone had come round selling the cards and I was at the age where one feels one should try anything once and keep an open mind. I only remember attending one meeting, which was held jointly with a somewhat more mainstream body called Jacari (Joint Action Committee Against Racial Intolerance) to hear R. Palme Dutt, a veteran Indian Stalinist, speak on the subject of "neocolonialism"—a subject I was interested in, having just returned from a Peace Corps–type voluntary service assignment in Senegal, where formal colonialism had just ended and neocolonialism, in the shape of a continued French economic, cultural, and even administrative presence on a substantial scale, seemed to be flourishing. I'm afraid I can't remember anything about Palme Dutt's speech, but what I do remember is that at the end of the meeting it was announced dramatically from the platform that news had just come in that President Kennedy had imposed a blockade on Cuba, and it was felt the meeting should not disperse without letting the president know of its strong feelings on the matter. Accordingly a telegram was drafted, initially opening with the words "Dear President Kennedy: One hundred members of Oxford University Communist Club and Jacari . . ." At this point some veteran politician present—I think it may have been Palme Dutt himself—interjected that perhaps such an opening would prejudice the recipient against the contents of the message, and it was amended to read simply, "One hundred Oxford students meeting tonight . . ."

I did come away from this meeting with a strong sense of the make-believe world that the far left inhabits. But I must have been sufficiently influenced by its ambience to feel that Kennedy had indeed escalated the crisis in an unwise and unjustified way by imposing the blockade, because I remember the next morning seeing one of my American liberal friends in the quad—one who I knew was often willing to criticize his own government for what appeared ungenerous or militaristic policies—and saying, "Well, Reid, are you ashamed of your president this morning?" To which he, to his eternal credit, replied, "You know, I'm not so sure I am."

Like everyone else—except, I suppose, those like Richard Perle who had known all along that everything would be all right—I was immensely relieved at the denouement of the crisis; and I was inclined to give Kennedy credit in retrospect for having kept his nerve. So, of course, were my American contemporaries, like Richard Burt.

BURT: I think it was a mixture of relief on the one hand and a sense of elation that, as Dean Rusk, the then secretary of state, put it, "the Russians blinked"—the feeling that our superior military power, coupled with a determined president, had caused Mr. Khrushchev to back down.

Andrei Kokoshin was seventeen at the time of the crisis.

KOKOSHIN: [I learned] that from our point of view our goal was achieved. We got some guarantees for Cuba, there was an American decision for withdrawal of missiles with nuclear warheads from Turkey, Italy, and . . . we returned to a more stable situation than it was before the Cuban missile crisis—though, of course, the price which we paid was very high. I mean, the tension was substantial, and we should keep in mind the lesson of the Cuban missile crisis and try to avoid it in a similar situation.

PLEKHANOV: By that time we were already used to the idea of a competition between the United States and the Soviet Union, and the Cuban missile crisis was an episode which provided a kind of ceiling to that competition—that one has to be very careful about that competition, and even though we may take great pride at having a lot of missiles (and later it turned out that the number of those missiles was not too great at that time), still, I mean, there are other ways to provide for your security; and so the Nuclear Test Ban Treaty [in July 1963] was a great educational exercise: a few months back we almost went to war with

> the United States, and now we're negotiating and we're able to produce a document which has a vital importance for security, it goes right into the heart of your nuclear deterrent.

I do remember arguing myself, for some time afterward, that it was unreasonable for the United States to object to Soviet missiles in Cuba when it had missiles that could threaten the Soviet Union from a comparable distance in Turkey. It was only very recently that I discovered that Kennedy himself effectively accepted this point during the crisis, and that Khrushchev's "climb down" was part of an understanding that also included the removal of U.S. Jupiter missiles from Turkey and Italy.[1] I suppose more serious students of international affairs were aware of that at the time, but for me—and I suspect for an awful lot of other people in the West—it was lost in the small print.

I can see how in retrospect, and for Americans especially, Kennedy's death might seem to mark the end of the good days when our generation felt basically optimistic about the world, and the beginning of the years of violence and disillusionment. But it wasn't so for me or, I would venture to say, for most people of my age outside the United States. It was a terrible shock, but we got over it. Chris Patten says of the Berlin Wall, Cuba, and the Kennedy assassination, "To some extent I associate all of those with the politics of being at university and that period of my life." It is not a time of life when one naturally feels very gloomy about politics, unless or until one feels personally and directly threatened. As I remember it, I did feel threatened intermittently by nuclear war, but most of the time the threat didn't seem sufficiently immediate to cast a deep shadow over my life. There were plenty of other things going on. British domestic politics became highly entertaining in the summer of 1963, thanks to the Profumo crisis: a minister had to resign because he had falsely denied, in the House of Commons, having slept with a prostitute who, it turned out, had also been sleeping with the Soviet naval attaché. The facts all came out, with much salacious detail about the lives of the rich and famous, at the trial of a society osteopath who was accused of living on the prostitute's immoral earnings. The "establishment" (itself then a term of recent coinage) was generally discredited, and the contempt for it felt by my generation, and my immediate elders, was expressed in a sudden explosion of the almost-forgotten art of political satire: it flourished even on television in the Saturday-night program "That Was the Week That Was," which, to the surprise and discomfiture of the authorities, quickly attracted an unprecedented mass audience.

The Conservative government was clearly on its last legs, and all sorts of fantasies were possible about how new and different a Labour government would be—especially for those of us not old enough to remember the previous one.

Of course, we were disillusioned with the Labour government when it came. I remember being incensed by its failure to use force to prevent the unilateral declaration of independence by Ian Smith's white supremacist regime in Southern Rhodesia, while force was still being used against the indigenous independence movements in South Yemen. When Harold Wilson came to Oxford to open the new Institute of Statistics I took part in a demonstration against him, shouting, "Out of Aden, into Rhodesia," under the cheerleadership of Tariq Ali, the Pakistani Marxist who was then president of the Oxford Union, where he attracted considerable publicity by organizing a replay of the famous 1933 debate on the motion "that this House would not fight for King and Country," as well as a marathon "Teach-In" (another fashion of the time) about the Vietnam War, in which Michael Stewart, the foreign secretary in Wilson's government, came and courageously—but unsuccessfully—defended the American position.

I did feel strongly about Vietnam, especially after the bombing of Hanoi started in 1966. But my overall memory of the sixties is still of a decade when politics was exciting and one felt an underlying confidence that history was moving in the right direction. I'm ashamed to say that the very difficulties and turmoil that the United States was getting into were part of the excitement. I felt, and I think quite a lot of my European contemporaries felt, at least to start with, an instinctive sympathy for the radical protest movements that were then surfacing in America. Chris Patten and I went together on our first visit to America in 1965: I remember being delighted—and I rather think he was, too, though neither of us took it all that seriously —by the popular protest song "Eve of Destruction," and also listening eagerly in Berkeley, California, to a sympathetic account of the student Free Speech Movement, given by a British friend who was studying there at the time, and feeling indignant that the movement had been misrepresented by the American press, with the exception of the *New York Times.*

It was interesting, therefore, to hear the accounts given by Richard Burt and Newt Gingrich—now respectively a senior official in the Republican administration and a prominent Republican congressman —of their own student days in the sixties.

Richard Burt is visibly a child of the sixties. Even though now an ambassador, after a spell in the influential position of director of politico-military affairs in the State Department, he still manages, with his deep-set eyes and his lock of gray hair falling over the forehead, to look at once youthful and decadent.

BURT: There was a kind of cultural revolution in the United States, at least on college campuses. I, when I entered college in 1965, I wore a coat and tie. You weren't permitted to have a woman in your dormitory room. When I left college in 1969 no one wore a coat and tie, there were mixed dormitories with mixed sexes, there was a good deal of drug use on college campuses. So there was a dramatic change in American society, which in large part, I think, was influenced by the Vietnam conflict. . . .

I think that the fact of protesting against American policy was representative of a major turning point in American society. The postwar period up until the late sixties had been a very tranquil period. The Eisenhower years were years of consolidation. Whole generations of Americans who had been in Europe during World War II came home, got jobs, went to school on the GI Bill, and got married, moved to the suburbs and had children. Those children grew up, like myself, in very tranquil surroundings. Suddenly there were protests, and the protests were not simply against a single American policy—Vietnam. They tended to be against a system, this system that had grown up in the 1950s which had made people comfortable but that many people in my generation felt was too kind of fat and happy; and so the act of protesting Vietnam raised questions about being kind of liberated—people's passions and emotions—and so it led people beyond Vietnam to question other elements and other aspects of society; and it was a fairly short-lived cultural revolution and by 1972–73 it was probably over.

Newt Gingrich must have graduated from Emory University, presumably still wearing a coat and tie, at about the time that Burt was entering Cornell. In the crucial late sixties, the high point of student protest and counterculture, he was already in graduate school. A cheerful, fresh-faced, all-American figure, he does not appear to have been personally marked by the permissive society. Consequently his analysis of what went wrong with his contemporaries in the sixties is less sympathetic, but not without insight.

GINGRICH: All of a sudden in the sixties you have four or five things happening at once. You have a very large biological upsurge of young people, the "baby boom" generation, of which . . . I was on the cutting edge (1943, when I was born, was the beginning of the big birth boom in America, and the baby boomers really come on when Dad gets home in 1945). So you used to have the biological, normal thing that when you have a lot of young people wandering around they have lots of energy: they want to rebel. Second, the civil rights movement had shattered belief in the fabric of the American establishment: I mean, after all, if segregation was that morally wrong, then what does it tell us about all those people in power who have accepted [it all this time]? Third, the Free Speech Movement starting in California—the whole sense of going bra-less, wearing short skirts, sleeping around. . . . I mean, just a general notion of "Why would we believe in all those silly Victorian systems?" Fourth . . . you had a left-wing radical strain in American life, people like George McGovern; and then, fifth, the morning that the rebellious young people, who knew the civil rights movement had discredited the establishment, who were in favor of Free Speech, were told they would be drafted, you suddenly had an explosion of—well, it was basically "protect yourself," self-protection: "I don't want to go get killed for some corrupt, establishment guy's war."

This questioning of the moral credentials of the establishment was even more pronounced in Germany at the same period. If the American establishment could be accused of having tolerated segregation, in Germany the older generation as a whole was tainted with the suspicion of complicity in the crimes of Nazism. What above all characterizes my contemporaries in Germany is that they are the first generation born too late to have participated in or had any knowledge of the Nazi movement even at kindergarten level; and the sixties in Germany were above all the period when that generation came of age and began publicly and collectively questioning its elders. Karsten Voigt, now a senior figure in the Social Democratic party, was one of the leaders of the student protest movement at that time.

VOIGT: We were very much interested to know what the Germans did during the Second World War, and what our professors did during the Second World War, and leading politicians did during the Second World War. . . . In the early sixties it was the Adenauer time, which I perceived at that time as a time of restoration under democratic circumstances, [of] economic growth, but social injustice. The second part of the sixties was represented by protest against this: protest against the brown [i.e., Nazi] past, of the democratic present, and protest against authoritarian structures which remained there in democratic postwar Germany; and where we tried to implement in international politics the values [in which] we were educated in postwar Germany. . . . We thought we could change not only Germany, but also Europe.

For the student movement was a European, if not a Western, movement —and we thought that as a fact of our international solidarity, as a fact of our protest, we could change our societies. . . . We were very optimistic, to a certain degree overoptimistic, about how much we could change. . . .

To a certain degree we were successful in overrunning institutions, changing institutions. And then we represented a new culture: this was fantasy to power . . . and it was not the old type of organized labor, disciplined labor, but we were overrunning them by new ideas, by individual behavior, and our expression was Peace, Not War—and Love, Not War. That means it was not only discipline: it was kissing the authoritarian and militaristic structure to death.

Matthias Wissmann, the Christian Democratic economic affairs spokesman, believes the student movement marked a crucial turning point in the political outlook even of those law-abiding students like himself, who took no direct part in it.

WISSMANN: Take the soldier coming back from the war, or the prisoner coming back from the war—I had people in my broader family who came back from Siberia in 1951. What they started to do was to build up what has been completely destroyed, and so it's understandable, I think, that this generation, in the time of the fifties, mainly was concentrating on restructuring their life, their basic needs—and I think this has been the incentive for the economic miracle. . . . And the problem of this development has been that at this time most of the people did not really think of other aspects of life. . . . The student movement at the end of the sixties has been fueled by this lack of philosophical, of nonmaterial thinking; and on the other hand, for those who have not been part of the student movement—like me—it has been an incentive to reflect on their own position, and to learn that a moderate policy [such as] I presented—and others, too—cannot only be based on economical elements: you need a vision, and a background which is more than material-based. For me the breakpoint of this is the student movement at the end of the sixties.

Josef Joffe, the much-respected commentator on national and international politics of the *Süddeutsche Zeitung,* also singled out this period when asked to name the event that had been most significant in shaping his outlook.

JOFFE: I would say no event in particular, it's a certain stretch of time: the late sixties—what the Berkeley generation went through, between Berkeley, Paris, and Berlin. That's not an event—it's a mood, it's a process, whereby basic patterns of behavior, both political and cultural, suddenly break up with a vengeance; and I think it was particularly strongly felt here in Germany, which after the war went through a kind of restoration period, with a kind of "stability *über alles*" mentality . . . and that suddenly collapsed with a vengeance in this country, with a whole generation becoming politically activist. And, being Germans, they do it more thoroughly than elsewhere, and so while Berkeley was soon over, and May 1968 in Paris soon became an episode, in West Germany the process set in motion then has never stopped: in fact right now we're witnessing all over Germany the sixties generation coming to power.

Was May 1968 in Paris only an episode? The Gaullist politician Jacques Toubon doesn't think so.

TOUBON: The victory of the Socialist party in 1981, from my point of view, is a kind of consequence of 1968, because those types of ideas, like less work, or "quality of life" [etc.] are, I think, 1968 ideas, and that's the basis of the Socialist doctrine in 1981 and the basis of the victory of the Socialist party, because the French people in 1981 dreamed about those kinds of ideas: working less but getting more money.

Although already a civil servant, and a supporter of the de Gaulle–Pompidou government then in power, Toubon was enough a man of his generation to enjoy what was happening.

TOUBON: I lived May '68 like a month of freedom, you know—of joy. I was walking to my bureau in the Finance Ministry—a half-hour walk, and it was very different from the bus or Métro, and I think for most people, in favor or not of the student rebellion, it was a period of . . . a kind of lightness, you know, in the air and in the spirit of the nation . . . quite exciting, arguments in the street—all these people around the barricade in the morning after the battle of the night, and that was a moment when some people meet who ordinarily don't meet at any time. . . . That's a kind of interesting and exciting period for young people, and I think for a lot of adults.

Certainly for me May 1968 was the high point of the sixties. I was twenty-four. I had just got engaged. I had obtained, as my first job, the position of assistant correspondent in Paris for the *Times* of London. In temperament I was still making the transition from student to journalist, and many of my friends in Paris were students. The Vietnam peace talks had just opened in Paris. The American press and TV circus descended in full strength to cover the opening ceremonies, and then found nothing else to report. "What about the riots in the Quartier Latin?" I suggested. "Yeah, the students. That's a good story, but unfortunately it's of no interest back home." Away they went. Two weeks later they were back: the whole of France was on strike, and de Gaulle had disappeared. There was, in the current revolutionary jargon, *vacance du pouvoir:* a vacancy of power. It was a beautiful morning, and the Communist trade unions were due to march. Rumor had it they might take possession of the Elysée in de Gaulle's absence. Anything seemed possible. A colleague, sent over specially from London, was invited to write a piece on the theme "France without de Gaulle." "No," he replied grandly, "I shall write the obituary of the Fifth Republic."

No good pretending I was impartial. At home I was a disillusioned Labour supporter, but I still thought of myself as left-wing. Though I admired de Gaulle for having got France out of Algeria, and agreed with his criticism of the Vietnam War, I was biased against him because he was keeping Britain out of the European Community (certainly the least of his crimes in the eyes of my student friends); because of his haughty and somewhat authoritarian style of government; because his government was, in conventional terms, right rather than left; because he was old and old-fashioned; above all, perhaps, because he had been in power for ten years. "France is bored," *Le Monde*'s political analyst Pierre Viansson-Ponté had diagnosed only two months before. Whether or not it was true of the nation, it was true of the young—and of the political journalists. "*Dix ans—ca suffit!*" ("ten years—that's enough!") was certainly one of the most potent slogans of the would-be revolution.

Of course it wasn't a revolution, though its leaders—some Marxist, some anarchist, some a bit of both—would have liked it to become one, any more than de Gaulle's state was fascist. There was some police brutality—unnecessary beating with truncheons, use of tear-gas grenades in enclosed spaces—but remarkably few deaths. As far as I remember I managed to count about ten, connected in one way or other with political events, in different parts of France between the beginning of May and the end of June: hardly enough to put a race riot in an American city on the front page that summer. There was just enough danger to make it exciting without being tragic. It was only three years later that I really understood the nature of what had happened, when I saw Ariane Mnouchkine's brilliant play *1789,* in which the original French Revolution is presented as a fairground drama, and the audience encouraged to play the part of the crowd. When I noticed sixteen- and seventeen-year-old Parisians around me chanting slogans against Louis XVI, with real enthusiasm, I understood suddenly that this was what had been happening all over France in May 1968. A whole generation of French youth had, without realizing it, joined in a theatrical reenactment of the great revolutionary *journées* of eighteenth- and nineteenth-century Paris. I remembered one of my student friends at the beginning of "the events" (as they were always called at the time, and for a long time afterward) jumping up and down with excitement and saying, "It's going to be the cops versus the students, it's going to be like during the Algerian War. What we need is some wounded. What we need"—he grinned nervously—"is a few deaths!" Of course. He had been too young to take part during the Algerian War. He had to have *his* revolution. And what do you do in a revolution? You tear up paving stones and tree gratings, and you build barricades—a complete anachronism when you are taking on the forces of a state that has aircraft and armored vehicles at its disposal.

But, of course, de Gaulle had more sense than to use aircraft or armored vehicles against students armed only with paving stones, and perhaps the odd petrol bomb. When it came to political theater, he was the master—and he played his part beautifully, even down to the dramatic twenty-four-hour disappearance when he went (as it was later revealed) to confer with the commander of the French armed forces in Germany. He arrived back and addressed the nation. The television was on strike, so he used the radio—which gave an extra dramatic touch, recalling his famous broadcast from London on June 18, 1940, urging the French not to accept Pétain's armistice with the victorious Nazis. He announced that he was dissolving parliament and calling a general election (thereby, in fact, granting the main immediate demand of the opposition, but making it sound like a decisive reassertion of his authority). He appointed the prefects (representatives of the state in the provinces) "Commissioners of the Republic" —a title that carried no specific powers but, again, recalled the administration installed by de Gaulle at the moment of France's liberation from the Nazis in 1944. And he asked the population to show him support, without mentioning that a mass demonstration carefully organized by his supporters was just about to begin. Gasoline, which, supposedly because of the strike, had been unobtainable for ten days or so, suddenly flowed like water, and most of France's population drove off to the seaside for the traditional Whitsun weekend (killing, needless to say, far more of themselves and each other in the process than had died from any political cause in the preceding four weeks). The crisis was over, except for a rather dull election campaign during which it soon became apparent that most French people over the age of thirty had been thoroughly alarmed by "the events"—especially, it was noted, by the fact that cars had been overturned and burned, which came to be seen as a kind of symbolic outrage against the material aspirations of the ordinary Frenchman—and that de Gaulle's supporters would be returned with a landslide majority.

It should never be forgotten that May 1968 coincided with the Prague Spring. For me at any rate—but it was actually a widely held view at the time—they were two sides of the same coin. There seemed to be an "objective" community of interest, if not an actual conspiracy, between those in power in the two halves of divided Europe, and between the two superpowers on whose support they respectively relied. It was the drab oppressivenes of the so-called "socialist" countries in Eastern Europe that had given socialism a bad name and, I thought, was helping reactionary governments to stay in power in the West—while obviously the regimes in Eastern Europe sought to justify their oppression by playing up the injustices of Western society as well as the "aggressive" or "imperialist" policies of the United States in Vietnam and elsewhere. Both May 1968 and the Prague Spring seemed like attempts to break out of this deadlock and to point to a better, freer, fairer future for Europe as a whole, for which Dubček's slogan, "Socialism with a Human Face," seemed as good as any.

It was in the Quartier Latin one night in May 1968 that I met Jan Kavan, a Czech student leader on some kind of exchange visit. He was a bit baffled by what was going on in Paris—understandably, since whatever oppressive elements there were in French society were very mild and subtle compared even to the mollified Stalinism of Czechoslovakia in the 1960s. Jan's father had been one of the victims of the Prague show trials in the early fifties—not executed, but imprisoned, and his health broken. So Jan knew all about the oppressive practices of the Communist regime. On the other hand his father *was* a Communist (like all the victims of those trials) and Jan had been brought up as one. At that time he, like many other Czechs, believed that Communism properly understood was not incompatible with freedom, and he was very anxious to rebut any suggestion that by advocating greater freedom one was furthering the interests of capitalism or of the West. He wanted to be seen as a *more* authentic left-winger and revolutionary than the Prague bureaucrats, so both by conviction and by tactical calculation he looked for allies in Western countries on the left, among Socialists or even, if possible, Communists (the Italians were more helpful than the French) rather than liberals and conservatives. So this encouraged me in my view that one should be against *both* orthodoxies, and both superpowers, rather than take sides between them. I was slipping toward the heresy later denounced by Jeane Kirkpatrick as the notion of "moral equivalence." (America, it should be remembered, was not looking too good just then. Martin Luther King was shot on April 4, and Robert Kennedy on June 5.)

Later in the summer Jan visited London and stayed there for some weeks as the houseguest of my fiancée, explaining to her each evening the latest developments in the Czechoslovak-Soviet drama. When the Soviet Politburo came to Czechoslovakia en bloc to settle matters directly with Dubček and his colleagues, Jan was overjoyed. He believed this formal recognition of the reformist leadership meant that they had won, and that the experiment of Communism in freedom was to be allowed to continue. Thus fortified, he went off on a visit to America, where he took part in the antiwar demonstrations at the Chicago Democratic Convention and got beaten up by Mayor Daley's police.

So for me the moment when the age of optimism ended is not November 22, 1963, but the night of August 20, 1968 (strictly, in the early hours of August 21), when the phone rang in my Paris apartment and the *Times* foreign desk in London said, "It looks as if the Russians have invaded Czechoslovakia. Please find out what you can." Of course I could find out nothing in Paris that could not also be found out in London, but I stayed awake for the rest of the night listening to the radio and contemplating the destruction of all my youthful illusions. In the days that followed there was encouraging news: the heroic passive resistance of the Czechoslovak population, the clandestine congress of the Communist party held in a Prague factory under the Russians' noses, the firmness of the kidnapped leaders and their return from Moscow unbowed, and still in office (having refused to board the plane without their colleague Frantisek Kriegl, whom the Russians had tried to keep). Jan came back to Paris and I remember a dinner in a Left Bank restaurant with Heda Margolius, widow of another show trial victim, who had just arrived from Prague and told us with a passionate mixture of rage and excitement what had been going on there. When one of us unthinkingly referred to the "illegal radio," she corrected us triumphantly: "No, clandestine—*illegal is the invasion!*" But I think we all knew it would make no difference in the end: the argument of physical force had been invoked, and on that level the Russians were bound to win. Moreover one had the strong impression that the Americans, wrapped up in their own problems, did not much care. Certainly they made no pretense of being able to do anything about it. It was easy to persuade oneself that they were glad that this potentially awkward challenge to their system—the notion of "socialism with a human face"—had been snuffed out. De Gaulle, furious that the invasion had destroyed his own dream of a "European Europe" independent of both superpowers, denounced it as a fruit of the "policy of blocs," which, he said, had been decided at Yalta and practiced ever since.

In October I got married, and on our way to our honeymoon in Turkey we visited Jan in Prague. The Soviet troops were visible on the roads and in the countryside, but "normalization" had not yet gone very far. Dubček was still nominally in power and people, even officials, expressed their feelings quite openly. The female immigration officer at the border who stamped our passports when we arrived, quite late at night, was actually in tears. "I wish you could have visited our country at a happier time," she said. She probably didn't realize how sincerely I wished that, too.

CHAPTER 5

Vietnam and Détente

For us in Europe, as will be apparent from the last chapter, Vietnam was really just a part of the general sixties scene—a larger part for some than for others. Of the European politicians and commentators interviewed, only Chris Patten named the Vietnam War as the most significant international event in shaping his outlook on the world. Karsten Voigt, who was such an active leader of the student protest movement in West Germany in the sixties, mentioned Vietnam only in passing, along with Algeria, Suez, and Iran, as an example of the policies of "our present allies" that his generation attacked. Matthias Wissmann remembers the shah of Iran as "a much bigger discussion" than Vietnam when he was at university in the late sixties. (The death of a student demonstrator during the shah's visit to West Berlin in 1967 was the point of departure for the most active phase of student protest in Germany.) Josef Joffe recalls the devolution to the West German government of emergency powers hitherto held by the Allied occupation authorities as "almost a more crystallizing event than Vietnam was," because the granting of such powers, however modest, to a German government was wrongly seen as a possible first step toward the return of fascism.

In France, as in Britain, I remember Vietnam being a major issue for the student left before 1968. It seemed rather odd that this should be so, for whereas the Wilson government in Britain was closely aligned with the United States, de Gaulle in France was criticizing the war, and annoying the Americans with several of his other policies, such as the withdrawal of France from NATO's military structure and his campaign for a return to the gold standard, and he was trying—not very successfully—to prevent the takeover of French industry by American-based multinationals. So on the face of it there was not very much to protest about. But my student friends were not satisfied with this. As far as they were concerned, France was still part of the U.S.-dominated capitalist world and therefore "objectively" supporting the American war effort. They demanded action against American interests in France.

Above all—and this, I think, was the real interest of the Trotskyist groups under whose influence they had fallen—they criticized the French Communist party (which was pursuing a cautious strategy aimed at winning electoral support and building an alliance with more moderate left-wing parties) for being too tame and—they claimed—insincere in its campaign against the war.* They were active in a body called the Comité Vietnam National, which refused to cooperate with the police in staging its demonstrations and was clearly seeking a confrontation in which the Communist party would be embarrassed by having to choose sides between anti-American demonstrators and the forces of the "bourgeois" state. But when the confrontation came, it was on domestic issues (essentially issues of campus discipline and the use of the police to enforce it), and Vietnam was forgotten. On the evening of Monday, May 13, 1968, I went to visit my friends in the "liberated" Sorbonne (it had been evacuated by the police and taken over by the students for nonstop political discussions) and tried to tell them that the peace talks between America and North Vietnam had opened that morning in the Majestic Hotel. A few months earlier they had been able to talk of little except Vietnam, but now they weren't interested. *They* were trying to tell *me* the real news that had just come through: there were barricades in the streets of Clermont-Ferrand.

I suspect the majority of French people, even politically minded people, were not greatly concerned about Vietnam in the first place —not in its American phase, that is. The French had had their own Vietnam agony, which had ended in 1954 and then been eclipsed by the worse agony of Algeria. Jacques Toubon recalls that American criticisms of French policy during the Algerian War, though he is now inclined to justify them by referring to America's need to keep on good terms with Arab countries that were already independent, were at the time "not very well appreciated" in France, "even among the

*In March 1968, shortly after the biggest and most violent Vietnam demonstration in London (outside the U.S. embassy in Grosvenor Square), I remember a French student telling me, at a fairly tame Vietnam-related event in Paris, that we in England were lucky: we could have a real, revolutionary Vietnam protest movement, because we didn't have a great big, cautious, reformist Communist party to get in the way! Hostility and disgust for the French Communist party is the consistent theme that links the present Cold War stance of France's "new philosophers," and many other less-known French intellectuals, with their "revolutionary" past in the late sixties and early seventies.

people who were in favor of Algerian independence." The substance of de Gaulle's Phnom Penh speech in 1966 was to say to the Americans, "You were good friends to criticize us over Algeria, even though we did not like it: I am now going to return the favor by criticizing your actions in Vietnam, even though you will not like it." As a faithful Gaullist, Toubon endorsed that position, and felt there was nothing much more to be said.

> TOUBON: You know, we have the experience of those kind of wars —colonial wars—and I think that the positions, the statements of General de Gaulle were full of wisdom. But I understand that the United States had at that moment some interests, and that it was very difficult to leave Vietnam. . . . I was not much impressed by the Berkeley affair or those kind of things. . . . I lived that really rather from afar. You know, French people had got rid of Indochina, and I think that French people hoped to be definitively out of this problem. It was a kind of protection for us.

As for Laurent Fabius, the future Socialist prime minister, he remembers feeling some "resentment" toward the United States, but was not affected in his own life and took no part in demonstrations.

> FABIUS: [Yet I do remember] images of death—people with arms which were cut, legs which were cut. It was not a question of understanding, it was more a question of feeling. . . . I was a youngster and a student, therefore I could not understand the reason of massacres everywhere. . . . I didn't like this view at all, because of the violence.

One should not underestimate the effect that the association of such images with America may have had, particularly at the subconscious level. Intellectually the new generation of European politicians may be no less convinced than were their parents of the superiority of the American political model to the Soviet one, or of the importance for European security of maintaining close ties with the United States. But their emotional, instinctive responses to America are clearly different, and the fact that the Vietnam War occurred at a formative period of their political development almost certainly has something to do with that. Irmgard Adam-Schwaetzer, now West German minister of state for foreign affairs, recalls that her feelings about the United States, very positive in the time of Kennedy, became "ambivalent" later in the 1960s as a result of reading *The Ugly American,* and that the Vietnam War seemed to bear out the picture of U.S. policies toward the Third World given in that book. She thinks, moreover, that this perception was typical of her contemporaries in Germany. At the time, she says, she and her "political friends" did not take any clear-cut stand on the issue "because the memory of the Khrushchev era [i.e., the Soviet pressure on West Berlin in 1958–61] still was too vivid . . . and we just knew that we had to associate ourselves with the United States to secure our freedom." But much later, in the 1980s, "the discussion of a specific role of Europe in NATO . . . in my opinion is a late consequence of this perception." And Volker Rühe, the Christian Democrat, says that although he himself was not greatly affected by Vietnam (being already aware of "the dark side of America, I mean the psychological damage that was done to young blacks through the race conflict," from experience working with black and Puerto Rican children from New York at a summer camp in the early sixties) and "never became a one-sided critic of the United States," he thinks "people who were younger than myself, and who were influenced by the Vietnam War as the first influence, tended to see America as the problem-maker." An example would be Ingrid Matthäus-Maier.

> MATTHÄUS-MAIER: [For people of my age Vietnam] was a very bad and terrible experience. And most of my friends were on the side of the Vietnamese people, not because we thought as Communists, or that we were Communists, but we thought that the Americans stood on the false side—that it would have been the task of Europe, and especially of the Americans, to help the people to develop and to have growth, economic growth, [so] that all people in Vietnam had enough to eat, that there could develop democracy—and we were very much upset that the Americans supported the dictator Diem, and we found it was really a very important injustice that they supported Diem against the Vietnamese people, and I think for many of my friends, and for me, too, it was a big issue—and we began to make politics. We were engaged [committed]. We made demonstrations in the streets, many thousands of young people, against the Vietnamese War. And that was not because they didn't like or love America: we were disappointed. We thought we are the world of freedom, of personal freedom, of democracy, and that doesn't go together that we support dictatorships there. And I think this has been a very bad thing for the image of America among the young people of this country.

For our American contemporaries, of course, Vietnam was a far more central formative experience—"more important than all the others," according to George Will, and no one seems seriously to dispute that. Richard Burt indeed admits to having been "so preoccupied with what was happening in the United States, with the civil rights movement, and in Vietnam, that in a way Czechoslovakia was a sideshow." Yet many now say, as Will does, that "the real Vietnam experience" was not so much the war itself, but "the experience of domestic dissent." One who emphatically agrees with that is Elliott Abrams, who began his rightward political journey in 1968 by resigning from the board of the liberal pressure group Americans for Democratic Action because of its refusal to endorse Vice-President Hubert Humphrey as the Democratic presidential candidate.

> ABRAMS: The real impact on me was the kind of "hate America" nature of the antiwar movement, which left a very bad taste in my mouth—and that was true both of the American antiwar movement and of the European antiwar movement; take Sweden, for example. That in an odd way had a greater impact, you might say, than the war itself.

Similarly Richard Perle says that, though he personally had doubts whether the war could be won, he suppressed them because he disliked the arguments of the antiwar lobby.

> PERLE: I was rather doubtful about the Vietnam War, especially as it was gathering momentum in the early sixties, because it seemed to me that the political infrastructure in South Vietnam just wasn't sufficient to deal with the determined effort of the North Vietnamese to take control. I never had the moral concerns that seemed to animate lots of others of my generation. It seemed to me that if the United States could contribute to a settlement in Vietnam that left open the opportunity for those in the South to pursue a nontotalitarian government, that that was a perfectly right and proper thing for us to do, but I did have reservations about whether the circumstances were such that we had a fair chance of succeeding. . . . I actually found some of the arguments against the war sufficiently offensive so that I was moved to set aside my own doubts about whether we could be successful, in order to defend the legitimacy of the kind of intervention in which we were involved.

And while many supporters of the war apparently had private doubts about whether it could be won, according to George Will the fact that it was not being won was the most unpopular thing about it with the public at large.

WILL: You have to understand about Vietnam that the general history of the period is mistaken. It is that there was general dissent from the government right along. Not true. If you look at the opinion polls —not of the elites, not of the college students, but the opinion polls— support for the government policy tracked with government policy right along, and even in 1968, when Gene McCarthy almost won—the average person thinks he beat Lyndon Johnson in New Hampshire: he didn't—when Gene McCarthy made a good protest showing in New Hampshire, it's not clear: we know from polls and analyzing the data that most of the people voting for Gene McCarthy wanted a more hawkish policy in Vietnam. So that the great criticism of the Vietnam policy is, we didn't win.

But *could* the war be won, given the nature of the government and society it was being waged to support? "There are those," as Richard Perle says, "who hold that the war was close to a successful conclusion at the point at which we terminated the bombing of the North." But Newt Gingrich thinks it could not have been won in the way—or at the pace—that it was fought:

GINGRICH: I thought it was essentially the right war at the time. I thought, though, that if we were going to fight it, we should fight it very fast. Democracies are not willing to tolerate their children being killed slowly. . . . They're willing, if a war matters, to win it and get it over with. . . . But democracies will not tolerate eight, ten, fifteen, twenty years of bloodletting. . . . We can't watch our own children gradually get killed, and we can't watch other people's children being killed.

The memory of Sam Gejdenson, a Democrat who was staunchly opposed to the war, seems to support Gingrich's point.

GEJDENSON: Here the United States was, fighting a war for somebody else. That government wasn't able to muster sufficient support to defend itself, and the government itself seemed so corrupt that it seemed impossible for even the United States to bolster it. So once again, almost like the Bay of Pigs, we were involved in what was going to be a losing effort, unless we were willing to go to incredibly cruel lengths in devastating the countryside—and the American public wouldn't allow an American government to go to the degree necessary. We couldn't do in Vietnam what the Soviets may well be able to do in Afghanistan.*

*Interview recorded in May 1986.

When I asked Lord Franks how far he thought the understanding of America's global responsibilities, which he encountered as British ambassador among the Americans who came home after World War II, had been successfully transmitted to the generation that has grown up since, he talked of the impact of Vietnam.

FRANKS: You have to make allowance . . . for the fact of Vietnam. This was a small-scale war which dragged on, caused quite a large number of American casualties, and was a humiliating defeat: the peace which had to be made was Vietnam's way, not America's way, and all Vietnam now belongs and is governed by North Vietnam, and so is Cambodia. This left a great scar on the American people.

Or, as Irmgard Adam-Schwaetzer puts it, "They had to learn in Vietnam that just being a big country doesn't mean you are successful." Joe Biden implicitly confirms these European assessments, and goes further: "It shattered our confidence, and our abilities, and our judgment." That could even be taken as confirming George Will's view.

WILL: A wise person said, toward the end of the Vietnam experience, that worse than Vietnam and more dangerous would be the lessons we chose to learn from it. A number of Americans—and I am emphatically among them—believe that we learned the wrong lessons: we learned that the United States should never act alone, we should only act multilaterally, preferably through international institutions, that the use of military force had had its day, that diplomacy must operate without force threatened or used.

Kenneth Adelman agrees.

ADELMAN: We always learn these historical lessons and apply them in the wrong way. We learn the lesson of Munich and apply it to Vietnam. We learn the lesson of Vietnam and apply it to Nicaragua. And it seems to me that as much damage is being done by learning these historical lessons and applying them to the wrong place as in forgetting history altogether. . . . I remember feeling that we should really see what's doable in the world and then take a stand there, and so it seems to me right now that we would have no argument in the United States on Nicaragua, for example, had there not been the damage of the Vietnam War.

It has often been remarked that the later stages of the Vietnam War coincided with the development of "détente" between the United States and the Soviet Union. Sergei Plekhanov, indeed, remembers finding this coincidence somewhat indecent.

PLEKHANOV: I remember very well how Nixon came to Moscow and was addressing the Soviet people, sitting at an ornate table in the Kremlin with his feet crossed, and recalling his visit to Leningrad; and he said that he was profoundly moved by what he'd learned about the suffering of and the deaths of the people of Leningrad during the war; and he quoted from a diary by a little girl whose name was Tanya—she died—and he said, "Now we must built a world in which there will be no more Tanyas dying," and so on and so forth. In the sense of an argument for détente that was okay, but that shocked me. That kind of had a very unpleasant ring to it, because right at this time the Americans were bombing Vietnam very viciously, and you know a lot of kids were dying there, and that touched me, that kind of struck me as very cynical.

MORTIMER: How did that make you feel about your own leadership—I mean, conducting this détente with the people responsible for killing the kids in Vietnam?

PLEKHANOV: Well, you see, we had no illusions about what the Nixon administration was all about. And, in fact, the war in Vietnam, that was going on, in which the United States was very clearly losing, not being able to gain its objectives in the war, and we saw the turn to détente as a kind of step forced by circumstances.

Kenneth Adelman agrees that détente became necessary "because the Soviets by the time of détente had become a real superpower in terms of nuclear armaments, which they were not before," but adds that it was only possible "because we had a president, Richard Nixon, who would not sell us down the river in any sense." But that is not enough to redeem détente in George Will's eyes. Détente coincided, he believes, "with the worst period of Soviet behavior in the postwar period: Angola, Ethiopia, Afghanistan, Nicaragua, all the rest, the sending of surrogate troops [Cubans] to areas not contiguous to the Soviet empire."

This, of course, is vigorously contested in Moscow.

KOKOSHIN: I think it's a totally wrong perception in the West that the Soviet Union tried to use this situation in order to expand its influence and assurance. We've had many discussions with our American and Western European colleagues on this matter, and tried to explain case by case all the situations, and you know that was the period when the last, I would say, relics of colonial empire disappeared—like Angola, Mozambique; there was a revolution in Ethiopia in that period, you know—and other events which had no connection with the policy of the Soviet Union. They were natural developments. And, of course, these countries, and revolutionary forces in these countries, they even needed support and help when they started to fight, and they then got into power—and that's the support from Europe, from the Soviet Union, or from Cuba, and I think we have all the legitimate rights to give them that support. But it was, of course, used by the right-wingers, by the conservatives, as a demonstration of the weakening of America and the Soviet Union using this for expansionist purposes and so on and so on. . . . I totally reject, personally, the notion that the Soviet Union used this "post-Vietnam syndrome" of the United States to fill their vacuum, as some American politologists say.

PLEKHANOV: When they say "Soviet expansionism," what they have in mind is the aid that the Soviet Union gave to Angola and Ethiopia and Afghanistan, trying to help these countries withstand foreign aggression. That was certainly not motivated by any design for global domination of the planet or something like that. But I can see how it could easily be painted in such terms because of the ideological background that exists. I mean, the Soviet Union is supposed to be expansionist because it's Communist, and the Communists are always trying to take over the planet—and so it was easy to put those events in those terms. At the same time, when the Americans were allegedly in their self-contained mood *they* were actually expanding very rapidly. If you take, for instance, the economic side of the question, American banking operations overseas never had grown at such a tempo as they did in the 1970s. The average annual growth was around 11 percent. I don't think there had ever been such a tremendous growth of overseas economic activity by any power in the world's history.

What went wrong, in Richard Burt's view, was "that détente was oversold."

BURT: The real problem was that the American people and the U.S. Congress were simply not prepared to give the president the instruments he needed to compete effectively with the Soviet Union. That is, what was shocking was not so much that the Soviets tried to and succeeded in sending Cuban proxy forces to Angola. What was shocking was that the U.S. Congress prevented the Nixon administration from responding to it;* and the fact that U.S. defense spending declined in real terms every year during the 1970s, whilst Soviet defense spending increased in real terms by maybe 4 percent per annum, shows that there was a fundamental misunderstanding during the 1970s amongst the American people, and a good deal of the political elite, about what détente was and how you maintained détente.

But George Will also believes that "there's been a second lesson" from the Vietnam War—a "sobering of America," in the sense of a realization that the results of American defeat and American weakness are worse than those of American arrogance.

One of those who learned this "second lesson" was Elliott Abrams.

ABRAMS: I think there was a kind of fatigue, the notion that we had tried the get-involved route in Vietnam and it was a huge disaster from every point of view—for the Vietnamese, for us, for everyone. In a way you might define it as asking the question, "Was the problem that we got involved, or was the problem that we lost?" And, of course, Carter's answer was "The problem was that we got involved," and Reagan's answer is "The problem is that we lost," and I think more Americans are tending to the latter view now. But I would say it was the feeling that mucking around in the world is just a big disaster and gets us into trouble [that prevailed in the seventies], and that view was quite understandable in the immediate aftermath of defeat, but as years went by and different people came to power—and not least we could see the result of this experiment in Vietnam and it was a million boat people, and it shocked the hell out of a lot of Americans. . . . So it feeds into what I think is a continuing sense of morality or moralism in US foreign policy: that is, that we should be concerned with what happens to the people at the receiving end. And what's increasingly clear, again, whether it's Nicaragua or Iran or Vietnam, is that what happened to them is awful. So that we have *a moral responsibility to stay involved.*

The "second lesson" has also been absorbed by some of America's allies, but they draw a slightly different conclusion from it. Yoshihisa Komori, senior political correspondent for Mainichi newspapers in Tokyo, spent nearly four years in Vietnam as a correspondent.

KOMORI: I came out feeling very resentful against the United States, not because they had intervened . . . but because of the way they decided to pull out abruptly, suddenly—that was just like ushering the

*Actually, this happened under the Ford administration.

Vietnamese people into the second floor and then after that they just take away the ladders leaving them upstairs: in other words, they had taught how to be anti-Communist, how to be truly, truly democratic in the American sense of the word, and then just in the middle of the process they suddenly, for their own benefit, turned around and then walked away.

It is hardly surprising that for George Will the fall of Saigon in 1975, with "all that film of the Americans being airlifted off the roof of their embassy . . . set the tone of the decade, the 1970s—one long damn humiliation." Yet both Koichi Kato, the Japanese defense minister, and Neil Kinnock, the British leader of the opposition, had words of praise for the American withdrawal. "A very, very bold decision, and we appreciated that decision," said Kato, while Kinnock felt moved to "say this about Nixon, that eventually . . . the withdrawal from Vietnam will get him a place in the history books when a lot of other people have been forgotten and when Watergate is absolutely gone into the past."

All the reactions to Vietnam so far quoted were at secondhand—though Perle did pay one visit there in 1973. In general, as George Will points out, "the opinion-forming class in the United States did not go to Vietnam. . . . It was fought by lower-working-class, lower-middle-class, whites and blacks." Abrams's admission that the nature of the antiwar movement had a greater impact on him than the war itself has already been noted. Of those so far mentioned, the one most directly affected emotionally by the war seems to be Pat Schroeder.

SCHROEDER: We would sit there and watch the news at night, and to have your classmates saying, "Oh my goodness, I know that person that just got shot down . . ." was really very intimate. . . . They were real people and they were people of our generation, people that my classmates knew, and, of course, my classmates were all living in stark terror that they were going to be called up next.

She makes the point that Rambo-style enthusiasm for further overseas adventures among present-day politicians tends to be in inverse proportion to actual war experience.

SCHROEDER: You know, somebody recently wrote an article about the Congress called "The Wimps of War," and it was about the members of the Congress who yell the loudest about adventurism and "let's go" everywhere were the ones who were not in a war. Many of them ducked all the way through the Vietnam War. The ones who were in it are *not* down there pounding the podium everywhere saying, "Let's bomb, let's nuke, let's go; Rambo, here we come!"

This point was also made by the only person interviewed who actually served in Vietnam, Senator Larry Pressler of South Dakota—certainly as un-Rambo-like a Republican as one could wish to meet. It was striking that Pressler spoke about Vietnam and its lessons more unemotionally than any of the other Americans. He said that at the time he had resented the fact that "you could avoid the draft by some ingenious ways if you were wealthy or well educated," and "that meant that some black guy had to go instead, or some guy who wasn't smart enough to know how to beat the system." But he had "gotten over being upset, because probably they saw it different than I did, and they served in another way, and they have their lives to lead."

All those interviewed agreed on the importance of the fact that this was the first war to be watched by a mass audience on television. Pressler said he agreed with Senator Barry Goldwater that a ground war on the scale of "the great wars where you put masses of men out there and you tell them, 'You stay out there until one or the other of you kills each other' " was no longer possible because "with television in the living room the mothers of America, the mothers of the world, wouldn't stand for it anymore, somehow it would be brought to a halt." (Though Gingrich, whose similar view was quoted earlier in this chapter, added, "It's not just the age of television: it's the nature of democracies.") If Pat Schroeder is typical of "the mothers of America," Goldwater is probably right. "It was awful," she told me, "you were watching it right there in your living room. . . . I suppose as a mother, as a woman, as somebody who watched friends be killed during that Vietnam War, I understand that war is not a game." And when Sam Gejdenson was asked for a personal memory, "something that just brings alive those years," he replied at once: "Well, I think probably the news footage—the news footage obviously played an important role in bringing the war home to us directly."

Richard Perle went further, arguing that television had crucially distorted the war, and this might even have affected the outcome.

PERLE: I went to Vietnam in 1973, having gathered an impression of what Vietnam must have looked like by what I saw on television along with millions of other Americans—and I expected to find a moonscape, a country devastated by war, with smoldering ruins everywhere. And, in fact, you had to get in a helicopter and go out of your way to find those physical manifestations of the war that was taking place. If you walked around Saigon in 1973 you were barely conscious of the fact that there was a war taking place—sandbags and barbed wire around the Ministry of Defense and a few other government buildings, but that was it. And you could travel quite considerable distances, but, unless you went to Khe Sanh or other places where there was active fighting going on, the signs of the war were far from evident. But what was on television every night was the footage that was taken at the scene of the battle, and so it gave the impression of a nation in flames, which was not the reality at all. . . .

I think it must have led to a discouragement and a pessimism and a revulsion on the part of people who, night after night, saw Vietnam being devastated by a war, the consequences of which in physical terms were confined principally to the battlefield—to villages here and there, and to a few areas where there is intense fighting—but much of the country was unaffected. . . .

The boat people are a testament to what that war meant, but you don't see that on television. I think if every night you could see people drowning, or could have seen people drowning in the immediate aftermath of that war, and if that had been the alternative alongside which a continuation of support for the South Vietnamese was judged, it might have come out quite differently. . . .

Again, television portrayed the bombing of the North as wanton and indiscriminate destruction . . . and that was a pretty ugly picture, and so the pressure to stop it was considerable, and once it stopped I think the die was cast and the outcome became inevitable.

Much of the same TV footage was seen abroad—not only in Europe but also in Third World countries—for instance, by the young Jorge Castañeda in Mexico.

CASTAÑEDA: I think the Vietnam War played a decisive role in changing most Latin Americans' of my age—of my generation—view of the United States. . . . I remember seeing the bombing on television: the pictures of the fellows shooting the little Vietcong fellow, the picture of the little boy burning running in the streets. You had very clear images running through the mid-sixties until 1968 of what the United States was doing in Vietnam: My Lai, the massacres, the bombs, the whole thing. I mean, it's all very, very vivid, and remember, by that time most of Latin America's middle classes were plugged into the worldwide television circuit. There were no dish antennas, there was no cable, but we still got the same television programs, the same images, the same press, we read the same magazines, and the pictures and the stories were all there. It was a global village already at that time, among the middle classes.

But if the war alienated much of the Third World from America, it also helped to alienate Americans from the Third World. Vietnam, after all, *was* the Third World. Americans believed they had gone there to help. It was part of the same generous vision that had led the young Larry Pressler to "hope that we could feed the world," the young Newt Gingrich to collect used books for Ghana, and President Kennedy to send out the Peace Corps. Joe Biden, too, had responded to that "noble notion" and looked forward to sharing his "Yankee ingenuity with the rest of the world, particularly the Third World."

BIDEN: [But] as I grew older, the Third World took on a different coloration. The Third World took on the coloration of napalm in bombs in Vietnam, and what many of my generation believe was an ill-fated venture, to say the least. We began to question whether or not we had the ability to impact on the Third World. . . . We saw it all—to use a slang American expression—come a cropper: we saw it all start to fall apart in Vietnam, and we began to question everything, from our humanity to our judgment to our ability to function.

Not only did Vietnam itself seem unresponsive to American generosity. In a number of other Third World countries the governments took it upon themselves to criticize what America was up to. As Olu Adeniji of Nigeria tactfully puts it, "Obviously, there was a lot of opposition to American policy in Vietnam, in several Third World countries, and obviously, also, a government that was involved in that kind of situation would feel that it was just misunderstood, and those who misunderstand, of course, are not likely to be the best friends of such an administration." Indeed. Not only the administration but many of the American people, including the idealistic young men and women just embarking on or thinking about political careers, began to feel cruelly "misunderstood" by those in the Third World whom they had been so anxious to help. The generous vision was beginning to go sour.

Finally, let's go back to Chris Patten and Ingrid Matthäus-Maier, the only Europeans to cite Vietnam as *the* formative international event in their political experience. They were also the only ones, of all the bright young politicians and pundits interviewed, to mention the effect of the war on the national and international economy.

PATTEN: I can remember hearing—I was in the United States at the time—hearing President Johnson announcing the sending of the first substantial numbers of combat troops to Vietnam. It sounded gung-ho and full of American enthusiasm. And the story of the next few years was the growing realization about the limitations of American power. The whole episode for the rest of the world, the whole dreadful sequence of events, I think had profound social and political and economic effects for all of us. I think it's very difficult not to see the Vietnam War as being one of the main determining factors in the economic problems of the late 1970s, and of the breakdown in the international economic concordat which had been established in the 1940s and had given us thirty or so pretty successful years. But the Americans, rather as in 1918 after the First World War, flooded the world with dollars, refused to pay for the war by tax increases because that would have made it more unpopular, and I think that contributed directly to the inflation from which we all suffered.

MATTHÄUS-MAIER: In order to finance this Vietnamese war America made new dollars. They really made this—new dollars, more and more and more—and they brought the inflation to the whole of the world, and so the impact of this huge inflation was a breakdown of the currency: it's a breakdown of Bretton Woods, and I think many people don't know that the Vietnamese War had also this impact on our financial markets—and now we have, as you know, trouble with our currencies. But Bretton Woods broke down because of the Vietnamese War.

In fact it was not just Vietnam, but the whole phenomenon of America's "imperial overstretch" (to use Paul Kennedy's phrase),[1] of which Vietnam was only the most acute and painful symptom. How and why that brought about the end of the monetary stability and economic growth that had characterized the postwar epoch I shall try to explain in the next chapter.

CHAPTER 6

The Rude Awakening

Ordinary people are affected by the effects of all the things that happen in the world. They were affected at the same time by the rising prices of petrol—and the shortage of petrol, perhaps. And they were affected in Europe by the higher rates of unemployment. They were, in other countries, affected by the protectionism that is creeping back into the system. And the ordinary man in the street doesn't really know whether he's being hit by a different exchange-rate system, or by Thatcherism, or whatever else is going on in the world—and he's right in not knowing it. I don't know it either, I think.

—JACQUES POLAK
Executive Director, International Monetary Fund, 1981–86

EXPERIENCE: THE "OIL SHOCK"

The world economic climate of the 1970s, which "Roosevelt's children" found themselves plunged into early in their political careers, was very different from that of the fast-expanding, optimistic, fully employed world of the fifties and early sixties in which they had grown up. The shock was felt first, and most acutely, in Europe, where it was associated with the sudden quadrupling of crude oil prices at the end of 1973. Matthias Wissmann recalls the effect in West Germany.

WISSMANN: The oil price shock in 1973—that really touched us. It even touched the young student with his car, who suddenly felt that the price was doubled. That led to the situation in Germany where one Sunday no one was allowed to drive: I think that was the only day in

German postwar history when no one was allowed to drive his own car. And that was a symbol for that radical change—and then all the issues came up: saving energy, dealing more carefully with natural resources, and then, taking it on a more intellectual level, the whole discussion of the Club of Rome, of the limitations of the world's natural resources, and of the limitations of growth: that really touched me, because that was a discussion that changed my thinking. I was, I think, one of the first at that time, being leader of the Young Christian Democrat movement in Germany, who was asking our party to concentrate more on antipollution policy. My conviction is still, if the Christian Democrats and the Social Democrats at the beginning of the seventies would have really dealt with this big new challenge, the Greens* would never have really existed. . . .

And so from 1973 on we learned in Germany, not only rationally but also emotionally, that economic miracles will not continue in a self-sustaining way, with growth rates year by year, no inflation, no unemployment—because, take the figures: in 1974 we had, I think, 500,000 unemployed people. In 1982 we had two million—and unemployment, I think, is the most personal, touching effect of economic problems. And so people understood: we have to work for our economic successes. [They are] not "delivered."

The Club of Rome report, *Limits to Growth,* published in 1972, plays an interestingly different role in different people's memories. Pierre Lellouche refers to it as a typical sixties fad—part of the ideology of May 1968: "Remember, these were the years of the economic boom: oil was very cheap, there was no unemployment problem. The Club of Rome was writing about zero growth as a goal—*as a goal!* People wanted to have no growth, and give people time to go on vacation, and all that"—whereas Wissmann clearly regards it as having been vindicated and made more relevant by the crisis of the seventies.

Right-wing Americans like George Will consider it part of the seventies disease: "The intellectual flirtation on the part of the Democratic party in our country with zero growth, Club of Rome, all that rubbish . . . It might be a good thing not to have economic growth, good for the air, or the chipmunks, whatever it was supposed to be." Jack Kemp lumps it together with the *Global 2000* report commissioned by President Carter (and published in 1980), "telling us that

**Die Grüne*—the radical ecological movement that has become a major force in West German politics in the 1980s.

the answer to energy price increases was to ride bicycles to work and to use less and to close down gasoline stations at night and not drive your car on the weekends—and that was so much against the grain of the American people that the American people decided to throw off that neo-Malthusian prediction of shortages and 'small is beautiful,' because it was against everything we'd been taught."

But Fouad Ajami, the Arab-American political scientist, sees it as a turning point in the history of the international system, marking the end of the postwar illusion "that the world was unlimited" and the opening of a period in which "there would be a real struggle over finite things . . . you couldn't incorporate everyone and feed everyone and provide for everyone . . . [because] the world is a zero-sum game that some people gain and some people lose, and the liberal model of infinite supplies is not a valid model." In this perspective American conservatives like Kemp and Will, with their tougher approach to the Third World, would be seen as having unconsciously accepted the Club of Rome message, but seeking to make sure the shortages are suffered by foreigners, rather than Americans!

Of course, the "oil shock" was the reverse of painful for some, as Prince Abdullah Bin Faisal Bin Turki, member of a junior branch of the Saudi ruling family that until 1973 had only a modest standard of living, reminds us.

ABDULLAH: I was sent on a scholarship, so it got me educated. The whole country benefited. People's incomes started to rise. We moved to a better house. People were doing better business. For the whole country we were able to build a lot of useful infrastructure, like ports, roads, telephones, hospitals. All the social services, which are the most important thing, improved. We had many more schools and educational outlets. The general standard of living improved. And it made us feel a tremendous involvement in world affairs, and we felt a lot of attention paid to our views. . . .

There was, of course, tremendous criticism of OPEC. I felt personally that it was rather unfair—because we did not invent the internal combustion engine, for the sole purpose of increasing our sales! We did not send our warships to your countries and force you to buy OPEC oil. On the contrary, it was the customers banging on our door, and many countries begging us to increase production. And we felt we were happy to play a positive role in the international community. . . . And this is why, of course, at the same time we had a very huge aid program to the poorer countries, and we contributed even to the richer countries through international organizations—the World Bank, the IMF, any other organization we could help with, the United Nations—apart from direct grants. . . . We also lent some Western countries money. So what more could we do, apart from forcing everybody to reduce prices?—Which you cannot do when there is demand for it anyway, when people themselves were bidding more and more.

But however innocent the oil producers might feel about it, for Europeans it was a case of *sentio et excrucior.* For Britain in particular the winter of 1973–74 was a traumatic moment, as the effects of the oil shortage were aggravated by those of a coal strike that turned into a trial of strength between Edward Heath's Conservative government and the trade union movement. Industry was put on a three-day week in an attempt to save fuel, and eventually Health called an election on the issue "Who governs Britain?"—and lost. Chris Patten, by then a Conservative party official of some eight years' experience, remembers this as the moment when Britain finally came face to face with her postwar decline.

PATTEN: I was a parliamentary candidate for the first time, in Brixton in south London, and I can remember the way in which the relationship between politicians and Parliament and the trade unions dominated the political argument, and I can remember a sense of hopelessness in actually coping with the argument. That was the first time I was hit by the sudden realization that life wasn't going to be quite the same again, and that the likelihood was that the whole of my adult political life was going to be spent coping with the consequences of Britain's relative economic decline, and trying to prevent that relative economic decline becoming absolute. I think that the politics of decline are inevitably what this political generation is going to have to cope with. . . .

I was working at the time for Lord Carrington, who was chairman of the Conservative party, and almost inevitably we became obsessed with the relationship between what was happening internationally economically, what was happening in the coal industry, and the timing of the general election—not an unreasonable thing for the chairmen of parties to think about; and our judgment was that the oil price hike and related developments had so fundamentally changed the economic scene that we would have to seek a mandate in order to require the sort of sacrifices from the public that were going to be essential if we were to cope with the oil price hike. I don't think that was a view that was widely shared—unfortunately, because I think that we could have won an honorable early election in 1973–74 on precisely those terms. . . .

I think that the period of government in the mid-1970s, particularly from 1974 to 1976 [Harold Wilson's second administration], because it didn't adjust as successfully as other countries were managing, and because the electorate were never brought face to face with the results of the oil price hike, was absolutely disastrous for this country. We're still in many senses living with the results today.

David Owen, who was minister of health in Wilson's government, does not really deny this.

OWEN: Inflation was just running amok, and you try running the largest outfit in the whole country [the National Health Service]—I mean, well over a million people—and the area health authorities, as they were then called: we were having to rejig their budgets every month. By 1975 we were up to 27 percent inflation, and it was a massively difficult problem. So oil had a very direct impact to me in 1974–75.

Yet the leaders of other European countries are not all that satisfied with their reaction to the crisis either—Laurent Fabius, for instance, who was to become prime minister of France in 1984.

FABIUS: It was very, very spectacular for us. We had no oil in France —remember that. . . . Suddenly I became aware that if we did not change, if we did not ask an effort from the people, there was a risk for France to become a small country. . . . It was a big shock, because we thought that everything was possible, and suddenly it was no longer true, and we had to revise our conceptions. It has taken time—it was true for the different parties, conservative and progressive—and, in fact, the revision of the conception came only in the eighties. We have been late, and it's only through international politics that we understood that it was necessary to change our method in France.*

Irmgard Adam-Schwaetzer describes 1973–74 in Germany.

ADAM-SCHWAETZER: The shock was not felt enough by the population, because the consequences then taken have not been very, very deep. So: we just couldn't drive our cars on Sundays for four weeks, or six weeks, but we took that with a smile, and we really didn't take any major consequences for our economies. I think this was one of the big mistakes European economies did make, at that time.

*The Socialist government of Pierre Mauroy (1981–84), in which Fabius served successively as budget minister and minister of industry, was obliged to abandon its expansionist economic policy in 1982–83 because of its disastrous effect on France's foreign trade balance.

But Josef Joffe says that the West German population had good reason to be less traumatized than those of other countries by the oil shock in the 1970s.

> JOFFE: In the first place the West Germans did relatively better than almost anybody in the West in weathering at least the first oil crisis, which was in 1973. By 1979, when oil went to $40 a barrel on the spot market, the Germans, along with everybody else, slumped into a worldwide depression—you almost have to call it a depression, from 1980 to 1984—but the first oil crisis was not really a wrenching kind of experience, because all the economic indicators will tell you that the Germans did rather well in coming out of it. . . . Real, serious unemployment did not begin in 1974, but in 1980.

In America, too, the worst effects of the crisis were not felt until the "second oil shock" of 1979. The United States recovered faster from the recession of the mid-1970s than its European partners.[1] But even if "objectively"—that is, in terms of statistically measurable economic performance—the effects were considerably worse in Europe than in North America, the psychological shock was probably about equal, given the boundless expectations and self-confidence in which postwar Americans had been brought up. According to Fred Bergsten, an economist who served in both the Nixon and the Carter administrations, "the 1970s were pretty traumatic for most Americans."

> BERGSTEN: All younger Americans had been used to unparalleled and constant prosperity in the postwar period. Even Americans who had lived in the Depression had gotten used to the new world. Double-digit inflation was a very new phenomenon here. Low growth and high unemployment were new phenomena.

Jack Kemp found that "the wages of the working men and women that I represented in Buffalo . . . were lower in 1980 than they were in 1967, measured in constant dollars after taxes." And George Will feels that the economic analogue to the Vietnam War, in undermining the confidence of the generation that grew up in the prosperity of the fifties, was "the slowdown of industrial growth around the world." Asked to suggest an image that symbolized that process in his mind, Will replied at once.

> WILL: Gasoline lines. You cannot imagine—I mean, every country would dislike gasoline lines, but—what that does to an American. We're a big country, we have low-density cities—people drive great

distances. To have to take your car—which is pretty close to being a sovereign right for the United States citizen to drive wherever he wants, whenever he wants, pretty much in any speed he wants—to take that and have to go queue up for gasoline: it's an absolute affront to the American. You can't imagine what a trauma that was—a consequence of a new feeling of dependency. "Three thousand cousins running Saudi Arabia run up the price of oil, and *we*'ve got to sit in line," Americans said. "Good heavens, this is not America!"

Dependence on imported oil was something Americans became aware of very suddenly and dramatically. But it can be seen as only part of a much more comprehensive process of growing dependence on the outside world and growing awareness of it. Sam Gejdenson describes graphically how this has affected his constituents in Connecticut. He describes the "incredible increase" in the American standard of living from the fifties to the seventies.

GEJDENSON: The Europeans and the Asians seem to be peripheral: if you wanted cheap goods you got them from Japan or Taiwan; if you wanted something with a little character maybe you got European goods occasionally, but basically what happened in this country was a function of what happened in this country, and the others were insignificant in their impact on our lives. . . . I mean, who thought about getting garments made in El Salvador, Yugoslavia, or Mexico, or Taiwan? What we did we made here: these were American goods, American equipment. Heavy equipment was American—whatever you Europeans or Asians did was kind of irrelevant to us. It was a nicety, it was cute to get something from another country—sometimes it was a good bargain, [but] the quality was always suspect.

That started to change, not just with Volkswagens and Toyotas, but with our electronic equipment; and it started to get more than just good value: it started to be *better* value, and it started to be products from all over the world. And we saw our parents lose their jobs. We saw communities wiped out by businesses closing down and moving overseas, and we saw American industry as a dinosaur—unable to move into the international markets, and not capable of reaching out and competing, and then small industry being too small, or uninterested.

BACKGROUND: THE FALL OF BRETTON WOODS

The international monetary system is generally considered a rather obscure and technical subject. It is usually covered only on the economic or business pages of the more serious newspapers. The scant coverage it occasionally gets in TV news bulletins makes little or no impact on the great mass of viewers, because they are unfamiliar with the background and there isn't time for it to be adequately explained. Consequently even well-educated people who take a serious interest in politics or international affairs often don't pay a lot of attention to this aspect of the subject; events in this area have to be of a very spectacular order before they make any real impression on the public at large; and a rising politician can therefore usually get by with a short all-purpose answer, recited parrot-wise—unless or until he becomes finance minister of his country. As Matthias Wissmann puts it, "The change of the world monetary system—the breakdown of Bretton Woods—that really did not touch the day-by-day life."

So it is no good expecting politicians and political pundits to reminisce about sterling or dollar crises that occurred when they were in their twenties in the enthusiastic and voluble way that they do about the Berlin Wall, the Cuba missile crisis, or Vietnam. Yet the difference between the fifties/early sixties and the seventies/early eighties, between the world we grew up in and the world we have had to cope with—whether as politicians and pundits or simply as citizens and parents—is so striking a feature of our lifetime that it cannot be simply shrugged off. It calls for analysis and explanation—and it is becoming less fashionable to explain it purely in terms of the sudden jump in oil prices.

The two "oil shocks" of 1973 and 1979 are still the most spectacular memories, but with the passage of time they are beginning to be seen in historical perspective. It has come to be more widely realized that movements in the oil price have to be looked at in conjunction with movements in the value of the currency in which that price is quoted, namely, the U.S. dollar. Both the great hikes of the 1970s were preceded by a steep fall in the value of the dollar, and the second one, that of 1979, did little more than restore the purchasing power that the producers had lost since 1974. Moreover, in 1988 there is still little sign of the dramatic recovery in the U.S. and other Western economies so widely and confidently predicted in early 1986, when oil prices spectacularly fell back to something close, in real terms, to their pre-1973 level.

Some people have remembered that an atmosphere of anxiety and gloom had characterized much discussion of the world economy for two or three years before 1973; and that the oil price hike did not come as a bolt from a perfectly clear blue sky. The immediate and apparent cause was the decision taken by OPEC to exploit the world shortage created by the Arab production cuts imposed during the October War. But those cuts would not have created such an immediate and acute shortage if the market had not already been extremely tight. World demand had outstripped supply, principally because the United States, in the space of about three years, had suddenly become a major oil importer. American tax policies had kept oil cheaper for American consumers than for those in other countries, with the result that "by the mid-sixties the United States was beginning to increase sharply the proportion of energy use to GNP, thus diverging sharply from a trend common to most advanced economies since the war." By 1974 its energy use per capita was five and one-half times the world average and more than twice that of Britain, France, or Germany.[2] The domestic oil industry, whose rapid expansion in the fifties and sixties had kept world prices low, was unable to keep pace with this galloping demand.

This can be seen as part of a general pattern of what was happening to the American role in the world economy—the very same pattern that Sam Gejdenson and his Connecticut constituents have piece by piece painfully apprehended. What has happened is that the central problem of the world economy as perceived by Keynes and others in the 1940s, the problem that was in a sense "solved" by making it the cornerstone of the new world monetary system at Bretton Woods—namely, the fact that the United States supplied almost everybody else with goods and services but also supplied virtually all its own needs, so that everyone else ended up heavily in its debt—has gradually been reversed. The United States today is still the richest and most powerful, and in absolute terms the most productive, country. But it consumes more of most things than it produces, and that is putting it in other people's debt. This change did not begin to become apparent to ordinary Americans until the 1970s, but it had already been underway long before that. Indeed, it can be argued that it was precisely the efforts of their rulers to conceal the change from ordinary Americans, and cushion them against its effects, that brought about the dislocation not only of the Bretton Woods monetary system but also of the world economy it was supposed to regulate. Alternatively it can be argued that since the American surplus was the premise on which the system was based, its disappearance was bound in any case to bring about fundamental change. But it still has to be asked whether the change needed to take so destructive and disorderly a form, and whether its costs have been at all fairly distributed.

The problem was not initially a problem of trade. America's overseas trade remained in surplus until 1971. The large annual balance-of-payments deficits that the United States was already running throughout the 1950s were occasioned by government expenditure—the Marshall Plan, the defense of Western Europe, and aid to developing countries—and by U.S. corporations investing abroad. Things were happening very much as Keynes would have wished: the great pile of gold and foreign currencies accumulated over the years through the surplus of American exports over imports was being put to work financing the recovery and growth of the rest of the world, and thereby helping to provide an expanding market for yet more American exports. In fact, by 1958 America's overseas "liquid" debts—that is, dollars which had gone abroad and could theoretically be brought back at any time to the U.S. Treasury for conversion into gold or foreign currency—already exceeded her monetary reserves. But until 1958 this overall deficit was caused only by capital outflows. The trade surplus plus "invisible" earnings (which include such items as freight, insurance, and banking fees and the income on overseas investments) remained high enough to cover the government's overseas expenditure. In that year the European Payments Union was dissolved and European currencies became convertible. This meant that American goods would now have free access to the European market. At the same time the Eisenhower administration took action to reduce the deficit by cutting foreign aid, military expenditure, and investment. It was expected that the American trade surplus would increase and the balance-of-payments deficit would be gradually eliminated. In fact, the opposite happened. Much of the aid and investment that Eisenhower had cut was "tied" to purchases of U.S. equipment.[3] The Marshall Plan had worked so well that, in a free market, European industries could hold their own against U.S. competition. Arthur Schlesinger talks about the Plan.

> SCHLESINGER: The Marshall Plan was a means . . . of setting West European democracies on their feet again economically, and it was a brilliant success in that regard. It was not devised as a means of extending American control over Europe. In fact it had quite the opposite effect, and the economic recovery of Europe created more problems for the American economy than it did solutions—competitive problems, I mean.

In 1959 the trade surplus fell abruptly, and the United States for the first time ran a deficit on "current account" as well as on capital flows.[4] This continued in the first half of 1960. It was calculated that, without the "compulsory" purchases of U.S. goods resulting from tied aid—both military and economic—the trade account itself would have been in deficit. As the 1960 presidential election approached, with the probability of a victory for Kennedy, who was pledged both to increase defense spending and to stimulate domestic growth, foreign holders of dollars for the first time doubted whether the United States could or would in practice sustain the gold value of the dollar, at $35 an ounce, which was the theoretical basis of the Bretton Woods system. They began selling dollars and buying Swiss francs or German marks—currencies that already seemed to have a sounder economic base—or gold, the price of which rose to $39 on the London market by the end of October. With the election less than a week away and promising to be extremely close, Kennedy was in the classic dilemma of the opposition leader who is accused of undermining confidence in the national currency. On October 31, 1960, he stated publicly that, if elected, he would defend the dollar at its existing parity. And, after a heated debate among his advisers, he confirmed this in a special message to Congress in February 1961, shortly after his inauguration.[5]

The current account, meanwhile, had returned to surplus and the immediate crisis passed. A "gold pool" was formed by the principal trading countries to keep the London market supplied with enough gold to maintain the official price. But the overall U.S. balance of payments remained in deficit. Kennedy's program of strong world leadership, in both armaments and economic development, would not permit him to make cuts in overseas expenditure; and his program of stimulating economic growth at home would not permit him to raise interest rates. Consequently the outflow of capital continued, which not only posed a threat to the dollar but also left a shortage of capital at home to finance the growth the administration was looking for. In 1963 it reacted by imposing an "interest equalization tax" on capital exports.

Clearly this was not the aspect of the Kennedy experience that marked the future political elite of America and Western Europe—or, for that matter, of Africa or Latin America. But when I asked Tadashi Nakamae, now one of Japan's most successful economic consultants, to name the earliest international event that directly affected his view of the world, and he replied, "The Kennedy shock in 1963," it was not the assassination but the interest equalization tax that he meant. Japan, he recalled, at that time "was heavily depending on American capital to expand, and to develop the Japanese economy . . . but that scenario was broken because of that measure." The experience taught him that whereas "the Japanese tend to think that changes are very moderate and very slow and very steady . . . American policy could change very drastically and very suddenly."

From the American point of view, however, the interest equalization tax had "indifferent success and unintended consequences"[6]—the main one being to give a big boost to the development of the so-called "Eurodollar" market: since the dollar was the main reserve currency in the world monetary system, there were by this time a great many dollars in the world outside the United States—indeed, it was only because foreigners (including foreign governments, but increasingly also foreign banks and corporations) were happy to keep dollars in their reserves rather than seek to exchange them for something else that the United States was, and is, able to run such large balance-of-payments deficits year in year out. In the late fifties and early sixties the lending and borrowing of these overseas dollars was developing into a specialized business, initially in London and then in other centers as well, and the dollar, besides being the yardstick of other currencies' value, had replaced the pound as the main medium of international finance and trade for the private sector. It was to this market that those wishing to invest dollars abroad turned, in order to avoid the interest equalization tax; and the more this market developed the more dollars there were around the world in the hands of the private sector: the more difficult, therefore, it became for central banks to control currency movements, and the more vulnerable the dollar—and other currencies—became to sudden gusts of speculation.

Fred Bergsten was beginning his career in government service at just this time.

> BERGSTEN: I was heavily involved in dealing with the U.S. balance-of-payments problem really from the start of my career in the early to mid-1960s, and so I was immediately with an issue that at least suggested that a little something was wrong with the U.S. economy, in that we were constantly running deficits, at least as defined in those days. There were various raids on our gold stock, our reserves were declining, questions were beginning to be raised about the omnipotence of the dollar and the centrality of the U.S. in the world economy. So from my very first professional experiences I was dealing with an area that was a problem for the United States, beginning to raise questions about our international superiority, and I suppose I developed a degree of humility from early on about what kind of role the United States could and would be playing for the future.

An alert economic analyst might also have seen a danger signal in the fact that productivity was increasing more slowly in the U.S. than in France, Italy, and West Germany, and at less than half the speed of Japan.[7] Larry Pressler says that when he first noticed, during the 1960s, the availability of cars and electronic products from Japan that were both better and cheaper than the American equivalent, he put it down to cheaper Japanese labor.

PRESSLER: [But on closer investigation] I became aware of great inefficiencies that we had in the 1960s, and still have, on our automobile manufacture lines. People get written into their contracts five or six weeks of vacation a year; managements skim off several thousand dollars in pay that they shouldn't; and the whole thing was inefficient. And government was inefficient, too. So it was inevitable that the Japanese would beat us at building cars—somebody would, because you won't go on forever with a situation like that.

However, perhaps none of this would have mattered very much if American domestic inflation had stayed at the low level of the early sixties. Kennedy inherited from Eisenhower's cautious policies an economy with a certain amount of slack in it, and therefore the stimuli he applied to it were not as inflationary in their effects as the foreign dollar-holders had feared: consumer prices rose by only 1 percent in 1961, 1.1 in 1962, and 1.2 in 1963.[8] But after 1964 this began to change, as Jacques Polak was able to observe from his privileged observation post at the IMF in Washington.

POLAK: In a sense Bretton Woods was a deal between the United States and the other countries. The United States would assure a stable core in terms of domestic monetary and financial policies, which permitted the other countries to attach their currencies to the dollar, and they would happily accumulate their reserves in dollars. That bargain really fell apart in the middle sixties—not, I think, primarily because the United States was running a balance-of-payments deficit, but primarily because the United States didn't continue with its totally stable financial, fiscal especially, and monetary policies; and that gave the feeling to the other countries, which, of course, had become much stronger in the meantime, like Germany and Japan, that being fixed on the dollar was not really a safe position for a country to be in.

Edward Bernstein had by then left the IMF to run his own consultancy. He served on two expert economic panels appointed by the Johnson administration between 1964 and 1968.

BERNSTEIN: Up to 1964 we had a very stable economy. It may have been one of the few periods in which unit labor costs in manufacturing actually declined: they were slightly lower in 1964 than in 1958. But after 1964 we had inflation being generated by the Vietnam War, and that's what really killed it. The discipline of Bretton Woods said, you have to keep your prices and costs stable, and if other countries do the same, then the exchange rates won't destroy the price competitiveness. But the United States was unable to halt the inflation. Its prices and costs outran those of Europe and Japan, and the dollar inevitably went down.

POLAK: You can put it on what happened in the mid-sixties in terms of the Johnson policies: both the Vietnam War and the War on Poverty at the same time; the unwillingness to pay for that by fiscal policy; and the unwillingness of monetary policy to become so tight as to make, in spite of those, balance-of-payments equilibrium and general financial stability possible—with the net result that you got a very large outflow of dollars, and many countries became concerned at being flooded with dollars if they maintained a fixed rate to the dollar.

Thus both the veterans of Bretton Woods—the Dutch IMF official and the highly respected adviser to the U.S. government—confirm Chris Patten's view quoted at the end of the last chapter: it was the Vietnam War, or rather the determination of the American body politic to have both the war and the "Great Society" at the same time, and not to pay for either by increased taxation, that brought about the fall of the Bretton Woods system. For the effect of inflation being higher in the United States than in its main competitors was to erode the trade surplus (as American goods became less competitive in world markets and foreign goods became more competitive in the U.S. market), thereby aggravating the balance-of-payments deficit, and so to increase the number of dollars held abroad, while reviving the doubts of those who held them about their long-term value. This, in turn, increased the pressure on the United States's diminishing stock of gold.

BERNSTEIN: In 1957 the United States had the same gold reserves it had at the end of 1950. But beginning in 1957 and running for another twelve years or so, the gold reserves in the United States fell in half, without any change at all in the growth of the money supply. We had gold convertibility of the dollar, but if you aren't going to restrain the growth of the money supply, you've got to run out of gold —and that's what we did.

By the late sixties it was obvious to everyone that the dollar was overvalued in relation to other currencies. But under the Bretton Woods system there was no mechanism for devaluing the dollar in relation to other currencies—it was they that were defined in terms of it rather than the other way round. The dollar itself was defined only by its supposedly immutable gold value, which is why the pressure on it took the form of an upward pressure on the gold price—a pressure deliberately increased by General de Gaulle, who when I started my journalistic career in Paris in 1967–68 was carrying on a kind of guerrilla warfare against the dollar and campaigning for gold to be restored to the center of the world monetary system on the grounds that it had a much more fixed and certain value than a paper currency whose quantity could be increased at will. The Americans, he said, were financing their ill-advised venture in Vietnam by printing more and more increasingly worthless dollars, which the rest of the world was obliged to accept because they were a reserve currency, and which, in the form of "Eurodollars," were destabilizing the whole world economy by careering back and forth like a loose cannon on board ship.

In July 1967 the French government quietly withdrew from the "gold pool": that is, it ordered the Bank of France to stop supplying gold to be sold in London at the official price. In November, just after the long-delayed devaluation of the pound sterling (widely seen as the dollar's outer defense line), this fact was leaked to *Le Monde,* giving further encouragement to the speculators.* In March 1968, after publication of the 1967 U.S. balance of payments and the intensification of the Vietnam War had dealt a further blow to international confidence in the dollar, with gold-buying on a larger scale than ever, the gold pool was abandoned. A "two-tier" market was created: the official price would henceforth be valid only for transactions between central banks (and the main central banks could be relied on not to ask for payment in gold, since this would be seen as an act of political disloyalty and a deliberate sabotage of the system). A "free market" was allowed for all other transactions, on which to everyone's surprise the opening price proved to be only $38 per ounce. The speculators had overreached themselves and

*The scoop was discreetly buried on an inside page, in the last paragraph of what appeared to be a long "color piece" about the gold pool and how it worked. But my colleague Paul Lewis of the *Financial Times* spotted it there, as he was surely meant to.

were in a hurry to collect their profits. The dollar was given a respite.

The Americans argued, with some justice, that they had done the world a great favor by providing, in the form of dollars, the essential "liquidity" for the unprecedented expansion of world trade and production over the previous twenty years, which would not have been possible if the world had had to rely on the limited quantity of gold in circulation. If and when the American balance of payments righted itself and the dollars all went home to pay for American exports, they suggested, the world would face an acute and deflationary "liquidity shortage." A lot of trouble was taken, in the face of vigorous French opposition, to provide for this ever-receding contingency by inventing a new financial instrument in the shape of special drawing rights (SDRs) on the IMF—in effect a new international currency, of which each member country received a quota. Some christened it "paper gold." But it was largely irrelevant to the immediate problem since there was no shortage of dollars in sight. Quite the contrary.

Whereas in 1944, as holders of three-quarters of the world gold stock, the Americans had insisted on its importance as the ultimate base of the new world system, they now argued that gold was really an irrelevance and an anachronism. They tried to frighten the speculators by suggesting that they might decide to "demonetize" gold by withdrawing their undertaking to buy and sell it at $35 an ounce, and that this price was actually much higher than would be justified by the industrial demand for the metal, once it ceased to be regarded as money. Few were convinced, and although I have a vivid memory of Signor Rinaldo Ossola of the Bank of Italy proclaiming *molto con brio,* after agreement had been reached to create the SDR at the Stockholm conference of March 1968, that "it is a great *victory* for the forces of *reason* against the blind forces of gold," I don't think anyone really believed that SDRs could actually replace gold—or for that matter replace the dollar.

Since they could not devalue against other currencies, and since it had become axiomatic that to abandon the official gold price of $35 an ounce would mean the end of civilization, the Americans tried to get other countries with balance-of-payments surpluses to *re*value their currencies against the dollar. But here again they were hoist with their own petard, having firmly ruled out of the Bretton Woods system all of Keynes's suggestions for treating surplus countries as coresponsible for imbalances and subjecting them to pressure to take corrective action equivalent to that imposed on deficit countries. Fred

Bergsten was one of those who came to the conclusion that the system had to be changed.

> BERGSTEN: There was an incredibly high degree of rigidity that had come to dominate the Bretton Woods system of fixed exchange rates. Getting the needed parity changes was extremely difficult. Countries even in obvious surplus or deficit resisted almost to the death changing their parities, and the whole decision-making system that surrounded exchange-rate changes was simply so costly politically as to be almost impossible to carry out in practice. I was convinced then, as I am now, that exchange-rate changes are a central element in the adjustment process, and unless you can have timely, adequate, effective exchange-rate changes you do not have a functioning international financial system. . . .
>
> I began to feel, from the mid- or late 1960s, that it would be desirable, both for the world and for the United States, to move away from the dollar as the lodestar of the system. I thought that world reliance on the dollar placed too much [burden] on the United States, and also created an excessive instability for the world as a whole.

Meanwhile the overheating of the U.S. domestic economy (with rising inflation and acute labor shortages) had finally induced the Johnson administration in 1967 to request a 10 percent income tax surcharge, which Congress eventually passed in June 1968, adding a $6 billion cut in government spending (mostly in "Great Society" programs) for good measure. As this had no immediate effect—with private borrowing and spending still roaring ahead—the Federal Reserve Board also switched at the end of the year to a tight credit policy. Nixon, coming into office in January 1969 as an orthodox conservative, continued these policies, with, at first, a healthy effect on the balance of payments, which in 1969 was actually in surplus for the first time since World War II, as money flowed back across the Atlantic to take advantage of high interest rates. By 1970 he had succeeded in producing a recession—but inflation was higher than ever (5.9 percent): "inflationary expectations, once aroused, proved to have a momentum of their own."[9] Americans were discovering the joys of "stop-go" policies and "stagflation"—hitherto thought of as a peculiarly British privilege. The Republican party paid the price in the 1970 mid-term elections, and business was increasingly unhappy. Nixon reverted to reflationary policies, which quickly put new pressure on the dollar: out went the short-term capital again, and the 1970 balance of payments showed a higher deficit than ever before.

These spectacular fluctuations in the capital account had partially distracted attention from the fact that from 1964 to 1969 the trade surplus had been declining steadily, as America's imports of manufactured goods consistently rose faster than her exports. In 1970 there was a temporary recovery (reflecting the fall in domestic demand due to the recession), but early in 1971 it became known that the trade balance was about to go into deficit, for the first time since the nineteenth century.

Nixon was unwilling to prejudice his chances of reelection in 1972 by a renewed bout of deflation. He and his advisers concluded that the overvalued dollar, and the strain of defending a fictitious gold price, were luxuries America could no longer afford.

On paper the Bretton Woods agreement could have been kept in being even without the special position of the dollar. The agreement, thanks to the careful stage management of Harry White, stated that "the par value of the currency of each member shall be expressed in terms of gold, as a common denominator, or in U.S. dollars of the weight and fineness in effect on July 1, 1944"; it obliged all members to support the parity of other members' currencies in transactions within their territories, but exempted from this obligation any member "whose monetary authorities, for the settlement of international transactions, in fact freely buy and sell gold within the limits prescribed by the Fund." In 1947 the U.S. had officially notified the Fund that it would buy and sell gold at $35 per ounce, thereby exempting itself from the obligation to support the parities of other currencies. In theory it would have been possible for Nixon simply to rescind this notification, thereby abdicating the special role of the dollar in the system and its (by now in any case purely notional) gold convertibility, but retaining the system of fixed parities. All member states would then have been on a theoretically equal footing, defining the parity of their currencies nominally in terms of gold but being obliged to defend this parity only through sales and purchases of other currencies. The dollar could then have been devalued like any other currency, and a new parity fixed in agreement with the IMF. Instead Nixon and his secretary of the Treasury, John Connally, decided to suspend indefinitely the convertibility of the dollar into both gold and foreign currencies, thereby freeing themselves to use the exchange rate as a weapon with which to defend the United States's national commercial interests. This was the decision announced on August 15, 1971, along with a temporary 10 percent surcharge on all imports and, on the domestic front, a ninety-day freeze of all wages, prices, and rents. This amounted to a scrapping of the whole Bretton Woods system and of the liberal internationalism on which the postwar economic order had been based: it was a leap into precisely the dirigiste, nationalistic economic policies that the Americans had found so objectionable in prewar Europe, and most specifically in Nazi Germany.

Not surprisingly, Fred Bergsten, who had left the administration some months before the decision was announced, had mixed feelings when he heard the news.

BERGSTEN: I remember coming home late that night, turning on the television and hearing that President Nixon had announced the policy package he had that day, and immediately thinking that the international monetary system as we knew it, and as I had been writing about it, had now been finished. I had a schizophrenic reaction. On the one hand I had felt for some time that the international monetary system needed to be changed substantially in the direction of more flexibility of exchange rates, and the action taken offered the possibility, though at that time by no means the certainty, of moving in that direction. On the other hand I was very unhappy with the way in which the United States broke up the old system. I had been in government for the first two and a half years of the Nixon administration, and had felt very strongly and had argued within that we should be making extensive efforts to negotiate reform of the monetary system. For a variety of reasons the U.S. did not really push negotiated reform and so, when the time came to break a lot of crockery, it was done in a rather brutal, unilateral way, without having paved the way through an effort to do it more harmoniously, which I would have strongly preferred.

Indeed, the package was hardly calculated to win friends for America elsewhere in the world, being an assertion of American power shorn this time of even the pretense that America was acting in the interests of the world community as a whole. Ironically perhaps, in view of French criticisms of the previous policy, it was in France that the reaction was sharpest and most articulate, and French politicians, unlike those in other European countries, do claim to have a clear memory of what they thought about it at the time. Jacques Toubon, who was close to President Georges Pompidou (being then the head of a charitable foundation set up by the president and his wife, Claude), may be assumed to reflect official thinking.

TOUBON: I thought it was very, very terrible news for the rest of the world, because it was the end of the period of monetary stability, and I feared that it would be a new period of instability and of crisis—and I was not totally wrong.

But Laurent Fabius, the future Socialist prime minister, could not help admiring the lucid self-interest of Nixon's decision.

FABIUS: I have a very precise memory of it because I was interested in economics at the time. I think it's a decision of immense importance, and a very intelligent one from the point of view of the United States. Because, as I understand it, under the system from Bretton Woods to 1971 the United States needed gold to back confidence in the dollar. But at one time . . . it became dangerous, because people were wondering, do they have enough gold? And therefore the new decision was taken . . . and at that time, because the United States had an immense role in the world economy, the dollar replaced gold as being the center of the international monetary system. Therefore it was, from the point of view of Nixon, a brilliant decision: at one time gold as the basis of . . . the strength of the dollar, at a second stage the dollar by itself, and people all throughout the world having to buy dollars if they want to remain prosperous—which is brilliant . . . I thought it was the best example you can have of what a leading country is and what it can do. Obviously, from the point of view of Frenchmen and Europeans it did harm, and I was not in favor of this decision, but it was a fact: therefore we had to adapt, and in terms of *realpolitik* it was brilliant. . . .

It did harm because we had gold, and our gold became, let us say, not worthless, but it has less value than before, and we had to buy dollars if we wanted to survive. Therefore it affected us very strongly.

In America itself, Jack Kemp, who in recent years has come to believe the subject is of considerable importance and has made demands for world monetary reform an important plank in his political platform, admits that he doesn't "remember exactly what my thoughts were when the whole Bretton Woods international monetary system was lifted, or disbanded, in the Nixon administration." But, as a newly elected "Tory Republican" congressman, with "very strong views about free enterprise and tax policy, and economic and social and foreign policy . . . someone who believed in the marketplace," he remembers "that intuitively, while I hadn't thought about it a great deal, intuitively I was opposed to trying to control inflation by putting controls on the wages of the working man and woman, as well as on prices. . . . [And] it was a big shock both culturally and politically to the United States to think for the first time that the dollar was not going to be as good as gold."

EPILOGUE: THE TRAGEDY OF JIMMY CARTER

Sure enough, Nixon's brilliant *coup de théâtre* of August 15, 1971, proved only a short-term solution to America's economic problems, while the new world monetary system (or nonsystem) of floating rates for which it paved the way* was to prove increasingly unstable from 1976 onward. Once reelected, Nixon relaxed his wage and price controls at the beginning of 1973, whereupon inflation shot up to "hitherto unimaginable levels,"[10] reaching 12.3 percent by the first quarter of 1974, when the first "oil shock" was only just beginning to bite. During 1974–75 the U.S. economy experienced a recession much more severe than that of 1970, while prices continued to roar upward (11 percent over the whole of 1974, 9.1 percent in 1975).

Then in 1975–76—helped by the fact that oil prices, after the big leap at the end of 1973, did not keep pace with the general inflation—the Western world began to recover, and in 1977–78—the first two years of the Carter administration—this recovery continued in the United States, while it slowed sharply in Western Europe. But this was achieved at the price of running record trade and current-account deficits and allowing the dollar to fall steadily against the mark, the Swiss franc, and the yen, in spite of a large influx of foreign investment capital into the United States.[11] The "second oil shock" of 1979 reflected, at least in part, a revolt by the oil producers against the steep decline in value of the dollars in which they were paid.† U.S. domestic inflation, which had slowed to 5.8 percent in 1976, was back up to 11.3 in 1979 and 12.6 in 1980—the highest annual rates ever recorded.

In the fall of 1979 the new chairman of the Federal Reserve Board, Paul Volcker, imposed a severe credit squeeze to combat inflation and restore confidence in the dollar, ensuring that 1980 would be a year of renewed recession, rising unemployment, nominal interest rates over 20 percent (which had an acute psychological impact even though much of their real effect was canceled out by the continuing inflation), and falling real incomes for many Americans. It was not a good year to be running for reelection—nor a good year to be remembered by, if it turned out to be your last. In sharp contrast to Richard

*A new set of parities was fixed officially by the Smithsonian Agreement of December 1971, but the United States accepted no responsibility for maintaining them by intervening in either the gold or the foreign currency market. By March 1973 this system had broken down and the era of floating rates began.

†The halting of Iranian production during the revolution in the winter of 1978–79, like the Arab cutback in 1973, exposed the underlying tightness of the market (due in large part to the U.S. recovery and its failure, up to that point, to implement an effective energy program), and so put the producers in a stronger position to restore their eroded purchasing power.

Nixon before him and Ronald Reagan after him, Jimmy Carter had got the political timing of his economic policies exactly wrong.

The result is that his name, perhaps unfairly, is indissolubly linked in the memory of most Americans, and not a few Europeans, to what George Will calls "the dreadful stagflation of the late Carter years."

> WILL: People in the United States began having a decline in real standards of living. A lot of people began losing ground, and there's nothing more central to the American experience than the expectation that tomorrow is going to be better than today: has to be, it's the law of nature. Jimmy Carter repealed the law of nature—no mean achievement! . . . The one thing you can never do to the American nation is what Jimmy Carter did in 1979: the famous "malaise" speech when he said, "We're all sick and tired, and we're kind of bad, and we ought to try and get better." Americans said, "We don't want to hear that, we want to feel good."

Chris Patten, who visited the United States in 1980, was struck by the contrast with the "enormous bustling confidence" he had met on his previous visit fifteen years earlier.

> PATTEN: The worries about international productivity comparisons, the worries that the American economy was going downhill, the worries that the American political system no longer gave America the leadership that she needed—the worry that even if America discovered more political leaders of really substantial caliber the existing political system would make it impossible for them to govern. I can remember one senator saying, "If only we had your parliamentary system"—I mean, an absurd proposition! Lloyd Cutler, who'd been one of Jimmy Carter's advisers, I can recall being asked to suggest ways in which the presidency could be strengthened in order to give America the clout she needed in the world. (We'd gone through, or were going through, the Iranian hostage crisis.) So from a period of great excessive exuberant overconfidence America had got into a position of excessive gloom and insularity.

If the first oil shock and the worldwide slowdown of economic growth in the early to mid-seventies were the economic analogue of Vietnam, the hostage crisis that dominated Carter's last, miserable year in office was clearly the political analogue of the second oil shock and the acute stagflation that then infected the U.S. economy. George

Will remembers it as the climax of a decade of humiliation. Larry Pressler, a remarkably fair-minded Republican, sums up the seventies as "a bad time overall," but thinks fortune played a part.

PRESSLER: I think it was a period of bad luck, in part—like Jimmy Carter getting caught with the hostages over there. Now I know that we say—some say—Carter was a weak president, and that; but I think Ronald Reagan's had some good luck, and what good luck, on the day of being inaugurated, to be able to welcome back the hostages!

Not surprisingly, Reagan supporters are generally critical of Carter's foreign policy, though with some interesting divergences of interpretation: George Will sees it as essentially a continuation of the détente policy inaugurated by the Republicans under Nixon, Kissinger, and Ford, while Newt Gingrich and Elliott Abrams see it growing out of the antiwar psychology associated with George McGovern, Nixon's Democratic opponent in 1972.

European views of Carter tend to break down fairly predictably on left-right lines. The Gaullist Jacques Toubon is even harsher than Chris Patten.

TOUBON: I feel very bad about Carter's presidency, really. . . . It was a period of American weakness, and I think that American weakness is not good for any people in Europe . . . America is for me the freedom guard, and that's why I say, when America is weak, I think it's not good for free people . . .

The Christian Democrat Matthias Wissmann is more sympathetic to Carter's human rights policy, but comes to a similar conclusion.

WISSMANN: At the very beginning, in 1976 when he started his presidential campaign and 1977 when he started to be president, I was quite impressed: human rights as an issue honestly taken was my impression; a leader who has not been afflicted with all the Watergate things; a new period. Later on I was very disappointed, because he has not been really a leader. He didn't know one day what he would do the next day, for example on the Soviet Union. And so I have no very simple judgment on his presidency. I think, for example, in Latin America he did something good with his human rights policy. Some changes from military dictatorship to democracy—like in Ecuador, like later on in Argentina and Brazil, would not have happened without Carter's human rights policy. But I think that is the only real long-term-oriented success of his presidency. For our relation to the Soviet Union, for a consequent policy toward Europe, it was not that much of a success.

For Wissmann's party colleague, Volker Rühe, Carter was damned above all by his inexperience and inconsistency.

RÜHE: We tend to be critical of people that are turned out by that political system in the United States with no international experience. So what is fascinating on the one side is that an outsider, somebody from the provinces, can become a president—I mean, without having been in the Bundestag like here, or in cabinets as a minister. But on the other side I think—especially as somebody from Germany with all its international problems, and the importance [of the role] the United States plays in this field—we are always looking for presidents who have as much international experience as possible. So I think this was something that was felt from the very beginning with regard to Carter, and not just by Helmut Schmidt, who also expressed this, but that was a pretty general feeling. . . .

What upset us was these changes in the arms control policy. At the beginning he tried to do everything the other way in the SALT process: maybe two or three years were lost, and then it was done again, almost the same way as the negotiations had happened before. And of course what struck people here was what Carter said when the Soviets invaded Afghanistan—I mean, that this was a surprise and shock to him: so that he gave the image of somebody who had misunderstood the Soviets.

Similar feelings were expressed by Irmgard Adam-Schwaetzer of the Free Democratic party, who dated her doubts about American leadership of the Western alliance from that period.

ADAM-SCHWAETZER: There was one thing we liked, and that was his moral position, but we felt right from the beginning that he would not be able to follow it straight through, so he would become a weak president—and indeed it happened like that. So it didn't make very much impact: it just showed that a politician should not go about things like that. . . . The real discussion on the leadership or partnership certainly began at that time in the Alliance.

Undoubtedly the most robust defenses of Carter, oddly enough, were provided by the British opposition leaders—David Owen, who dealt with the Carter administration as foreign secretary in the Labour government under Jim Callaghan, and the present Labour leader, Neil Kinnock.

OWEN: You had a U.S. secretary of state and a U.S. president—Carter and Cyrus Vance—who wanted to work with the United Nations; and we were prepared to use the United Nations, and that meant mobilizing a sufficient number of votes for us to carry the day—carrying Africa with us, carrying various other continents with us; and it was quite an exciting period actually in terms of international diplomacy—the lead being taken by the United States, and they were active. It came unstuck really with the Iranian revolution, and that's eventually what toppled Carter from office. But I believe that style of American leadership which Carter introduced was actually right. The trouble was that he got himself too bogged down in detail, and didn't carry conviction with his own people.

KINNOCK: I was in the States on the day that President Carter was elected. . . . I spent two or three days in the campaign, and when it all started it was such a refreshment, there was such a cleanliness about the whole thing that you could actually taste it. And the unfortunate thing I think is that the whole of world events, as well as big chunks of the American establishment, conspired—initially accidentally, but then deliberately—against Jimmy Carter, so that by the third year of his administration I think he was on his knees, and after that it was downhill. Which was sad, because I think we actually need that sort of outgoing attitude and that sort of self-confidence about America—that isn't chest-beating but is deep enough to be certain, so that people are not overreacting all the time—to be a major characteristic of American relationships with the remainder of the world. . . . You see, I think that what Carter was doing, like a lot of the other American politicians over the last century and a quarter that I admire, was to treat the American people as being mature. "We don't have to make these arguments again"—I think that's the view that was being taken: "We don't have to bang the drum in order to prove that we exist. We are so big, we are so rich, we are so democratic, we're so free—let's take it for granted, not in any complacent sense but in the sense that we don't have to keep on proving it: right, let's move on to the next set of obligations."

Perhaps that *was* Carter's message. If so, the tragedy is that he got it across to Neil Kinnock much better than he did to his fellow Americans. It must be so, or surely at least the representatives of his own party would have spoken up for him. But none of the three Democratic legislators we interviewed did so. Pat Schroeder paid tribute to the man Carter appointed to represent the United States at the UN—"I think Andy Young did very well in the UN; I think we need more sensitive people like Andy Young in the UN rather than people who are using it as a forum to rabble-rouse and feel good because they can go in and blow up once a day at everybody." But even then the name of the last Democratic president of the United States did not pass her lips.

CHAPTER 7

The View from Japan

Japan today has the second-biggest economy in the world. It has the biggest trade surplus, and the biggest credit balance. At present rates of exchange the average Japanese citizen will soon be earning more than the average American. Clearly Japan is a major participant in the world economic system—and, potentially at least, in the world political system, though the extent and nature of its political role remain for the moment rather ill defined, as we shall see. A survey of "tomorrow's world leaders" that did not include Japan would certainly be inadequate.

Yet Japan presents special problems in a survey of this kind. While its industrial and commercial success is founded in part on an extraordinary openness to ideas from the outside world, Japan has also succeeded, perhaps to a greater degree than any other modern society (China being the most plausible exception), in preserving its social and cultural specificity—in other words, what makes it different, and also difficult for foreigners to penetrate. In formal terms, Japan has adopted a "Western" economic and political structure—free enterprise capitalism and parliamentary democracy. But it does not seem to have adopted in any profound way the thing that most reflective Westerners see as central to their culture, the central premise on which both capitalism and "pluralist" democracy are based, namely the cult of the individual. The Western notions that a person is best fulfilling himself or herself when competing successfully with other individuals, and that conflict and contention, canalized within limits but publicly displayed, are creative and valuable to society as a whole, seem to have remained largely alien to Japanese culture. A much higher value is placed on the cohesion and harmony of the group—the family, the nation, the firm—and the individual is expected to contribute to the collective success of the group while respecting its structure and his or her place within it. Conflict within the group is regarded as embarrassing rather than healthy, and usually resolved by compromise. Its public display is, whenever possible, avoided. (The minimal role played by lawyers and law courts in Japan, as compared with most Western countries, has often been noted.)

The above observations are anything but original. In fact they amount to tiresomely familiar *idées reçues.* The very last thing I would claim to be is any kind of expert on Japan—having only visited it for the first time in the course of preparing this book—and I have no doubt that someone who really knows it could easily produce examples showing that all these Western commonplaces are absurdly oversimplified if not plain wrong. No society as rich and diverse and dynamic as Japan obviously is could really be reducible to such generalizations. In particular, there is clearly an important part of Japanese society that is interacting with the outside world in all sorts of ways and being affected by it, culturally as well as materially, and one of the things hardest for a foreign visitor to gauge is how far those people, who inevitably will be his main direct interlocutors, are (a) representative of Japanese society as it is, and (b) indicative of the direction in which, or speed at which, it is changing. In fact, that is one of the main things I asked them about—but, as we shall see, their answers were neither unanimous nor clear-cut.

In any case the immediate problem was that the Japanese equivalents of Neil Kinnock, Laurent Fabius, Volker Rühe, or Joe Biden were not at all easy to identify. The same party has been in power for the whole of Japan's postwar history, and its most prominent leaders are all in their sixties or seventies. There is no prospect of its losing power in any foreseeable future, so it would be difficult to present opposition leaders (who in any case are equally venerable) as the likely national leaders of tomorrow. Younger members of the ruling party, I was told, would be reluctant to thrust themselves forward, or to say anything that might be interpreted as critical of their elders.

In the event two of them—Koichi Kato, minister of state for defense at the time of my visit (and being groomed like Lord Lundy, in the view of resident foreign correspondents in Tokyo, "to be,/The next prime minister but three . . ."), and Kaoru Yosano, a member of parliament closely associated with the then prime minister, Yasuhiro Nakasone—did agree to be interviewed, and showed themselves on the whole less reticent than I had feared. But there was also a doubt whether politicians were the right people to be interviewing in Japan, given the fact that so much of Japan's participation in the international system goes through the private sector. We therefore decided also to interview a number of obviously up-and-coming Japanese businessmen, whose experience had given them significant knowledge of the workings of the world economy and Japan's place in it. Being very sophisticated people, they understood the requirements of the Western media and agreed to lay aside, for the purposes of the interview, the restraints on self-expression that men* of their age and position in the various hierarchies to which they belonged would instinctively have respected had they been speaking for a Japanese audience. And we did find, in Yoshihisa Komori, then senior political correspondent of Mainichi newspapers, an internationally minded "pundit" well able to hold his own with George Will, Pierre Lellouche, Christine Ockrent, and Josef Joffe.

Having thus rounded up a Japanese squad of "Roosevelt's children," I soon discovered that the postwar world they grew up in was significantly different from the one we in the West, or for that matter in the Third World, have experienced. Japanese people of my age do not share my memories of a childhood and adolescence colored by confidence and optimism about rising living standards and a progressively better organized, more equitable world order; nor was their political horizon dominated by the East-West division and the Cold War.

There are, as one would expect, points in common with the experience of their contemporaries in West Germany, a state that has followed the same trajectory from devastation and total defeat to astonishing economic success and political rehabilitation. But there are also very striking differences, by no means all of them attributable to the decision taken by Truman after Potsdam "that I would not allow the Russians any part in the control of Japan." My Japanese contemporaries, I found, grew up with a very strong sense of a terrible collective *misfortune* that had befallen their country. They were aware that the nation, or its leaders, had brought this disaster on itself by adopting and cultivating a militarist, expansionist form of nationalism and that this error must not be repeated. Kaoru Yosano, for instance, speaks of what he believes is the universal feeling of all generations in Japan that "they have the 'original sin' of waging war forty-five years ago"; and Tadashi Nakamae, the economic consultant, recalls that "since we entered into the primary school we have learned not to have weapons, or not to have military prowess."

But the phrase "original sin" was, I think, used metaphorically. I

*We were, alas, unable to identify any women who could plausibly be presented as leaders of tomorrow's Japan.

did not find any preoccupation with the issue of moral responsibility for the disaster, or with what Japan had done to others as opposed to what it had brought upon itself, or any disposition to see those issues as sharply divisive in Japanese society, whether between generations or otherwise. I caught no echo of that great questioning of its elders about the past by this generation, when it came of age in the sixties, which was obviously a major feature, if not a turning point, in the postwar history of West Germany. It has been written[1] that the assumption by General Tojo,* at the Tokyo International Tribunal, "of full responsibility for the war, thereby absolving both the Emperor and the people of Japan from guilt, raised him—with national relief—to a position of a national hero and man of loyalty." Perhaps that partly explains why the defeat of 1945, catastrophic as it was, seems in the last resort to mark a less absolute break in the continuity of Japanese history, and to have been less disruptive of the cohesion of Japanese society, than it was in the case of Germany.[1]

One has to remember, also, that Japan found itself participating, after as before World War II, in a world order constructed and dominated by Europeans and people of European origin, in which it felt (and was considered) a newcomer if not an outsider. Germany, even though defeated, occupied, and divided, clearly belonged to what remained the dominant culture. She was still at the center of things, even if for a time more passive than active. That perhaps explains why young Germans growing up in the fifties and early sixties seem to have shared the general confidence and optimism that reigned in the West at that time to a greater extent than their Japanese contemporaries, and to have been a little less affected by the feeling of vulnerability and fragility from which the Japanese suffered.

In any case the Japanese experience as it emerged from the interviews seemed sufficiently different to be better treated in a chapter of its own. Inevitably, it starts from the war. Several of our Japanese interviewees, like Norbert Gansel in Germany, were just old enough to have fragmentary memories of the war itself; and, like Gansel, Hajime Shinohara—now deputy general manager of the planning division in the Bank of Tokyo—remembers the night bombing as "a beautiful scene . . . with the beautiful big flame beyond the scenery." Yoshi Komori has "a memory of being rushed to one of the nearby air shelters by my mother—that was a standard practice at the sound of the siren: even at night I was rudely awakened by my mother—and

*Japanese prime minister, war minister, and chief of general staff, 1941–44; executed as a war criminal, 1948.

then being herded to that shelter, which was more like a cave in my neighborhood, even though it was almost in the heart of Tokyo."

Yutaka Ohtaka, managing director of Showa Shell, remembers being moved out of Tokyo at the age of six or seven to "a very local place" to escape the bombing.

> OHTAKA: There was nothing to eat, you know. It was a really poor and difficult situation. And when the war finished and I came back to Tokyo it was extremely difficult for me to go upstairs, even—[I was] so much exhausted. And when we came back the old houses—you know, my parents' houses—were burned down, and the first thing we had to do was to make the shelter, and to find very basic things like food.

Komori has a very precise memory of the war ending.

> KOMORI: I was four when Japan surrendered at the end of World War II, and I was just old enough to realize—though not in any coherent way—what was going on around me; and I have a distinct memory of seeing my father sitting in front of the radio listening to the emperor's surrender speech. It was the fifteenth of August 1945—a sunny, hot day, at noon; and I knew that almost everything around us was just shattering, and not by any internal force but by the outside forces of what we used to call fiendish, demonlike Americans, who were just destroying everything around us. . . . I think it dawned on me, in a very childish, primitive way, that whatever we might do or whatever sense of values or order we may build in Japan, that would still be subject to destruction by external forces. I hope I'm not exaggerating, but I think that's—put in a more coherent way—I think that's the perception I had at the time.

Again the Japanese experience resembles the German in that even those too young to remember the war itself have vivid memories of the acute poverty that followed it: times when such things as chocolate, chewing gum, or bananas were a rare and desperately longed-for treat. Komori believes this memory of "the days when Japan was very, very poor" may have reinforced the feeling "that Japan is still a very vulnerable country and the Japanese economy is a 'fragile blossom,' as Zbigniew Brzezinski called it—that it was susceptible to sudden change, that it could collapse suddenly." And, like their German contemporaries, the Japanese have as a result grown up with what Koichi Kato calls a "small-country mentality," which would certainly have surprised their grandparents, and which, as he says, makes it difficult for them now to adjust to the idea of Japan being a rich country with a certain responsibility in the world, and a partner of the United States (an opposite but analogous problem to the difficulty the British had in adjusting to no longer being an equal partner). However, Kato believes that this mentality is more difficult to overcome for the older generation, which was directly traumatized by the defeat, than for his own, which has grown up since; and Yosano told us that the "younger generations," including his own, "well know that we are not a very small country, we are a medium-size country which has to assume more international responsibility vis-à-vis the Free World." Yet even a businessman as young and successful as Kazuhiko Nishi, founder and owner of the ASCII software empire, still thinks of Japan as a "small island country in a small archipelago in the far east of the Asian continent," which cannot aspire to be a world power but must live by its wits and "be clever enough to be friends with almost everybody in the Western countries."

Many of those interviewed echoed Norbert Gansel (again) in stressing the difference between the immediate postwar generation and the younger one that, in Nishi's words, "does not remember being thirsty, does not remember the lack of food, or does not understand the miserable situation of the defeat of the war." They tended to see themselves as an intermediate generation—readier for change, more internationally minded than their elders but less so than their juniors.

YOSANO: I'm already forty-seven, and in my heart I still have aftereffects of the last war . . . although I don't remember [it]. But the next generation of Japanese people are free from all the influences, or all the effects of the last war. Their mind is free to think anything; they are free from all the obsessions of the last war, of the past Japan. So I think they are ready to assume all the responsibilities, all what Japan has to do in the world. And although I belong to the "young" generation of our party, I think the *next* generation has a very flexible mind and they have more adaptability to the changing world and the changing situation in which Japan is placed.

Among the characteristics of this new generation are, apparently, a greater propensity to take holidays, as well as greater opportunities to travel abroad.

YOSANO: When I joined a private company in 1968 I had twenty days' paid holidays, which I theoretically could use freely, but . . . no one was using those paid holidays, so I did not take even one . . . for my pleasure. But nowadays the new generations have a feeling that twenty days' paid holidays is their right, which is to be used.

KATO: Visiting a foreign country was a very special opportunity for privileged persons in the older days. But nowadays the younger generation spend their holidays in London, or, of course, in New York. So they are ready to buy foreign things, to respond to a foreign stimulus.

That was the politicians' view. But both Yoshi Komori, the journalist, and Masao Katsurauma, manager of the controller's department in Toray Industries, felt it was their generation that had most appreciated the chance of contact with the outside world, and that their juniors were liable to be more blasé about it.

KOMORI: If you compare my generation, people in their forties, with the generation of those who are in their fifties and sixties, you can say for sure that we are more willing to see Japan play a major role, or more of a role, in world politics or the world economy. But I'm not sure that the younger generation—people in their thirties or people in their twenties—are even more willing than we are in that respect, because, in a way, we feel that my generation has been at the forefront of the kind of Japanese who really started exposing themselves to the international community, or outside world.

KATSURAUMA: Our generation was quite willing to go abroad to work. In my case I have experienced working in Bangkok for four years. At that time I was quite willing to go abroad, no matter whether to advanced countries or developing countries. But my subordinates, generally speaking, are rather reluctant to go abroad, because they are quite satisfied with their life in Japan.

A possible reason for this reluctance was given by Nishi, who, though himself a frequent and enthusiastic traveler to the United States, said he had personally experienced racial discrimination there. He had, for instance, been shown to the worst table in an empty restaurant (even though "wearing a really nice shirt and suit"), or placed in economy class on airplanes when holding a first-class ticket —"that type of prejudice: it's sort of taboo to discuss in public, but I would say there is such existing."

Indeed, almost any kind of criticism of the United States seems to be covered, if not by a taboo, then certainly by a strong inhibition. Those wartime feelings of hatred for the "fiendish, demonlike Americans" have been well and truly sublimated, or transformed into admiration for a power that, as the Japanese have learned from positive as well as negative experience, it is much better to have as a friend than as an enemy. The official attitude was beautifully expressed by Koichi Kato in an anecdote of his first encounter with his country's conquerors.

KATO: When I was six years old I was staying at a small village because I had been evacuated from home, because of the bombing in the city. And to that small village American occupation forces—military forces—drove over, and we met American soldiers. They were very tall. They spoke a different language, which I couldn't understand; the language I spoke *they* couldn't understand—that was a kind of culture shock to a small boy living in a small village.

My father was the mayor of that village; so the lieutenant colonel of the occupation military forces came over to my father's place, and my father took me to show the foreigners. And this lieutenant colonel and the other soldiers were all smiling, gentle, kind to a very small boy like me: that was a shock—and they gave us a very good impression about American people, and the lieutenant colonel gave us bottles of Coca-Cola: that was a strange taste. And the most shocking fact for us was, the lieutenant colonel allowed me to bring home the empty bottle of the Coca-Cola. You know, at that time bottles or glasses—this kind of item—were so precious after the defeat of the war. And I felt the affluence of American society.

Besides that, when we tried to drop the bottle from the second floor of the house, the bottle did not break. That was so shocking: it impressed me about the thickness of the glass of the bottle—that means the quality of American products.

As a result, he says, America for him became associated with "affluent society, richness, quality, generosity, and different language," hence "different culture"—impressions that have stayed with him, even though "now the cars we produce are sometimes much better than American cars, and we have lots of good glass bottles."

Yoshi Komori, who, being a journalist, not a minister, can speak his mind without causing a diplomatic incident, and also from living in America and frequenting Americans in Vietnam has acquired a rather un-Japanese candor, has a slightly different memory of his own childhood view of the occupying forces.

KOMORI: Almost everyone coming from my generation had experience of having seen American occupation authorities, symbolized by

GIs just walking around the major streets of Tokyo, and that planted in us, in a very subtle way, two kinds of perceptions with regard to how to cope with international events—with whatever happens in the outside world. One is a sense of helplessness, because whatever our government leaders might do that would still be vetoed by the occupation forces—and I could cite many examples. I mean, that's for the public record: Japan was an occupied country.

And also the second kind of perception that came to us as a result of being exposed to the occupation era was that to be nationalistic, or to try to be truly independent, whatever you might interpret that word to mean, you have to be critical of the United States. So anti-Americanism and a sense of national independence would go hand in hand. And very few Japanese would probably publicly admit it, but I think that's the seed that was planted very, very deeply in the minds of Japanese people in our generation. . . .

My own personal encounter with my first American happened to be with an American of Japanese ancestry—a noncommissioned officer, probably—who happened to be living in my neighborhood, and he and his family used to park a huge car only a few blocks from where I lived. And somehow, maybe just for the heck of it, I and my peers would do something to the car—eventually flattening one of the tires, or just taking some air—a little bit—out of it. And then finally this American noncommissioned officer found out who was doing it; and then he came over to my house—that was really a dreadful experience—and he threatened us (which I deserved) that he might report it to the police, and eventually he might report it back to the occupation authorities: that was the ultimate threat to me.

So my image of America or Americans in my childhood was really negative: I would call it may be something beyond our reach, and that would make you very resentful or critical at the beginning, though in a very primitive way.

Everyone, it seems, had a sense of Japan's smallness and poverty compared with America's size and wealth.

KATSURAUMA: [I remember being] told by one of my relatives that 70 percent of the total wealth of the world belongs to the United States. So my first impression about the world is how big is the United States, and I never thought that anytime in the future Japan could be compared with that country.

A major experience, therefore, for every Japanese of this generation has been the discovery that Japan is, after all, a great economic power. As Hitoshi Seki of the Japan Productivity Center puts it: "It's a weird feeling that when we were kids Japan was nothing to mention —probably fiftieth in the world, something like that—and suddenly we find the nation being ranked second in the Free World, and it's a real weird feeling, among all the countries our country being the one that achieved the highest and most rapid growth."

Different events or experiences brought this fact home to different people. Some mentioned the first Western "economic" summit (held at Rambouillet in 1975), when they were astonished to find that Japan was considered important enough to take part. Others, more specialized in finance, went back to 1968 when Japan's foreign currency reserves broke through their $2 billion ceiling—reaching $3 billion in February 1969 and $4.5 billion by 1970, so that the yen had to be revalued (it seems quaint now, but was "a great big swing for our economy" then) from 362 to 357 to the dollar, and for the first time since the war shortage of foreign exchange was no longer a constraint on Japan's economic policies. Another important discovery (not precisely dated) was that the label "Made in Japan," which in childhood "used to mean a shoddy product," had come to be seen in the outside world as "almost equivalent to quality." For Yoshi Komori the moment of truth had come in 1970, when he spent two months in America as a roving correspondent.

> KOMORI: Simply on the West Coast . . . the number of Japanese cars I saw was much, much more numerous than I had seen in 1963–64. And then some really peculiar awakening dawned on me, that Japan might not be as poor as we had always been led to believe.

Or again there was the realization that Tokyo's skyscrapers were as big as New York's and that there was virtually nothing one could bring home from Europe or the United States—not even green asparagus—that was not already easily obtainable in Japan. Yutaka Ohtaka of Showa Shell dated the breakthrough from around 1964, when the "bullet" train came into service, the road network was developed, and Japan successfully hosted the Olympic Games.

But since it is the comparison with the United States that most interests the Japanese, discoveries of American weakness have been no less important than those of Japanese strength. It is above all the inconsistency of American policy, the suddenness of its chops and changes, that Japanese find unsettling—perhaps even more so than Europeans. Nakamae's "Kennedy shock" (the interest equalization tax of 1963) has already been mentioned, as have Komori's feelings about the American withdrawal from Vietnam. In between those came two if not three "Nixon shocks": the rapprochement with Communist China (of which the Japanese government had not been warned), the removal of the dollar from the gold exchange standard, and—according to Komori—an embargo on the export of soybeans, which are a key ingredient of the Japanese diet.

Koichi Kato, who was a career diplomat and a China specialist before becoming a politician, tactfully emphasizes that the Sino-American rapprochement was also a spectacular volte-face by the Chinese, and at least as embarrassing to the Japanese Socialist opposition as it was to the Japanese government. After it, he recalls, the Chinese stopped criticizing the U.S.-Japanese security treaty, and insisted on dropping what had been a routine sentence on this subject from the joint statements published when Japanese Socialist parliamentarians visited China. (Kato also said that for him both the Cultural Revolution, which he observed from the Japanese consulate general in Hong Kong, and the Sino-Soviet border conflict had been important formative experiences. These events had cured him of utopian illusions about socialism that, he said, were prevalent among Japanese students when he was at university, and had taught him that "the national interest went over the ideology." It struck me that this experience was more or less parallel to my own—and that of many other Europeans —over Czechoslovakia.)

But it was, apparently, the Nixon dollar shock that made the biggest impact on the Japanese—a much more direct and immediate one than it did on most Europeans.

> KATO: That was also a shock, because we were allowed to rebuild our economy and develop it under the very soft protection of the fixed rate; so the floating system put us [like] a very protected child into the very cold water—that change in the currency system gave us the cold reality of the world economy.

The other politician, Kaoru Yosano, actually named this as the event that first made him aware of Japan's new standing in the world, because he felt that Nixon had abandoned the United States position as "the sole leader in the world economy."

Among the businessmen, Tadashi Nakamae said that after Vietnam and the Nixon dollar package he felt that "everything could change, and very drastically, so we have to prepare for the very sudden and very sharp change." Hajime Shinohara, who had been recalled from his honeymoon on August 16, 1971, to help his bank sort out the consequences of Nixon's announcement, not unnaturally remembered it as "the first occasion for us to be shocked by the power of the United States market declining," having previously always advised his clients to price their exports in U.S. dollars, as *the* stable currency. And Yutaka Ohtaka of Showa Shell named this as "the biggest event" of his lifetime since the end of the war.

> OHTAKA: Since then the whole structure of the world economy has changed. . . . I would think that maybe eighty or ninety percent of my time is now spent thinking or coping with problems which arise from changing the exchange rate, and the changing exchange rate is as a result of the floating system, which is caused by this decision by the United States in 1971.

Nakamae described the last fifteen or twenty years as "a history of the repetition of shocks, for Japanese." No doubt the one that stands out most clearly in the minds of ordinary Japanese, perhaps even more than ordinary Europeans, is the oil shock of 1973, to which Japan, the world's biggest oil importer, was peculiarly vulnerable.

> KATO: Japan is a resources-poor country, but we had worked very hard to have good, rich lives. We had worked for years: in the late sixties we began to have enough food to eat, and decent clothes to wear, and good transportation systems, and even cars. At that time the older generation, and even ourselves, thought, "Well, finally we came to this living standard, but is this true? Isn't this a kind of fluke? Because in terms of resources, in terms of the land we have, we're quite a vulnerable country for maintaining this richness." This kind of uncertainty about Japanese richness was very strong in our deep mind. Then came the oil shock: we thought, "This is it. This is the end of our little dream."

> KOMORI: I saw the effect of the war in the Middle East in the supermarkets in Tokyo. I think that was the first recognition for most Japanese that international events do have significant and almost direct impact on our daily lives. . . . The toilet paper disappeared! People started talking about the shortage of oil, and any products that would use oil or petroleum or related products were just running out, so we believed; and people started rushing to the supermarket. . . . Many people started buying up even toilet paper: the "toilet shock" or "toilet paper panic," as the newspapers called it.

But the extraordinary thing was, as Komori says, that "Japan was just about the only major industrialized country that muddled through without great failure." Although Japan did suffer from high inflation in the seventies (higher than the United States and much higher than West Germany, but not as high as France, let alone Britain or Italy), and though it did not retrieve its phenomenally high growth rate of the sixties (an annual average of 10.5 percent from 1960 to 1973), it did get back to 6.5 percent by 1976, and was able to sustain rates of 5 percent or over through the remainder of the decade. It was done partly, as Kato says, "by rationalizing the use of energy"; partly by taking a sudden bold leap into "Keynesian" economics, running enormous budget deficits and running up government debt until (from practically zero in 1970) by 1980 it was a higher proportion of GNP than in any other advanced country—a "very tragic result," according to Yosano, "we won't be able to solve it for another century"; but most of all perhaps, as Hitoshi Seki says, thanks to the "unique flexibility of the Japanese economy" and the willing cooperation of the Japanese workers in "raising the productivity of Japanese corporations." Komori felt that most Japanese consider this remarkable recovery "the result of luck rather than a result of any calculated strategy," and remain attached to "the perception that Japan is a vulnerable country, susceptible to outside changes," but most others said that it had strengthened the confidence of the Japanese in their economic future—as one might well think it should. For Hajime Shinohara, the banker, the consecration came in 1978.

> SHINOHARA: When the Japanese yen went up to 175 and when President Carter took major steps to protect the United States dollar—that was, as far as I know, the first occasion for the United States to take measures to adjust the domestic monetary and economic policy for the sake of the exchange rate. . . . That is one of the most important things, I should suppose, as far as Japan and the United States's relations are concerned, that not only Japan but also the United States committed [themselves] to adjust their own domestic monetary policy targeting to keep a reasonable exchange rate . . . and in other words that this might be the first occasion for Japan to recognize herself that now we are the equal partner with the United States in the implementation of their own economic policy and political policy as well.

Whether the Americans saw it quite like that is very doubtful. Certainly they did not keep their side of the bargain. But that a Japanese banker should think of his country as having the right to help decide American domestic policy was a kind of revolution in itself. Japan had come a long, long way.

PART III

Where Are We Going?

CHAPTER 8

All Quiet on the Eastern Front?

Forty years have passed. "FDR's children" have reached, or are fast approaching, middle age. Their careers as professional football or basketball players, if they had them, are over. They are entering that time of life when a politician, if he is to achieve something for his supporters, or get his name in the history books—and most politicians aim to do both—needs to start getting his hands on real power. In the years to come some if not all of these men and women will be among the world's key decision-makers. Having described, in part I, the world order they grew up under, and having traced, in part II, what they regard as the formative experiences of their lifetime, in this final part of the book I shall look at what they see as the world agenda for their generation.

In chapter 1 we saw that the main shadow cast over the otherwise rather sunny adolescence of politically minded young people in the West in the 1950s was the shadow of Soviet power and the danger of East-West conflict; and that the containment of Soviet power had come, by the late 1940s, to be seen as the most urgent item on the international agenda by leaders on both sides of the Atlantic. Although the North Atlantic Treaty is not directed against any named adversary—simply committing its signatories to consider an attack against any of them in Europe or North America, from whatever quarter, as an attack against them all—there was and is no doubt in anyone's mind that the threat that NATO is there to repel is a threat from the Soviet bloc.

Well, NATO is still there. American forces—some 325,000 of them—are still stationed in Western Europe, nearly forty years after the treaty was signed, although no one at that time seems to have expected or intended that they would be there for so long. Membership in the Atlantic Alliance, the Western power bloc centered on the

United States, remains clearly the primary geopolitical relationship in which Western Europe is involved. And, as Newt Gingrich says, the Alliance has been very successful in its primary aim of maintaining "a peaceful, free Western Europe." We may not like what goes on on the other side of the frontier, or the methods used by the Russians to keep the frontier closed. But at least on our side of it we have gone unmolested.

When you are unmolested for forty years, it gradually becomes less easy to believe that anyone really wants to molest you. What seemed such an urgent task in the late 1940s has come to seem a rather humdrum, tedious, routine affair, as well as exceedingly expensive. Not surprisingly the question has been asked on both sides of the Atlantic, is it really necessary? Some people have remembered, or have found out, that until the outbreak of the Korean War in June 1950 the main policy-makers, in Washington and in London, were skeptical about the notion of an actual Soviet military offensive in Europe. They saw the danger as primarily political. But today, in any purely political struggle in Western Europe, the presence of American forces and missiles seems more likely to be useful to pro-Soviet or neutralist political parties than to their opponents—and the likelihood of pro-Soviet parties winning any such struggle seems in any case rather low. The French Communist party has gone into what seems a terminal decline, which its three years as junior partner in the Socialist government (1981–84) did nothing whatever to arrest. The Italian Communists have—genuinely, in the view of most observers—distanced themselves from Moscow and pledged their support for NATO; and, even so, the other Italian political parties have proved much more able and more willing to keep them out of government than seemed likely ten years ago. And meanwhile historical research has cast grave doubt on the notion that the Korean War was part of any Soviet master plan to take over the world by force. Stalin himself, it seems, was taken by surprise by the North Korean attack on the South. Could it be that we are defending ourselves with all these expensive and terribly destructive weapons, and with all these masses of armed men, against a threat that never really existed in the first place? As Newt Gingrich says, this is something about which Western Europeans need to make up their minds.

GINGRICH: I mean, is the Soviet Union a threat or not? If it's not a threat, and you're comfortable with us not being there, why are we staying? We're not coming to dinner, we're there to protect you. If you don't need to be protected we should leave. If on the other hand you think you need to be protected, then we by God better have a partnership and be serious about it.

Clearly an assessment of the nature and intentions of the Soviet Union, and a program for dealing with it appropriately, must be items at the head of the foreign policy agenda for tomorrow's leaders, both in Europe and in the United States.

AN EVIL EMPIRE . . .

Undoubtedly the most memorable characterization of the Soviet Union in recent times is President Reagan's "evil empire." While this choice of language has been widely criticized in the West as unduly provocative, or inappropriate for the head of one state to use about another, especially when the fate of the world depends on some sort of working relationship between the two, it is striking that very few people other than active, card-carrying Communists have really taken issue with the substance of it. Certainly no mainstream politician in the West, left or right, American or European, seems to have anything positively good to say about the Soviet system. Not only does Newt Gingrich affirm, as one would expect, that it is indeed "an evil empire . . . by any human standard." Not only has Larry Pressler, a much milder and more conciliatory Republican, "come to believe that the Soviet Union's operations are evil, will resort to evil very quickly in terms of killing people or in terms of accomplishing their goals or whatever they want." Even some of the most scathing European critics of Reagan's policies make it quite clear that they regard the Western political system as infinitely preferable to the Soviet. The widespread American belief that Western Europeans in general have an unduly and dangerously benign view of the Soviet Union* was hardly borne out by our sample. Here, for instance, is Chris Patten on a trip to the Soviet Union in 1981.

PATTEN: Two or three things most struck me about the Soviet Union. The first was the extent to which nothing had changed very much: the xenophobia, the extraordinary bureaucracy that one reads

*Gingrich kindly attributed this to the fact that Europeans "for two decades now have been fed balderdash" by their American allies. "Prior to Reagan, there was no American willing to stand up and say things like 'The Russian dictatorship will probably lie to you if they have a nuclear power plant go bad. . . . We bring you tourists, they bring you radiation. Now whom do you want as an ally?' " Europeans, it seems, are assumed to be too dumb to work this kind of thing out for themselves, if the American leadership omits to point it out to them!

about in Tolstoy, was still present. Secondly, one had the awful feeling of people's personality and integrity being downtrodden, not just for decades but for centuries. I remember the sense of slight insult at one's guides traveling in a couple of hours early in the morning just to get apple juice for breakfast by taking one down to breakfast in the hotel. I can remember feeling rather shocked that the boutiques around our international hotel were only available for people with dollars or sterling or credit cards, and not available for Russians. I can remember, too, breaking out of the Museum of State Industries in Yerevan in Armenia—not the most fascinating museum I've ever been to—and seeing great street markets full of privately produced produce, with at either end the state butcher's with long queues for rather scraggy bits of meat. It did remind me of the virtues of market economics.

Chris Patten, as readers of this book may have noticed, is not the kind of Conservative who automatically springs to the defense of unregulated market economics in any and every context.

Even Neil Kinnock, the Labour leader, is quite clear on which side of this fence he belongs. He has, he says, "always thought that whoever I talked to from the Soviet Union, it was essential for them to understand that we regarded the barbed wire and machine-gun towers and the Wall [in Berlin] as physical evidence of the weakness of the system"; and he recounts with some relish how he replies to Soviet criticism of our society's deficiencies.

KINNOCK: Whether it's unemployment, or violence on the streets of New York, or the actions that have had to be taken in respect of Northern Ireland . . . I had to say to a very senior representative of the Soviet administration last year, when he brought up those arguments, "Well, look, I tell you, you give me a system in which everybody's got an identity card, everybody has been fingerprinted, we can get as many police on as many street corners as we want, and we can lock off those areas that are potential sources of trouble with barbed wire, and I will give you a serene society of complete peace. It won't be much fun but it'll be peaceful!" And the argument got more furious until we had to part on fighting terms.

And Pierre Lellouche—certainly no uncritical pro-American, as we shall see—stresses that the Soviet system scores no better for equality than it does for freedom.

LELLOUCHE: I went to the Soviet Union once—I cannot go anymore because they don't like what I write. I discovered what the system was:

I talked to people who refuse the system and people who were in the system. I discovered the most unequal system in the world. Those who are in the *nomenklatura* live in fantastic apartments, have French perfume, French dresses, Japanese TV and hi-tech and so on at home, and the others have nothing. . . . It's the most incredibly unequal system.

So the end result of that is, it's turned me unfortunately perhaps too much into a cynic: there is no longer an ideal cause for which I would die—except my freedom, and the way of life we have here, and they are very precious. And if one day I get into power I will gladly offer a trip to Berlin and Moscow to any young people who so desire, to go look for themselves.

. . . BUT IS IT EXPANSIONIST?

So the argument, in fact, seems not to be about the reality of the Soviet system as it operates internally but about (a) how far the internal unpleasantness of the Soviet system implies, or is accompanied by, a threat to those of us who for the moment have the good fortune to be beyond its reach; and (b) what, if anything, one can or should be doing to try and change it, given that no one seems to think that going to war with the Soviet Union is a good idea.

On the first point, Newt Gingrich feels that the case is proven by the experience of détente.

GINGRICH: The radical left of the government—Carter-Mondale—basically said, "If only we talk with the Russians, they'll be nice." Well, they invaded Afghanistan, they shot down the Korean airliner, they are supporting terrible dictatorships in places like Ethiopia and Cambodia. . . . And the problem the left has in Europe, and the left has in America is, every couple of years the Soviet empire will do something so horrible that it knocks down all of the lunatic left arguments how "if only we're nice, they'll be nice" and it reminds us that they're really tough, nasty, mean people.

For Richard Perle, there is a clear parallel with Germany in the 1930s.

PERLE: I would like us to be remembered as having understood the mistakes of the generations that preceded us, and above all the single most catastrophic mistake in this century, which is the failure to recognize that the totalitarian regime of the Nazis represented a threat, even at great distances, to all of those who saw too late the need to respond to it. And I hope that we will, having learned that lesson, succeed in sustaining the argument that we must not again permit a totalitarian power—at the moment it's the Soviet Union—to achieve such a dominating strength as to be able to impose its will and its values, values with which we profoundly disagree, on the rest of us.

From the other end of the American political spectrum, Sam Gejdenson draws the same parallel, at least implicitly—comparing those who refused to boycott the 1980 Olympics or join in other sanctions over the Soviet invasion of Afghanistan with those who insisted on "business as usual" with Germany, or tried to thwart Roosevelt's efforts to get weapons to the British, during the period before Pearl Harbor.

GEJDENSON: I mean, here was the Soviet Union invading Afghanistan, and Europe kind of went along, business as usual. . . . To me that was the Soviet Union invading, maybe not a white country—and maybe that's why there wasn't that kind of outrage—but there should have been more of a memory. The Soviet Union should have paid a much higher price for that, and it didn't.

In Newt Gingrich's view, the Soviet Union is bound to seek to expand, because the very existence of the Free World constitutes a threat to it.

GINGRICH: I think the main threat for the foreseeable future is the Soviet empire. I mean, it is an empire, it is essentially a political aristocracy of three or four million people who use the secret police to live fairly well on the backs of 250 million other Soviet citizens, and who could survive only through power. By definition all of us are a threat to the Soviet empire, because we're free, and as long as we're free, people keep leaving the Soviet empire. The Berlin Wall wasn't enough. And I think in that sense we need to understand that as long as we're free the Soviet empire has a deep vested interest in our defeat, because we're a permanent, living proof that it's an inhuman and a destructive system—because we prove you can live without a secret police.

Perle, however, sees the Soviet expansionist drive as more geopolitical than ideological.

PERLE: The Soviets take rather a long view, and they regard themselves as the dominant force on the Eurasian land mass, at the extreme western end of which is a cluster of countries that we call Western Europe; and I think they'd rather like to clean that out, in the sense of dominating the whole of the Eurasian land mass. . . . And as long as we recognize that the Soviet ambition is, in fact, to dominate the whole of the Eurasian land mass, and make the necessary defense effort so that that can't be accomplished by force of Soviet arms, then I don't see any reason why we can't go on protecting the democratic West for the indefinite future.

As for the view current in the late 1940s that the Soviet threat was primarily political or ideological, rather than military, Perle holds that the exact opposite is now the case.

PERLE: I think it's a very considerable threat in one dimension only, and that is in its possession of military power; and the Soviet Union is not a very effective competitor in any other sense. If anything, it's a less effective competitor ideologically today than it was fifteen or twenty years ago, when you could still find people who believed in the egalitarianism that Marxism purports to advance. But it's bankrupt now ideologically. I think that has been true from the beginning, but better understood in the aftermath of Solzhenitsyn and a generation of disappointed intellectuals—with the Stephen Spenders and George Orwells of an earlier period and the more recent writings of some French philosophers. The treatment of dissidents in the Soviet Union, I think, has contributed significantly to that—men like Solzhenitsyn and Sakharov and others—and now there are very few people left who believe that the Soviet model is worthy of emulation.*

Perle is—or was, in May 1986—remarkably dismissive even of Soviet culture, repeating the old joke about "the definition of a Soviet string quartet: it's a Soviet symphony after a visit to the West." He clearly had no inkling of the extraordinary flowering of Soviet literature, drama, and cinema that was even then beginning to be revealed, as *glasnost* gathered pace.

PERLE: There's nothing left but military power. . . . The only thing that keeps the Soviet Union in the game of international competition is its military capability. It's got nothing else to offer the world.

*Sergei Plekhanov is convinced, however, that this is going to change as a result of the Gorbachev reforms: "In peaceful competition in ten or twenty years I think we will be able to provide a very attractive example of a system which provides the best potential for development of individuals."

From this flows a prescription for Western policy.

PERLE: I think as long as we maintain a balance of military power, the Soviets, who are conservative by nature, not terribly adventurous, will show restraint in the use of that military power. But where they think they potentially dominate a military situation, where there's a vacuum that they alone are in a position to fill, then I think we have to expect that they will act aggressively. Afghanistan strikes me as a good example: they calculated correctly that the Western response to the invasion of Afghanistan would be feeble, and it was, and so they didn't hesitate to cross an international border with their own military forces, and make war against essentially unarmed Afghan people—and this despite the fact that they already had in place an Afghan leadership that was well disposed toward the Soviet Union. We've seen the same thing recently in South Yemen, where the Soviets were actively involved in overthrowing a Marxist government in order to replace it with a still more ardent Marxist government.

So they're prepared, where they believe it is safe to do so, to use military force, to dispatch their surrogates, whether they be Cuban or East German or others, to engage in subversion and the application of military power. And the best way to prevent that, and to prevent the further encroachment of Soviet influence, is by maintaining sufficient strength, and will, and resolve, to confront them rather than yield to their military advances.

Needless to say, this view of the world is firmly rejected, if not stood on its head, by Perle's opposite number in Moscow. According to Viktor Mironenko, the first secretary of the Young Communist League, those who think the military power of the Soviet Union much greater than its economic success "definitely underestimate the economic potential of the Soviet Union."

MIRONENKO: We have had certain difficulties, even serious difficulties, in the development of economics, and some remain even now. But at least the last year or eighteen months since April 1985* clearly show that we are capable of solving our economic problems, and to underestimate the economic possibilities of the Soviet Union is simply silly. The Soviet Union has demonstrated its ability to overcome economic difficulties and to achieve foremost positions in production and scientific and technical progress many times.

*Since the beginning of Gorbachev's reform program. The interviews in Moscow were recorded in December 1986.

As for the military power of the Soviet Union, the Soviet Union has never aspired to any supremacy in military strength. . . . The thing is, we have to have a look at the history of our country. In 1917, people themselves have chosen their fate.* The revolution was completely peaceful, there was practically no armed resistance—there was no serious resistance inside the country. In 1918, the beginning of the civil war, foreign intervention. By 1920 we had just finished one war, and had barely ten to fifteen years to pull up the economy somehow, and in 1941 we were forced to enter another war. We lost twenty million people—the best of the [first] generation which grew up under socialism. We lost practically the whole European part of the country. Industry was ruined, agriculture as well. And what happened after the war? Winston Churchill's speech at Fulton,† well known to you—the Cold War. Then nuclear arms: it was necessary to destroy the monopoly the U.S.A. had in nuclear arms. Then intercontinental ballistic missiles—and I could enumerate further. In my opinion there isn't a single person in the Soviet Union who is not convinced that each time we had to answer, against our wish, attempts on the part of others to attain military supremacy.

Yet it is not only Americans who see the Soviet Union as expansionist. On my side of the Atlantic, Jacques Toubon, though he doesn't see any immediate threat to the peace in Europe, does think that the Soviet system is aggressive.

TOUBON: And I think that from Trotsky's "permanent revolution" to Gorbachev it's not very different in the spirit, of extending the Marxist revolution all over the world. . . .

The Marxist regime has no longer any appeal for people even in Third World countries. . . . I think that in the Soviet Union power is concentrated in the hands of politicians and head officers of the army or navy—which are the same people—and I think this concentration of power has a kind of aggressive internal motion.

The system is becoming "less dynamic," in Toubon's view.

TOUBON: I think that the Soviet Union is now a kind of enormous bureaucracy, and I think that the people who are now governing the Soviet Union are a kind of *fonctionnaires*—more than Khrushchev or

*In fact, the Bolsheviks seized power by force in November 1917. The elected Constituent Assembly, in which their Social Revolutionary rivals had won a majority, was dissolved as soon as it assembled in January 1918.

†The "Iron Curtain" speech, March 1946.

Stalin, who were the builders of the Soviet Union or were the fighters of the socialist movement.

But this, he thinks, makes it more rather than less dangerous, since the bureaucracy has "a sort of internal movement," and is "very, very difficult to stop."

In Britain, the Social Democratic leader David Owen speaks of the Soviet Union's power.

OWEN: . . . and the ruthless way in which they will protect their ideological purity within what they consider to be their own sphere of influence. We saw that in Poland. There was an illusion which some people wanted to maintain in the West, and in Europe, that Solidarity was something which was crushed by the Polish forces. It's nonsense. Solidarity was suppressed by Soviet power. They masterminded every single part of the suppression of Solidarity, and to this day are still the dominant influence in Poland, and we should not forget it—and there is a tendency to forget it.

Afghanistan was a slightly different issue. I had visited Afghanistan when I was a student, in 1959. I spent quite some weeks living up in the mountains with a group of tribesmen. So I kept a pretty close eye on Afghanistan—and indeed we were stopped from driving in our Land Rover from Herat to Mazar-i-Sharif in the north because of Soviet troop maneuvers: that was back in 1959. So the Soviet Union has actually been pretty strong in Afghanistan for well over thirty years, and what they were worried about was being booted out of Afghanistan in humiliating circumstances as part of the consequence of the Islamic revolution [in Iran]. So I think that their movement into Afghanistan was more defensive than offensive. But once there, of course, they have achieved a very considerable strategic position, an important strategic position. But having sort of clambered up most of those mountains and ridden across those hills I've never had much doubt that the Afghan tribesmen would do to them what they had very successfully done on a number of occasions to the British. I mean, after all, they were the one people who consistently defeated the British at the height of our empire, and I always thought that the Soviets would get a bloody nose, as indeed they are getting.*

Even the West German Social Democrat Karsten Voigt, whose prescriptive views on dealing with the Soviet Union are different, and

*Recorded in October 1986.

who since the early seventies has cultivated direct contacts with Soviet officials probably to a much greater extent than any of those quoted so far, talks about what he learned from these contacts.

> VOIGT: One of the preconditions of détente is that you can negotiate on an equal basis. And they would only take you seriously if you have something in the background, in power terms. . . . I learned from them what might not have been the intention of their side, how important their view of the United States was—at that time they were fixated on the United States—and how important military power was for them. I never took the United States [to be] so important as the Soviets [did]. I never took military power as so important as the Soviets—but I learned a little bit about it from their side! . . .
>
> This doesn't mean that they want war. This doesn't mean that they have the intention to attack. I differ from that. But this means that they take military power as part of their history, as part of their ideology, as part of their identity. They take it more seriously than postwar Germany.

Josef Joffe also thinks that Germans, at least of his generation, no longer take the Soviet threat seriously.

> JOFFE: I would think that this generation—I'm not speaking for myself now, I'm trying to portray this generation—is fundamentally different from its parent generation in the view it takes of the Soviets. Of course, the Soviets did change. I mean, Gorbachev is not like Stalin, and the Berlin blockade happened a long, long time ago. So did the Berlin Wall. So did the Berlin ultimatum. And the Cuban missile crisis. So whereas the immediate postwar generation world view was surely shaped by the experience of the Soviet invasion, of partition, the threat against Berlin and so forth, this generation has taken the stability which we have enjoyed since the Cuban missile crisis for granted, and therefore refuses to see the Soviets as the kind of looming threat that motivated their parents' generation. There's almost, I would say, a readiness to impute more benign intentions to the Russians than to the Americans.

From my own observation I should say that similar views are not at all uncommon in Britain, especially among the grass roots of the Labour and Liberal parties. In fact Neil Kinnock's reluctance to come down on one side or the other, even now, over the Cuba missile crisis can surely be seen as a symptom of "moral equivalence" astigmatism, which can easily affect one's view of international affairs even if one is quite lucid about the relative merits of the two social and political systems.

The French, by contrast, appear quite exemplary in their robust anti-Sovietism. Pierre Lellouche explains why.

> LELLOUCHE: Well, ironically, because we used to have a very strong Communist party, which embodied, if you like, the Soviet model at home. We could see every day, in reading *L'Humanité** and hearing Georges Marchais, and before him Thorez—we could see who it was looming at us. They are exactly a mini–Soviet Union within French democracy, and for a long time we've had a fight.
>
> After the war the Communist party in France had a lot of prestige because of its role in the Resistance. So it had a lot of intellectual influence . . . and there was a phase in the fifties when intellectual France was rather pro-Soviet—the Soviets still had the aura of being a model of freedom, and so on, and the U.S. was seen as a neoimperialist, neocolonialist power. That began to shift in the late sixties, essentially because of Czechoslovakia—and that was a fantastic event, including in my personal life, as the Soviet tanks entered Prague. Then you have Solzhenitsyn and all of the Gulag and so on, and then Afghanistan. And the historical fight between Jean-Paul Sartre on the one hand and Raymond Aron, who for years had been talking about the nature of the Soviet Union but nobody was listening, was finally won in the seventies by Raymond Aron, which explains why the non-Communist left, such as the Socialist party, became "Aronien," and also pro-American and anti-Soviet—very, very anti-Soviet—when Mitterrand arrived in power, and why increasingly, as the influence of the Communist party declined, the aura of the Soviet Union declined as well.

Christine Ockrent gives the same paradoxical reason for the lack of such a strong anti-Soviet consensus in Germany and Britain as there is in France: "Because you have no Communist party!" It is suggested that there has been a kind of crossover, with the countries of southern or Latin Europe, which have or used to have important local Communist parties, becoming more or less unanimously anti-Soviet, while those of northern Europe, which had such a consensus in the immediate postwar period, have now forgotten why they had it and are prone to the temptation of "moral equivalence"—the view that Europe is the helpless victim of a struggle between two equally amoral superpowers, neither of which is intrinsically more frightening than the

*Daily newspaper published by the French Communist party.

other. There is no doubt something in this, but I think weight should also be given to Joffe's point.

> JOFFE: The French did their anti-Americanism bit in the sixties under de Gaulle, and they worked round that, and they have suddenly rediscovered anti-Sovietism. I think it also helps if you are less dependent on the Americans than the Germans are: the French have their own nuclear weapons. They can in the end have the feeling of being the masters of their own security fate, in a very fundamental way.

AND CAN IT CHANGE?

Now for the second question: what is to be done? Newt Gingrich has a program of sorts for the evil empire.

> GINGRICH: I think in the long run you have to be for decolonization, because you have to allow people to have power over themselves now. Decolonize the Ukraine, and Byelorussia and Central Asia, and all sorts of places: we only have one last nineteenth-century empire left, and I think we should decolonize it at some point, or encourage it to decolonize voluntarily as the British empire did.

Jack Kemp, not content with mere encouragement, says, "I really believe their colonial empire can be shrunk: we don't want just to contain, we can destabilize their colonial empire," while George Will thinks that "if we keep our nerve and keep the pressure on, and allow the natural resentments and rivalries and nationalisms that are so strong in Eastern Europe to continue to grow—Hungary, Poland, and all the rest—the Soviet empire, which is an irrational artifice, is doomed in the long run." But, he concedes, "it's a matter of a very long haul."

Not surprisingly, these views tend to be combined with skepticism about any hopes placed in the new generation of the Soviet elite, which is rising to positions of importance under Mikhail Gorbachev, as an agent of change from within.

> WILL: I think they have everything in common with all the other generations of Soviet elites. I think it's a marvelous reproducing machine in the Soviet Union. The socialization process, insular and narrowing, brutalizing, ignorant, that churns up that final leadership pool from which the top leaders are drawn, just reproduces *itself.*

Christine Ockrent agrees.

OCKRENT: I don't think one can really say that because Mr. Gorbachev is younger he is less of a Soviet Communist. I think it is ridiculous and shallow and dangerous. . . . As much as I know there is still a Wall in Berlin and the Soviets are still in Afghanistan and they are still in Angola, together with East Germans and Bulgarians and Cubans, and they are still very present in Ethiopia and in other parts of the world. Then there is really no saying that Mr. Gorbachev has abandoned any of the traditional goals of the Soviet system, and in his own logic, why should he?

Even Richard Perle, who does think that "hopefully in time we will see a change in Soviet objectives—a recognition that it has gone as far as it will be permitted to go in exercising influence over the remainder of the European continent—and then the basis may exist for a more normal relationship," says it would be premature to suppose this change is already happening.

PERLE: Those sentiments have arisen every time there's been a change of Soviet leadership: it wasn't so very long ago when the head of the KGB, Mr. Andropov, became the general secretary of the Communist party of the Soviet Union, and the next thing we knew we were being told that here was a man who drank scotch, liked jazz, read Western novels, appreciated modern art, and was a kind of secret dissident. . . . You've got to hand it to the Soviet propaganda machine for having persuaded the Western world that the number-one policeman in all the world, the head of the KGB, which runs a massive complex of repressive institutions, including the Gulag, was in fact a kind of closet liberal! So I think the proof of the future Soviet policy has to lie in the evidence that there's a change. I mean, there's a tremendous momentum in that system, and I don't see the change thus far. Gorbachev, who's intelligent and tough, has exhorted his people to drink less and work more—and that doesn't sound like much of a reform package to me.

The above remarks were recorded in the summer of 1986. Richard Burt, speaking in October, gave a similar assessment, but with slightly more positive nuances.

BURT: I have friends and some professional contacts—Soviet diplomats I've dealt with. Some of the younger ones have been very pleased by Gorbachev's ascension. They believe that this will breed a new life into the Soviet system, but so far I'm not very impressed by what Mr. Gorbachev has done. In fact, I haven't really seen any real effort to reform the system, and, of course, it's the system that's the problem in the Soviet Union. Gorbachev has said that he doesn't want people to drink alcohol, he wants to stamp out corruption, he wants people to be more efficient. He's brought new people into positions of authority—but that's kind of the traditional Soviet approach to enhancing the system. He hasn't undertaken the kind of structural reforms in the Soviet Union that are really necessary to change Soviet society. There isn't a process of decentralization of decision. There isn't a process of reforming Soviet agriculture and giving people larger private plots and introducing incentives. I suspect that those decisions will not come, if they come at all, until the 1990s. When Mr. Gorbachev realizes that just trying to enhance efficiency on the margin is not working, then he will face the decision of whether he's really prepared to undertake major structural reforms in the society, or instead rely on the traditional props of Stalinism—and how he will decide it's much too soon to say.

A VISIT TO MOSCOW

In fact, by the time I was able to get to Moscow in mid-December 1986 it was becoming clear that Gorbachev had reached the point of decision much sooner than Burt had anticipated. It so happened that my interviews with the three Soviet figures offered to me as representatives of the postwar generation—Viktor Mironenko, head of the Young Communist League, and the two senior officials of the U.S.A.-Canada Institute, Kokoshin and Plekhanov—were all conducted on Friday, December 19, 1986. The previous night, riots in Alma Ata, capital of Kazakhstan, had been openly reported (though no film was shown) on Moscow television, which suggested they had been "incited by nationalist elements"—something hitherto unimaginable in the official Soviet media. That morning, which would have been Leonid Brezhnev's eightieth birthday, *Pravda* carried an outspoken attack on the disastrous corruption, inertia, and inefficiency that had marked his years in power. And that same day I happened to be at the Soviet foreign ministry when the announcement was made, in a press conference ostensibly held to explain why the Soviet Union was ending its moratorium on nuclear tests, that Academician Andrei Sakharov had been released from internal exile and would be allowed to resume his scientific work in Moscow. (It later transpired that a telephone had been specially installed in his apartment in Gorky so that he could receive the news of his release in a personal call from General Secretary Gorbachev.)

I was as yet unaware of any of these developments when I interviewed Andrei Kokoshin early that morning. But I was impressed by the strong language he used to explain the thinking behind the Gorbachev reforms, and the uninhibited enthusiasm with which he espoused them.

> KOKOSHIN: I think that we're really entering a very important new phase in our development, and if I look at this situation from a historical perspective, I should tell you that we achieved a very important historical goal in the Soviet Union: we got the rough overall military strategic balance with the United States, and we are now quite confident that we can maintain it. Now, we paid a very high price for it, of course—economically, politically—but we are very proud of this achievement, and maybe we have the greatest security for the Soviet Union, and for all nations of the Soviet Union, and for our allies, that ever they had in their long and very difficult history. . . . But now we have domestic issues first of all on our agenda—you know: more efficient economy; more active and I would say more long-term-oriented social policy; higher level of education, of cultural development, and so on; democratization of our society—because for many decades we lived like in a fortress, trying first of all to save the basic achievements of the great October Revolution. Now we really need to change this mechanism—which helped us to survive, but in many respects it's not good for the further development; and there is objective need for substantial reform—revolutionary reform, you know—and we are working very hard at it. . . .
>
> You know, we are discussing, for example, the problems of the youth. In our country we have a problem of bureaucratization. The youth movement is not isolated from the issue as well, and we have problems of bureaucratization of the Young Communist League, for example—too much paperwork and not enough work with the young people on the street; too much, I would say, regulation from the center, not enough support of the initiative from the bottom—and many other issues.

I was able to gain some firsthand experience of the problems of "bureaucratization" in the Soviet Union in general, and the Young Communist League (Komsomol) in particular. As we were recording these interviews for television, our requests for them had to be channeled through the state radio and television organization, Gosteleradio, which—although we named a number of Soviet officials and journalists we wished to interview—clearly decided at an early stage in the proceedings that since we wanted spokesmen of the next generation of Soviet leaders, the Komsomol was the appropriate official body that must be approached. The trouble was that for months on end they were unable to get an answer from the Komsomol bureaucracy. Thus although our producer had what seemed very promising exploratory talks with Gosteleradio in Moscow in April, and we initially hoped to be able to go and film there in June, it was not until October that we were told that Viktor Mironenko (who had been installed by Gorbachev as the new head of the Komsomol, presumably charged with shaking up the bureaucracy, in July) was willing in principle to grant us an interview, and not until mid-December (when we had threatened that any further delay would mean the complete exclusion of the Soviet point of view from the series) that we were finally given the go-ahead to come.

Even then we were very nearly refused visas on a technicality on the day before we were due to leave, and even after we arrived in Moscow a definite time had not been fixed for our interview with Mironenko, and our hosts at Gosteleradio were clearly extremely nervous lest he should prove to be unavailable at the last minute.

It was impressed on us that Mironenko was certainly a man with a future, since he had reached the dizzy height of first secretary of the Central Committee of the Communist Youth League of the USSR (to give him his full title), as well as membership in the Presidium of the Supreme Soviet and candidate-membership in the Central Committee of the CPSU, at the unusually early age of thirty-three. When we eventually met him, in his palatial office at the Komsomol headquarters, he seemed less a typical youth leader than the Soviet equivalent of a "young fogy"—a chain-smoker with thinning hair, prematurely aged by the responsibilities of office. Speaking through an interpreter —the only one of our interviewees to do so—he uttered a series of almost clergymanlike expressions of goodwill toward mankind in general and the American people in particular, coupled with anxiety about the dangers to world peace arising from U.S. government policy; and backed up his argument with quotations from Ernest Hemingway and (more surprisingly) G. K. Chesterton—for both of which authors he professed a long-standing admiration. He admitted to finding the debureaucratization of the Komsomol an Augean task, and also seemed worried by the news from Kazakhstan—the riots being both in themselves a setback for Gorbachev's policies (they were a protest against his replacement of a corrupt but indigenous local party leader with an ethnic Russian) and also potentially useful to his opponents as evidence of the kind of disorder to which the new policy of *glasnost* (openness) would lead.

"The time of solutions by force," Mironenko said, "has gone for good, no matter how much some may miss it and pine after it." This was a lesson he had learned from the Helsinki conference, but it applied equally, he said, to domestic policy.

> MIRONENKO: The thing is that perhaps the very fundamental idea of domestic policy at present is to rely more completely on the initiative of people themselves, to deepen the democratization of society. The idea is to give greater possibilities to man to use his own abilities—physical, spiritual, mental, intellectual, and any other. For me, as leader of an organization of youth, such policy is appealing, and youth has taken it up as if it had been expecting it for a long time. That is quite clear in the country now. And there is another idea I would like to stress: this policy is characterized by a sincere dialogue with the people. I am sure you know that this has not always been so in our country. At times it was too tempting, in the interest of educating people, or some political interest, not to mention one thing, to slightly prettify another. Those times are gone as well, and it is a good thing.

But are they really gone, I wonder? Is not the phrase "slightly prettify" an example of the very phenomenon it purports to describe? And as for not mentioning things, while the mentioning of the Alma Ata riots on television was clearly an important advance, the release of Sakharov—and of many other dissidents in February 1987—went unmentioned in the Soviet media, although announced (prematurely in at least one case, that of Yosef Begun) to the foreign press. At the time, however, I merely asked Mironenko whether he felt that, with Gorbachev's arrival in power, the Soviet Union was entering a new era.

> MIRONENKO: I would not put it that way. The thing is that the arrival of Mikhail Sergeevich Gorbachev at the leadership of the party has meant very serious changes in the political life, in the domestic and foreign policy, of our country. Marxists have their own understanding of the role of personality in history, based on a seminal work by one of the classic figures of Marxism, Valentin Grigorievich Plekhanov, which mentions the role of personality in history. The role of personality in history is very great, but the personality usually appears when it

is objectively needed, or required. And there was this need in our society. That is how I would put it.

That, indeed, is how he did put it. Clearly one feature of Soviet society still to be reformed is the style of official discourse. What the French call the "wooden tongue" *(langue de bois)* is still clacking. Clearly, too, the personality cult is a well-entrenched aspect of Soviet political culture. It reminds me of a letter published a few years ago in the *Financial Times* from the press attaché of the Iraqi embassy, who, while protesting vigorously about the use of the phrase "personality cult" in reference to the Iraqi president, went on to explain that, just as France had its Napoleon, England its Cromwell, and America its George Washington, so Iraq had its Saddam Husain, to whom Iraqis felt a natural devotion.

Still, my overall impression of Moscow was a good deal less unfavorable than I had expected. Of course, in a three-day visit, shepherded much of the time by a Gosteleradio representative, I could not claim to have met a representative cross-section of Soviet people, let alone any oppressed minority. But I was struck by the absence of that *universal* gloom and dourness that earlier visitors had described. Most of the people I did meet were cheerful, friendly, and polite. None looked at all undernourished. None seemed nervous about being seen or heard talking to a foreigner—as I have found people in, for instance, Iraq or South Yemen.

I must be careful not to exaggerate. No one in my hearing criticized Gorbachev—though there was perhaps a hint of sarcasm in the waiter's tone when refusing our request for wine with lunch: "Two o'clock, Gorbachev time." All those with whom I could have any extended conversation, including those formally interviewed, were in some sense representatives of the establishment, and strongly committed to supporting the Gorbachev reforms. What was striking was the explicitness and confidence with which they expressed themselves. They not only claimed to feel secure and confident about the Soviet Union's place in the world order: they actually sounded as if they were.

None of them alluded directly to the astonishing reversal of styles that had occurred between the leaderships of the two superpowers—with vigor and decisiveness suddenly beaming out from the Kremlin, while the White House, with the outbreak of the Irangate scandal in November, had even more suddenly begun to appear elderly, fumbling, and uncertain—but the psychological effect was clearly there. A speaker like Kokoshin could now sound more credible, including probably to himself, when asserting with pride that his country had achieved "a rough overall military strategic balance with the United States." Plekhanov could even sound as if he meant it when proclaiming his confidence that Soviet Communism would once again become an attractive model for the rest of the world. But most striking of all, to me, was Kokoshin's willingness to make an explicit connection between these external developments and the need for "democratization of our society," for "revolutionary reform" in the internal Soviet system, and to admit openly and on the record that "for many decades we lived like in a fortress."

On a less exalted level, what he said was borne out by the attitude of Pavel, the "guardian angel" provided for us by Gosteleradio: a highly educated and sophisticated man in his thirties who clearly believed in the job he was trying to do—to facilitate the production of sympathetic or at least objective Western television programs about the Soviet Union—and was equally clearly frustrated by the way the system made this task all but impossible for him to carry out.

The atmosphere reminded me of Spain at the end of the Franco regime. The society had clearly outgrown the political superstructure it had been supporting. The system remained restrictive, and no doubt often very brutal, but the wholesale mass murder of Stalin's time seemed as remote from the Moscow of today as the abject poverty and implacable violence of the Spanish civil war had seemed from the Madrid of 1975. As in Spain, there was a new elite, both more aware and less afraid of what was going on in the outside world, and anxious, for its own sake and that of the country, that the latter should no longer appear conspicuously more backward or uncivilized than its main political and economic competitors. That elite was the audience to which Gorbachev was appealing, and for the moment it seemed untroubled by any fear that he might fall, and the old guard regain control. Not, of course, that it expected the Soviet Union to be transformed into a parliamentary democracy. But it did expect the Communist party dictatorship to be exercised in a more liberal, enlightened, and above all more open manner.

On my last day I did have a brief encounter with the Russia I had been warned against before I went—appropriately enough, in Red Square. A policeman saw me pointing my camera at him, beckoned me over with a gruff "Komm," motioned to open the camera, pulled out the film, exposed it, and handed it back to me. Feeling rather foolish, I recounted the incident self-deprecatingly to Pavel, who had not been present but came to the airport to see us off. He expressed surprise and irritation. There was no law, he said, against photographing policemen. I tried to find extenuating circumstances. Perhaps, I suggested, the policeman thought I had been photographing the large black limousine on its way into the Kremlin, for which he had just been holding back the crowd. "So what?" said Pavel. Well, I said, presumably the car had someone quite important inside. "So what? You should have protested."

He knew, of course, that if I had protested, I would have achieved nothing, except probably causing our whole party to miss its flight home. But I think that *he* might have protested, had he been with me. He *had* been with me the day before at the Foreign Ministry, when the release of Andrei Sakharov was announced; and he clearly felt the day was past when a Soviet citizen had to regard an argument with a policeman as lost before it started. (In fact, it was only a few weeks later that a KGB official in Kiev was actually dismissed for harassing a Soviet journalist who had exposed corruption.)

So I was a little surprised, when we interviewed Kenneth Adelman in London in early February 1987 (admittedly just before the first large-scale release of Soviet political prisoners), to find him still asserting, "I can't see that Mr. Gorbachev has changed much in the Soviet Union since he's taken office"—though, of course, as a government official, he had good reason for being cautious.

> ADELMAN: I have a good friend, who was an adviser to Dean Acheson when he was secretary of state, who has done research recently showing that there have been fifty-three times in the postwar era when an American president or secretary of state has said, "It's the turning point in U.S.-Soviet relations," because of changes in the Soviet Union—because of a "new era" in the Soviet Union. I am not about to tell you right now it's number fifty-four.

A MORE POSITIVE VIEW

A few days earlier the West German foreign minister, Hans-Dietrich Genscher, had made his Davos speech calling on the West to "take Mr. Gorbachev at his word." But even in the summer of 1986 there had been a noticeably different emphasis, on this point, in the way that leaders of the moderate left in Western Europe expressed themselves—especially when they were out of office. Both Laurent Fabius and Karsten Voigt said they felt, from their personal contacts with the Soviet leadership, that it was becoming more open to the outside world. At least, Fabius said, it was now possible to have a discussion with one's Soviet interlocutor, rather than simply listening to a prepared statement recited parrot-wise. Voigt gave this description of the current state of mind of his Soviet contemporaries.

> VOIGT: I think they are now on the one hand, after Gorbachev, in a mood where they really believe that they can change the country. I think they are more optimistic than they have reason to be, for changes in the Soviet Union are very difficult to implement. But they are very optimistic, for they have now a leadership which is energetic, and which really gives the impression of efficiency, which is very important for them.
>
> On the other hand I think they still know that they are very much behind in economic terms, compared with the West, and they are asking for equality, but in many aspects they have the feeling of inferiority. . . .
>
> At least it's a change in style. But it's also a change in substance. When I compare the people whom I met in the early seventies, in the older generation, and when I compare my relationship and my type of talks with them nowadays, it's a deep shift. Their private behavior is different. They are much more relaxed. In style they are more Western —that doesn't mean that in thinking they are more Western—and they are much more relaxed, less dogmatic in their behavior. But that doesn't mean that they are not rooted in the perception of Soviet interests and of the Soviet political system. They are modernizers, but they are not typical Westerners. On many aspects of their behavior and thinking they have much more experience about the Western world than any other generation after the death of Lenin, but this doesn't mean that they want to take over every aspect of Western life. And, so far, I think this generation over there is a more credible competitor for us, for they have certain elements of efficiency, which makes them more efficient when they compete with us.

Sergei Plekhanov, with his uncannily perfect American English and his ability to integrate the terms and concepts of Western political science into an unrepentant yet flexible Marxist analysis of world events, is an excellent example of the kind of people Voigt is talking about. I asked him, as a specialist on American politics, whether there were any aspects of the Soviet-U.S. relationship he would have handled differently if he had been in charge, or had the chance to play them over again.

> PLEKHANOV: Well, I think I would have paid greater attention to the domestic peculiarities of American domestic politics and the policy

process. It's a large and complex country. The ruling class in the United States is not monolithic. Even the "foreign policy elite," which is only part of the ruling class, is complex and big enough, and one has to be patient and one has to see the problems that various groups have in building their consensus; and one has also to take into account the historical traditions.

Plekhanov sees the last twenty or thirty years as "a period of growing wisdom, growing ability to handle the problems," and professes to feel "more optimistic now about what will happen in the next ten or fifteen years than I was, for instance, twenty years ago when the Cold War was in full swing." He agrees that the Cold War "did try to start up" again in the 1980s, "but I think it didn't really have a chance to grow to the extent that it did grow in the forties and fifties, because I think that we're already seeing a change of gear in world politics. Trends toward détente are unmistakably developing, even though this is not a linear movement—there will be setbacks, but I think the worst part is already behind us."

Interestingly, this view seems to be more or less reciprocated by Elliott Abrams, now in charge of U.S. policy in Latin America, who, even if he would not use the word "détente," feels confident that "the U.S.-Soviet relationship . . . is an increasingly mature relationship." But Plekhanov does not share Abrams's confidence that "neither the U.S. nor the Soviets will allow Third World local conventional conflicts to escalate into U.S.-Soviet conflict."

PLEKHANOV: A war need not start in Europe itself. When you have a confrontation between the two military blocs—an institutionalized confrontation, all those scenarios and military plans, operational plans, for all kinds of strikes against each other—and when against that background you have a local crisis developing somewhere, and when you have military strategies tied to the development of those crises—for instance . . . there has been a shift in NATO strategy toward using the military machinery of NATO in local situations which need not having anything to do with Europe—when you have that sort of "horizontal escalation" scenarios working on the minds of the military planners, then odds are that the powder keg will blow up.

Nor does he share the complacency of Kenneth Adelman, who thinks, "Looking at forty years, the U.S.-Soviet relationship has been managed very nicely by both sides. . . . There are other things that we could do to help the situation, but by and large the big picture is one of a pretty good success."

Plekhanov doesn't agree.

PLEKHANOV: The world has been saved from a very, very tragic fate during the forty years of the nuclear age not so much by the wisdom of statesmen, although the wisdom of statesmen did play a role . . . but . . . quite a few times by sheer luck. By sheer luck—especially now that we are more and more dependent on technology, and the war can start as a result of some computering mistake or something. . . . You know, it has never happened in world history, there has never been a situation where for four decades you would have such a huge buildup of military power without that military power being used in a war. . . . It's easier to imagine why a war would take place than it is to imagine that we would be able to avoid it, if we continue on the same course of the arms race.

DIVIDED GERMANY . . .

In Europe, at any rate, the spheres of influence have been long since defined, with neither side seriously challenging the other's right to do as it pleases even—since 1961—in its sector of Berlin. Europeans can feel grateful for that, inasmuch as their continent, so terribly ravaged by war in the first half of the century, has been characterized by a remarkable absence of international armed conflict in the second half. Western Europeans have the additional bonus of being free, and most of them probably do not sleep much less easily at night because that bonus is not shared by Eastern Europeans, though their feelings of moral outrage can be aroused from time to time by dramatic events like those in Hungary (1956), Czechoslovakia (1968), or Poland (1981)—one per decade seems to be roughly the ration—much as their conscience about poverty in the Third World can occasionally be aroused by a spectacular natural disaster.

That is true of Western Europeans in general, but it is surely less true of the Germans. The Germans are not reconciled to the division of their country. That doesn't mean that they are actively working for reunification, or have any real expectation that it could happen in a politically meaningful time scale.

GANSEL: You could ask the question of somebody who lost a leg when he was a little child, how he could manage with only one leg. But he only knows of the lack when he sees that other people have two legs. I mean, we had to grow up with that. We have to live with it.

It is not, so to say, a natural situation—the division of Germany—but I don't see any situation where the other leg can be given back to us.

It is not practical politics—as Volker Rühe also emphasizes.

RÜHE: I remember some journalists from Great Britain in 1984 when Honecker was about to come, or was scheduled, and they were asking me, "What is Chancellor Kohl, who's talking to Honecker about German reunification, going to—?" and I said, "Wait a minute, you're completely wrong. I mean, they are *not* talking about German reunification. Honecker would not be ready to spend ten seconds on that subject. They are talking about the reunification of German families.

But, precisely, reunification of families is not the kind of topic politicians can easily forget about. While German reunification may not be on the agenda, relations between the two Germanies emphatically are.

RÜHE: Some people advise us to close down the German question, say, "That's it." This is unhistorical. I also think it's not moral, because people in East Germany have the right of self-determination. But I think what's important for foreigners to understand is that twenty-four hours after the democratic parties in West Germany would close the German question, and say, "This is it," nondemocratic parties would take up the issue of German reunification, of the self-determination of all Germans. The first would be the Communist party in East Germany . . . and there would also be a nondemocratic party on the right, with a lot of moral support for the self-determination of all Germans. So also from a pragmatic point of view I think it would be very stupid indeed to leave this issue to nondemocratic forces.

Until the end of the 1960s, the official West German approach to this problem was principled rather than practical. Recognition was withheld from the German Democratic Republic, and, under the "Hallstein Doctrine," the Federal Republic broke diplomatic relations with any country that established them with the GDR (though the Soviet Union, from 1955 onward, was treated as an exception). Irmgard Adam-Schwaetzer of the (liberal) Free Democratic party recalls that time.

ADAM-SCHWAETZER: For us the election in 1969 was very important, because the static "big coalition" [CDU-SPD] was replaced by the coalition between Social Democrats and Liberals, and we looked forward to developing democracy but also developing our own relationships to the Eastern countries, because we felt that . . . it was just not enough to secure our own freedom here in the West. . . . We found out that by following up that dogmatic position [the Hallstein Doctrine] we would isolate [ourselves], so it was very important to get out of that, which we felt was a trap, and only a coalition between SPD and FDP at that time could find out that way.

Over the next three years this new coalition, led by Willy Brandt, embarked on a complex diplomatic process known as *Ostpolitik,* resulting in treaties with the Soviet Union, Poland, and Czechoslovakia—in which West Germany accepted the postwar frontiers—a four-power agreement on Berlin, mutual recognition of the two German states, and their admission to the UN (1972): a kind of final ratification, by the international community, of the postwar division of Germany. The Christian Democrats opposed this policy at the time, but Rühe now stresses the element of continuity in it (pointing out that his party had already begun nibbling at the edges of the Hallstein Doctrine during the sixties). It is clear that the renewed human contacts with the East which it has made possible, limited and unsatisfactory though they may be, are valued by West Germans of virtually all shades of political opinion.

GANSEL: I believe that West Germans ten or fifteen years younger than myself have much more *gesamtdeutsch* ["whole-German"] sentiment and consciousness than we have, which is partially due to the policy the Social-Liberal government has pursued since 1969 to try to make, as we say, "the Iron Curtain transparent," or open up for relations again, between families, the places where your parents were probably born—cultural exchange and, well, today that a school class with its teacher goes for a trip to Dresden or to Leipzig in the German Democratic Republic, whereas in our times you were put on a blacklist when, in the Young Socialist movement at the end of the sixties, we had connections with the youth of the Communist party in the GDR—connections which collapsed after Prague. When somebody from there came to see me in Kiel the car of the secret police was waiting at the corner and was watching what was going on, and we knew that we were put in the files. I mean, this has changed and this is a good thing.

. . . AND DIVIDED EUROPE

For Germans, therefore, the experience of détente in the seventies, rather than confirming the essential nastiness and expansionist nature of the Soviet Union as it apparently did for Americans like Newt Gingrich and George Will, has shown that the East-West relationship does not have to be wholly static, that it can be improved, at least in small but significant ways, by patient and conciliatory diplomacy. The results of this proved to be more tangible than those achieved by standing pat on positions of principle and issuing ritual denunciations of Soviet iniquity. And Germans are acutely aware that the "German question" cannot be considered in isolation.

> RÜHE: There is no isolated, national solution to the problem. That's impossible. It's only possible in a larger European framework. . . . You can only overcome the division of Germany by overcoming the division of Europe. The Soviet Union will never allow a change in Germany, because it knows this would mean immediate change in Poland and elsewhere. So it's the division of Europe. Germany's only part of it. And in the meantime we have to work for the people that are living now and can't wait for history to improve the situation in general.

But Karsten Voigt believes that, by a careful and patient extension of *Ostpolitik,* he can give history a helping hand.

> VOIGT: The precondition of my policy is not that I underestimate the importance of military power for politics, but the goal of my policy is to make it less important: that means especially make it less important in the relationship between East and West. So my strategy is to demilitarize the East-West conflict. But I don't assume that it is already demilitarized, so I'm dependent on the United States . . . to balance this military power on the other side. But my *goal* is not this dependence. I am not frustrated by this dependence, but I will want to change it in the direction of less dependence; and I *can* change it: first, by Western European cooperation, and, second, by diminishing the importance of military power in the East-West conflict.

On paper at least, there is a clear convergence between this and the Soviet view of European security, as explained by Sergei Plekhanov. According to him, Europe remains "foremost" among Soviet security concerns.

PLEKHANOV: We're a Eurasian power, but most of our population lives in the European part of the Soviet Union. The two world wars were fought largely in Europe, and the greatest concentration of military hardware and soldiers is still in Europe, and the main scenarios in existence in the world today about a world war again have to do with the possibility of a European war. There is a contradiction, I think—a fundamental contradiction—in Europe: that there is no way you can fight a war there, and yet at the same time this is the place where you can find the most preparations for a war; and that contradiction will have to be resolved. If it is resolved in favor of the military side then it will be the end, not only of Europe but of the world. So it has to be resolved the other way, by means of removing most of that hardware and matériel and the nuclear weapons, and reducing drastically conventional armaments—turning Europe into a peaceful and diverse continent and creating, you know, a different kind of security system for Europe which is based not on the division of Europe into East and West but on the realization that this is a single continent.

Voigt brushes aside the argument of the American (and some European) hawks that détente was discredited by Soviet behavior in the Third World.

VOIGT: In those areas where we negotiated and where we had treaties in the region of Europe, they were sticking to the treaties and the situation remained stable. So it's not the problem that we had too many treaties, but that we had too few treaties. Our problem was not, and our goal was not, to blow up détente in Europe, but to include other areas in this process of détente.

He agrees that the Soviet Union did not live up to many of the human rights provisions of the Helsinki Final Act, but points out that on Western insistence this did not take the form of "a formal binding treaty." He sees it rather as "a charter which is defining the goal of our future cooperation." No doubt he would be heartened by Viktor Mironenko's claim to have been convinced by Helsinki that "regardless of political and philosophical differences, and other differences, rational political leaders, responsible to their people and for the future of mankind, given goodwill, can certainly find adequate solutions to existing problems"; and thus, "through my acceptance of the results of the Helsinki conference," to have been "prepared to accept what is now taking place in the domestic and foreign politics of our country" (the Gorbachev reforms).

A EUROPEAN DÉTENTE?

In between the purely German and the pan-European aspects of the problem, the Germans perceive another level that not only Americans but other Western Europeans (or perhaps I should say "Western Europeans proper"), such as the British and French, tend to overlook: a forgotten entity called "Central Europe," which was a casualty of World War II and its aftermath.

RÜHE: We understand that Poland is a central European country, and when you talk of "Eastern Europe" this is very much misleading, really. East Germany: that's central Europe. Poland is central Europe, Czechoslovakia is central Europe, and not so long ago they belonged, together with Hungary and Austria, to a completely different political setup.

VOIGT: I think that most "Eastern European" countries among the smaller states feel themselves to be central European, and they feel deeply rooted in central European culture—and they very often criticize when I call them Eastern Europeans. This has to do with democratic traditions and cultural pluralism, which in a certain degree they now try to integrate into a political system which is not pluralistic, but they are not afraid about pluralistic thoughts, while pluralism has not such a tradition in the Soviet Union. . . . They might harmonize the view with Soviet power inside the alliance, so far as officials are concerned, but they are defining their specific national interest in the framework of this alliance, in a much more explicit way than ten years ago, and they have a feeling of their identity as national states in Eastern Europe. But they have also a feeling of their specific interest together with us, especially in the situation where they have tried, to a limited extent, to influence the policy of the two superpowers, and where they tried, sometimes even with higher energy than Western European statesmen, but in a more difficult environment, to give expression to their specific views. And on both sides I have the impression as if the two sides try to cooperate across the borders of the bloc systems—but on each side doing this with one eye pointing to their respective big partner and saying, "But we stay there in the alliance, with solidarity." So we have on one side still the blocs, we have the alliances, but we have also a formal and informal network of . . . cooperation [cutting] across the bloc systems and state lines.

But how far could the Soviet leadership be expected to tolerate such a development?

VOIGT: The discussion is going on in the Soviet Union about the role of Western Europe, and the discussion is starting about the role of Eastern Europe—and this is a very complicated discussion, but it's obvious that the Soviet Union would prefer a situation in which we increase our differences with the United States, and in which they can harmonize every aspect of life between them and Eastern European states. But this will not work. . . . We will only give expression to our specific interests in relationship with the United States if the Soviet Union is also willing to respect our specific interests to a higher degree than it is now; and, on the other hand, if we express our specific interests, some—and increasingly more—Eastern European leading people might have the same temptation.

How far, then, is this ambitious program for overcoming the division of Europe through détente endorsed by other Western European leaders? Neil Kinnock certainly seems likely to back it, though in Voigt's eyes (not to mention those of the Americans) he would probably be found insufficiently aware of the need to have military power (including U.S. nuclear power) behind you if you want to be taken seriously by Moscow. Kinnock says that when détente started in the seventies he found "the prospect of what it could produce . . . quite exciting" but was and still is "very reserved about its possibilities," apparently because he doubted whether either side was sufficiently serious about it. As with the Cuba missile crisis, he is reluctant to put the blame for its failure more on one side than on the other.

KINNOCK: Such is the mirror relationship of the world, given two superpowers, that you can ultimately, I suppose, find out where the first offense took place, but what you know is that with the first offense there will be a mirror reaction, and within a matter of months the burden of guilt will be the same on both sides. [But] I think it was simply efforts to prove that American politicians weren't soft on the Commies that started to wear it down—and then, of course, the outrage of Afghanistan put a stake right through its heart.

He adds, though, that "in retrospect the fact that it did take place does mean that the chance of it being resumed is that much greater: it's always easier to build on what exists than to start the business of invention."

Chris Patten is a firm supporter of détente, provided it is not tainted with any hint of "moral equivalence."

> PATTEN: I think one has to attempt to discover a modus vivendi with the Soviet Union and Eastern Europe. I think one has to make as many contacts, both personal and on a broader front than that, as one conceivably can. The only alternative to trying to find a way of surviving together is to blow up the world. But having said that, I don't think there are any circumstances in which, however much one supports multilateral disarmament, one should go in for moral disarmament as well. It seems to me to be a most gross absurdity to pretend that there is no moral difference between the sort of society represented by the Soviet Union—and the sort of society imposed on Eastern Europe—and what we, however imperfectly, try to do in Western Europe and in the United States.

In France, Jacques Toubon, describing himself as "from that point of view very Gaullist," thinks the Iron Curtain "is not a permanent situation," and feels deeply "that people on both sides of the Iron Curtain are the same European people and that they are the same culture," with the same "historical, human roots—and I hope that some day this cultural identity would be translated by political union." He thinks the Western way of life "could in the future be extended to the Eastern countries," pointing out that already "in Moscow they are drinking Coca-Cola, and I think it's a very important event," but seems to lack any very specific ideas on how this process could be encouraged. Pierre Lellouche, on the other hand, has very clear ideas. He stresses that "the key to withdrawing the twenty Soviet divisions in the GDR is in Moscow, not here," but thinks that trade can be used "as a political tool to get liberalization, to get movement on the human rights front."

> LELLOUCHE: Our long-term interest is certainly to create as many links as possible with Eastern Europe, and that would complicate the life of the Soviet, if we do it properly. If we simply are there to help the Soviet sustain its military empire in central Europe, then it's wrong So we have to walk a tight line there—be careful what we sell, and under what terms. . . . What I'm arguing for is a policy which is based on a very strong stratum of mutual deterrence, not on a policy of military weakness. I think the basic condition for balanced political dialogue with the Soviet Union is mutual respect—and they respect your military forces and your ability to strike at them. So if you have

a strong stratum of deterrence you can build a balanced political relationship.

He believes—like Richard Burt—that the détente of the seventies went wrong because after Vietnam the United States (not Europe!) reduced its defense spending: "They thought they had fixed the Soviet Union through a political relationship, and the Kissinger years were years of slashing the defense budget."

To sum up, then: The rising political elite in Western Europe, as in the United States, has no illusions about the Soviet political system being benign. There are differences of view on how fundamentally aggressive and expansionist the system is, not between Europe and the United States but within both. There is, however, general agreement that it is a system that takes military power very seriously, and that those who wish to be taken seriously by it in any political argument need to be sure they have military power behind them. But there is doubt whether this point has been clearly taken by public opinion in northern European countries that have not had strong local Communist parties in the postwar period. These countries—including Britain and West Germany—seem somewhat more prone than others to feel that the domination of the world in general and of Europe in particular by two superpowers is a bad thing for which both superpowers are more or less equally to blame.

There was in 1986 slightly greater optimism among Western Europeans than among Americans about the possibility of the Soviet system changing from within, either spontaneously or as a result of contact with the West, carefully modulated by Western governments. This optimism tended to be more pronounced among Socialists or Social Democrats than conservatives, especially in West Germany, but Germans in general are more sensitive than others to the human benefits of détente, and to the specific character and aspirations of "central European" nations, including the Communist leadership of those nations, which find themselves lined up willy-nilly as loyal citizens of Soviet-controlled "Eastern Europe." By 1988, however, the picture was further complicated by the enthusiastic American reaction to Gorbachev ("Gorbymania") on the one hand, and the distinctly nervous reaction of European governments to the new U.S.-Soviet détente with its hints of a denuclearized Europe on the other.

In general, one can say that there is no clear-cut division between a "European" and an "American" view about the Soviet Union. But there is a tendency on each side to attribute views or attitudes it dislikes to the other. The problem may be less one of East-West than of "West-West" relations—which are what I propose to look at in the next chapter.

CHAPTER 9

The Troublesome Frontier Province

THE FRONTIER SEEN FROM ROME

ABRAMS: I think there is a sense that the United States has more and more clearly been defining its global interests—first in Asia because of this phenomenal economic growth, and now we tend more and more to look south; and Europeans don't. And not only do they not, but they seem to be trying to constrain us from doing so. . . . There is a feeling that Europeans thought it was great when America was interested in Europe, including in defending Europe, but as our interests tend to grow and vary there is a sense of resistance from Europe, from the NATO countries, and that meets with a certain degree of annoyance.

Abrams, of course, is paid to "look south," but his view that there is a "reduction in the centrality of Europe in American diplomacy, American thinking about the world" is quite widely shared. Pat Schroeder, an opponent of the administration and the representative of a western state (Colorado), voices the kind of political pressure that American diplomacy has to respond to.

SCHROEDER: We have neglected our hemisphere much too much, that's why I say, "What in the world are we doing in Europe?" I mean, you're a European partner: terrific, fine! But we have a hemisphere we have totally neglected, and we better get off our tail and do something about it.

Pierre Lellouche comments, too, about changing perspectives

LELLOUCHE: The generation of postwar Americans, mostly East Coast, who made the Marshall Plan, who made NATO, who were culturally very close to Europe, are increasingly going out of business. They're old and retiring, and they're being replaced by younger people coming not so much from the East but from the South and West of the United States, with different, completely different, views about the world. . . . You have a much more nationalistic, materialistic nation, oriented toward the fulfillment of its own needs—and the rest of the world, well, if it wants to join, all the better: if it doesn't want to join, well, it's too bad. And essentially the new Americans look at Europe with some interest, but not much: a lot of indifference, a lot of exasperation, when Europe does not follow what the U.S. thinks is good for the Free World. You know, in Reagan there's a lot of what I would call "Californian Gaullism"—it's nationalism plus unilateral decision-making.

Joe Biden, himself senator from an East Coast state—one of the original thirteen colonies—points out that the demographic center of the United States moves steadily westward year by year, and now corresponds more or less to the geographical center, well to the west of the Mississippi.

BIDEN: Those folks on the West Coast clearly have a more keen and genuine interest in things Pacific—the Pacific Basin. Quite frankly, we trade more with other parts of the world than we do with Europe. We have equally as much of our military wherewithal facing to the west rather than to the east. . . . And secondly I think there is a change generally, an attitude that Europe is prosperous now, that your combined population exceeds ours—and Americans are asking the question of people like me, who hold high public office: Why are we spending all that money to have all those troops in Europe?

Thus Americans see a triple shift since the 1950s in the interplay of geopolitical forces: there is the westward demographic shift within the United States itself, reflected in the composition of its political elite. There is a raising of the economic stakes in East Asia and the political stakes in Latin—especially Central—America. And there is the success of Europe itself in recovering economically and stabilizing politically after the alarms of the immediate postwar period. All of these combine, it is suggested, both to reduce America's overall politico-military capacity relative to that of the rest of the world, and to move Europe, in particular, lower down on the U.S. foreign policy agenda.

GINGRICH: We're no longer who we were. In the fifties we were so big, and we were so rich, and we were so powerful, we could sustain the entire Free World. We can't do that now—and frankly, *you* can't afford the redundancy and the inefficiencies of the current NATO process.

Biden feels that Americans see Europe as a kid brother who has now grown up and should be able to look after himself—or, alternatively, like the American woman in the cigarette commercial who has "come a long way, baby!"

If there is one point on which the new generation of American politicians seems to agree irrespective of party affiliation, it is, in the words of Larry Pressler, "that Europe should bear more of the defense effort." Pat Schroeder, a member of the Democratic majority in the House of Representatives, describes the frustrations of serving on the Armed Services Committee.

SCHROEDER: Every year we meet with our European counterparts. Every year we say, "You ought to do a little more." They all say, "Amen, Charlie, amen, Charlie." They leave. Next year we get back together and we say, "Hey, guys, you didn't do any more!" And they say, "Oh, I know, but next year—amen, Charlie." Our government is so embarrassed, we classify what our allies do, because we figure if it ever got out on the streets of Peoria that they have never met their targets, we as politicians would have great trouble explaining to the farmers why they're in trouble but we are sending even more money and more troops overseas because they [the Europeans] never meet their commitment. I mean, that doesn't make any sense to me, so that to me is very frustrating. . . . Maybe they see it differently—I have tried to listen to how they see it differently, but I never understand it.

Let's just bring it down to a narrow frame everybody understands: chemical weapons. I don't think we should make chemical weapons in the U.S. We have no use for them in the U.S. Who are we going to use them against? Canada? Mexico? I mean, crazy. There is no way we would ever use chemical weapons in the U.S. There is no threat, and the military agrees on that. Why do we make chemical weapons? Well, we make chemical weapons because the Russians have them and we're afraid they would use them in Europe, that's why. The Europeans get together and say, "That's right, you should make chemical weapons and you should store chemical weapons in the U.S. We won't make them . . . and we won't store them." Well, if you won't store them, they don't do any good, because if they are stored in Denver, Colorado, which is where they have been stored, you are never going to get them to Europe in time. It's not like the Russians ring up and say, "We want to make this as interesting as possible: we are going to give you full notice, get everything you need"!

Josef Joffe, the West German journalist, is ready to concede that such criticisms are well founded.

JOFFE: Europe is not capable, and certainly not willing, to shoulder the burden of defending itself. We have tried that for thirty-five years and we haven't succeeded. . . . The Europeans have acquired a rather comfortable place in the world, being protected by Americans and being free to invest their resources elsewhere than in the military.

But Volker Rühe, as a spokesman for West Germany's ruling party, disagrees, pointing out that there are "500,000 German soldiers" in the Federal Republic's own armed forces, and that it is the only NATO country currently expanding its military draft: "there is no military draft in the United States." Curiously, in Britain it is Chris Patten, a member of the government in office, who is ready to acknowledge "a degree of truth" in the American argument "that one reason why their deficit is so high is because of the defense burden which they are carrying, and that if we in Europe carried a little more of our own defense burden, their deficit wouldn't be so high," while Neil Kinnock, the leader of the opposition, springs to the British government's defense, claiming that "proportionately we dedicate more of our resources to the defense of free Europe, as well as our own country, than does the United States of America." In France Jacques Toubon, general secretary of a party that admittedly had returned to office only three months earlier, put up a somewhat tentative defense: "I admit that the American administration could take this point of view, but I think that now in France, in Germany, or in Britain or in Italy, we take a very large part of the burden." The defense expert, Pierre Lellouche, was much more polemical.

LELLOUCHE: If you look down at the hardware and the men who actually defend Europe, 80 percent of the defenses in Europe—talking about land armies or air forces, and so on—are manned by Europeans. So it's completely wrong to say that Europeans are freeloading. Similarly, after Vietnam, from 1968 to about 1978, for ten years, the U.S. defense budget went down in real terms by 2 or 3 percent per year, and the load of defense was carried by the Europeans, who kept increasing it. Now what you have in recent years, under Reagan in particular, is a burst of rearmament for a few years—as usual in the U.S. As you know, the rearmament curve in the U.S. is zigzag—because there was the first zigzag in Korea and there was one during Vietnam, and a third one during Reagan, but each time it's a very few years . . . it goes up very abruptly and then goes down, because of the political processes in America—they cannot sustain a long-term defense effort, whereas the Soviets, of course, go up slowly but surely for decades, and that makes a difference after a few decades.

In Europe, therefore, during recent years, you've had a stagnation of defense budgets contrasting with the Reagan peak, but now, of course, the American defense budget is going to go down again and everybody is going to stagnate. So in reality what you have is increasing defense costs that are staggering, because of the amount of new technologies in weaponry, and at the same time an increasing difficulty of all Western democracies to cope with that expenditure.

Who is right and who is wrong? It is largely a matter of perspective. The total armed forces of the Western European members of NATO (not including Greece and Turkey) outnumber the total armed forces of the United States, and amount to six and a half times the number of American forces stationed in Europe. So, since the vast majority of Western European forces are stationed in Europe, it cannot be too difficult to arrive at a definition of "the defense of Europe" in which European soldiers outnumber Americans by a factor of four to one. Equally it is no doubt true that Britain contributes a higher proportion of her resources "to the defense of free Europe, as well as our own country" than does the United States. But the American complaint is, precisely, that the Europeans behave as if there were only Europe to be defended, whereas they, the Americans, have to think in global terms. And if one looks at defense expenditure in general, whether as a proportion of all government spending or as a proportion of gross domestic product, the United States was already top of the NATO scoreboard in 1980, and was way out in front by 1983.[1] (Ironically, its nearest rival for the proportion of GNP spent on defense was Greece, politically the United States's least favorite ally, whose defense effort is directed primarily against another NATO member, Turkey.)

Much of the American defense effort, in other words, is outside NATO and, according to Joe Biden, Americans question lukewarm European involvement outside NATO.

BIDEN: Why isn't it that, when there's a problem outside of NATO that obviously affects the Europeans as much as it affects the Americans, why isn't it that there is an equally strong reaction? I remember after that great man the Ayatollah Khomeini, that idiot, took power, there was a great concern about "Well, what does this mean now? Will this give the Soviets an excuse to move into the Persian Gulf? And what will it mean if Iran blocks the Strait of Hormuz?" and so on and so forth, and we'd say, "Well, what are we going to jointly do?" And you all would say, "What do you mean, 'jointly do'? That's outside NATO, that is nothing to do with NATO." And we'd say, "But wait a minute: you import more oil from there than we do. Why is it our responsibility to keep the Strait of Hormuz open and not equally your responsibility? Why don't we jointly sit down and conclude what we would do if that would occur?" . . . There is this feeling, I think, in Europe that anything beyond the purview of NATO is something that almost *de facto* should not be discussed for any joint effort, whereas the feeling on the part of the United States, as it's moved into this period of greater limits than it had in the past, [is] "Wait a minute, why do we jointly agree to protect Europe, and the United States says, 'We'll take the rest of the world'?"

Personally I rather doubt, having followed events in the Middle East quite closely during the period in question, whether any discussion quite on the lines suggested by Biden occurred, either in NATO or in bilateral contacts, between the U.S. and European governments. I know that both Britain and France do usually keep naval forces in the vicinity of the Persian Gulf, and I should be surprised if they did not discuss contingency plans for joint action with the U.S. government to keep open the Strait of Hormuz and to protect shipping in the Gulf, should that be necessary to ensure a continued flow of oil —if not at the time of the revolution in Iran, then certainly after the outbreak of the Iran-Iraq war in September 1980. In 1987, when this argument did come to a head as a result of the escalation of the "tanker war" and Kuwait's request for reflagging of its tankers, a number of European states did join the United States in sending warships to the Gulf to help defend neutral shipping against Iranian attacks.

Such differences as do arise in this area between European governments and the U.S. usually stem not from European refusal of American requests for joint action but from European misgivings about the propensity of the United States to do its military contingency planning unilaterally and out loud. Europeans often feel that U.S. policy-makers exaggerate military threats and underestimate political ones, especially in the Middle East, and that their military activities are liable to be politically counterproductive. That said, it has to be admitted that "Europe" as such, as opposed to its member states, has not so far developed much of a capacity even for political, let alone military, action to defend its interests outside NATO, partly because the European Treaties do not cover security and one member of the EEC (the Irish Republic) is formally neutral; and that in practice European governments, with the partial exception of Britain and France, often seem to behave outside the NATO area as if they had decided that "since we cannot compete with the superpowers in military terms we may as well get on with making money and leave the security considerations to the Americans, hoping they do not make too many disastrous mistakes."

What cannot be disputed, in any case, is that Biden's summary reflects all too accurately how the relationship is perceived from the vantage point of the U.S. Congress; and the view from the administration is not much different.

> ABRAMS: [On the part of the Europeans, there's been] a kind of effort to restrain the United States, and to view American involvement elsewhere as a big pain—as an annoyance that reduces American attention to what we should really be thinking about, which is Europe. If that gets worse it will really harm the NATO alliance a lot, and I think Europeans really face a question over this period, say till the end of the century, of whether they're going to join us in some of these global activities or whether they're going to retire from the scene and have a kind of "little Europe" foreign policy—which obviously we hope is not the case, but may well be the case.

Matters are made worse by the fact that in the one area where Western Europe *has* developed a capacity to act collectively in defense of its interests, namely trade, those interests can often conflict quite sharply with those of the U.S.

> BIDEN: One of your successes has been the Common Market. It now competes with us—and some of us think on occasion unfairly—in ways that impact on American jobs, whereas that was never a consideration before, in the fifties and sixties.

> SCHROEDER: The interesting thing that has happened in the world is that our military allies are also our trading competitors. So we put on our military hats and we're buddies. We take those off and then we

become trading competitors, and we have not found a way to deal with that dual role.

And, increasingly, Europeans are perceived as being "resentful" toward the United States.

BIDEN: I think there is the belief on the part of Americans that because the United States had been generous at a time of great need to the Europeans, that the Europeans are resentful of that . . . not resentful enough that they don't want to have a relationship with us, but . . . that they're just going to tweak us wherever we can be tweaked.

Early examples of this "tweaking," at least as felt by Pat Schroeder, were the European attitudes during Vietnam . . .

SCHROEDER: At first you are very angry that the Europeans who were supposedly your allies aren't helping. I think that is an initial response of many Americans: "We went to help them for democracy on their turf, and now here we are fighting for democracy in Asia, and where are they? What's this? How selfish can you be? Decadence, selfishness!" . . . But then, as you got more into the history of what was really going on you understood why they had not bought into this . . . and I think not all Americans got to that second level.

. . . and, more especially, the airlift of arms to Israel during the Yom Kippur War.

SCHROEDER: I must say when I got to the 1973 war in particular I was very distressed that the Europeans would not allow us to land, on bases that Americans manned and Americans built, to refuel . . . and no matter what you say about the Middle East, Israel is a democracy and so, I mean, that is different: you couldn't say that about South Vietnam, but you can say that about Israel and you can say that it is carrying on some of the Western European traditions, and when you see it invaded and someone says, "No, you may have built this base and this may be your base, but you can't land here: we don't approve of the war," we all said, "Wait a minute, what is this all about?"—and that, for me, has been very troubling about Europe.

But what seems to have gone beyond mere tweaking, as perceived by the entire American political establishment, was the European refusal to support the U.S. bombing of Libya in April 1986.

BIDEN: [Americans] are truly confused. I mean, they don't understand. They say, "Well, wait a minute: all these bad things are happening in Europe, I mean these rotten Libyans are shooting British policemen from their embassy. . . . We don't understand. Why would they not want to do that? It must be they don't like us"—rather than understanding the complexity of each individual European country's relationship with their own populace and with the Libyans or with things in the Mediterranean. But—and I think that's something Europeans miss—it would be different if Americans thought you liked Libya, but they don't. They say, "Well, we know Europeans don't like the Libyans—look what the Libyans have done to them. Therefore it must be us, it must be the United States that they don't like, and that's why the French won't let us fly over their territory, because they don't like us, or that's why British public opinion seems to run so strongly against Margaret Thatcher: it's because they don't like us."*

According to Richard Perle, there is "disenchantment" in Washington "with what is seen . . . as a pusillanimous attitude on the part of weak governments in Europe that are not prepared to defend their own territory against terrorist attack," and this is seen as the latest symptom of a characteristic European sickness, which contrasts with American vigor.

PERLE: I think the Europeans have become, in the last decade or two, a persistent voice for caution, always rounding the edges, always compromising, always blurring the issues that we in the rest of the world have to face. And American decisiveness from time to time has proved to be correct and effective. It's hard to get a decisive decision out of a European government these days, and I think one of the sources of tension between the United States and Europe at the moment is the desire to avoid clear-cut and decisive decisions. . . . We're in a somewhat different political situation, and can afford to make decisions and carry them out.

The Europeans complained about Grenada, but the people of Grenada aren't complaining: they were a lot better off as a result of that decision. No government in Europe in recent memory, with the possi-

*MATTHÄUS-MAIER: "I was in America a short time after the Libya raid, and the Americans can't understand how people in this country [Germany] think about that. I give you a personal impression: my grandmother—I think a conservative person, she's not on the left wing—when I telephoned to her just two days after the Libya raid . . . she said, 'Oh, it is so terrible!' and 'I feel [for] these children in the streets of Libya—and they [did] it during the night, and I remember during the night in 1944, 1943, I had to run with my little boy in the cellars in order to escape the bombs on our houses.' . . . Although she hates terrorism, she was against this American raid, and I think these are things that Americans must think about."

ble exception of Mrs. Thatcher, has been prepared to take the sort of decisive action that President Reagan took in his first weeks in office with the air controllers' strike. I mean—unheard of to deal decisively with a labor dispute of that sort in Europe! And I think in part the European approach, which is to compromise always, has led to a drift in European policy; and by contrast the vigor and decisiveness of American policy—which won't always be right—is on balance proving not only to protect our interests, but, I believe, in the long run to protect the interests of the democratic world.

Elliott Abrams has an explanation for the pettiness and indecisiveness of European policy.

ABRAMS: I'm not sure this is terribly diplomatic, but I do have the feeling that you can divide Europe between the great nations of Europe that we think of, such as England and France, and then others which have traditionally been somewhat more insular, and which are smaller, and which have a somewhat different foreign-policy history; and perhaps the advent of the Common Market, and of a degree of European integration, such as it is, has had a kind of "lowest common denominator" impact, and is tending to push the great nations of Europe in the direction of the other foreign policy. And that's unfortunate.

The Young Turks of the Reagan administration, it will be noted, were, at least until Irangate became public, as confident in their own judgment as they were contemptuous of that of the Europeans. This was perhaps a long-delayed revenge for generations of European superciliousness toward the supposedly crude and unsophisticated Americans.

PERLE: There was a time when our diplomatic establishment, at least, looked to the Old World as a source of wisdom and propriety in complex and delicate diplomatic negotiations and affairs of state, and there was a tendency even to defer to their judgment. I think that's gone now—not least because the judgment and wisdom of the Europeans so manifestly failed twice in the first half of this century, and led to two very bloody world wars—and Americans are far more confident today that we can make determinations about the kinds of policies that will succeed and those that will fail, and we're far less inclined today to defer to the wisdom of older societies, whose presumed historical experience in fact turned out not to endow them with the special wisdom necessary to keep the peace.

Now we've done a pretty good job of helping to keep the peace, of

> helping to rebuild Europe. Indeed, the Marshall Plan, the reconstruction of Europe, the nurturing of the institutions of European defense, and even European integration—these are American ideas. These were not the ideas or the concepts of striped-pants European diplomats, [but] kind-of-crazy Americans, who put together the postwar structure of Europe, and it's a structure that's lasted longer than any the Europeans were able to put together for themselves. So we're a little less inclined to take the sage advice of our elders these days.

The result is, as George Will says, that "the kind of fellow feeling that existed between those [Americans and Europeans] who fought the war and built the Marshall Plan and did all that, just doesn't exist"; or, in Newt Gingrich's words, that the Americans, "at levels the Europeans should not underestimate, are tired."

> GINGRICH: We are tired of having our troops in Germany and being told that we should be grateful that we're there. We're tired of having blocked the Soviet empire from making West Germany into another Afghanistan, and being told that it's our fault, because we're not nice to the Russians. We're tired of frankly doing a heck of a lot more to save your citizens from terrorism than you are, and then being told that we should be more reasonable. . . . We look on at things like the English policewoman being killed in London and nothing effectively being done except kicking a few Libyans out, and . . . we're befuddled—I mean, we don't understand. We watch the French basically buy off Arab terrorism, and, I mean, I understand that there is a French attitude that the world is not moral, so one should never make moral decisions, so if you can buy off the terrorists, why not? But that's un-American. I mean, as an historian I understand the French; as an American I'm befuddled by it. Because we are a moral nation: that doesn't mean we don't sin a lot, it just means that we happen to think sinning is sin. . . .
>
> And I think, finally, we're a little tired of being nagged at—I mean the significant segment of America that says, "You don't want our missiles? Fine. You don't want our troops? Fine. When we leave, and you and the bear share the continent alone, good luck!"

The threat that America might reduce or pull out its troops from Europe if Europeans do not behave better has become a regular feature of such philippics, though usually the speaker is careful to put it in quotation marks: this is not what he or she personally thinks, please understand, but it is what others think and, if Europeans are not careful, it might become a majority view. Thus Elliott Abrams thinks that if Europeans do seem to be settling for a "little Europe" option, "in the long run . . . there would be an effort here, probably successful, to reduce the American military presence in Europe," while Joe Biden says that European success in competing for world markets will prompt Americans to ask, "[Since] the Europeans have figured out how to unify in terms of taking care of their economic interest, why haven't they been able to do that in terms of their physical interest? . . . Why do all those American troops have to be there?"—and it is, he says, "a difficult argument to answer." Newt Gingrich asserts that "a large segment, particularly of my generation, of left-wing Americans . . . would pull out of Europe in a weekend," and that this kind of feeling is fed by European behavior of the type exhibited in the Libyan affair. He even suggests that American tourists might be pulled out as well as troops—something many European hotel-keepers thought had already happened in the summer of 1986.

> GINGRICH: You know, France may, Italy may, have to worry about Libya: we don't have to. Let me tell you: nobody in Europe has thought about the fact that we have a real easy way to avoid American tourists' getting killed. We can quit issuing passports. I mean, we are a huge country, we can just say, "Don't go to Europe for the next ten years: you Europeans want to clean up the terrorists, we'll come back. You don't want to clean up the terrorists? We ain't coming!"

(It's interesting to note how willing some of these supposedly libertarian American right-wingers are to suggest state interference with individual rights, such as the right of the American citizen to a passport!)

Larry Pressler, one of an influential group of senators of both parties who voted for the Nunn Amendment—an attempt, so far unsuccessful, to make the maintenance of U.S. troop levels in Europe conditional on rises in European defense spending—gives a rather harmless-sounding interpretation: "It really wouldn't withdraw any troops, but essentially what it says is that the Europeans should do more, and we should eventually get our troops out—in a very general way."

But George Will sees it as reflecting "a certain chilly cost-benefit analysis in the turn of mind" of the new generation of legislators.

> WILL: That's why you have a leading younger American senator, Sam Nunn—well, certainly one of the rising stars of the Democratic

party—casting a cold eye on the size of our commitment in terms of men and material in Europe, and on the logic of the American forces as a tripwire.

NATO, Will points out, no longer has the aura of achievement and endeavor for his generation of Americans that it did when they were growing up, in the days of Truman, Acheson, and Eisenhower.

WILL: All of those people have left the stage now, and NATO is just something that's been there for as long as anyone can remember—"Oh, NATO? Of course, NATO. So what?" It's like the Post Office—just always there, and people can't imagine a world without it. They can say, "Well, it's, I suppose it's useful, but how useful?" And certainly the postwar generation, the people we're talking about, are much more open to questions about NATO. I mean, something comes along like the terrorism and the raid on Libya, and we get cooperation from some countries and signally bad cooperation from others—the Italians and the French conspicuous among them—and Americans say, "Well, who needs this?" Americans get the feeling that we're defending Europe as a kind of act of altruism, and they don't feel like doing that.

America would not, Will thinks, actually withdraw its commitment to Europe, but "you would see a rethinking of the size of it and of the logic of it. It's the logic that gets interesting when you begin to get strategic defense and you begin to get negotiations, anyway, about mutual and balanced force reductions of conventional forces, and you get theater nuclear forces:* it's not clear the role the United States has in a conflict on the central front of Europe."

These developments leave it "open to discussion," in his view, whether the United States might withdraw its troops from Europe while leaving the "nuclear guarantee" in place.

But it is not at all clear that such a guarantee actually exists. Ernest Gross discusses what it was that reconciled Truman and his advisers to keeping American troops in Europe in the late 1940s.

GROSS: There was no way in which the United States could really commit itself to use the American strategic nuclear weapon in a war in

*"TNF": nuclear weapons designed for use in a regional conflict confined to a "theater" of operations close to the USSR, such as Western Europe or the Persian Gulf. Also known as "intermediate-range nuclear forces" (INF) because they come in between tactical and strategic weapons. The best-known examples are cruise and Pershing II missiles, and on the Soviet side SS-20s.

> Europe. There is no way—if for no other reason than that under our procedures, as you know, the incumbent president of the United States has the sole and exclusive authority to decide upon the use or non-use, and the circumstances of use, of nuclear weapons: it's impossible for that personal grant of authority to be delegated or shared in a treaty. And I think that people who talk about the "nuclear guarantee" of the North Atlantic Treaty simply ignore that. . . . There is no such commitment possible in advance of the presidential decision.

It was doubts—especially German doubts—on this point, of American willingness to use nuclear weapons in defense of Western Europe, that led to the deployment in Europe of American cruise and Pershing II missiles. But even before they were deployed, President Reagan had proposed the "zero option" under which deployment would have been canceled if the Soviet Union were to dismantle all its SS-20s in Europe.

> OWEN: [But] the basic, fundamental German position, and the majority in NATO, was that you needed that American presence with nuclear weapons anyhow, irrespective of SS-20s. So in a sense we were wrong to offer the "zero option"—"Take out all your SS-20s and we'll take out all our cruise and Pershings." Now that has actually been negotiated by the United States the Europeans are rather unhappy about it, and I think they've only got themselves to blame.

David Owen was speaking just after the Reykjavik summit of October 1986. At the time Soviet acceptance of the zero option was conditional on the abandonment of Reagan's Strategic Defense Initiative ("Star Wars"). But Gorbachev dropped that condition in a speech on February 28, 1987. By putting forward the so-called "double zero" option (extending downward to five hundred kilometers the range of weapons to be included in the new treaty), he adroitly stirred up new confusion and mutual suspicions within NATO. Secretary of State George Shultz quickly accepted the offer, arguing that it amounted to an offer of something for nothing since the United States did not have any missiles in Europe of the range in question. He insisted that the obsolescent Pershing IA missiles in West Germany would not be affected, because they belonged to West Germany and not to the United States.

This was scarcely a tenable position, since it was only the missiles themselves that were West German. The nuclear warheads did indeed belong to the United States, and for Moscow to accept their exclusion would have been tantamount to recognizing West Germany as a nuclear power. Inevitably the West German government came under intense pressure, and in August Chancellor Helmut Kohl announced that if the treaty went ahead on the lines proposed he would phase out the Pershing IAs and not replace them. Partly thanks to this concession, the treaty was signed at the Washington summit in December, and promptly endorsed by all of America's NATO allies. But the affair, coming as it did after disagreements about SDI and about Reagan's attitude at the Reykjavik summit (both of which seemed to many Europeans to imply U.S. willingness to abandon the nuclear defense of Europe), left a serious legacy of mistrust and policy differences within the Alliance. The Germans were not happy that an attempt to forge a common European position on "double zero" had been preempted by a statement supporting the U.S. attitude from Margaret Thatcher during the British election campaign; and they were very unhappy to find that the only land-based nonstrategic nuclear weapons left in Europe would be very short-range ones, whose targets could only be in one or the other half of Germany.

They argued, therefore, that the next stage in nuclear disarmament negotiations must address these weapons. By contrast, the United States was principally interested in negotiating a 50 percent cut in strategic weapons, while the British and French were more preoccupied with the imbalance in conventional forces and chemical weapons and were extremely hostile to any suggestion of removing short-range nuclear weapons before these imbalances had been redressed. Under pressure from his allies Kohl came out against a "third zero" (abolition of short-range nukes), but in response to German public opinion he also refused to commit himself to modernizing the short-range weapons as had been agreed in principle back in 1983. A NATO summit held in Brussels in early March 1988 papered over this issue without resolving it: Kohl persuaded Washington not to press it for the time being but ran into very sharp criticism from Mrs. Thatcher, while the French president and prime minister (about to stand against each other in a presidential election) were transparently on opposite sides of the argument.

Only one interviewee, Pat Schroeder, admitted to being personally in favor of reducing U.S. troop levels in Europe—though she was under the erroneous impression that "there are more troops there than there were twenty years ago": in fact, there are about 100,000 less. She was also the only person to express concern about the welfare of the troops themselves:

SCHROEDER: With the fall of the dollar recently we saw people taking a one-third pay cut in four months. That is very hard for people to do—and I've got to tell you, they don't live a very pleasant life in Europe. I mean, I have got to say to your Europeans, I am shocked at how they treat our black troops. That hurts me to say that, because they would say no, no, they're not racist, and I would say, we as a family have vacationed in Europe many times: been eating in a restaurant, my blond-headed son gets up and asks for the restroom, and of course they show him, and in will come some of our troops, clearly our troops—they have got the ghetto-blaster and you know they are ours, they are red, white, and blue!—they ask for a restroom and they say no, and it just pains me—and when I go over and talk to them they have got all sorts of stories about how they get treated traveling around Europe. . . .

You put the European economies together and they are bigger than ours: I mean, there is no reason that we have to be there. It is not isolationism; it is not pulling out of the partnership. The problem the U.S. has is that we have so many responsibilities in our own hemisphere, and everywhere else, and we only have about 3 percent of the world's population. So why should we be so heavily implanted in parts of the world where (a) they are very economically viable, (b) if they had the same percentage of people in uniform in Europe that we do, of their civilian population, you wouldn't need one American troop? I mean, so why do we do that? I mean, I can't make a good excuse.

After a day or two in Washington listening to this kind of thing, it is not difficult to agree with Pierre Lellouche's assessment: "The Americans are moving out. . . . I just don't see Europe with 350,000 U.S. troops at the end of the century."

ROME SEEN FROM THE FRONTIER

If Americans got the message from the Libyan affair that the Europeans "don't like us," as Biden suggests, were they right? Not according to opinion polls, which "regularly show that most Western Europeans both like and respect Americans."[2] It is American policies and leadership that tend to be unpopular in Europe, not the American people or the American way of life. Indeed, Biden himself might not be so far off the mark when he says, "I think the thing you Europeans genuinely question about us is our judgment: I don't think you question our intentions as much as you question our judgment." But he is probably also right to sense a certain resentment bred by overlong and excessive dependence. Chris Patten gives a good summary of the things on which dislike of America and Americans in Europe is based.

> PATTEN: First of all there is good old-fashioned snobbery, represented in a cultural sense by, on the left, Graham Greene, and on the right, Evelyn Waugh. Secondly, I think there is some resentment at America's success and material affluence and power in the world—it's the same sort of resentment, I daresay, which was felt by young people in the 1940s when all the girls were getting nylon stockings from GIs. Thirdly, I think that there is a European distaste for American enthusiasm and the Americans' tendency to invest everything they do with a sort of moral fervor—and we don't care for that rather Canningite approach to the world now that we can't run the crusades ourselves.

The third, of course, could be regarded as an aspect of the first. Patten might be reluctant to acknowledge this, since he obviously feels the distaste for "moral fervor" and the "Canningite approach" in politics very strongly himself—though he is honest enough with himself to admit that our distaste for American activism springs at least partly from our own passivity.

Personally I think that almost all Western Europeans of our generation feel a degree of schizophrenia about the United States. There can be very few of us who do not admire or feel excited by some aspects of American society and culture, and I suspect there are also very few of us who do not feel at least a twinge of jealousy at America's greater economic dynamism and overwhelmingly greater political power. In my own case, I think I have tended all my life to be critical of American policies partly because America was the "status quo" power, and I wanted to be on the side of change, which I tended to think should and would be for the better. It is ironic to realize now that that optimistic view of history reflects my upbringing in the optimistic world of the "American peace"—and would be regarded by many as a typically American outlook. I think a lot of the pain Americans have experienced in their relations with the rest of the world in the last twenty or thirty years arises precisely from the difficulty they have in recognizing themselves as a "status quo" power: that is not how they are brought up to see themselves, and is certainly not what they feel to be their historical vocation. But it is partly because of that, because we know that Americans share our values and aspirations, that they want people to be free, and believe that the world can be a better place than it is—that we leftish or liberal-inclined Europeans are particularly prone to criticize and demonstrate against American policies that we disapprove of. If "anti-Soviet" demonstrations are generally not as frequent or as well attended as "anti-American" ones, it is essentially because Europeans have lower expectations, both of Soviet behavior in itself and of their own or their governments' ability to influence it, than they do in the case of America.

> MATTHÄUS-MAIER: [During the Vietnam war] many people told us . . . "Why don't you demonstrate against the oppression of personal rights in the Soviet Union?" We did, and everybody knew that is a system without personal freedom, and therefore we loved to live here [in West Germany] and be friends with the American people, and that we live with other values—and it was clear, a system like the Soviet Union, which even theoretically does not have these values, then you can't be so disappointed about this system.

That's one side of it. The other is what Patten calls "snobbery"—the pleasant feeling of persuading yourself that you belong to a superior and more sophisticated culture: a pleasure one is the more prone to indulge in if one needs to compensate for feeling inferior in other respects. And, it is fair to say, we are often encouraged in that by our American friends, members of the East Coast liberal intelligentsia (or perhaps more accurately, in Gingrich's phrase, "the cultural elites on the two coasts"). They pride themselves on their cosmopolitan, European-oriented culture and feel the same mixture of contempt for the provincials who have taken over in Washington, the same concern that those provincials enjoy so much popular support, and the same anxiety about what ill-advised, if not terminal, adventures they may get up to. Twenty years ago it could be embarrassing for a liberal Englishman to encounter American Anglophiles, who were usually staunch conservatives. Not anymore. Today's Europhiles are the liberal critics of neoimperialism, global unilateralism, or whatever; and European writers who echo those criticisms are welcome in the pages of the *New York Review of Books,* or for that matter the *Los Angeles Times.*

> MATTHÄUS-MAIER: The conservatives in this country [West Germany] want to blame the Social Democratic party for the so-called anti-American movement, but there isn't one problem where we as the Social Democratic party [do not] see very important movements, or even parties and groups, in America to thinking exactly the same as we do. For example, about Nicaragua: when I was together with a friend

of mine, a Republican congressman, we discussed Nicaragua and my husband and I told him our position, that we do not agree [with U.S. policy], and as we finished he said, "Oh, you speak like the churches in my country!"

Patten recalls that when growing up he felt for the United States "certainly a good deal of admiration, and a bit of envy because, after all, to use the rather overworked Harold Macmillan metaphor, we regarded ourselves as Greece and looked with a certain amount of mild contempt at what Rome was up to."

Macmillan identified Greece with Great Britain, but the metaphor is equally if not better applicable to Europe as a whole. Ancient Greece, we were taught at school, was where humanity made its great intellectual and cultural breakthrough. But the Greeks, perhaps just because they were so intelligent and individualistic, were too quarrelsome to found a stable political order. The torch was passed on to the Romans, who had great military and administrative skills, but perhaps were not quite so subtle and imaginative. They incorporated Greece into their empire but adopted its culture, and employed Greeks in privileged positions as tutors, physicians, and advisers. Eventually, of course, after several centuries of Pax Romana, the empire split—and the half of it that lasted for another thousand years was the eastern, Greek-speaking half with its capital at Constantinople.

Probably few of today's Europeans are thinking that far ahead. But many of them, especially in the political elite, do like to think of Americans as rather crude, unimaginative people—well-meaning, useful to have around, good at keeping out the barbarians, refreshingly vigorous and self-confident, but badly in need of good advice, too obsessive in their quest for wealth and power, above all too unsubtle and obvious in the way they go about it. According to Pierre Lellouche, America is "a profoundly ahistorical society: they are not interested in history, nor are they interested in the rest of the world. Historically we have been different, and we still have this interest in the rest of the world. We should preserve that, and we should try to establish a different kind of model."

This sense of having greater historical depth than the Americans is something the European elite shares with those of some other cultures. The same criticism of American attitudes was voiced by Jorge Castañeda of Mexico, when I put to him the American argument that the Latin American debt problem is the result of mistaken economic policies pursued by Latin American governments.

CASTAÑEDA: Americans do not know history, they don't read it, they're not interested in it, they don't like it, and so they disregard it completely. . . . Nobody created these enormous state-owned sectors of the economies and these enormous Latin American welfare states out of ideological conviction. . . . What happened is that this is the result of thirty, forty, fifty years of economic development, of stimulation, of a necessity to deal politically with certain problems—of all sorts of contradictions which now the Americans want us to forget, as if all of that did not exist and the world began on January 20, 1981, when Ronald Reagan was inaugurated president of the United States. It's not true, and consequently it's not going to work. In addition to which we have the problem of what is going to happen on January 20, 1989, when Ronald Reagan no longer is president of the United States and when most likely, as often happens in the United States, the next administration will not think that the previous administration's ideas are the best in the world.

When I remarked to Pierre Lellouche that most Americans would be surprised to be told they had no sense of history, and that all the American politicians we interviewed had peppered their replies with references to the American Revolution, Washington, Jefferson, the Monroe Doctrine, etc., he almost exploded with contempt.

LELLOUCHE: It's a totally parochial kind of history—*c'est tout!* The only history they are interested in is their own, and it's all two hundred years, that's all. The rest of history, whether it's Indian or Chinese or European, is sort of belonging to another planet. That's why they cannot understand countries that are as important as India. If you take a policy like U.S. policy in the subcontinent, in India, it's the most stupid policy you can dream of: they are allied with a conservative Islamic dictatorship, Pakistan, against the biggest democracy of the world, with 800 million people—admittedly not the nicest country, lots of faults in it and so on, but, I mean, any good-sense policy would say, "Right, look, if I'm a superpower I'm going to be allied with the Indians rather than the Paks"—right? I mean, you would do that if you were doing *realpolitik.* And why can't they have a decent relationship with the Indians? . . . Because they cannot accept from the Indians, first of all that they are very rich people in culture and tradition, and then very proud people, and they cannot accept to deal with them on equal terms. For them it's a question of how many dollars per capita—very much as in a dinner party in the U.S. the whole question revolves round how much taxes you pay, how much you make, and if you don't make a certain amount, you don't belong to certain strata of society and you are, in fact, excluded from a great deal in America.

Now what America allows you to do is to make that kind of money, whereas in Europe it's much harder to actually become rich. In America you can still do that, but look toward the future: do I want my children to be educated in a country where the only kind of value is American history, and the dollar? Forget it.

Not many Europeans would speak quite so candidly in public—and few even in private could articulate their views with quite the same panache, just as few Americans could quite match the unscripted eloquence of Newt Gingrich or Pat Schroeder. But it would be unwise for people on either side to assume that the feelings so expressed are not real, or that they are unrepresentative. They are not, perhaps, to be taken as the speaker's final and considered judgment. But they come from the gut, and that may be more important.

West Germans may in general be a little more reticent about giving lessons to the United States in matters of civilization and political *savoir-faire* (though Helmut Schmidt, at least, has long since overcome any such inhibitions), but they do feel entitled to treat Americans quite condescendingly in matters of economics. "We don't need Milton Friedman," says Matthias Wissmann with a laugh.

WISSMANN: We have the ideas of Ludwig Erhard,* and our own European way. That means we have to learn from America, but they have also to learn from us; and if you take the economic performance, I don't think that we are worse in 1986 than our American friends are. That means I am still fascinated about the country, about the way of living, but I know that there are aspects of life—take Social Security—which I don't want to transport completely to our country.

While Wissmann remembers being enthusiastically pro-American in his youth and has clearly become more critical since, Karsten Voigt, who was very anti-American in the sixties, now describes himself as "a learned Atlanticist," meaning that he has learned to appreciate the importance of cooperation with the United States, "especially in the security field." But when I asked him whether his general feeling about the U.S. had become warmer he thought not.

*West German economics minister, 1949–63, and "father of the economic miracle"; chancellor, 1963–66. Already in the late fifties Erhard annoyed Americans (including secretary of the treasury Robert Anderson) by lecturing them on "how to overcome the problems of the American economy"! See Roger Morgan, *The United States and West Germany, 1945–1973* (London: Oxford University Press and Royal Institute of International Affairs, 1974), pp. 80 and 93.

VOIGT: Not warmer, but I would say cooler. At that time it was very warm, but in a negative sense. . . . 1974 was the first time when I ever went to the United States, and at that time I had already a lot of experience not only in Western Europe but also Eastern Europe. . . . I was one of the first who had contacts to the East, but one of the last ones in this political scene who had contacts to the West—not to Western Europe, I mean now to the United States. And my relationship was very conflictual to the United States. But step by step I learned that there are some people in the United States, even in the administration, who have similar views as I have; and that even if I want to make détente with the East, I don't want them [the Russians] to define the conditions of common security by unilateral power, and so I need to balance them in one way or the other by our relationship with the United States.

That's what I call a more rational relationship with the United States, but I wouldn't call it emotionally too warm: it's a case of interest. I have a warm feeling—personal relationship—with many persons, and I think this country [the United States] is an exciting one, but the United States was never my ideal of a society.

Older West Germans, Voigt explains, felt "that the United States brought them democracy."

VOIGT: [But] I was brought up in a democratic Germany. When I became sixteen, seventeen, eighteen, we *had* democracy in Germany, and my relationship with the United States was that they were less social-minded than we were, and that on the question of peace and war they were more going in the direction of atomic weapons, and that in the Third World—which was a very emotional question for me, as for most people in my age group on the left—they were suppressing countries . . . directly or indirectly, and this led me to situations where I compared them, in certain occasions, to the behavior of the Soviet Union in Eastern Europe. . . .

[Today, having got to know America at first hand,] what is really impressive in American society is their capability of frank discussion, and their capability to give rights to every individual subject—in certain aspects of civil rights they are better developed than our society. On certain other aspects of their democratic life—corruption, importance of money, importance of big business, a lack of industrial democracy and social justice—our democracies in Western Europe mostly are better. So on certain values of democratic society I share their values —sometimes I even look up to them—and on certain other aspects even of democratic values, social justice, industrial democracy, I think they can learn from us. And in power politics, I think we have to maintain our relationship with them.

Such is the complex background of European feelings about the United States against which the European reaction to Ronald Reagan has to be seen. A poll taken in Britain in February 1986 found that, although two-thirds of those asked said they liked Americans, over half did not trust Reagan's judgment and thought America was at least as big a threat to peace as Russia. Those who said their confidence in the U.S. as a world power had decreased outnumbered easily those who said it had increased. In December 1985—nearly a year before the Reykjavik summit and the Irangate revelations—Reagan was thought "trustworthy" by only 40 percent of Britons sampled. He did a little better in West Germany (52 percent), France (56 percent), and Italy (61 percent)—but the same poll showed that 47 percent of Italians were prepared to trust Mikhail Gorbachev. As many as 14 percent of the West Germans (and 10 percent of the Italians) thought Gorbachev trustworthy and Reagan not.[3]

Among the politicians, Chris Patten said it was "interesting" how quickly America had "bounced back" after the "excessive gloom and insularity" of the Carter years.

PATTEN: For the rest of the world we're all happier and the United States are best served when they find a *via media* between the moralizing overconfidence and self-righteousness on the one hand and the pessimistic insularity on the other.

He clearly felt that the "bouncing back" had gone well beyond this golden mean, and dismissed any suggestion that the America of the 1980s could be compared with that of our youth in the 1950s.

PATTEN: I don't myself think that one invasion of Grenada or one bombing raid in Libya, or any amount of enthusiastic exuberant verbiage, actually transforms the realities about the limitations on any nation's power in the world today. . . . I think American might has been used in a successful and beneficial way on a number of occasions—I think it *was* in the 1940s. I think it also needs to be used constructively and with a degree of restraint, and I think the greater the moral fervor the less likely it is to be very constructive and restrained.

Volker Rühe complained of the lack of continuity in American foreign policy—in this respect it seemed, paradoxically, that the Reagan experience had been a continuation of the Carter experience—but suggested that Reagan had not turned out to be as bad as he first looked.

> RÜHE: It happened the same way again. I mean, in the beginning Reagan said in arms control he would do everything the other way round—forget about SALT II and things like that, and no summits, or not much interest in summits. But in practice there was good cooperation—especially after there was a change of government here*—and good consultations, and apart from some of the topical problems we have now† I think the president has also moved into the middle and made in many fields a cautious and pragmatic policy, quite different from some of the rhetoric that was used in the first election campaign.

Rühe would probably agree with the *Economist*'s interpretation of the opinion polls, that "Europeans have never woken up to the fact—as Americans did in 1979 and 1980—that Mr. Reagan is actually a warm, vague, and rather sentimental old gentleman. This has prevented them from noticing that his foreign-policy actions, as distinct from his words, have been cautious, modest in scale, and fairly conservative." But this seems too reassuring. As the same article pointed out, nearly three-quarters of Americans approved of the bombing of Libya, while nearly two-thirds of Western Europeans condemned it. American support for Reagan was surely based on something more than warmth, vagueness, or sentimentality, and it was that something which by and large, rightly or wrongly, made Europeans uneasy—though it is now fashionable for European politicians to admit that the Libyan affair might have been avoided, in the sense that the Americans might not have felt obliged to resort to military action if the Europeans had agreed sooner on political or economic sanctions against Libya. Rühe even wondered aloud (echoing Abrams's concern that European decision-making was governed by the "lowest common denominator"), "if it's right, for instance, for countries like Great Britain and Germany to hide behind communiqués that are done by twelve countries. When it comes to essential questions we cannot hide behind these communiqués, but the countries which carry most weight politically, militarily, economically, have to come to an agreement with the United States on major world issues."

Another European criticism of the Reagan administration—ironic

*Helmut Kohl replaced Helmut Schmidt as chancellor in September 1982.
†This interview was recorded in June 1986.

in view of the constant American demands that Europe take a greater share of responsibility within the alliance—is that, in Irmgard Adam-Schwaetzer's phrase, it treats Europe like "a small kid you have to take by the hand." In her view the "discussions" or "difficulties" between Germany and the United States arise from the "growing self-confidence of the Europeans" and their demand "to look at us really as a partner and not as a vassal. . . . We are always confronted with the word 'anti-Americanism,' " she says. "It's not really anti-Americanism, but it's our demand to be treated as a partner." Neil Kinnock, while indignantly denying that he has ever, either in Britain or elsewhere in Europe, "either in the general public or amongst politicians of any party, caught any whiff of a mood of neutralism," warns Americans.

> KINNOCK: [They must understand] that the failure to accept every jot and tittle and every movement and degree and nuance of American policy in every respect is not in any sense evidence of a desire to break off relationships: it's free people acting like free people, and at base, of course, that is the foundation of our alliance. Now the moment that we have to act in a deferential form—and I don't think anybody's asked us to, but if that should ever become current—then the pressures really would be on, and they couldn't benefit anybody at all, not on this side of the Atlantic, nor the other side of the Atlantic.

Is there, in fact, much neutralism in Western Europe today? Josef Joffe summarizes some opinion poll findings that bear on the subject in West Germany.

> JOFFE: First, pro-American feelings have always been strong in this country: those who feel that they essentially like the Americans are well above 50 percent in the opinion polls. Second, there is no visible increase in pro-Soviet feelings. Third, the real significant change over the past five to ten years is that those people who say we must be equally cooperative with the Americans and the Russians have increased rather rapidly. Now, is this neutralism? I don't think so. Is it something which has loosened the emotional ties of the West Germans to the United States? I would say yes, in a cautious way, and it reflects the feeling of a generation on the front line, which is dependent on a foreign protector, and therefore would like to be on good terms with its primary opponent, which will decrease insecurity, and also decrease dependence on the protector.

And with this has gone a revival of specifically German patriotism.

> JOFFE: None of those things that are part of the normal upbringing for a French, British, or American child took place here—I mean patriotism, the flag, national rituals, etc. Those had been so heavily discredited in the past, and the state we had here in West Germany, the Federal Republic, was, according to the official lore, destined to disappear anyway for the sake of a single unified Germany. . . . And I think what we're witnessing now is also a search for national symbols, a search for national identity. So the Greens, the "peace movement," etc., is all part of a reaction to that emotional and symbolic void that was left here after the war. . . .
>
> I think that nationalism, if you want to call it that, is very different from "traditional" nationalism in Germany. It's almost escapist. It's like "Stop the world, I want to get off" . . . It's not "Deutschland Über Alles," it's "Leave us alone! . . . Why can't we be like everybody else? Why can't we get rid of those superpowers? Why can't we push them back? Why can't we just opt out of world politics and live happily ever after?"

The French attitude, as already noted, is different. Ronald Reagan could hardly hope for a better press anywhere than he got from the Gaullist leader Jacques Toubon, who stressed his happiness at Reagan's election "because I felt that the American people were happy, because Reagan corresponds, from my point of view, exactly at the moment to the spirit of America, and for me, liking America, I was very happy with the American people's happiness," going on to give a positive verdict on Reagan's leadership of the Western Alliance and even to assert, unfashionably, that Europe had benefited from Reagan's economic policies.

What is it that makes the French more pro-American, or less anti-American, than other Western Europeans in the 1980s? Pierre Lellouche, whose condescending attitude to American culture has already been noted, suggests it is partly because France has regained confidence in her own culture.

> LELLOUCHE: You know, there is a rebellion against American cultural symbols which is characteristic of some parts of the right and some parts of the left. It's still there but it's dying, because people understand that we have a very strong cultural base in this country, that nothing is going to threaten it. We have a very good cinema and good music, etc., television very alive—so what's the problem? So we can import

Disney World right outside Paris, and we reconcile it with national culture and there is no problem there, because there is a limit to Americanization and . . . there is no inferiority complex.

But more important, probably, is the fact that de Gaulle cured France of its *political* inferiority complex.

LELLOUCHE: I think we've had our crisis over anti-Americanism and we've rebelled, we've got our independence. . . . We got American troops out. There's a very strong feeling of autonomy, and a capacity to deal with the threat alone, and with our lives. Also there has been a shifting perception of American strength: it used to be thought, especially during Vietnam and before Vietnam, that America was over-powerful, and that was dangerous. Today, quite frankly, nobody really has that feeling, and it's more the feeling of dealing with somebody nearly equal. There is no such gap as there used to be in the past, so there is no need to rebel.

Christine Ockrent spells out de Gaulle's achievement.

OCKRENT: We are all Gaullists, you see, we've all become Gaullists . . . I think it is the French nuclear defense system, the French civil nuclear industry. Nuclear power, French independence—these are magic words and magic ideas which everybody in France agrees about, whatever their political labels.

She recalls that public opinion was by no means unanimous, at the time, in support of de Gaulle's removal of France from the NATO military command in 1966, but adds that "no one in his right mind would put that into question again."

Jacques Toubon alsc suggests that France is better able to act in defense of Western interests outside the NATO area—for instance, by her military intervention to thwart a Libyan takeover in Chad, or the Kolwezi expediton in 1978 (when French troops suppressed an Angolan-backed leftist insurrection in southern Zaire)—because "we can self-determine more than other European countries like Britain or Germany. . . . We are not part of the military organization [of NATO], but we are part of the Alliance."

Elliott Abrams acknowledges this, and draws a very interesting conclusion from it.

ABRAMS: Look at France: I mean, the country that withdrew from NATO, and that has its own nuclear force, ends up being the country that in a way is most involved around the world, most willing to use force around the world, with a foreign policy that, oddly enough, is most like ours. So you could make an argument, I think, that the reduction of this kind of American [military] presence might not necessarily mean that the relationship would degenerate. It might actually be healthier. It hasn't hurt in France, and you could argue that it's helped.

Toubon, too, was attracted by the suggestion, which I put to him, that other European countries might become better allies for the United States if they followed France's example and pulled out of NATO's military command.

TOUBON: That's a very interesting question, you know, and that's why I feel that the decision of General de Gaulle in 1966 could be perhaps one of the best decisions for the Western alliance since World War II. That's a question we can ask.

But Lellouche also has a warning.

LELLOUCHE: [Be wary of] the semi-Gaullism that you find elsewhere in Europe, which is not Gaullism carried to its logical conclusion of having one's own weapons and one's own autonomy and defense—which I would share, you know: as a European there's nothing more that I would have okayed than a Europe capable of defending itself together, and it can—but these people are semi-Gaullists in the sense that they are anti-American and rather pro-Soviet, but they don't want to carry the consequence in terms of being able to defend themselves.

But, I asked Pierre Lellouche, wouldn't it be good for Europe if we could have a further dose of Gaullism, this time applied to other European countries like Britain and Germany, where one could imagine political leaders coming out for increased defense spending and nuclear weapons but also for greater independence from the U.S. and possibly for the removal of American troops and weapons from their territory?

LELLOUCHE: I don't think that's how you should say it, because if you say it this way you are going to get yourself a huge problem. First of all you are going to precipitate the withdrawal of America, which you don't want to do. Second of all you are going to present what you are doing as an anti-American, anti-Alliance thing, and therefore it's not going to work—certainly not in Germany, where if you present a

European effort as an anti-American effort it is going to freeze all the establishment, which is still very strong.

Maurice Couve de Murville, who was de Gaulle's foreign minister at the time of the French withdrawal, agrees that—because of the question of nuclear weapons—the French solution "can't be applied to all countries, especially to Germany." And Josef Joffe, too, accepts it as axiomatic that the Germans "can't have their own nuclear weapons like the French" and therefore "it's very hard for me to see how they could decrease their dependence [on the U.S.] without falling into the arms of somebody else."

THE FUTURE

So what is to be done?

GINGRICH: Something the Europeans need to think through is, do they want to be part of a worldwide alliance of freedom, and contain the Soviet empire, or do they want to become Finland? Now those who want to become Finland just need to understand that if one morning Russia decides to invade Germany, like it decided to invade Afghanistan, if we're not there we may not come. Because you can make a very good twenty-first-century argument that the United States can play the role of Britain in the nineteenth century: we can be in splendid isolation, we can be a worldwide trading partner, we can be the hi-tech country of the planet—and we don't need to have half a million people in Europe to do that.

While this warning is addressed to Europeans in general, other Americans are more specific about *which* Europeans they see pushing things toward this conclusion.

BIDEN: The Germans have their Greens, you have your Labour party now, that has seemed to me to become more radicalized than it ever was. . . . If Labour were to get into power, the conclusion is that we should have nuclear weapons out of England, and I imagine there would be reconsideration of our position in NATO before it was all over—your position in NATO.

Richard Perle doubts "that any British Labour party will be elected on that platform."

PERLE: But if it were to come to pass, and if we were instructed to leave the United Kingdom—even though we're there by agreement, and by a series of agreements that have helped to protect the peace for a good many years—we would obviously have no choice but to leave. But I find it a bit presumptuous for the Labour party to say at the same time that they would remain faithful members of the North Atlantic Alliance. This is, after all, an alliance in which the United States has pledged to come to the defense of the other members, including the United Kingdom, with nuclear weapons if necessary. And it seems to me hardly fair for a British government to ask the people of Kansas or Minnesota or Louisiana to risk a nuclear war in defense of the United Kingdom, while they're throwing us out of the United Kingdom. So I'm not sure that Mr. Kinnock has thought through carefully the implications of the solidarity of an alliance in which one side breaks with the agreed-upon defense strategy and defense structure. And, in fact, I think in practice the Labour party would moderate its views, and would discover in office that it's not as easy as all that.

Needless to say, Neil Kinnock insists firmly that this time Labour will carry out its defense policy—not only phasing out Britain's independent nuclear deterrent but requesting the removal of American nuclear weapons from Britain as well.

KINNOCK: Of course that doesn't just mean nuclear disarmament. It means doing our job within the North Atlantic Treaty Organization, within the Alliance. And I take heed of the recommendation of Field Marshal Lord Carver, who said last year, and has said it repeatedly before and since: let us discharge ourselves from this delusion of nuclear grandeur and do the job that we're good at doing. And that job at which we're good is sustaining guard on the Central Front [i.e., in Germany] and looking after our naval obligations in the North Atlantic, and seeing that we've got an air force which is effective for the purpose of preventing danger to our country and to neighboring democracies.

Now that's in the nature of our commitment. Some of the criticisms, indeed I think a great many of the criticisms which come from the United States, come from people who have a preconception about the nature of the Alliance which is not really based on its foundations. The Alliance was conceived, indeed constitutionally established, as a partnership of equals, which although different—very different in terms of economic and military power—were nevertheless regarded as having the status of participants, whose views and contributions combine to put the democracies together for the defense of democracy.

This feeling that behind American criticisms of Europe's performance lies a determination to keep Europe in a subordinate role in NATO is by no means confined to the British Labour party.

LELLOUCHE: [The Americans] don't like to go through the cumbersome process of an alliance and so on, and [have] a very ambivalent attitude vis-à-vis the Europeans: they would like the Europeans to, as they say, "get their act together" and pick up the defense cost and establish their own autonomy, political and military; at the same time they are not ready to live with the consequences of that. They are not at all ready to live with Europeans who would say, "No, I disagree with the policy in the Middle East, I disagree with the policy in Central America, I disagree with the nuclear policy, and we propose x, y, or z." Now, of course, they are getting the worst of both worlds.

VOIGT: Very often Americans now, especially in this administration, understand transatlantic alliance as an element where they go and we follow. And then afterward they are frustrated that we don't follow. . . . And what I fear in the American policy is not that they are impatient with us, but that they don't understand that times are changing—that I have to respect that they are getting more American and less European, and that at the same time the same procedure is going on in Europe: we are also becoming more European.

As for the threat that the Americans might pull their troops out if Europeans do not accept their leadership, Voigt says that he thinks the Americans should stay.

VOIGT: I think it's in the European interest that they stay here; I think it's *their* interest. If the Americans would act against their interest, then I would regret it. But I would not capitulate, only to live up to their expectation. For an alliance cannot be maintained stable if both sides are trying to pressure one another. Certain pressures might be impossible to avoid, but I think pressures of that type would not work anymore. . . . If the Americans more or less want to leave NATO . . . we as Europeans couldn't do anything about it. I would regret it. I would try to argue against it. But to use this type of pressure to change the behavior of the others, this would not work. I think it will only have a negative effect.

We are, as Voigt says, clearly "now living in a period of suppressed frustration on both sides." Richard Perle professes to be not terribly worried.

PERLE: I think it's a kind of marriage which will have its rocky moments, but divorce would be so much worse than continuing, I think it's unlikely that that will happen. I don't see anyone rushing to switch sides just because there are differences within the family—and the differences are not terribly fundamental.

JOFFE: [But] we have to distinguish between coolly calculated interests and what you might call "national psychology." Coolly calculated interests tell the Europeans, "You can't do it without the United States," and coolly calculated interests tell the Americans, "You'd be foolish to yield the single most important strategic, economic, and demographic area in the world to Soviet domination." . . . But on the other hand we are all democracies . . . and democracies have attitudes, beliefs, feelings, and an alliance of democracies is an alliance of electoral majorities. If there are too many people on either side who are beginning to question the *realpolitik* benefits of the Alliance, and if there is too much psychology and ill-feeling and fear and resentment coming in, then the best-laid, coolly calculated political scheme may go awry.

This is a fear echoed by Richard Burt, from his privileged observation post in the U.S. embassy in Bonn.

BURT: I think there's a process of mutual resentment under way between Europe and the United States. I think there's a feeling in the United States that the Europeans are just too weak. The Americans find it difficult to understand how, say, the European Community, with its 300 million or so people and combined gross national products which exceed that of the United States, can't do more to protect themselves and to play a larger role on the world stage. In Europe I think there's a sense that the United States is just too strong—that the United States is not taking the concerns of its key allies into account, that the United States is more apt to act unilaterally now than it was before: this was the argument that you heard with the strike against Libya. And so I think there is this process of mutual resentment which feeds one another. What I think is the greatest threat to the European-American relationship is this action-reaction process of American unilateralism and European parochialism.

In other words, while there may be very few people on either side who actually want to break up the Alliance, we could arrive at that result through a chain of reciprocally misinterpreted actions, reactions, and overreactions, especially if, as happened in the Libyan crisis, politicians have to respond to—or, particularly in the case of opposition leaders, seek to exploit—popular feeling aroused in opposite directions on opposite sides of the Atlantic. It could turn out that, while both sides want the Alliance to continue, each side reads into it things that are unacceptable to the other. Thus Perle warns Kinnock not to expect that he can remain in NATO if U.S. nuclear bases are expelled from Britain, while Kinnock and Voigt warn the Americans not to expect the Alliance to continue if the price is unquestioning European acceptance of U.S. leadership. David Owen, at least, takes the American warnings seriously.

> OWEN: We can't always rely that the United States is moored into European security. I believe they will be, if we conduct ourselves prudently; they will continue to remain, but this whole idea of "kick 'em in the teeth" and tell them to clear out of bases in this country [Britain] without that having a tremendous impact back in the United States is naive—politically wholly, totally naive—and, in that sense, there *is* a special relationship: being kicked in the teeth by any other European country might be tolerable, being kicked in the teeth by the U.K., by the Brits, will strike most Americans as "No, that'll be a kick not in the teeth but in the groin," and they'll react and they'll say, "Hold it!"; and it's absurd to believe that it won't happen.

A whole series of events, from the Yom Kippur War in October 1973 to Reagan's failure to consult his allies before the Reykjavik summit, suggest that there is no longer the instinctive pulling together of the Alliance in a crisis that there was in Kennedy's time. It may be true, as Joe Biden (who would clearly have liked his compatriots to see him as the new Kennedy) says, that "an enlightened leader, quite frankly, in the United States could go a long way to making things better." The trouble is that many Europeans' belief in the capacity of the American political system to produce such a leader has been badly eroded, and in their present state of mind they might not be that easy to convince that any new leader who does emerge really is enlightened.

> OWEN: The best type of American presidency is one which is, if you like, a bit halfway between the Carter role, which was too apparent to

the American people as being led by the nose by others, and the Reagan style of leadership, which is leading everybody else by the nose. There's a happy mix between the two, and we haven't yet had an American president who's got it right.

Certainly an essential feature of enlightenment in this context would have to be an ability to understand and respond to the point made by Karsten Voigt when he says, "I never asked for American leadership: I always ask for common leadership of Europeans and Americans." (It was Kennedy, after all, who first called for a balanced and interdependent "Atlantic Community" whose "two pillars" would be the United States and a united Europe.) But that, of course, means that Europe would have to produce equally "enlightened" leaders at the same time. (Even Kennedy's seemingly enlightened proposal encountered suspicion and hostility from de Gaulle, who denounced it as a mask for American domination of Europe, and effectively torpedoed it in 1963 by vetoing British entry into the European Community.) The chances of achieving that combination in any given four- to five-year period are probably no better, and perhaps worse, than those of hitting the jackpot with any given pull of the handle on a slot machine.

It is clearly, in the abstract, desirable that Western Europe should have its own independent defense system. As we have seen, the Americans did not expect, when they signed the North Atlantic Treaty, to have to keep troops in Europe indefinitely; and many of the new generation of American politicians clearly feel quite strongly that Europe should by now be capable of defending itself, at least in conventional terms, without American help. They are probably right, too, in thinking that prolonged and excessive dependence has bred an unhealthy state of mind in too many Western Europeans, leaving them prone to escapist nationalism, pacifism, "moral equivalence" heresy (if not actual neutralism), or just a preference for grumbling about American policy rather than facing up to real political choices. The counter-example of France, which by an intense effort has cured itself of at least the more extreme and visible forms of dependence and has emerged remarkably free of all these symptoms, is certainly telling.

So why not, as Jacques Toubon advocates, "an independent European defense, based on cooperation between Britain, Germany, and France essentially, and . . . independent from the American system," but ready to stand "beside the American people and American soldiers . . . on some battlefield," as French, Italian, and British soldiers did in the Multinational Force in Lebanon in 1982–84? Because, says

Josef Joffe, the free ride that the Europeans are having at America's expense is simply too comfortable for them seriously to contemplate giving it up.

> JOFFE: [It leaves them free] to nourish their economic miracles, to engage in détente diplomacy, to take certain risks in terms of diplomacy, because they know Big Brother is there to ensure them against the unpleasant consequences of their credulity: that's a wonderful world to live in!

But perhaps it does not have to be all or nothing. The Europeans do not need to aim for *complete* independence, which even France, after all, does not claim to have achieved. If they could only take some significant steps in the direction of greater self-reliance, they would do much both to raise their own self-respect and to win back the respect of their American allies. One obvious step—and one that Neil Kinnock ought surely to consider as an alternative to scrapping Britain's independent nuclear capability—would be for Britain and France, Western Europe's two nuclear powers, to start cooperating in matters of nuclear defense. Pierre Lellouche certainly thinks so.

> LELLOUCHE: Absolutely, that's one of the things that I hope for in the long term. I think that we've missed a great deal of opportunity in both countries because of very silly psychological reflexes that date back to Nelson and Napoleon, but eventually we'll get there.

But the possibility of involving the West Germans in the development of a European nuclear deterrent seems very remote indeed. Even such a keen advocate of European independence as Karsten Voigt is firmly against it. Though he has no objection to Franco-British cooperation, and says he would like the French to inform the Germans "about their planning procedures, especially . . . those systems which are targeted on German soil," he thinks the inclusion of West Germany in a European nuclear power "would have a destabilizing effect in Europe, and between East and West." And he accepts that the implication of this, given the need for military power to balance that of the Soviet Union, is, for the foreseeable future, a degree of continued dependence on the United States.

Pierre Lellouche agrees that "we will always need America to deter the Soviets," just as "in a sense we will always need the Chinese to be there, too, simply because of geography and size and so on: we need multiple points of problem for the Soviets to deter them." But he is convinced that the specific U.S. nuclear commitment to Europe (insofar as it ever existed) is being gradually withdrawn.

LELLOUCHE: I think that's a long-term trend that started about the time of Sputnik. You know: the moment the U.S. became vulnerable to a Soviet nuclear strike for the first time in history, they had to qualify their nuclear commitment. De Gaulle left [NATO] and we built our nuclear force. NATO went into a long convoluted debate about "flexible response" and so on, and we had the Pershing affair . . . and now we have SDI, which is another attempt by the US to sort of shelter themselves against that Soviet nuclear threat. Clearly now in the U.S. there is a consensus amongst the liberals and conservatives, an alliance of the bishops and the generals, of McNamara and Kissinger, that you can no longer defend Europe by threatening the first use of nuclear weapons, unless you can convince the Soviets that you will use very short-range weapons that will be used in Europe and not reach Soviet territory.

So I think there is not much we can do except between the French and the British to spend as much money as necessary to stay in the nuclear business, and gradually turn these national weapons into the armory of a European deterrent, so that the Soviets know very well that if they take on Germany, they also take on the two European neighbors of Germany.

On the conventional side, Lellouche argues, we have to slow down the American withdrawal as much as possible because American soldiers in central Europe constitute "a guarantee of doubt [in the minds of] the Soviet leadership: they would have to deal immediately with the other superpower and there is no quick grabbing of Europe without getting into a war with the United States." But he takes into account the demographic changes now occurring in the United States (with the rapidly increasing proportion of blacks, Hispanics, and Asians).

LELLOUCHE: It's just not reasonable for any European to believe that he will have this same contingent of American troops at the end of the century. We have to try and slow it down, but make sure we can cope—and that means find a way in which we can integrate the conventional power, which is not at all irrelevant, which exists among the main European countries. Let me tell you, as Schmidt once said in 1984 in the Bundestag, if you could get thirty German and French divisions together—fifteen each—well armed, and behind that you would have the French and British nuclear weapons, the Soviets would think twice. The Soviets are not risk-takers. When they invade Czechoslovakia, which has no great military history, frankly, they go in with half a million troops.

Lellouche believes, therefore, that it is possible for Europe to combine its own (Anglo-French) nuclear deterrent with a credible forward defense based on "modern, well-equipped conventional forces." It is, he says, essentially a question of political leadership, and of "rationalizing defense costs."

LELLOUCHE: Because if we continue trying to pay for national weapons that are different, like seven types of tank, fifteen types of artillery, six or seven types of aircraft, we are going to die, because no one in Europe can afford those costs any longer: so we have to spread the industrial and the financial burden among the Europeans equally. If we can't do that, let's be clear, within ten years there won't be a European defense industry and we will be buying American and Japanese stuff—and at least the industry knows that if the governments don't.

The West German Bundeswehr would remain, as it is now, "the cornerstone of conventional defense in Europe," though needing to be supplemented with increased French conventional forces "in part because they [the Germans] don't make babies anymore and therefore their demographic curve is gravely in danger"; and once the Germans have overcome their "very great allergy to any kind of nuclear weapon"—which Lellouche believes "with good political management" they can—"nothing prevents a coordination of decision-making at least on tactical nuclear weapons between France and Germany, and Germany and the U.K., or perhaps the three together. After all, earlier this year [1986] there was an agreement signed between France and Germany which is really a mini-revolution in French strategic policy, giving the Germans right of consultation in time of crisis on the usability of French tactical nuclear weapons."

All this, he insists, must not be presented as something anti-American but explained as "a necessary reinforcement of the structure because the NATO Alliance is not going to survive the present imbalance between the American contribution and the European contribution and the feeling on both sides." Such ideas seem to have a lot in common with those of Karsten Voigt, who declares himself "strongly in favor of a European pillar." Voigt thinks we must accept that the age of unquestioning trust between Europe and the U.S.

based on "common feeling, common experience from every aspect of political life and culture, which was typical of the direct postwar period," has come to an end.

> VOIGT: But this doesn't necessarily mean the end of the Alliance. We have to find a new basis for the Alliance, and I think the new basis can only be the basis of more solid pillars on both sides, where we respect common views and different views.

Matthias Wissmann feels much the same about the political structure of the Alliance as Lellouche does about its military structure. It "was always," he says, "my conviction that we need more European imput," but if European input has been limited so far that is the fault of the Europeans, not the Americans, "because normally the Europeans do not really know what they want together."

> WISSMANN: We Europeans now as a Community of Twelve must strengthen our own common will and integrate our own foreign policy and security policy, and my understanding is, many people in America —even political leaders—would like to see us as being stronger, and so in that context not the Americans are the obstacles: we are our own.

Christine Ockrent feels much the same.

> OCKRENT: I think it's up to Europe to stand for itself. It's forty years now that Europe has tended to rely on America. Whenever something goes wrong it's America's fault, and whenever something goes right it should go better. I think it's a terrible guilt of the previous generation, and probably ours, that somehow Europe as such has not been built more carefully. I think that the real failure is there, and I think it's Europeans' responsibility, not Americans'. I think that those who created the idea of a united Europe were not able to give it an emotional impact strong enough to bring a real popular mood, and I think it's again up to the Europeans to face their own fate. I think we should let go that sort of attitude of always being dependent upon somebody else, when we feel that we're weak and unprotected and "What's going to happen to us?" Well, my God, let's stand for ourselves!

But in order to do that, she adds, Europe has got somehow to be made more inspiring for ordinary Europeans; and she thinks there is more chance of persuading young people that Europe is an ideal they should wholeheartedly work for "than what our politicians and our media tend to think."

> OCKRENT: I think that in that very, very generous generation—it's a generation which follows the heart rather than the mind—I think that somehow Europe is something they relate to, and I think there is a need in that generation for ideals. . . . I think Europe can very well be one of those, as long as it doesn't have the face or the shape of those buildings in Brussels. I think there is room for a European crusade of a kind, and I am using that word on purpose. I think it's a generation —and that's something that Geldof has understood very well—it's a generation that needs to give and it needs to feel that there is something to do in the world, that things are not just there never to change or just to sit by and enjoy.

She agrees that young people are more inspired by causes like Ethiopia or the Vietnamese boat people than by an abstract ideal of Europe, but feels that the one could be harnessed to the other, "if politicians could do things in such a way that Europe would give to Ethiopia, that European democracies as a set of values would actually be fighting against evil, whatever evil is."

Volker Rühe can remember being inspired by the signing of the Treaty of Rome when he was fifteen, at a time when the young idealists of the day were burning down customs barriers between European countries. Matthias Wissmann can remember being inspired, at the age of thirteen or fourteen, when those "two old charismatic leaders," Charles de Gaulle and Konrad Adenauer, came together to the baroque castle in his home town of Ludwigsburg and spoke about Europe. He began then to understand, he says, "that Germany alone, France alone, Britain alone will not really be able to solve their problems," and ten years later, by then already active in politics, he was one of thousands of young people marching down Whitehall to celebrate Britain's entry into the European Community, "and even for a young German who has not been afflicted in the period which was such a catastrophe for the world, before 1945, it was really touching that we all were singing the national anthems of Britain, of Germany, of France, of Italy." So Europe has been able to inspire young people in the past. Perhaps it can do so again, as Chris Patten suggests.

> PATTEN: [If] the problems Europe is seen to be wrestling with seem to most members of the public to be serious problems, like unemploy-

> ment, like protectionism, like our economies, like—though I realize one can't do it through the European Community—our strategic position in the world, between the United States and the Soviet Union.

It clearly is a problem that the European Community, which has come to represent "Europe" politically in most people's consciousness, is formally an economic community, lacking the competence to deal with defense, since defense is the crucial area in which Europe needs to be seen to exist if it is to be taken seriously politically whether by its own inhabitants, its American allies, or its potential adversaries. Lord Gladwyn may be right in saying, "It would have been far better if Europe had been built up on the Treaty of Brussels"—the Treaty of Economic, Social and Cultural Collaboration and Collective Self-Defence signed in March 1948 by Britain, France, and the Benelux countries and later expanded to form the Western European Union (WEU), including West Germany and Italy. Instead it was built on the Coal and Steel Community, founded in 1950, and then, after the abortive attempt to build a European army in the early fifties, on the European Economic Community founded by the Treaty of Rome in 1957—all initiatives from which Britain held aloof, so that when she belatedly changed her mind and sought admission in the early sixties, de Gaulle was able to delay her entry by ten years. Britain eventually entered a Community whose structures and practices had developed without her, and therefore took little account of her own particular needs and interests; and at a time when the great postwar economic expansion was just ending and the time of troubles beginning. The result was that much of the Community's energy, throughout the seventies and early eighties, was consumed in dispiriting wrangles between Britain and her partners, and all too often its institutions have seemed neither inspiring nor relevant to the main problems that European societies now have to confront.

The member states have developed, in parallel to the institutions of the Community itself, reasonably efficient machinery for political cooperation, and have also institutionalized thrice-yearly meetings of their political leaders under the name of the "European Council." They obviously do talk about security in a general sense, but one that falls far short of even beginning to formulate a common defense policy. This is partly because one member, Ireland, is outside NATO and formally neutral; partly because another member, Denmark, objects on principle to any extension of the Community's competence that might infringe national sovereignty; and partly because a third member, Greece, although a member of NATO, has since 1981 had a government that is temperamentally much closer to the Non-Aligned Movement.

Therefore the serious work on European defense cooperation has to go on elsewhere—either in WEU, which has been partially revived for the purpose, or within NATO itself, or through various ad hoc meetings. But it seems to go on rather slowly. The main emphasis so far has been on rationalizing defense costs through joint procurement, which everyone agrees is desirable in principle but which proves very difficult in practice, because each country's armed forces have their own particular preferences, and each country's arms manufacturers have their own vested interests.

But behind the technical difficulties, it seems to me, lies a crucial psychological difficulty. Human beings notoriously only unite when faced with a common threat or a common adversary. The main military threat to Western Europe is agreed to come from the Soviet bloc. As long as that threat appears to be adequately contained by NATO in its present form, there is no strong incentive for Europeans to develop any new European response to it; and whenever the threat does look more menacing than usual, its effect is rather to reinforce the Europeans' sense of dependence on the United States, making some of them cling closer to Washington's skirts while others wish they could opt out of the East-West conflict altogether.

In the postwar world it is hardly possible to define a European identity except by emphasizing whatever makes Europe different from America. Otherwise one would be describing a "Western" identity. Consequently it is only insofar as European interests are seen to be different from those of America, and either inadequately protected or positively endangered by America, that the political will to organize an effective European defense system is likely to emerge. It may be true *now* that the Atlantic Alliance has broader and deeper support in France than in other Western European countries, because of the relative independence France's defense policies have given her. But de Gaulle was only able to get his countrymen to make the effort involved in achieving that independence by convincing them they were threatened by American hegemony. And it is surely significant that in this survey the two most articulate exponents of the need for a "European pillar" in NATO, even if both of them rationalize it as a way of strengthening the Alliance, are Karsten Voigt, who admits that he started from a strongly anti-American position, and Pierre Lellouche, who is convinced that the Americans cannot be relied on to defend Europe in the long term. There is a manifest contradiction, indeed, between Lellouche's exposition of the reasons why it is unreasonable to expect the Americans to stay and his insistence that one must not give this as the reason for seeking to strengthen Europe's contribution to the Alliance. Of course he is right that by giving that reason one will upset a lot of people and thereby possibly stiffen opposition to what one is proposing. But if one does not give that reason, how will one obtain the positive support that is needed for an arduous program of military expenditure, which will take resources away from social services, in a peace-loving and compassionate society? Why should people bother?

I tend, therefore, to agree with Josef Joffe that people will not bother, unless or until they have to. That means that Europeans and Americans are likely to go on irritating each other more and more, and that before very long people like Pat Schroeder will be in power in the United States—people who say, very reasonably, "If the Europeans won't bother, why should we?"—and they will take public and visible steps to reduce American expenditure on European defense in various ways, including the withdrawal of at least a part of the American forces. (The troops might be needed, after all, in Central America, or even—who knows?—in southern Africa.) That is the moment when Europeans might wake up to the need to do something about their own defense, in quite a hurry.

Why does Irmgard Adam-Schwaetzer think it "absolutely necessary" that in the next few years European peoples and leaders get away from their "egoistic standpoint, and come together more and formulate our common standpoint"?

> ADAM-SCHWAETZER: Because we are confronted with Russia and the satellites around. We are living in Europe, in a place which is quite different from the United States. The United States is far away from Russia. So Western European countries have to get together to formulate their own standpoint, because otherwise they might not be taken seriously enough to secure their own security.

The reasoning may sound a little abstract at present. But if the American troops were on their way home, it would suddenly begin to sound extremely concrete.

CHAPTER 10

The Japanese Surplus

GEJDENSON: As we grew up, in the early years, as we were just starting to be conscious of what happened in the world, the power of Europe and Asia seemed to be very minimal, trying to pull themselves up after the war. Our economic contact with, for instance, Japan in my town was at the Lincoln Store, and there was this one little counter of kind of second-rate toys that were stamped out of old American Coke cans, or whatever they made it out of—and that's what Japan meant to you: it was cheap, it didn't last very well. They tried to hide where it came from: they even made a city named "USA," so that they could stamp "USA" on it and hide "Japan." Now, American companies may be doing the same—trying to hide the "USA" and get "Japan" up there.

The appearance of quality Japanese goods on the American market in the 1960s was, as we saw in chapter 6, one of the things that first made both Sam Gejdenson and Larry Pressler aware that parts of American industry were relatively inefficient and ill equipped to face foreign competition. Since then it has become an American habit, in George Will's words, to "compare our commercial and technological competence more to the Japanese than to the Europeans. Ask the average American what they get from Europe: they'll say cheese and whisky. What do you get from Japan? You get cameras and calculators and cars and motorcycles, and all our television sets—that sort of thing."

Not surprisingly, Japanese competition has also cut a swathe through European industry, even that of West Germany, the other great industrial and commercial success story of the postwar era. It has led, Irmgard Adam-Schwaetzer says, "to the fact that in Germany certain types of industry just don't exist anymore. There is no photo apparatus that is sold in Germany still built in Germany"—an extraordinary thought when I remember that in my childhood it went without saying that only German cameras were any good.

> ADAM-SCHWAETZER: [It happened] somewhere in the seventies: I do not know exactly when. But there have been two reasons for it. First of all, labor became very expensive, and for these cameras you have to do a lot of handwork; and, secondly, the Japanese developed cameras far more sophisticated than the German cameras—or the other way round, the sophisticated German cameras have been very expensive and nobody could buy them, so the Japanese came with their sophisticated cheap cameras on the market, and really everything had to be given up. Even light cameras: they are still of very high value for professionals, but even these light cameras are not built anymore in Germany.

Japan's economic strength has become proverbial. Japanese foreign trade constitutes 10 percent of all international trade, and Japan now has a current account surplus comparable to that of the United States after World War II. As we noticed at the end of chapter 7, Hajime Shinohara, one of the leaders of the new generation of Japanese bankers, feels that his country is now "the equal partner of the United States" in economic and political decision-making. Japan's political role, he adds, "depends on the expectation or perception of the rest of the countries rather than Japan. In other words, say what sort of function you expect to be implemented by Japan, and I should say we are ready to assume that role."

And he confirmed that this would include an increased contribution to the defense of the Free World. Japanese politicians, however, are much more cautious on this point. Koichi Kato, as defense minister, asserted that "in our deep mind we feel that a country without big military power cannot be a strong political power, and we are determined not to become a big military power." Kaoru Yosano agreed that Japan had no intention of developing a military capability to back its international influence, but thought it would find ways of using its economic strength to "contribute to the stability and peace of the world," for instance, by shouldering more of the burden of aid to developing countries.

Under article 9 of the Constitution with which General Douglas MacArthur endowed the Japanese in 1946:

> War, as a sovereign right of the nation and the threat or use of force, is forever renounced as a means of settling disputes with other nations. The maintenance of land, sea and air forces, as well as other war

> potential, will never be authorized. The right of belligerency of the State will not be recognized.[1]

By 1950, however, the Americans had changed their minds, being now more preoccupied with the danger of Communism than with a possible revival of Japanese militarism. They began pressing Japan to rearm, and in 1951, as well as a treaty of peace, they signed a Security Treaty, which stated, "Japan will itself increasingly assume responsibility for its own defense against direct or indirect aggression, always avoiding any armament which could be an offensive threat or serve other than to promote peace and security."[2] Thus Japan does, in fact, have armed forces, officially designated "self-defense forces." Even so, the Japanese have consistently remained more faithful to the spirit of MacArthur's original injunction than their American allies would have wished. Even in 1986 their defense budget remained approximately 1 percent of GNP (it was 0.999 percent in 1985, compared with 7 percent in the United States), and "Japan continues for most purposes to be defenseless against outside aggressors."[3] Not surprisingly, Japan incurs, even more strongly than Western Europe, the accusation of taking a "free ride" at America's expense, or competing commercially with the United States while sheltering behind an American security umbrella. The point is made gently by Joe Biden . . .

> BIDEN: Japan has to step up to its role in the world in a way different than it's now performing—and I realize that's not an easy thing to do. The United States imposed a constitution upon Japan that they now use as a shield against further participation in their responsibilities in the Pacific Basin.

. . . and more bluntly, in her inimitable style, by Pat Schroeder.

> SCHROEDER: Japan is probably the worst. I mean, they never spend more than 1 percent, and in 1978 they gave us a pledge they were going to at least take care of the thousand-mile perimeter around Japan. Well, we got the pledge and I don't think it's been taken care of.

George Will confirms that his generation probably feels even more dissatisfied with Japan's defense contribution than with that of Europe.

> WILL: I mean, it's one thing for a steelworker to lose his job to Japanese imports of steel and cars, but then to say, "One reason they're

so good at that is that they're not bearing their fair share, they're getting a free ride in the defense of the free world!"

And Europeans themselves take up the cry. Laurent Fabius's reaction to the Japanese is "to understand them, and at the same time to say, 'Well, now, because you are powerful, you have to share the burden of the world.' "

George Will thinks there's a good chance of getting them to do so, as "the trauma of their war experience fades, and the Japanese moderate, centrist population understands the degree to which they have, as the great commercial power of the Pacific Basin, special responsibilities." It might even, he suggests, "become a point of national pride." Indeed, Koichi Kato's national pride did seem to be nettled by the criticism "that we are a free rider in the defense field." Japan, he asserted, had "the eighth largest military equipment in the world," though he admitted that "in comparison with our GNP it's not big money." But he stuck to his guns—or rather, to the lack of them.

KATO: When we were defeated we made up our mind that we were not going to be a military power again. If we would, that would give certain irritation to the neighboring countries, especially China and Korea. So we decided to become a big nation without military power. It's a very innovative experiment. Up to today we think we have succeeded.

But Yoshi Komori, a journalist with sensitive political antennae, not bound by the constraints of the official line, thought otherwise.

KOMORI: I think Japan will be assuming more burden with regard to security, reluctantly as it might be. I think we are coming to realize gradually that in order to maintain this free economy, free market, we have to pay a price for maintaining it, to some extent.

And the price would be "increasing our defense budget." He did not think, however, that Japan would be willing to post forces outside the country, "even in twenty years." As for nuclear weapons, they, of course, are generally assumed to be unthinkable for Japan. But Kaoru Yosano left us with this thought.

YOSANO: Japan has reached the level in terms of technology that we will be able to produce a nuclear explosion device any time—perhaps within a year or two. . . . My feeling is that we should not have nuclear weapons. But the younger generation: I'm not certain whether they have any resistance to nuclear weapons or not. I fear that.

Since these interviews were conducted, a long-awaited five-year defense plan, prepared by the Japanese Defense Agency under Kato's direction before he left the government in July 1986, has been published, setting 1990 as the target date by which Japan should be able to defend its own strategic sea lanes and air space. The 1 percent ceiling on defense expenditure has, apparently, been removed. One suspects, however, that well before some Americans are satisfied that Japan is really bearing its due share of "the burden," others will be worrying about the implications of Japanese rearmament.

Less controversial is the argument that Japan should do more to help the Third World.

GEJDENSON: Japan is a country with half our population, half our gross national product—their per capita gross national product is equal to ours—they've got to take a more important role. If they're not going to do it in defense, then we'd like to see them do more of it in foreign assistance to many of the developing countries.

This point seems to be readily conceded by the new generation of Japanese leaders.

KATO: As I said, we are not going to be a political power, but we have to contribute to the development of the developing countries, especially in Asia. So we have to increase our foreign aid to these kinds of countries—not only in terms of money we are going to spend but also we have to give them certain assistance in terms of the managerial expertise we have, like how to organize farmers, in terms of land reform or irrigation reforms, how to make vocational training for carpenters or engineers—this sort of thing.

Komori agreed: Japan should give more assistance to Asian countries, and less of it should be tied to the purchase of Japanese products.

Yosano, too, thought Japan was "ready to transfer more of our conventional technology to developing countries," and that government aid to these countries would increase, but he drew attention to a difficulty: while Japan as a nation is a massive net creditor, its government is heavily in debt (to its own citizens). The private sector leaders, while endorsing the principle, seemed more cautious and uncertain about how exactly it should be done. Masao Katsurauma thought Japan should transfer advanced technology and know-how to less-developed countries, to help them catch up, but Hitoshi Seki demurred. "Our technology," he said, "is something of a strategic asset, and if you are practical, I don't think we can easily give them up." He would prefer Japan to provide "the software in human management," to which he felt there would be less political resistance.

Hajime Shinohara, the banker, felt Japan's contribution to solving the "so-called debt problem or accumulated debt problem of Third World countries" should be to concentrate on exporting capital to Southeast Asia and the Pacific, while "the United States or New York market should cope with the Latin American countries" and "the London or European market should be ready to serve the African and Eastern European countries." And Iwao Koga, the oilman, urged his colleagues to "think about the Japanese future," which he saw as threatened by the rapid industrialization of Korea, Taiwan, and Southeast Asia. The overall impression I took away from these interviews was that Japan is very far from the frame of mind where one could hope for a really imaginative assistance program on the scale that her financial surplus, and the plight of the Third World countries, would justify. Even Kato's suggestion of a kind of Japanese peace corps—showing Thai farmers how to irrigate their land, or organizing vocational training for Filipino carpenters—was somehow not easy to believe in. It may be just prejudice on my part, but I did not sense in Japan a great burgeoning of the Marshall or Kennedy spirit.

The shadow of World War II still lies over Japan's relations with the rest of the world. Whereas Marshall and Kennedy spoke as leaders of a victorious power, confident that the world was waiting for their leadership, the Japanese, whatever their economic victories, are dogged by the memory of the disastrous outcome of their last bid for political hegemony. While it is now fashionable again for Japanese to emphasize their interest in and concern for their Asian neighbors, and even to present themselves as spokesmen for Asia in the councils of the West, there is little sign of any eagerness among those neighbors for a revival of the Co-Prosperity Sphere. As Yoshi Komori, a shrewd and somewhat detached observer of his compatriots' foibles, says, "Japanese media often talk about Asia and say that Japan is in a much better position to be able to comprehend how the other Asians would think and feel than British or Americans, but I'm not so sure about that."

What is it that makes the Japanese such formidable commercial competitors? Part of it, undoubtedly, is simply their willingness, for whatever combination of cultural, historical, and psychological reasons, to work extremely hard without demanding constant pay raises.

BERNSTEIN: Japan is the only country I know of which has lower unit labor costs in manufacturing, meaning their export industries, than they had ten years ago. In the United States we're up 35 or 36 percent. The average for the European countries is around 45 percent.

Kaoru Yosano, indeed, regards his compatriots as a nation of workaholics, psychologically incapable of leaving their offices after working hours (though this, he says, is changing in the generations after his own). But he does not think this is the cause of the trade imbalance.

YOSANO: The trade imbalance is caused by two factors, I think. One is that we produce good-quality goods, which meet with your standards and with your taste. And at the same time . . . for instance, take London: I was surprised to find that in London there are about fourteen thousand Japanese people living there.* I don't know what they are doing, but I am sure that they must be selling Japanese goods every day. But we don't have so many British people stationed in Tokyo. . . . I think we will not be able to find more than a hundred English tradesmen stationed in Tokyo trying to sell your goods to Japan.

In other words the Japanese are much more determined about exporting to other countries than other countries are about exporting to Japan. The whole Japanese economic structure, according to Yoshi Komori, "has been that we depend on export—export, export, export!—and we don't think about noneconomic aspects of our dealings with other countries. . . . We were led to believe that as long as we keep producing fine products, as long as we keep exporting them as much as we can to the other countries, to the needs of the people in the other countries, everything would be fine for Japan."

But increasingly people in other countries, instead of being grateful for having their needs met, are concerned about the danger to their own industries. And the danger may be greatest for Europe, which, according to Laurent Fabius, has not yet felt the full impact of the Japanese export strategy, which has been concentrated on the United States and Asia: "But it can come a time where U.S. of A. will say no. It will come a time when Asian countries will compete with Japan. . . . And at that time, if it goes this way, it will be very, very dangerous for us."

Many of Japan's competitors, particularly in the U.S., accuse the Japanese of "dumping"—that is, of targeting a particular sector of

*According to the Japanese embassy 13,127 in 1985.

another country's market and going all out to destroy the competition, even by selling at a loss. The most common reaction of Japanese businessmen to this accusation is to assert that it simply reflects the frustration of Europeans or Americans who find the Japanese moving into a market where they are not used to competition—recently, for instance, in the provision of financial services. But some, like Hitoshi Seki of the Japan Productivity Center, are willing to admit that the criticism is true.

> SEKI: I think we have not been quite aware of the consequence of our targeting special markets and exporting quite suddenly and drastically, and I think we should change this kind of strategy; and I think most Japanese companies are becoming aware of the result, and that those kinds of things could backfire. So I think from now on Japanese companies will be a little bit more considerate, so to say.

All Japanese seem to accept that their trade surplus has become an international problem and must somehow be reduced—"But, please," added Yosano, "do not expect that we can do it in two months or three months: it takes at least three or five years." In fact, the immediate effect of the steep rise in the value of the yen after the "Plaza Hotel" meeting of finance ministers in September 1985 was to further increase the surplus measured in money, whether dollars or yen (because the dollar value of Japan's exports went up, while the yen value of her imports went down—the well-known "J curve" effect of currency changes, amplified in this case by further savings in energy consumption as well as the declining oil price). Thus by 1988 the surplus was running at $7 billion to $8 billion *per month,* but in volume it had begun to fall during 1986. The rapidity and magnitude of the parity change—from 250 yen to the dollar in May 1985 to 160 yen exactly a year later—came as a severe shock to many Japanese manufacturers, and made them sharply aware of the vulnerability of an industry too exclusively oriented toward exports.

The Mitsuboshi Cutlery Company, at Seki City in central Japan, is a good example. It produces exclusively for the export market, accounting for nearly 40 percent of Japan's cutlery exports—and selling 65 percent of its products in the United States. Its manager, Mr. Ito, told me how he had struggled throughout the winter of 1985–86 to keep pace with the rising yen by cutting his prices, but was unable to do so, and lost 20 percent of his business in six months. Up to May 1986 no workers had actually been laid off, but the price cuts had been shared out between Mitsuboshi and its suppliers (subcontractors)—

reducing earnings throughout the region—and, he claimed, the company was now producing at a loss. The trouble was, he said, that at the new exchange rate he could no longer compete with neighboring countries like Korea and Taiwan, whose currencies are pegged to the dollar and which, moreover, he complained, benefit in both the United States and Europe from the "generalized system of preferences" (GSP) accorded to underdeveloped countries, whereas his products are subject to import duties. He felt the only answer was to set up "new factories outside Japan in underdeveloped countries, like Indonesia or some Caribbean countries," but such a move would be resisted by his fellow directors, who belonged to the older generation (the president of the company being his father-in-law) and felt an overriding loyalty to the local employees and subcontractors. His own view was that these should be encouraged to change their jobs, or find a market for their goods inside Japan, as he himself was now trying to do: it was preferable, he now felt, to rely on the domestic market for at least 50 percent of one's sales. But he was also aiming to get into the import business, and turn his offices in New York and London, hitherto exclusively concerned with sales, into buying agencies for goods to sell in the Japanese market.

In any case there is clearly a limited future in Japan for such low-tech industries, as Kaoru Yosano said he was trying to convince the bureaucrats of Japan's powerful Ministry of International Trade and Industry.

> YOSANO: Those areas of industry which are competing with Korea, Taiwan, Hong Kong and Singapore—they are losing and they are sure to lose. For instance, take toys, textiles, spoons and knives and forks: they are sure to lose because their technology is so simple, they [the other countries named] can do the same thing very easily; and although we cannot abandon them at this instant, in the long range we have to retreat from those areas of industry which are competing with the "NICs"—newly industrialized countries.

It was generally accepted that Japanese industry, built up since the war partly by very large injections of foreign capital, must now reinvest its profits in the countries that it exports to, as well as in the developing countries that constitute its most threatening competition.

But all these changes are being accepted only slowly and reluctantly. The dominance of the older generation in Mitsuboshi's board of directors is typical of "most of Japanese economic society," according to Yutaka Ohtaka, who as managing director of Showa Shell is one of the rare exceptions. "For example, the average age of the leaders of the Japanese Management Association is already about sixty-eight, or even say as much as seventy," and the head of it is over eighty. Only when his own, more internationalized generation takes over, Ohtaka feels, should we expect "a lot of changes." But, he warns, resistance to change comes also from the state bureaucracy, since government offices still play an important role in economic planning, and in his view young bureaucrats are liable to be just as bad as old bureaucrats.

The government of Yasuhiro Nakasone (1982–87) was committed to shifting the Japanese economy away from its export orientation, and this was the main purpose of the recommendations of the Maekawa Report, produced with much fanfare in the spring of 1986.

> SEKI: The problem is the resistance of internal industry and some other people who resist changing that nature of Japan, and so it's a tug of war in a way, I think. If the administration has a strong-enough kind of leadership, the change will be possible, and if not, Japan will remain as a country of export-oriented economy, which in turn may not allow them to reduce the surplus, in which case the roof of the U.S. Congress will blow up and protectionist measures will be passed—which is quite an unfortunate thing.

But the kind of change required is twofold. The reorientation of Japanese industry away from exports is only half the story, the other half being Japan's openness to imports. Of course, the Japanese like to suggest, as we saw Yosano doing just now, that the low level of Japanese imports is all the fault of the importers for not trying hard enough. Oil and whisky, two products that Japan does import, were both cited to me as not having taken advantage of the rise in the yen to make their prices more attractive to the Japanese consumer. In the case of oil, this reflects the pricing policy of the Japanese importing companies, rather than the oil exporters. Iwao Koga, who represents one of these companies, was clearly on the defensive when I interviewed him jointly with three other businessmen representing different sectors of the economy, who accused the oil companies of operating a price ring and pocketing the difference between the yen price and the reduced dollar price. He said it was a matter of waiting a few months for the fall in prices to work through the stocking and refining process, and pointed out that his industry was legally obliged to keep three months' supply in stock. He might have added that it would by no means obviously be in Japan's national interest to encourage a rapid expansion of oil imports, given the experience of the 1970s.

As for whisky, Hajime Shinohara, who proclaimed his strong affection for this product, said that he had asked his local distributor why the price of imported alcoholic drinks did not go down when the yen went up after September 1985, "and the answer was simple, that the original producer wouldn't agree with the decrease of the prices, to keep with the image of the quality of their product: it's not the Japanese fault, it's rather the exporter's fault, I should say." If this is correct, the producers have presumably calculated, with or without the benefit of market research, that those Japanese who drink imported whisky in preference to the local product do so essentially out of snobbery and are positively attracted by the fact that it is more expensive, and that even at a lower price there is not much chance of capturing a mass market. The *Economist** suggests two reasons why this might be so:

> In Japanese pop-and-mom shops, pop gets goods on sale-or-return from associates of big groups that employed him before retirement. He then does not stock imports which he cannot return if no sale; so it hardly matters that foolish foreign exporters to Japan (those wrongly told they should always operate exclusively through a Japanese intermediary) often get an agent who obeys big groups by telling pop not to sell competing foreign goods save at prohibitive margins.

In fact Yosano certainly could find "more than a hundred English tradesmen stationed in Tokyo" and trying to sell British goods to Japan if he looked for them (well over a hundred British *companies* belong to the British Chamber of Commerce in Tokyo, and they must have an average of at least two expatriate representatives each) and quite a few thousand other foreigners as well. Japan is far too important a market to be ignored, especially in times when business is difficult in most other parts of the world. No doubt would-be importers to Japan are not always as imaginative or as well informed as they should be, but you do not have to talk to many of them before you realize that their problems are not all of their own making. Foreign banks, in particular, have the greatest difficulty in getting authorization to set up offices in Tokyo and operate on the financial markets there.

Needless to say, the complaints of European and American business about Japanese protectionism soon find their way into the mouths of politicians. Irmgard Adam-Schwaetzer in Germany, for instance . . .

*April 26, 1986.

ADAM-SCHWAETZER: There has been, to our opinion, unfair trading by the Japanese. The Japanese still have their specific regulations before they let goods into Japan, which means it is really a market closed in itself and you have difficulties to get in, whereas our markets are open.

. . . and, of course, Pat Schroeder in the USA.

SCHROEDER: I want to tell you, in Colorado we are competitive in beef. We have got the most competitive packing house in beef in the world. . . . We also have a lot of environmentalists in Colorado. They are out picketing the Japanese, saying, "Why are you killing whales?" The Japanese ambassador says to me, "We are killing whales because we have to have protein. You know this is outrageous. Tell your people: this is unfair, this is wrong." And I said, "It is going to be hard for me to explain, because we have protein in Colorado and you won't let it in, and they're not whales—and we'll send you all you want, and you won't let it in." So it's not that we are not competitive. We are bloody competitive. We can't get in, and yet the others come the other way. I believe in reciprocal free trade, but also you have to have an even playing field, and that's what's very hard.

One Japanese at least who admits that many of these criticisms are well founded is Yoshi Komori, and he is not inclined to let his countrymen get away with attributing this closedness to the peculiarities of Japanese "culture." In the first place, he says, culture by definition is always changing.

KOMORI: I think we have a tendency to overemphasize the Japanese unique culture. I would respond to that by saying that the culture of every country is unique, and somehow we grew up thinking that Japan is more unique, more different, special compared to other countries, and that has been used to justify this closed nature, with barriers of various sorts to imports. . . .

And again, there are some instances of the closedness of the Japanese market that one can hardly attribute to the Japanese culture, when you have a double standard: for instance, they require that the importers of American or foreign pharmaceutical products would have to submit a lot more data, or would have to go through a lot more experiments to prove that this would be harmless . . . and for the reason that Japanese and Americans, or Japanese and Europeans, are "physiologically different"! I don't think that can be justified by cultural uniqueness: that's just an excuse to protect the Japanese domestic pharmaceutical manufacturers.

The Japanese have also, of course, been adept at developing home-made products to compete with imports—Japanese whisky being a classic example. And though in the case of such luxury articles the genuine import may retain a certain cachet (one sees the odd Rolls-Royce, for instance, and some other expensive makes of foreign cars, in the streets of Tokyo), the general Japanese view remains that "made in Japan" is best, and exhortations from the prime minister to "buy foreign" have done little to change this.

YOSANO: In July 1985 Mr. Nakasone has proposed that every Japanese should buy foreign goods at least of $100 value. So I went home and conferred with my wife and two boys, that "I am going to buy you anything, but which must be of foreign origin, and the maximum or minimum buying is $100," and I gave them three days to think about that. But their conclusion is that there are no attractive goods of foreign origin, but they rather want straight cash!

One area of the Japanese economy many foreigners would particularly like to see open up is the capital market, so that the yen could take on a greater role as an international currency. Here, too, Koichi Kato, as a minister, gave the diplomatic answer.

KATO: Yes, I think the yen is going to be one of the international currencies, with the dollar and the mark. The three currencies are going to be major factors in the international monetary system. For that purpose we have to liberalize the currency market.

Kaoru Yosano also thought that because "the yen is a very strong and stable currency," trade and capital transactions would inevitably shift to it "in the middle-range view." This would mean, he pointed out, that Japan would have to "assume more responsibility" both in managing her domestic economy and in helping to harmonize the growth of the world economy as a whole—an implicit criticism of Japanese policy up to now, but also of the United States, which has clearly not lived up to the responsibility of managing a world currency in this sense.

The view that this was a responsibility Japan could not and should not avoid was shared by the banker Hajime Shinohara: "It's our duty," he said, "because in the Free World the Japanese economy has a share of more than 11 or 12 percent." Among the other businessmen, Masao Katsurauma thought it "could be detrimental to the Japanese economy in the short run" because it would restrict Japan's freedom of action in monetary policy, but in the long run would increase Japan's national security by giving foreigners a stake in her prosperity. Hitoshi Seki thought the yen would not replace the US dollar, which was bound to remain the dominant currency in the international market, but maybe would "grow up to be number two, almost on a par with the deutsche mark," and this would have a "more stable effect on the [international] currency market, if there is a second strong currency rather than [i.e., as an alternative to] the U.S. dollar." However, he felt this process was being held up by the fact that "the yen is not so freely available outside the country," because the Japanese Finance Ministry and the Bank of Japan were not ready to give up control of it. Yutaka Ohtaka agreed that the government was proceeding in this direction slowly and hesitantly, and appeared to be back-pedaling on its decision to introduce a completely free "offshore" money market in Tokyo. He thought this might be an example of the fact that Japan has a "slow decision-making process . . . but once it is agreed at the preparatory stage, then the actual implementation will be quite quick and . . . done quite thoroughly." But the journalist Yoshi Komori, as usual the most skeptical, felt that not only the authorities but the "majority of people" were not ready for this change in Japan's international role: "I think again as a result of this feeling—in a way it's a feeling of insecurity and in a way it's a feeling that Japan is not quite a major country, or major player, or not quite in the major league."

The same feeling of insecurity is thought by some to lie behind another peculiarity of Japanese economic behavior much remarked on by foreigners—and often complained of, since it, too, can be held responsible for Japan's trade surplus—namely, their propensity to save money rather than spend it. Children in Japan, it seems, are told by their parents to save rather than spend—but in what country are they not? The fact that grown-up Japanese actually do it may partly be explained by the relative inadequacy of the Japanese social security system (compared with that in other industrialized countries)—a theory supported by the fact that, according to Tadashi Nakamae, "contractual savings—basically pension fund contributions, life insurance policies, etc." have rapidly increased in the last fifteen years at the expense of household savings. Indeed, in his view, "Japanese households do not have enough savings anymore: that is why in Japan at the present stimulating domestic consumption is very difficult." But he also sees the habit as having a philosophical base.

NAKAMAE: That is a philosophy, I think, based on the very old Japan when the Japanese economy was so poor. That is why we have to work very hard: we have to keep the savings as high as possible. But now I think the younger generation is quite different. We realize, we understand the necessity to work hard, but also we realize the necessity of the youth to spend more.

The "youth" themselves also realize this—perhaps a little too much so, according to Iwao Koga, who speaks for parents the world over.

KOGA: I think of myself as the middle-aged generation—I mean, I'm now just over forty years old—but as far as I can see the younger generation are just interested in only their clothes and their food and their leisure. . . . They know how to enjoy themselves and they know how to use their money for their private things, but they never think about how to stock their own property or something like that. . . . They just want to enjoy the now, not the ten years later or twenty years later.

Provided the younger Japanese do not grow out of these habits, foreign anxiety about Japan should cure itself in time. Meanwhile, another explanation given for the high savings ratio is the scarcity of land in Japan, which makes investment in real estate prohibitively expensive and therefore obliges the Japanese to keep their savings in more liquid form. According to Ohtaka, "It's almost impossible for the third generation to buy land and build a house," and this may be the reason why the Japanese are so famous for living in "rabbit hutches." Certainly the low standard of Japanese housing is an argument constantly advanced by the Japanese to prove that their country is not "really rich"—and no less constantly cited by critics of Japanese economic policy, native and foreign alike, as something on which Japan, since it *is* so rich, could and should be spending more. The contradiction between these two arguments is only apparent. In fact, the one backs up the other, as Iwao Koga shows.

KOGA: Japan is still relatively a poor country compared with the Western countries in terms of the "social stock" [housing, etc.], despite the fact that it has accomplished a high standard as measured by GNP growth ratio and so on. In this aspect I don't think those criticisms coming from Western societies are groundless. Therefore I think Japan should make an effort in expanding domestic demand in order to raise the level of the social stock, as well as the standard of living of the Japanese people.

But, ironically, it is this very "poverty," according to Yoshi Komori, that makes the Japanese feel insecure—and therefore incites them to save rather than spend.

> KOMORI: Just living in Tokyo, commuting to your work in the packed subway or other train, living in a very small, shabby—shabby by the Western standard—apartment, just gives you the feeling that you're not really rich. People talk about Japanese affluence, but where is the affluence? You have to work six days a week. . . . And this feeling is also reinforced by the fact that Japan has always been plagued by major natural disasters—earthquakes and typhoons and all that. So it's going to take a long time until we reach the point where we are free of that fear.
>
> MORTIMER: But you have the money to improve your standard of living, if only you spent it. Why is it that the Japanese insist on saving more than any other country in the world?
>
> KOMORI: I think that also stems from that feeling that you really have to prepare for the unknown, unpredictable future—mainly disaster—and that feeling again is reinforced by the fact that Japan has to depend on imports of raw materials. In other words, economically we cannot survive without depending upon other countries' resources, and this somehow makes Japan essentially fragile, economically fragile—at least in the minds of most of us.

But Tadashi Nakamae believes the rise in the yen, and the consequent difficulties of the export industries, are forcing Japan in the direction of "domestic expansion, especially in the infrastructure investment, including housing," because "if Japan does not take very strong domestic stimulations, the Japanese economy will fall into very sad recession." The Japanese, in fact, seem to be much more willing to listen to (if not to act upon) advice of this kind than the Germans, that other showcase of recovery whose export-led growth seems to proceed from a somewhat similar psychology—what Josef Joffe calls "a mild underconsumption pattern, meaning that our wages all remained a bit lower and grew a little less fast than others, that our prices as a result inflated less rapidly than those of others, which meant that the West German economy could always maintain a competitive edge by being a bit more deflationary than others."

Whatever the explanation, the Japanese habit of saving certainly puts them at the opposite pole to the Americans who have, as Fred Bergsten points out, "a uniquely low rate of savings among the industrial countries."

BERGSTEN: What is particularly discouraging about that is that the American low savings rate has been about the same for a hundred years. We had the same low savings rate even before we had a tax system, let alone the particular kind of tax system we have now. So it's not very encouraging to look to improve our savings rate by changes in our tax system. It is one of the great mysteries why different countries have different rates of savings, but they do seem to be structurally embedded in national economic behavior, and most resistant to policy change. Certainly everything under the sun had been tried here in the United States to raise the rate of savings. It stubbornly resists that. Indeed in the last two years it's been much lower than even the historical norm, despite all the efforts of so-called supply-side economics to raise it.

Not surprisingly, their high savings rate is one thing the Japanese do rather resent being criticized for. Apart from the fact that it is, as Hitoshi Seki says, their own business what they do with their hard-earned money, there is also the point made by Hajime Shinohara.

SHINOHARA: For the sake of the world economy, it's a great important thing, I should suppose, that one country is still keeping a high saving ratio, with a very large size of economy, and is prepared to export capital toward the rest of the world. Since after the first oil crisis happened in 1973 every country is suffering from the shortage of new capital inflow, whereas Japan may be able to export capital for the sake of the rest of the world for years to come.

The fact is that, thanks to their high savings rate, the Japanese are not only able to finance their own government deficit (which as a proportion of GNP is as high as that of the United States) but also to finance that of the United States as well. For once the politician Kaoru Yosano puts the point more bluntly than the banker.

YOSANO: In straightforward words we are actually financing the financial debt of the federal government of the United States. We export about $50 billion to the United States market, which is actually financing their huge financial deficit. And although the United States is blaming us for the huge trade imbalance, I hope that Japan should be modest enough not to try to make our point too clear. But I hope that the United States should be a little *more* modest, to think of their own situation, how not well managed their financial structure is. You know, they are spending more money than can be raised from the financial market of their own country. Now what is happening is that they are using their high interest rate to absorb our capital, which in turn finances their financial deficit. Therefore, on our part we will do our best to reduce the trade imbalance, and their position, to be frank, should be that they will make their best effort to reduce their financial deficit.

Which is the subject of the following chapter . . .

CHAPTER 11

The American Deficit

THE PAPER-DOLLAR STANDARD

The Bretton Woods international monetary system had come to an end on August 15, 1971, when Richard Nixon announced that the dollar was no longer convertible into gold.

Theoretically, the system did not have to have one central, gold-convertible currency. To give the dollar that role, or at least to spell it out, was something of an afterthought: a dotting of the *i* by Harry Dexter White to reassure the New York bankers. The dollar's predominance in 1944 was dictated by the facts—the overwhelming strength of the American economy, its chronic trade surplus, its consequent accumulation of three-quarters of the world's gold supply. During the fifties, and especially the sixties, the costs of running the world (what some call America's "imperial role"), combined with those of the rapid rise in American living standards (what one could perhaps call the "imperial life-style"), and the rise of competitor economies in Europe and Japan had eroded the foundations of that central pillar of the system. First the U.S. gold stock was run down, then America began to suffer from inflation, and all the while the trade surplus was diminishing until, in 1971, it disappeared. In the 1940s the world had desperately needed dollars to buy American goods. By the 1960s the world was awash with dollars and, at the exchange rates as they were then fixed, goods from other sources often seemed better value than American ones. The dollar was no longer an unquestionably safe store of value.

Given that this was the problem, a logical solution might have been for the U.S. government to withdraw the dollar from its central role in the system, fix a new parity for it, and undertake to maintain that parity by buying and selling other currencies as necessary—the obligation accepted by all other countries participating in the system. But this would also have meant subjecting U.S. economic policy to the same discipline as those of other countries—the discipline that requires a government to take account, in managing its domestic affairs, of the effect its decisions will have on the supply of, and demand for, its national currency outside the country.

Nixon did not accept that. He renounced the United States' theoretical obligation to buy and sell gold at a fixed price, but also refused to undertake any obligation to buy and sell foreign currencies at a fixed rate. The U.S. government, in other words, abdicated from any responsibility for deciding the value of the dollar. During a transitional period, between December 1971 and March 1973, this responsibility was effectively undertaken by foreign governments, since they assigned a dollar value to their own currencies and bought and sold dollars as necessary to maintain that value. This system quickly proved untenable.

> POLAK: With the United States no longer the absolutely trustworthy and reliable financial center of the world, there was really no hope that the Germans or the Japanese, nor for that matter anybody who wasn't a small country quite clearly in the American circle of interest, would want to fix its currency to the dollar again, and that basis therefore for a fixed rate system that would cover the whole world had disappeared.

So the world moved into the era of floating rates, in which currency values were left to foreign exchange dealers to determine simply by balancing the supply and demand on any given day (except in Europe, where a small-scale "replica," as Polak puts it, of Bretton Woods was developed: the European Monetary System [EMS], in which "Germany took over that role of the totally reliable, conservative, stable, very-low-inflation center, to which other countries like the Netherlands and Belgium, and I would say also France and Italy, were very happy to peg their currencies").

The baby, one might say, had been thrown out with the bath water: the whole world system had been dismantled because the dollar was no longer up to playing a central role that was, on paper, incidental to the system rather than essential to it. One could put it that way—except that the bath water was still there. The dollar, even after it ceased to have a fixed value in relation to anything—after the government that issued it had formally abrogated any responsibility for deciding or maintaining its value—and in spite of the fact that over fifteen years its value has varied much more widely in relation to all the other major currencies than they have varied in relation to each other,[1] nonetheless continued to play a central role. Even in 1986 that role was not really questioned by people like Hajime Shinohara, who deals with the currency markets day by day.

> SHINOHARA: As far as foreign exchange is concerned, the dollar has been the center and is the center still, and will be the center for the foreseeable future. We say, "Buying marks, selling sterling, selling the French franc, buying the Swiss franc," and so forth, and on these occasions we never say, "Against what?" because we are quite sure all the time: against the United States dollar.

And the same is true of ordinary people when they travel abroad, as Kazuhiko Nishi, the Japanese software wizard, points out: "I don't think the yen is a strong currency. I mean, I can't use Japanese yen in London to buy anything. [But] I can use U.S. dollars to buy things in London, if it's a tourist shop."

But why has the world continued to make such extensive use of a currency of uncertain value, which on the face of it is only the national currency of one nation, rather than agreeing on an international unit?

> FABIUS: [Because] the world is dominated not by gentle feelings but by relations of strength, and it was in the interest of the leading countries, and especially of the United States, to have their own currency as the international one. For years and years—it's a tradition of French governments, whatever they are—we have asked for reform of the international monetary system, with an international unit . . . and tried to build some sort of zones—the Japanese zone, the European zone, and the American zone—and with an important part played by the Third World countries. But to date we did not succeed, because of the fact that we are not, probably, strong enough.

The theory is an attractive one—especially to people like me who find politics more interesting than economics and have a sneaking predisposition to see the world in Humpty-Dumpty's terms: "Who is to be master? *That's* the question!" But one must beware of swallowing it too easily or in any simplistic form. *Before* 1971 the Americans clearly did bring heavy political pressure to bear on their allies to go on keeping dollars in their reserves; to abstain from exercising their nominal right to exchange dollars for gold at the official price; and to support the dollar in the gold and foreign exchange markets. *Since* then it seems difficult, if not impossible, to prove that they have in any sense forced the rest of the world to go on using dollars. All one can really say is that after Nixon's coup they participated only halfheartedly in the attempt to reach an agreed reform of the international monetary system, undertaken by a "Committee of Twenty" set up by the IMF.

A large majority both of professional economists and of policymakers in other governments at that time favored a system of fixed-but-flexible exchange rates in which the special drawing right (SDR)* would gradually assume the role of the central yardstick of value.[2] But George Shultz, as U.S. secretary of the Treasury from 1972 to 1974, and even more openly his successor William Simon, insisted on allowing the dollar to float freely and so blocked any effective reform.[3] In the words of a recent specialist study of the subject, "The most powerful country, the United States, gradually lost interest in international monetary reform and saw, instead, many benefits for itself in the way in which the system was developing 'spontaneously' "[4]—that is, in the direction of a *de facto* dollar standard, sometimes called the "paper-dollar standard" to distinguish it from the gold-backed dollar standard of 1944–71.

Clearly, whatever its economic troubles and mismanagement, the United States was still far too important in the world political and economic system for it to be thinkable, even for a moment, that the rest of the world could agree on and implement a new international system without its full participation; or that, in the absence of an agreed international unit, any other national currency could replace the U.S. dollar in international transactions. Whatever the balance or imbalance of its foreign payments, the United States remained in absolute terms much the biggest economy in the world.

> PATTEN: The great dollar is supported by that continental-wide market itself, and I think the Americans can get away with things which an individual European country, or any other country in the world, couldn't get away with. Maybe we could get away with them if we had a European currency.

So the world had to adapt itself to the system of floating rates, which initially pleased the Americans well enough, but came as rather a shock to everyone else. As Yutaka Ohtaka says, "It was just like uncharted water, where no people had experience except those who were already, say, seventy years old or eighty years old at the time of the U.S. decision"—a slight, but only slight, exaggeration. But it turned out to be the Japanese who adapted to it most successfully, and

*The IMF's "paper gold."

so, not surprisingly, they tend to be the readiest to speak up in its defense today.

Tadashi Nakamae thinks the floating system was inevitable, "as far as the international economy is so volatile, especially affected by oil price or international inflations"; and the minister, Koichi Kato, agrees.

> KATO: Even if we had maintained the fixed-rate system, we would have been forced to adjust this fixed rate to the economic fundamentals after a certain time interval. So that requires certain political judgments or international negotiations, and if that kind of political factor was too big, then it would distort the economic factors. So the floating system, with the "invisible hand" to lead this kind of adjustment, would be better.

But, he adds (remembering, perhaps, that this application of Adam Smith's doctrine to the currency markets is no longer quite as fashionable on either side of the Pacific as it was a few years ago): "Of course, too much radical fluctuation would cause lots of trouble to the countries concerned. So a moderate fluctuation system, if we can establish [it] . . . that system would be ideal." Clearly extreme variations of the yen-dollar rate were *not* justified by "economic fundamentals": certainly not the rise of the dollar to 278 yen in 1982; and while the Japanese may have benefited from that in the short term, it can hardly be said to have facilitated their adjustment to whatever much lower rate the economic fundamentals eventually produce. (By April 1988 it was down to 124 yen, and experts were divided into those who thought this was about right, those who thought it an "overshoot" that would soon correct itself, and those who believed the dollar needed to fall even further to restore U.S. competitiveness.)

The experience of the dollar's precipitate fall in the winter of 1985–86 had in any case been quite enough to convince Mr. Ito, the manager of the Mitsuboshi Cutlery Company in Seki City, that "fixed is much better than floating," though his hope that a new fixed rate for the yen might be as low as 180 yen or 200 yen to the dollar was surely forlorn.

Fred Bergsten, whom we met in chapter 6 as a critic of the "incredibly high degree of rigidity that had come to dominate the Bretton Woods system" before 1971, admits now that "the flexible exchange rate system has not been effective."

> BERGSTEN: It has permitted, even induced, constant—even growing—misalignments in currencies, which have had all sorts of distorted

effects, and partly because of that we've had a creeping erosion of the international trading system. . . .

The floating dollar has had a very disruptive effect on the lives of ordinary Americans. In the late 1970s, for example, the sharp decline of the dollar, which was unjustified by underlying economic factors, significantly accelerated our inflation rate and, in turn, required a very tough monetary policy response by the Fed [Federal Reserve Board] in 1979, which began the move to high real interest rates, bankruptcies, severe recession in the early 1980s, and the like—very big effects. Perhaps even more profound was the enormous overvaluation of the dollar that we saw from roughly 1982 through the beginning of 1985. That, by moving our trade into deficit by $150 billion, cost us something like three million jobs and moved the United States into being the world's biggest debtor country, interest on which my children, and probably their children, will be paying: a very heavy price for the next decades.

For much of the period 1982–86, Bergsten explains, "the dollar was overvalued by 40 percent in terms of the underlying price competitiveness of the American economy."

BERGSTEN: That means we were, in essence, taxing all our exports by 40 percent, we were subsidizing imports coming into the country by about 40 per cent—no wonder that we had a $150 billion trade deficit last year [1985] and an enormous outburst of trade protectionism, which was seeking to defend American firms and workers against that currency valuation simply by stopping the goods at the border. . . .

[Of course] currency misalignments can . . . occur under both fixed rates and flexible rates, but the unfortunate history now is that it's worst under flexible rates. The dollar became overvalued by about 20 percent at the end of the Bretton Woods period: we know that because the two devaluations in 1971 and 1973 accumulated to about 20 percent, and that pushed the U.S. back into surplus. This time, under flexible rates, the dollar imbalance probably was in excess of 40 percent at its peak [in 1985]—twice as great as the imbalance that we had under Bretton Woods: much worse under the system that was supposed to obviate the risk of this kind of currency misalignments.

Bergsten, who served in the Carter administration, can now observe all this with detachment, if not relish, from the vantage point of the private Washington think tank he has founded, the Institute for International Economics. Joe Biden and Jack Kemp, though of opposite parties, are serving legislators who have to cope with the pain that these phenomena cause to their constituents. It's been particularly harmful, Biden says, in the chemical, textile, and automobile industries. By the time these interviews were conducted, in May 1986, the dollar had come a long way down again.

BIDEN: [I hope that] we are now going to see some righting of that imbalance. The problem is, though, once a market's lost, unless you in turn are able to get to the point where you undercut the other fellow's position, you may not get the market back. And I think we're going to have to work awful hard to resist the temptation—and so far we've been successful in resisting the temptation—of instituting protective measures.

Jack Kemp, probably the first would-be presidential candidate (and the first former professional footballer) ever to make international monetary reform his hobbyhorse, feels it is "the one thing in the economy that touches everybody's life,"

KEMP: And it's the one thing that has been so destabilized that it has caused such disruptions of trade and commerce and industry, and unemployment, and inflations and deflations, that this fundamental systemic destabilization of how money should work, how it should operate, how it should perform, seems to me to be at issue not only in the United States but all over the world. And it's the one thing that we have failed to address as urgently as I think it should be addressed.

It was, in fact, Europe, more than the United States, that suffered from high unemployment in the first half of the 1980s—and this, too, according to Edward Bernstein, "is probably a consequence of the volatility of exchange rates."

BERNSTEIN: Let me see if I can explain it: the United States kept a very tight monetary policy, it raised interest rates, and itself sustained two recessions very quickly one after another—1980 and 1982—to stop the inflation. It was very successful in that, but as it raised the interest rates and the dollar began to appreciate, in mid-1980, the Europeans also cared about inflation, especially the Germans, and so, as they feared that a depreciation of their currency against the dollar would make prices rise very rapidly . . . their method of defense was to tighten monetary policy in turn. To put it another way, the United States, in its attempt to stop the inflation of the United States, generated

> a flood of policies everywhere duplicating what the United States did, that is to say raising interest rates—but with this difference: in the United States we simultaneously generated a very big budget deficit. The Europeans weren't prepared to do that, and I think this is one reason that in Europe you have so much unemployment.

And so gradually the experts in all three main areas of the industrial capitalist world—Japan, the United States, and Western Europe—have been forced back to the conclusion that animated the founding fathers of Bretton Woods, that—in Fred Bergsten's words—"the exchange market is a prize too important to be left to free forces."

> BERGSTEN: [The exchange markets,] like any markets, reflect all sorts of factors unrelated to the underlying competitiveness of national economies: capital flows, interest differentials, "safe haven" considerations, psychology, expectations about political changes. It's very rational for individual players in the exchange markets to take those factors into account and move the exchange rates accordingly. The problem is, the exchange rate has a job to do: the job of the exchange rate is to equate the competitive positions of national economies, and to leave their trade and current-account positions in a more or less balanced position. The exchange rates cannot do that when they are pulled around by political, psychological, and other vagaries—and so it's an area where, I'm afraid, governments and central banks will consistently have to take a view as to the appropriateness of rates, and take action to avoid exchange rates that get way out of line and create huge economic distortions.

By this point the reader may be wondering why on earth the United States should have persisted for so long with (and even now not really abandoned, though the present secretary of the Treasury, James Baker, is certainly more interventionist in his approach to the exchange rate than was the man he replaced at the beginning of 1985, Donald Regan) a policy that has had such manifestly disastrous results. The answer is, as Fred Bergsten explains, that in the short term it had great advantages.

> BERGSTEN: I'm fond of saying that we now know the miracle of supply-side economics: the miracle is that the foreigners supplied the money, and the flexible exchange-rate system made that possible by providing an attractive means through which foreign investment would

come into the United States and reconcile the massive budget deficit with the pickup in private investment here in 1983 and 1984.

I think that's only a temporary solution to our problems. I think we will get crowding-out of the domestic economy at some point in the future, when the private capital inflow dries up. But it's certainly prolonged the economic expansion the United States has been achieving, and probably was the main vehicle that assured President Reagan's reelection in 1984.

AMERICAN DEBT, WORLD PROBLEM

One might have thought that the floating exchange-rate system, in which the value of each currency is determined purely by the balance of supply and demand, would be the most brutally effective in enforcing "discipline" on national economic policy-makers, since the effects of their decisions are visible day by day in the currency markets. But it doesn't work like that in practice, because the effects are felt by the ordinary trader, not directly by the government itself—as is the case under the fixed-rate system when the government has to be ready to buy in any amount of the national currency that does not find another buyer at the official price (if the currency is "weak"), and to supply any amount of the national currency that may be required by holders of other currencies who do not find a seller at the official price (if the currency is "strong").

Under the floating-rate system the strength of the currency ceases to be a matter of direct financial consequence for the government and becomes instead a political problem: what happens to the currency only matters to the government to the extent that it matters to those on whom the government depends for support. It is likely to be very important to the government of a small country whose economy depends to a very large extent on international trade. It matters much less to the government of a vast country, like the United States, where foreign trade has traditionally represented only a small percentage of the economy as a whole. Although Jack Kemp now says that "it was a big shock both culturally and politically to the United States to think for the first time that the dollar was not going to be as good as gold," he also admits that he doesn't remember what exactly he himself thought about it at the time. George Will is probably nearer the mark when he says that the exchange value of the dollar was *not* an important part of the economic/psychological trauma of the seventies for most Americans, because "the average American doesn't relate to that." If it *had* been important to most Americans, the exchange rate and the balance of payments would surely have been at the center of American political debate throughout the seventies and early eighties, whereas, in fact, it was not until the 1986 mid-term election campaign that the opposition party—the Democrats—began to focus on the foreign trade deficit as a major political issue.

In two respects, the role played by the dollar in the international trading and monetary system was useful to American policy-makers in prolonging this relative indifference of the public to the exchange rate even after (as Gejdenson noted) trade with foreign countries began to affect the lives of large numbers of ordinary Americans in the sixties and seventies.

First, because most foreign trade is priced in dollars, exchange-rate movements tend to have a less direct and immediate effect on the United States than they do on other countries. Suppose, for instance, that the dollar goes up against the pound sterling—or, as it is more likely to be perceived, the pound goes down against the dollar: in Britain the price of imported goods will immediately rise, while the British exporter will at once be receiving more money in pounds for each sale he makes, unless or until he decides to take advantage of this by lowering his dollar prices and trying to capture a larger share of the foreign market; but, unless or until he does that, the price of imported goods in America will remain the same, as will the amount in dollars that the American exporter receives for each sale—unless or until *he* decides to reduce his prices because sales of his goods in Britain are falling off.

Second, the exchange rate itself is not affected by the balance of payments in America in such a straightforward way as it is in other countries. When other countries use their own currency to settle import bills, that currency comes back to them—either to be spent on their products, or to be exchanged at the central bank for gold or other currencies. But because the dollar is still a "reserve currency" —one in which foreign governments and firms like to keep all or part of their monetary reserves—the dollars used to pay for American imports do not all come back to America. This means that the U.S. balance of payments deficit does not automatically have the same effect, either on the exchange value of the dollar abroad, or on its value at home (in the form of inflation), that a deficit on a comparable scale would have on the currency of any other country. When another government spends more money than it is taking in, that money is liable either to cause inflation at home or, if it is spent on imports, to cause a balance of payments crisis and a collapse of the currency. In

America it can be spent on imports and *not* cause a collapse of the currency: the inflation is "exported" to other countries, wherever the dollars end up.

In a free-enterprise society, where the state does not directly control the production and distribution of goods, the government has two main levers with which to influence the behavior of the economy: the tax system ("fiscal policy") and the control of credit and the money supply ("monetary policy"). The latter has much more immediate effects on the exchange rate than the former: if you restrict credit and make money expensive, the higher interest rate attracts money from abroad, pushing up the value of your currency in relation to others; if you make credit easier and interest rates lower than elsewhere, your currency goes down. This limits the extent to which most governments can afford to rely on monetary policy, and obliges them to react to economic trends by manipulating the tax system. In America this is difficult because taxation is controlled by Congress, and the executive (unlike that of Britain and most other democracies in the industrialized world) cannot rely on a disciplined parliamentary majority to endorse its decisions. Consequently American governments have to rely, to a greater extent than most, on monetary policy—which is why it is especially convenient for them not to have to worry too much about the exchange rate.

So while it is not quite fair to suggest that the Americans since 1971 have been deliberately using their political power to force the rest of us to conduct our business in dollars of uncertain worth, it is true that by continuing to use dollars, whatever our own motives, we in the rest of the world have made it easier for the American government to frame its policies without worrying about their effects on the relations between the American economy and those of other countries. But America is not actually immune from the laws of economics. The same causes do in the end produce the same effects there as elsewhere. The "paper dollar standard" simply acts, or has acted, as a cushion that delays these effects, and therefore allows much larger distortions to build up than could otherwise occur. Thus in the 1970s, when the Americans "exported" their inflation by running large balance-of-payments deficits, this did eventually cause the dollar to fall steeply, and this in turn did eventually—as Bergsten says—have inflationary effects in the United States itself, obliging the government for the first time to modify its domestic policies for reasons primarily connected with the exchange rate.

In the first half of the 1980s the process was reversed: while taxes were reduced, in obedience to the dictates of "supply side" economics, without any corresponding reduction in government expenditure (in fact, defense spending was sharply *increased*), monetary policy was used to forestall the inflationary effects that this would otherwise have had. By raising interest rates the government enabled itself to finance its budget deficit through borrowing. Normally this has a *de*flationary effect, because it soaks up money that would otherwise be available for private investment and consumption. But in this case the deflation was "exported," like the inflation before it, because the high interest rates attracted enormous amounts of capital from abroad—notably from Japan, as we saw at the end of the last chapter, but also from many other countries where capital was not so easily spared, and where governments (as noted by Edward Bernstein) tried, with only very partial success, to stem its flight by raising their own interest rates, thereby deflating their own economies. In financial terms the flood of money into the United States easily swamped the trade deficit, and pushed the dollar sky-high—but the economic effect of this was, in time, to aggravate the trade deficit by making imports absurdly cheap in dollars and American exports absurdly expensive in foreign currencies. By 1985 Americans were beginning to notice the depressive effect that this had on American industry, and the Reagan administration, like its predecessor but for the opposite reason, was obliged to start paying some attention to the exchange rate.

This long disquisition is necessary to explain why, if the Americans tend to see the Japanese (and to a lesser extent the West German) trade surplus as the main problem in the world economy today, almost everybody else tends to see "the American deficit" in that light—by which they sometimes mean the foreign trade deficit, sometimes the government budget deficit, and most often both, for the two are generally seen as being closely related to each other: the budget deficit, and particularly its rapid growth after Reagan's arrival in the White House, is, in Fred Bergsten's view, "the basic cause of our trade deficit."

BERGSTEN: [Previously] there'd been a fairly close balance in the United States between our domestic production levels and our consumption, with a modest trade deficit or surplus. But when there was this sharp increase in government's demand on resources, on top of a reasonable level of private consumption and investment, we wound up consuming more than we could produce, and we wound up investing much more than our domestic savings would support; and the result was huge inflows of goods (that's the trade deficit), and huge inflows of capital.

Thus the budget deficit was responsible for a huge increase in imports, but it also depressed exports.

BERGSTEN: The high interest rates sucked in capital from around the world, and that drove the exchange rate of the dollar through the ceiling. So there was a pretty straight causal relationship between the budget deficit and the trade deficit, working through the exchange rate of the dollar, which was pushed to levels that simply rendered most American goods uncompetitive in world trade.

Was this necessarily bad for the rest of the world? There are those in Europe who think, like Josef Joffe, that "the kind of super-Keynesian deficit spending that Reagan has engaged in for the past several years" has played a "good part in pulling the Western world out of its 1980s depression," or who ask, like Jacques Toubon, "What is better for us, a large deficit and economic recovery or a narrow deficit with American recession? That's the choice, and I think that the economic recovery since 1982 was the leading factor of the German or British or Italian and—my real hope now—French recovery."

But theirs seems to be a minority view. To most Europeans these alleged benefits appear dubious,* and such recovery as there was (in Germany, notably) to have been achieved as much in spite of American policies as because of them. As Chris Patten sees it, "We all have higher interest rates, and therefore I suppose lower rates of economic growth, partly because of the price that the world has to pay for funding the American deficit." The British government, he thinks, "would have been able to relax our own fiscal stance rather more"—run a larger deficit of its own—"if we hadn't been obliged to carry such a heavy interest-rate burden."†

There was, in fact, as Fred Bergsten points out, a complete lack of harmony between the United States and other industrialized countries during the period 1980–85: "The United States was sharply increasing its budget deficits by 4 to 5 percent of GNP, and therefore, of course, pushing interest rates sky-high. Germany, Japan, the U.K.

*"In sharp contrast to U.S. experience," writes the British economist Stephen Marris, "the recovery in the other OECD countries has been the weakest since World War II: unemployment continued to rise, and there was virtually no pickup in the share of investment in GNP." ("Deficits and the Dollar: The World Economy at Risk—Summary," *Policy Analyses in International Economics* 14 [December 1985]: 6.)

†Stephen Marris agrees: "A less expansionary fiscal policy in the United States, coupled with less restrictive fiscal policies in other major countries—and hence less appreciation of the dollar—could well have produced a stronger recovery in the rest of the OECD area with a lower rate of inflation." (Ibid.)

were sharply reducing their budget deficits by 3 to 4 percent of GNP." Edward Bernstein argues that, in view of this, European governments did not need to follow the United States in raising interest rates, even though had they not done so the dollar would have risen even higher, "because while it's true that the prices of raw materials in sterling or in deutsche marks would go up as the currency fell relative to the dollar, it was also true that the world recession was keeping these prices down"; while Tadashi Nakamae says that if Japan and Europe had expanded more rapidly in the early 1980s the American trade deficit would not have increased so fast, since they would have consumed more of their own products (instead of exporting them to America) and more imports from America as well. But, according to Stephen Marris,[5] "had other countries followed the same course [as the United States] there would have been a strong world boom leading rather quickly to a new outbreak of world inflation." And Irmgard Adam-Schwaetzer is certainly not convinced that Europe was saved by Reagan's deficit spending. Even the more modest deficit spending undertaken by the Federal Republic itself after 1977 (at American instigation), she says, "just meant that for a short time the development of unemployment was not as much as it would have been, but on the other hand it meant also that the reconstruction of industry did not take the pace it should have done. So this meant that we have been forced five years back with reshaping our industry to future needs; and in addition the interest rates we had to pay, and the strain on the budget we had since that time, meant that nevertheless unemployment did rise. It rose enormously at the beginning of the eighties."

Everyone agrees that the high U.S. interest rates, necessitated by the huge U.S. budget deficit, led to higher interest rates around the world than the performance of local economies would otherwise have dictated, and thereby maintained the dollar "artificially" at a far higher level than would have been justified by the famous "fundamentals"; and that this greatly aggravated the trade imbalance, especially between the United States and Japan. This in turn gave a powerful stimulus to what is seen as another of the great economic evils of our time: the revival of protectionism—the idea that national industries should be "protected" by restricting imports or imposing a tariff on them. This has been especially marked in the United States, which always used to be the great champion of free trade but now is assailed by doubts. Despite the successful conclusion of the latest round of tariff negotiations, the "Tokyo Round," says Fred Bergsten, "trade protection has been on the rise for the last ten or twelve years."

BERGSTEN: I think the two things taken together—the financial [i.e, currency misalignments] and the trade erosions—really raise some serious questions as to whether we can get international economic cooperation and effective transactions back on track, or whether we're headed toward some serious disruption of the world economic order. . . .

My greatest concern for U.S. foreign policy now is that the continued overvaluation of the dollar and massive trade deficits will produce a huge burst of [protectionism.] I think America's greatest foreign policy risk right now is that our own Congress will unleash a burst of trade protectionism both on ourselves and on the world, which if it went to extreme forms, as in the current legislation being considered by Congress,* could, I think, severly disrupt the whole world economy.

Protectionism was, of course, a widespread response to the ravages of slump, financial crisis, and monetary instability in the 1930s. Bergsten feels that many of his own contemporaries, who are not old enough to remember this, "did not experience the lessons of the past and had not learned them adequately. That's why some in my generation, in the Congress, for example, are pushing stupid protectionist trade policies, because they've forgotten the lessons of the 1930s and don't realize how heavy the costs would be of essentially opting out or copping out of the world system. That would be bad for America. It would be disastrous for the world."

Chris Patten agrees, describing protectionism as "the real threat to all our futures." We have already seen that Japan is far from guiltless in this respect, and that Japan's "unfair" practices are one of the main arguments used by politicians backing protectionist measures in the U.S. But protectionism, it seems, is always what someone else is doing to you, not what you are doing to them. Seen from Japan, for instance by Kaoru Yosano, protectionism is essentially an "emotional conclusion" on the part of Japan's competitors and customers that calls for tact and self-restraint on the part of Japanese exporters.

YOSANO: Even after saying a hundred logic[al arguments] that protectionism is bad for the United States, bad for Japan, bad for the rest of the world . . . because it is a result of emotion we have to be very careful that the rise of protectionism cannot be prevented by words or by logic.

It is no good having logic on your side, he points out, if you end up losing your client: "We have to live up to their emotion." Hence

*Interview recorded in May 1986, at about the time when the Democrat-controlled House of Representatives passed a trade bill described by President Reagan as "kamikaze economics."

the need for Japan to limit its "poker winnings" in order not to "lose gambling friends." As for Hitoshi Seki, the bright young man of the Japan Productivity Center, he thinks that "free trade in its true notion is already dead," given the proliferation of non-tariff barriers throughout the world.

THE DEBT AND THE "DEBT PROBLEM"

One of the effects that Fred Bergsten fears, if the protectionists in the U.S. Congress get their way, is that "it could certainly trigger a renewal of the Third World debt crisis, and that could plunge the world into a very deep state of uncertainty." Other speakers, on all three continents of the industrial North, feared that this could happen even if present policies (not always as liberal as policy-makers like to claim, especially where imports from the Third World are concerned) continue unchanged.

YOSANO: The present accumulated debt in developing countries, like Brazil, Argentine, Peru, Mexico, Poland, Rumania—I think this has reached the point of $900 billion. And I don't see any trend that this accumulated debt will decrease, but this will rather increase, and if we mishandle this accumulated debt problem, our whole system of economy might collapse, especially the banking and finance system. This worries me very much.

FABIUS: Imagine that Mexico refused to pay the debts: there are many international banks which are deeply involved in the lending to Mexico. If Mexico doesn't pay its debts, there is a bankruptcy of many banks. . . . The international banking system can go bankrupt . . . and it's a catastrophe. It does not take place because, once more, we are buying time in order to avoid catastrophe. But the solution—the deeper one, the development of the Third World countries—is not there.

BIDEN: The Third World debt is staggering. Now none of us are going to be in very good shape if in fact the Third World goes into a deep recession. It's real simple: the money owed is not only owed to American banks, it's owed to British banks, it's owed to French banks, it's owed to Japanese banks. And the collapse of the banking system in any one of those countries, or a portion of it, has an impact that reverberates throughout the whole economy.

The reason why a default by major borrowers in the Third World seems likely to so many people is that in the last six years there has been "a net outflow of real resources" from the world's poorer countries to the richer ones—something considered as "a perverse and dangerous anomaly . . . by every school of economic thought,"[6] as developing countries have struggled, on the insistence of the IMF and the main lending countries, to meet their interest and repayment obligations by maximizing their net foreign-exchange earnings—expanding exports and reducing imports, which has meant cutting the living standards of their people and in most cases sharply slowing, if not actually reversing, their economic growth.

PATTEN: There is, of course, a profound nonsense about our attitude to the Third World debt at the moment, because if the Third World was to do what we claim to think that they should do to cope with it—that is, to make a really radical adjustment in their balance of trade position—then we'd be totally kiboshed because we wouldn't be exporting any goods to the Third World.

Moreover, as Ingrid Matthäus-Maier points out, industrialized countries tend to put up tariff barriers against Third World products as soon as the latter become competitive with their own, and in the case of agricultural products the European Community deprives countries like Argentina of their markets even in third countries, because it insists on dumping its own agricultural surpluses at subsidized prices.

But Elliott Abrams, dealing with Latin American countries at the State Department, seemed remarkably relaxed about the debt problem when we interviewed him in May 1986:

ABRAMS: I think the largest single debtor is Brazil at about $102 billion right now—huge transfers out—and Brazil grew at 8½ percent last year. So it is not the case that debt and growth are necessarily incompatible. But there's an answer to the question of outflows, and it is to get money flowing in; and the money that you flow in is investment money. It isn't new debt. The last thing they need is new debt. What they need is money that will help them grow, money that will create employment. In many Third World countries job creation is probably the largest single problem, because it has political implications-that is in terms of internal stability. This is certainly true in a country like Mexico, which needs to create a million jobs a year. Foreign investment can do that—money that comes in to put up factories and things—and that is the way the money should be flowing in; and that will happen if, but only if, they adopt internal economic policies that lead to that investment. And, you know, in a number of Third World countries part of their problem is that a huge amount of money owned by local citizens has flown the coop and is sitting in Swiss banks, and American banks, and so forth—and it's really ridiculous to ask us to put more money into those countries, where nationals of those countries are sending their money out! So they're going to have to adopt policies that attract their own investment, and then it will attract our investment as well. . . .

Jorge Castañeda, however, will have none of this. For him, this problem, too, is directly attributable to the American deficit.

CASTAÑEDA: There is no question that, if real interest rates, today and since 1981, had remained at their historical levels, in other words between 2 and 3 percent, there would be no Latin American debt problem. Every expert, every finance minister, every IMF or World Bank bureaucrat will tell you this. Now Reagan says that high interest rates in the world have nothing to do with the massive $250 billion yearly American [budget] deficit. But the only person who thinks that is Ronald Reagan. Everybody else in the United States, and in Europe and in Latin America, thinks the opposite, beginning with his own economic team, his own chairman of the Fed, his own secretary of the treasury. So whose fault is it that Latin America has a debt problem? The Latin Americans who contracted the debt, or the Americans who created the deficits which have increased interest rates which have created the debt problem? There is not always a debt problem: there is a debt, and then there is a debt problem. The important point is to see what transforms a debt into a debt problem, and the answer is high interest rates. . . .

The real problem is that if someone in the United States—the banks, the administration, somebody—does not really begin to try to address this problem, we're going to be facing a next fifteen or twenty years of very dramatic, conflictive, tense relations between Latin America and the United States, because it is not possible for countries with such massive problems of poverty, backwardness, lack of education, health difficulties, to be exporting massive amounts of resources to the United States. This cannot go on, and the more it goes on the more bitterness you create.

The fact that some of the resource transfer is being done *by* Latin Americans is beside the point. You can make a debating point by saying, "Well, yes, but it's the Latin Americans who are removing some of the money." Well, yes, you could win a debate by saying so—but that's not the problem. The problem is that you have this massive resource transfer, because of the debt, because of high interest rates, and because the Americans do not want to do anything about all this. Who removes the money is, I really think, a secondary, irrelevant matter.

And if this is not changed—in other words if you don't go back to the situation where we have resources coming *from* the industrialized countries *to* the developing countries in order to stimulate their development, or at least, let's keep it even, no resources flowing in any direction, but certainly not *us* financing *their* deficits—if we don't do that, then the relations are going to deteriorate enormously. . . .

You can have individual countries in individual years having high rates of growth. That will happen. It has happened in the case of Brazil—8.5 percent in 1985—perhaps it'll happen in another country in this year or next year. That's not the point. The point is that, as a continent and as a general rule, since 1981 the Latin American economies stopped growing, and they have not returned to a path of sustained economic growth since. Nor is there any reason to believe that the majority of the countries of the continent will return to such a path in the near future, until the debt burden is removed. . . .

Now, as to the question of how you get the rate of investment up again: to begin with, Latin America has traditionally had, since the postwar period, a very high level of investment as a percentage of GNP—in the low twenties in Mexico, Brazil, Argentina, etc.: in other words, a rate of investment comparable to Japan, Western Europe, etc. So it's not a new problem of trying to get a high rate of investment: we have had one traditionally. It has dipped in the past few years, and it has dipped for a series of reasons: lack of confidence in the economies, high interest rates in the United States—once again, the same old problem. How do you counter a real interest rate in the United States of 9, 10 percent, which we had in 1983 and 1984? That means that your local interest rates have to be extraordinarily high, and that means that people stop borrowing and stop investing.

The only short-term solution, he concludes, to enable the Latin American economies to start growing again is "some form of write-off, no matter how disguised, how conciliatory or how negotiated you want it to be"—and this need not be primarily at the expense of the taxpayer in the lender countries.

CASTAÑEDA: The question is how you share the burden of the debt among everybody involved: the lenders, the borrowers, and the international agencies; among the lenders, how you share the burden between the banks, the stockholders—and the United States government, that is to say, some of the taxpayers. But it's not direct: it's not that you take the Mexican debt and you make every American citizen pay for it. It's not that simple, and by simplifying in that way the Reagan administration is simply trying to make it appear that there is no solution to the debt problem other than "Keep the Latin American countries solvent and paying," whereas in fact they are insolvent because they are paying.

But is it just high interest rates that have attracted so much capital into the United States? No, says Jack Kemp, who made his name in the late seventies and early eighties as the man who put supply-side economics on the American political agenda.

KEMP: If it were, they'd invest in Third World countries with higher interest rates. People are investing in the United States of America for the rate of return, and for the safe harbor that it is; and that should encourage other countries who want to finance long-term investment or borrowing to make their own investment climates more attractive, by lowering tax rates on savings and investment and entrepreneurship.

And George Will enthusiastically agrees.

WILL: We have a deficit—a public borrowing requirement, as you people call it. That's a bad thing, but . . . one reason we're able to finance it so effortlessly, and hence pile up so much public debt, is that so many foreigners are so eager to send their money here to lend it to us. I mean, we're borrowing from abroad a sum equivalent to 40 percent of our national debt—deficit—because the reason they'll send their money here is the economy's so good. It's a great haven for money.

This point is conceded, in part at least, by Fred Bergsten.

BERGSTEN: The world does have a very high degree of confidence in the American economy, and I think rightly so. A lot of the foreign investment here is motivated purely by "safe haven" considerations, and a lot of it—which has an important interest-rate element—is in part motivated by the strengths, stability, outlook for the American economy.

[But] my concern is that that's a bad thing for the United States, because it pushed the dollar to such overvalued levels that it created

> a massive trade deficit. It has moved us from being the world's largest creditor country to the world's largest debtor country in just three years, has cost us millions of jobs, the export of lots of our factories and technology and production overseas, and has built a legacy for the future which I think is appalling in its cost to the American economy. It bought us a few years of economic expansion, but so could an alternative program have done, without distrupting our whole international trade and financial position and putting us in a totally unsustainable position for the future.

Laurent Fabius considers that it is the international role of the dollar that has enabled the United States to behave like this.

> FABIUS: They have been able to have an enormous budget deficit, which would not be the case for some other country. In other countries, when you have a budget deficit, you must cut it because you have to pay for it. But if you have the currency [used] throughout the world, you can keep on and issue bonds . . . and if you pay interest on the currency, people have to put their money in your country.

WILL AMERICA RECOVER?

The drawbacks and dangers of the paper-dollar standard are by now apparent to just about everybody. The dollar retains a central role that it originally acquired as the currency of the country with by far the largest financial and trading surplus in the world—reflected, at the time, in that country's near monopoly of the world's gold stock and therefore appropriately symbolized by the dollar's convertibility into gold at a fixed price. It clearly no longer qualifies for that role now, not because it is no longer convertible into gold (that, again, is merely a symbolic reflection of the economic facts) but because it is issued by a government that is the world's largest debtor, and based on an economy that, however big and important, is in massive and apparently chronic deficit in its transactions with the rest of the world.

It is partly by exploiting the dollar's central role and lack of fixed value that the United States has been able to build up these extraordinary deficits, which no other nation could have got away with. In so doing it has aggravated the instability of the system, alternately driving the dollar down to try and retrieve its competitive position, and driving it up so as to finance the budget deficit without resorting to inflation. This has subjected world trade, including the foreign trade that now plays a major role in the U.S. economy itself, to huge distortions and uncertainties, and thereby spurred the rise of protectionism around the world, but especially at home in the United States.

What is to be done? Since the problem arises from the U.S. deficits, the most comfortable thing to think is that the United States is going to pull round. The "system," having weathered the present patch of rather choppy water, would then right itself and steam smoothly ahead. That, broadly, seems to be the view of Tadashi Nakamae, who thinks there is "no alternative" to the dollar as the main international currency, and that the world economy is in any case entering a "deinternationalization period," as most major countries' import bills fall (because of the drop in the oil price) and they "need to reduce exports in order to balance the trade account"; thus over the next ten years or so "self-sufficient economies in major countries will develop, and international trade is less important relative to the whole economic activity." Japan in particular, he says, will reduce its trade surplus by cutting exports and increasing domestic demand, and thus assist the "recovery of the U.S. economy from the very sharp imbalance in trade and in budget deficit." The United States "will continue to be the number-one country," becoming more powerful because of the great expansion of U.S. productive capacity in the last seven years or so—the fruit of supply-side economics—which only the overvaluation of the dollar has so far prevented from being used. So much so, indeed, that "the recovery of American power and how to cope with it" will be a major problem for the world in the next twenty years, "especially for Europe and the Japanese," whose strategy is "based on the assumption that American economic power has been deteriorating and will continue to deteriorate," and that therefore whatever else went wrong one could always increase one's exports to the United States: "Now is the time for the United States to use their own production capacity, and then Japanese and European industry will suffer from excess supply capacity problems. They can't continue to increase export to the United States"—and the result will be "very deflationary pressure on Europe and Japan."

I met no one else who believed the world economy is entering a phase of "deinternationalization," unless artificially induced by the rise of protectionism or a general recession produced by the default of Third World debtors and consequent collapse of the international banking system. Much more popular is Edward Bernstein's view that "the kind of world we're going to have is a world in which production—in which finance—has become completely internationalized," and that this is what makes it impossible to get back to the Bretton Woods system, which was based on the assumption that capital flow between countries could be controlled by governments and central banks. But Nakamae's view about the imminent and spectacular U.S. recovery is, naturally, popular with many Americans who, as George Will says, "are feeling in the 1980s that the disparity on behalf of America is widening again"—that America is heading back toward the kind of world dominance she enjoyed in the fifties. It is popular with Jack Kemp, who, despite his concern about the lack of stability and discipline in the world monetary system, is of course happy to bask in the successes attributed to supply-side economics.

KEMP: The Malthusian predictions of doom and gloom, both economically and socially and probably internationally, have not proven to be the case, as people have grabbed once again the reins of the future. I feel like there's more confidence in the West, and that freedom is working, and it can work, so that our future indeed from my standpoint is brighter today, say, than it was ten years ago.

It is even popular with Joe Biden, who though an opponent of Reagan and of Reaganomics has clearly taken to heart George Will's point that "the first thing an American president has to do . . . is to make the American people feel confident about their role." He rounded off his interview with us with a peroration that sounded like a rehearsal for an inaugural speech in January 1989.

BIDEN: We're a big, big country, and capitalism works in this big, big country. And there is this feeling, rightfully or wrongfully, that my generation has now, not unlike we had immediately after we were stunned by Sputnik: once we got rolling again it was like, "My God" —you know?—"let's go!" There is this quintessential—and again it's chauvinistic to say this, but I don't know how to be any other way—there is this quintessential American character, this notion there's nothing we can't do. . . .

The nation has just caught its breath. I mean, the Reagan administration has not done much to help, other than allowed us to catch our breath. The Americans basically sat down and said, "Well, wait a minute"—in the last eight years—"Where do we go from here? Who are we? What can we be?" And they've come out of it saying, "We are what we've always been." We are still, notwithstanding the relative nature of our strength and our economic prosperity, we still are capable of doing great things—great things for ourselves and, I believe, great things that will impact favorably upon the world.

With optimism about America goes, often, a certain pessimism about Europe. Nakamae, indeed, confesses to feeling "very pessimistic for Europe," because he feels that Europeans are complacent about American competition and have delayed making the necessary capital investment to modernize their industry. He thinks that "if the weakness of the European economy is realized by Europeans, then Europe is very likely to become more isolated," retreating into a self-sufficient trade block, while the United States and Japan would be part of a more dynamic and open Pacific area. Newt Gingrich has similar thoughts.

> GINGRICH: The greatest economic threat we face is East Asia, and it's a good threat. I mean it's a threat of free people working their tails off manufacturing products, and being aggressive and inventive, and improving the quality of life on the whole planet. So it's a positive threat, but it's a threat. If Europe is not able to rethink the limitations on change, limitations of public housing, limitations of psychological and cultural attitudes, the lack of labor mobility, etc., Europe is going to become a backwater. . . .
>
> I was stunned with this fact, which I learned only a couple of weeks ago: Taiwan, by itself, has more manufacturing exports than all of Latin America. . . . I mean little Formosa is a bigger player in the world market than Argentina, Brazil, Mexico, and Colombia combined. . . . Now Europe, if it can't modernize into the information and industrial revolution—and I think there are very real doubts of it now—Europe becomes relatively less and less important economically.

And George Will is pessimistic about Europe because he believes the Europeans are pessimistic about themselves.

> WILL: What alarms me about Europe, both as an ally and as a happy place, is a kind of pessimism that "maybe we, the Europeans . . . can't quite cope, not only with terrorism but with our welfare states and our cities and with educating people and training for a dynamic industrial world."

But very different was the note sounded by Matthias Wissmann, with all the strength of the formidable West German economy behind him. He referred to a book by an American journalist, *The World After Oil,*[7] which had described Germany as "dying economically" and America and Japan as the economic and technological superpowers of the future. This, he said, had reflected the mood of the early eighties.

"But today, four years later, I think the picture is going to change again." Germany was now more than ever in the lead, or at least competing, in new technology.

> WISSMANN: So I personally know that we have still big problems, but that we are able to compete with Japan and the United States. Take one example, in comparison with Japan: Japan has an impressive big industry, but nearly no successful small and middle industry, whereas this country here has hundreds of thousands of innovative, successful, future-looking small and middle entrepreneurs and people working for them. . . . Year by year [he added, with a legitimate puff of local patriotism] more young enterprises are built in Baden-Württemberg than in the whole of Japan. Baden-Württemberg is the only part of Germany which has a positive trade balance with Japan—and Baden-Württemberg is more like the Germany of the future than the Ruhrgebiet. . . .
>
> So this depressive shock for Europe, starting with the beginning of the seventies, I think is now more or less away, and Europe, with Germany and France and others as cornerstones, will be able to compete with the Americans, and the Americans know that it would be a mistake to underestimate European competitors.

Perhaps it is not surprising that the French, just across the Rhine from Baden-Württemberg, tend to make their hopes for Europe conditional on the achievement of effective European unity. Jacques Toubon agrees with the Americans that Europe suffers from "a kind of smoothening of the economic determination, of the will to make profits," though he emphasizes that this is not true "on the moral side" or on questions like defense. Laurent Fabius confesses to being worried about Europe's economic future, because "very strong efforts" are needed to meet the challenge of Japanese and American competition.

> FABIUS: [But] I think we Europeans, if we gather together, if we understand that we are not big enough countries but we have to join up, then we can be really a very strong power. . . . I think we can give the best of the technique, and add something else, which is probably culture, and a sort of magic between economic efficiency and the quality of life . . . and at the same time the sense of human values, the idea that we are not concerned only with our problems but also with the problems of the foreign world. All that can give really a particular strength to our continent, if we think in terms of continent and not in terms of country.

Building Europe, Fabius feels, is "the only important thing" for his generation of politicians to achieve. He does not agree that Europe has "lost its way."

FABIUS: No. Europe has lost time, but it has not lost its way—it's different. We have wasted time. We have thought that we were the best. Then we have discovered that we were not the best. Our first reaction was to say it's because *they* have done this and because *they* have done that—and [now] we are in a new period where we understand that it's because of *us,* but that we can overcome these difficulties. Therefore I'm optimistic for Europe, because now the analyses, the diagnoses, are good. Sometimes the will is lacking, but the new generation, which has nothing to do with frontiers, which wants to build something . . . with unity—I think the new generation can make it.

But the most dismissive of the "fad to talk about 'Europessimism' and all that thing that comes from the Reagan administration" is Pierre Lellouche. "I am profoundly convinced," he says, "that you will get the same words applied to the U.S. a few years from now. Mark my words, because it has already happened under Carter, and these are cycles." Certainly it will take more than mere chest-beating assertions of American self-confidence to cure the specific problems of the American economy that are disrupting the world system. What signs are there that anything is really being done to bring the budget deficit under control?

In Fred Bergsten's view, only one man has stood in the way.

BERGSTEN: I think it's very easy for the United States to reduce its budget deficit. I think frankly only one person stands between us and a sharp decline in the budget deficit, and that's President Reagan. The Congress has been very willing to slow the pace of the defense buildup; despite elections coming every two years the Congress has been quite willing to raise taxes—they did so in 1982 and again in 1984; but the president has resisted both those components of a deficit-reducing package. The president has very strong views: he obviously gives very low priority to reducing the budget deficit compared with some of his other, more structural policy objectives. But I think if the president were to change his view, we would, within a matter of a couple of weeks, have a budget package that would significantly reduce our deficit and really be on the way to curing a lot of economic ills.

The Gramm-Rudman-Hollings "deficit-reduction" (or "budget-balancing") law, enacted in late 1985, was not in itself such a package but an attempt by the American political system to force itself to produce a package, by making failure to do so automatically trigger cuts across the whole range of federal expenditure. According to David Stockman, who was Reagan's budget director until August 1985:

> The defense cuts would be so draconian as to amount to unilateral disarmament; a large portion of the IRS [Internal Revenue Service] staff would be fired and we would collect no revenue at all; life-saving new drug applications would pile up at the Food and Drug Administration unreviewed; our airports would become a parking lot for cars, people and planes because the FAA [Federal Aviation Administration] would be too short-handed to manage even a fraction of the normal traffic.[8]

Sam Gejdenson, as a member of the Democratic majority in the House of Representatives, explains what is politically at stake.

> GEJDENSON: The battle now is one where a significant portion of Congress is trying to bring the reality home to Ronald Reagan that, if you want to continue to allow either one—the deficit to continue to rise (and it's risen over a trillion dollars in the last five years) or if you want to try to continue to take away feeding programs for the poor and for the elderly in this country—that we're going to bring that pain home to you. We're going to bring it home in defense—and some of it, sadly, is going to fall on foreign assistance as well. There is a fight on by many of us to try to limit that damage, clearly, in places like Haiti and the Philippines where the problem is so immediate. But there are many in the Congress who say that this president's got to understand that the blue smoking mirrors, the fairy tales of cutting taxes and increasing defense spending, just don't work; and there has to be an alternative, and this is it.

No wonder, then, that the names of Gramm, Rudman, and Hollings (the three senators who sponsored the bill) became a talisman for those, all over the world, who saw the U.S. budget deficit as the main cause of disorder in the world economy today. In Japan, notably, Hajime Shinohara saw it as "the first hint" of a change in policy that might, by reducing America's thirst for capital imports, bring about a more balanced world monetary system, while Masao Katsurauma thought that "to keep up with the Gramm-Rudman-Hollings law is very important for the dollar to keep its reliability." By May 1986 Fred Bergsten could observe cautiously that "long-term interest rates in the United States have come down very substantially over the last six to nine months [and] on some readings there is at least the beginning of a significant reduction in our budget deficit through the Gramm-Rudman process—through the congressional unwillingness to finance the kind of defense buildup that the president wants."

Joe Biden was confident, in May 1986, that the Gramm-Rudman process would succeed in bringing the budget deficit under control, and added that "in a strange way that's going to put pressure on Europe . . . because there's going to be increasing pressure . . . to say, well, one of the logical places we can reduce military spending is by reducing our presence in Europe." Sam Gejdenson, too, thought that "the implications for America's allies are that they have to pick up some of the burden. . . . Certainly the Japanese and others can play a much bigger role in foreign assistance." Fred Bergsten, however, saw no risk "that the budget-cutting exercise will have a serious adverse effect on U.S. foreign policy," given the momentum already achieved by the defense buildup, whereas it would be "a big plus for American foreign policy" to head off the risk of protectionism by "getting the dollar exchange rate down a good bit further and getting our trade balance back into some reasonable equilibrium."

By April 1988 the dollar exchange rate had indeed got down "a good bit further" (126 yen, 1.69 deutsche marks), but the consequent improvement in the volume of trade flow was disappointingly small, and even less impressive when translated into money (since the effect of depreciation is to make a given volume of exports cover the price of a smaller volume of imports, or a given volume of imports require a larger volume of exports to pay for it). The monthly U.S. trade deficit averaged $12.5 billion in the three months from November 1987 to January 1988, but the February figures, announced in mid-April, just when the Group of Seven finance ministers (the five mentioned above plus those of Canada and Italy) had got together again in Washington to reassert their commitment to a stable dollar, again showed a sharp increase in the deficit, to $13.8 billion, in a month when deficits are normally lower than average.

This seemed to confirm the gloomy forecast issued by the International Monetary Fund just before the G7 meeting that the U.S. current account deficit, which had been $160 billion in 1987, would be reduced only to $140 billion in 1988 and $130 billion in 1989. It promptly sent Wall Street (which had just recovered from the previous October's "Black Monday" crash) into a new dive, while the dollar slipped further down against both the yen and the deutsche mark.

The bilateral imbalance between the U.S. and Japan remained as wide as ever, in spite of the appreciating yen and the rapid growth of Japan's domestic economy—and the latter in any case was not certain to last, since Japan's political leaders, who in 1987 had at last kept their promises to adopt stimulative policies, were now turning back toward fiscal retrenchment. The IMF's judgment was that on the basis of current policies and exchange rates international payments imbalances should shrink in the short term, but would still remain at unsustainable levels.

The IMF saw little scope for further improvement in the U.S. current-account deficit without either renewed action to cut the budget deficit or a further fall in the dollar. The former being ruled out politically, at least until the presidential election, the latter seemed almost unavoidable, given the unlikelihood of overseas investors being willing to continue to finance such deficits at current interest rates. Higher U.S. interest rates would not be an acceptable price to pay for propping up the dollar, since they would weaken growth throughout the world, exacerbate the debt crisis (so far contained but by no means solved), and add to the problems of the American banking system. They might also trigger new turbulence on stock markets around the world.[9]

In short, the remarks made to me by Larry Pressler in June 1986 still seemed every bit as relevant nearly two years later.

PRESSLER: I don't know why people aren't more alarmed about the deficit and about the amount of credit that's been expended around the world. You're sort of thought to be an old curmudgeon if you talk about it. . . . Everybody would verbally agree with you, but when you start really trying to do something about it, when you really start to cut spending, even Ronald Reagan abandons you. For example, on a Social Security vote, when we all jumped off the cliff and said we'll eliminate the COLA [cost-of-living allowance] . . . Ronald turned around and said he was for extending it. He was running for reelection . . . and so we all went back and voted him in again, and got on record as being for it. This president—and I support him strongly—hasn't vetoed a single appropriations bill, while Gerry Ford vetoed fifty (and he got beat, incidentally).

So the point is, there's a rhetoric about it but there isn't a practice. Even the president doesn't practice, and the Congress doesn't, and the international banks haven't, and states haven't—state and local governments have unprecedentedly high debt. So I predict (and I'm not a prophet of doomsday), unless we do something about it we're going to have a 1932-type experience again, and I think it has to come in the next ten to fifteen years.

"WHERE DO WE GO FROM HERE?"

When that is the considered view of one of the more thoughtful younger senators of America's governing party, it is surely foolish to bank on America reestablishing itself as the stable center of the world's trading and monetary system. Even on the most favorable assumptions it must be unrealistic to imagine that the United States is going to regain the massive credit balance with the rest of the world from which the dollar's central role originally derived; and even if it did, how long would it last? What guarantee would we have that America would not again abuse its central position by breaking the rules of economic and financial management that other countries have to observe? Is it not high time to replace the dollar with an international currency such as Keynes proposed, in which all countries would have to settle their foreign payments and to which all countries would have access on equal terms to finance their trade and investment? Could not the SDR be adapted to serve this purpose? Jacques Polak, the IMF veteran, remains skeptical.

> POLAK: A currency derives its base value from being the currency of a country: it's the thing with which, in a country, you can buy something. With the SDR you can't even buy a cup of coffee in the cafeteria here [in the IMF building]! I'm not paid in SDRs. And so the SDR cannot have a value of its own. It has to have a derived value, originally in terms of gold—and gold, of course had a derived value from the dollar—and currently as a package of currencies. Currencies are things that exist sort of "in the blue." They are currencies of countries, and that's the only reason why they're worth something.

To me this argument does not seem conclusive. Was the value of gold really derived from the dollar, or was it the other way round? In the last resort, surely, any currency (including gold) derives its value from the willingness of people to accept it in payment for goods and services, which in turn depends on their confidence in the willingness of other people to accept it in payment for other goods and services at a later date. In the case of gold, that confidence derives historically from the fact that it is both beautiful and scarce, and today essentially from its unequaled historical track record of being sought after and fought over by human beings through the centuries.

In the case of national currencies it derives from the monopoly of their creation held by national governments, so that the value of any given currency depends essentially on people's confidence that the government in question will not abuse its monopoly by creating too much. But national governments are not the only institutions capable of inspiring confidence. Currencies issued by private banks have been quite acceptable at various times and places in the past, and there seems no a priori reason why the IMF should not pay its staff in SDRs, if its board of directors chose to do so, provided that it undertook to convert those SDRs, on demand, into national currencies at the going rate. If that condition were fulfilled, private banks in different countries would be quite happy to accept SDR deposits from clients and no doubt open SDR accounts for them, so long as national governments did not impose regulations to prevent them from doing so. And if the IMF staff were paid partly in SDR-denominated tokens or luncheon vouchers, these would no doubt quickly become acceptable in the staff cafeteria and meals there would be priced accordingly.

In fact, of course, an international currency would not need to circulate physically to fulfill its two main functions—as a unit of account in international transactions and as a form in which those involved in such transactions on a large scale (governments or central banks, and firms engaged in foreign trade) could hold their monetary reserves, knowing that the value of these would thus remain more or less constant in terms of the various national currencies being paid in and out. The present use of the dollar for these two purposes is not really dependent on its acceptability over the counter in Oxford Street, London, convenient though that may be for Japanese tourists.

Strictly speaking, a unit of account can be chosen quite arbitrarily by the parties to any given transaction. If the SDR is not more widely used for this purpose than it is, that must be in part because, as at present defined, its value contains a large dollar component, and is therefore not so much more stable than the dollar itself as to make it worthwhile breaking old habits and forming new ones. As for its use as a reserve asset, that is limited partly by the same consideration and partly by the fact that there is not enough of it around.

Both these defects could be remedied by decisions of the IMF—but the IMF is, of course, a multinational institution and such decisions could only be reached by agreement of at least the five or ten most important members. The problem is not technical but political. However bad things look under the present arrangements, they are not yet bad enough to generate the political will required for agreement on such a radical alternative.

The most likely prognostic, therefore, is that for the time being at least we shall continue using dollars, but that gradually other, more solidly based national currencies—notably the yen and the deutsche mark—will figure more prominently alongside the dollar both in accounting procedures and in monetary reserves.* Tadashi Nakamae thinks that such a balanced system, with several major currencies in wide circulation, is preferable to one where one country plays a central role, because the latter is only stable if that one country has a very big trade surplus to fund its export of capital (which was how the Bretton Woods–Marshall Plan system originally worked), and this, of course, implies that most other countries run trade deficits and fall into debt. (But that does leave open the question of where, if international trade were balanced and no country enjoyed a large surplus, the capital to finance its expansion would come from.)

Fred Bergsten believes that "there is certainly no alternative to the dollar for international transactions, at least in the majority of cases."

> BERGSTEN: [But already] some other national currencies are playing a key role. The deutsche mark has done so from really the early 1970s. The yen is now increasing very sharply its role. In fact we are moving into an international multiple-currency system, with the dollar still by far the dominant single element, but other currencies playing an increasing role. So far it doesn't look like any international monies —the special drawing rights at the IMF, or the écu (European Currency Unit)—are really going to play any significant role in transactions.
>
> As a *numéraire* [a unit of account] anything can play, and both the SDR and the écu are being increasingly used. But for transactions purposes, real international business and finance, it'll continue to be the dollar for some time, I think, with an increasing share taken by the deutsche mark, yen, and perhaps a few other national currencies in regional transactions.

In somewhat similar fashion Irmgard Adam-Schwaetzer, while agreeing that "theoretically" there is a need for a more stable medium of exchange and store of value than the dollar, asks about practical applications.

*In March 1988, for example, Britain experienced its first political crisis over the exchange rate of the pound *in relation to the deutsche mark.* The pound-dollar rate was hardly mentioned.

ADAM-SCHWAETZER: But what would that mean practically? It would mean practically that you have to build up something very synthetic. We have something like that in the European Community—we have the écu as a currency between the countries—and it's okay for a number of states with about the same economic power, but trying to install something worldwide would mean most probably more chaos than anything else.

Edward Bernstein, as one of the architects of the Bretton Woods system, accepts that the standards it set were "not standards that could be kept forever."

BERNSTEIN: [But] it's my hope that, because we have these international institutions in which to cooperate, we will find a gradual change in the present system—which is too volatile, too uncertain—which would give us more flexibility than even Bretton Woods gave us, but still some element of stability, and I think we will find it in time.

And that hope is echoed by many of the "successor generation."

PATTEN: We have to believe again in the efficacy of coordinated intervention in the markets. I don't think it's fair to argue that just because of improvements in electronic communication it's impossible anymore for governments to establish a rather greater degree of sanity in the exchange-rate market or commodity market or whatever. So the first thing is that governments should start to believe, not excessively, but should start to believe again that they can actually, working together—as many of the European countries have done through the EMS—they can, working together, create a much better framework for economic development than we have at the moment.

Fred Bergsten thinks that over the next twenty years "we will move back toward much greater fixity of exchange rates."

BERGSTEN: Probably not all the way back to a rigid Bretton Woods or even EMS system, but one in which countries keep their currencies in fairly close bounds and work together very consistently to try to maintain exchange-rate relationships that do reflect underlying reality. That in turn will produce the second change, which I think is inevitable, namely, increasingly close cooperation among the major countries on the conduct of their national economic policy. It may never go so far as to be called "international policy coordination" or anything very formal, but I think inevitably, because world economic interdependence will continue to grow, the countries will be forced in their own interest—not out of some altruism, but out of their own interest—to coordinate their policies much more closely and to take national actions much more cognizant of what's going on in the rest of the world. . . .

Countries maintain economic sovereignty in a nominal sense, but in real terms they're already very interdependent and their own fortunes are very heavily affected by what goes on elsewhere. It's simply a matter of recognizing that, and trying then to govern those international events in an orderly way, rather than letting them hit you in an unexpected and disorderly way and then having to react with crisis response. . . .

It's difficult to say what the relative role of the United States in the world economy will be over the rest of this decade, or for another twenty years. Between the end of the war and roughly the mid- or late 1970s Europe and Japan were in a catch-up phase, and so the U.S. position was declining. Now you see a continued rapid pace of growth in some of the developing countries in Asia, and until recently in Latin America. But we may now have come fairly near to stability in terms of the relative share of the United States, in gross world product, for example. Likewise with the role of the dollar in international finance: the mark and the yen are playing an increasing role, but whether they will go much further is not clear.

So we may now be approaching a fairly stable balance among the roles of the different countries. That would be helpful because then one would know what was his underlying sense of relationships on which to base the kinds of cooperative approaches that are needed now to stabilize the world economic performance, to the benefit of all countries.

"Policy coordination" has become a kind of American mantra for getting other countries, particularly Japan and West Germany, to lower their interest rates and increase domestic demand so as to act as the "locomotive" of world growth, making it easier to reduce the American trade deficit and offsetting the deflationary effect of the hoped-for reduction in the budget deficit. Bergsten proudly cites an example of how it should be done.

BERGSTEN: . . . from my personal experience in the Carter administration, where we were seeking "locomotion" from our German and Japanese colleagues, which succeeded at the Bonn summit in 1978 to generate a coordinated global expansion program. I think the Bonn summit in 1978 is to this point a milestone—one of the very few instances where the major countries really did explicitly agree on an internationally coordinated package for economic expansion, where each country accepted its share of the responsibility for that and went home and actually implemented what it had agreed to do. That's an image of great success. The thing fell apart a few months later because of the second oil shock, but I think at least it offers some promise of what could be done again in the future.

But the Germans, unfortunately, have much less rosy memories of that period. This time around, said Irmgard Adam-Schwaetzer, American suggestions that the counterpart of the reduced American deficit should be increased spending by the "surplus powers" (West Germany and Japan) would not get much change out of the Germans.

ADAM-SCHWAETZER: No, not anymore. We have done that once. You remember in 1977 Helmut Schmidt conceded to the other six economic countries to play a leading role in such an expenditure campaign, and the outcome was very bad, very negative for us. . . . The deficit spending meant that the interest we had to pay did increase. The state had to borrow the money and we had to pay interest, and it meant that the interest we had to pay did increase from year to year to an enormous amount, and finally in 1982–83 we really feared . . . that by just this interest-spending we would cut down our own possibilities of political decisions, so much that we had to shift our own policy to the austerity policy we are following now since three or four years.* . . . So this would never be done again.

Germany, says Josef Joffe, is much less powerful than the Americans think.

JOFFE: If you look at the numbers, the Germans are still a long way from the power of the American economy. I don't think the Germans could have any of the kind of sway over the world economy that the Americans are imputing to them. I mean the numbers just aren't right.

And he feels that the Germans are quite happy to be just a middle-sized country and to avoid taking responsibility for the management of the world monetary system and the global economy.

*Recorded in June 1986.

JOFFE: Look, what are the Americans getting out of it? Mainly criticism for whatever they do: their interest rates are either too high or too low, the dollar is either too dear or too cheap. If yours is a global reserve currency, it gives you certain pleasures but also exacts a price —and Germany is a medium power, it's a nation of sixty million with a GNP to go with it. It is in no way a great economic power, prosperous and well managed as it is.

Ingrid Matthäus-Maier, representing the Social Democrats (in opposition since 1982), was less complacent, but saw the solution in a stronger European currency block as a shield against the dollar's volatility.

MATTHÄUS-MAIER: The European Monetary System—that means a sort of fixed currencies within a floating system—is a good thing, because it brought to Europe a sort of stability—a stability of currencies —and that was a sort of push to try to have similar economic policies. . . . Before the system some countries made an inflationary policy and others a very solid policy, and now everybody is forced to make a noninflationary policy. . . .

Our idea in the Social Democratic party is to support the European Monetary System in order to have three currency regions—the dollar region, the yen region, and the écu region—so that when the dollar has problems we don't get the same problems in Europe, and I think that is one very important field where Europeans must work more together. . . . I think in order to avoid this very erratic coming up and coming down of the dollar we have to have a strong European currency: then we have not to rely so much on the American dollar.

So, although Jacques Polak claimed to detect "a new spirit" after the May 1986 Tokyo summit—a "great interest on the part of the Big Five, or the Big Seven,* to coordinate economic and especially financial policies"—it was easier to agree with him when he said: "Coordinating of economic policies is a wonderful name, and I'm very happy to see that the main countries are going to try very hard to see what they can achieve in that direction. It will take quite a while to see what that, in fact, produces in terms of actual policies, and in the willingness of countries to adjust their policies, for their own long-run benefit, at perhaps the expense of some immediate domestic difficulties."

*In addition to the Group of Five, Canada and Italy attend the annual "economic" summits of the main Western powers—though Italy in February 1987 threatened to boycott them, on the grounds that the real decisions were being taken behind her back in the Group of Five.

And Fred Bergsten certainly did not think that Tokyo 1986 had repeated the alleged triumph of Bonn 1978.

BERGSTEN: The Bonn summit in 1978 was a concrete agreement by each of the major countries to take specified policy changes to improve the world economy as a whole. The Tokyo communiqué in fact ignored any serious action to deal with the immediate economic problems. It put out a blueprint which could, over time, evolve into meaningful coordination of national policies, but which is going to take many months, if not years, for us to know whether it really has any practical impact.

There was, he said, no "automaticity" in the Tokyo agreement.

BERGSTEN: [There was only] an effort to assure international compatibility but no mechanism that assures that compatibility will be achieved. If a country deviates from its chosen path, there's no mechanism to force it back in place. It's not even clear that meetings will be held, because somebody has to blow the whistle on somebody else, and we know that countries are frequently reluctant to haul each other into court.

Similarly, the euphoria that followed the Paris agreement to stabilize currencies in February 1987 was quickly dispelled when it became apparent that there was no real commitment by either Japan or West Germany to adopt the kind of expansionary policies being urged on them by the United States.

Laurent Fabius, for one, does not believe the political will is there for the kind of policy coordination that is needed. People are aware, he thinks, of the importance of the issue, "but it means sacrifices—and it means sometimes [he was speaking from recent experience] to lose elections to ask sacrifices from people who are your electorate. And all political people don't lack intelligence: they are intelligent, but sometimes—and it can apply to me as well as to anybody—people are lacking in courage."

Even though politicians may be persuaded intellectually that economic catastrophe is possible, he added, they find it difficult to act on that belief.

FABIUS: What strikes me is that we are thinking in terms of short-term issues more than long-term issues. Maybe because my generation has not had direct knowledge of a big economic catastrophe, therefore

> we are trying to solve short-term problems, to win elections, and not enough thinking in terms of long-term problems which really are important. . . .
>
> Every year when I join international monetary conferences, I listen to people saying, "Be careful, because next month, next year, it will be a real catastrophe." And one must say that all the elements are gathered for an international catastrophe: you have the enormous debt of Third World countries, the problem of North-South relations, the imbalance between rich and poor, the absence of an international monetary system. All that is a sort of enormous burden which is here, like that, but at the same time it does not take place. Why? Because countries like the United States, France, Germany, and so on have an interest in the working-out of the system. Therefore, we are paying in order to buy time. But it is only time that we buy. Not a solution: time.

Larry Pressler, too, thinks serious coordination will not happen "until there's a major crisis, unfortunately—and when it's done it will probably be very repugnant to a lot of our thinking." I asked him what form he thought the scenario of catastrophe might take.

> PRESSLER: The U.S. deficit might be so high that it would cause great inflation or an interest jump that would slow our economy down dramatically. The stock market would collapse. Foreign money would no longer come into the U.S. to finance our deficit. We'd be forced to raise interest rates dramatically. One thing would trigger another, and it would get worse and worse, and you'd see basically the collapse of our economy for a period of time. I'm not a doomsday-seeker, but this could happen, very easily. This would be followed by defaults on all the Third World countries' debts to banks and governments: countries would say, "We're just not going to pay." That would close all of our big banks, including the biggest names in banking, overnight. That would be followed by the Europeans, who depend so much on our trade and our money system. So it would be a world depression, and it wouldn't be just strictly under the mechanical monetary system, but it would be based on what we have developed during all these prosperous times.

On some readings, we may already have seen the first act of this scenario in the autumn of 1987. But it is still difficult, when all you can remember is twenty years of rapidly growing prosperity followed by fifteen years of "shocks" that have slowed down our progress and thrown some millions of our less-fortunate fellow citizens out of work, but not stopped the rest of us from living very comfortably, to take such flesh-creeping scenarios seriously—especially as we have been hearing them in one form or another for several years without any of them coming true. As Chris Patten says, "If you manage to cope with living with a time bomb in the sitting room for several years, you get into the stage where you forget that it's actually behind the sofa."

CHAPTER 12

The Revolt of the South

"WE'VE JUST NEVER BEEN GIVEN THAT CHANCE"

The first oil shock, in 1973, coincided with and drew attention to the demand put forward by the Third World for a "new international economic order" (NIEO). The framework for this had been outlined for the first time at the fourth summit conference of the Non-Aligned Movement, held at Algiers in September 1973, only weeks before the Yom Kippur War triggered the great oil-price hike, which was, in fact, only the most spectacular of a number of sharp increases in commodity prices about that time, resulting partly from a long-term cyclical upswing (the "Kondratieff curve") but aggravated by inflation in the industrialized world and the depreciation of the dollar after 1971.[1] This gave a new self-confidence to the Third World countries, whose main role in the world economy was the supply of raw materials.

Their leaders were profoundly disappointed with the results of the "Development Decade," as the UN had unanimously designated the 1960s on the initiative of John F. Kennedy. Already, at the previous Non-Aligned summit, at Lusaka in 1970, President Nyerere of Tanzania had argued that the members of the movement should "help each other rather than waiting as individuals for help from the great powers," and put forward a plan to convert non-alignment into a "trade union of the have-nots."[2] Now the energy crisis and the rising demand for raw materials seemed to provide the leverage through which the industrialized world—the "North"—could be obliged to take notice of Third World demands, which came under three main headings: stabilization of commodity prices so as to protect both consumers and producers from abrupt swings in the market; free access for "Southern" products—including manufactured products—into "Northern" markets; and increased "capital transfers," both official and nonofficial, from North to South (the words "aid" and "investment" tended to be avoided); with, as a subsidiary item, the transfer of technology as well. All of this was summed up as a global redistribution of power and resources from the haves to the have-nots.

The oil-price increase imposed a much heavier burden, proportionally, on the economies of poor oil-importing countries than it did on rich ones. In spite of this the oil producers saw themselves, and were for a time accepted, as the vanguard of the have-nots. They were going to use the clout that oil had given them to secure a fairer economic order for all. And it is true that, but for their insistence, the governments of the "North" would probably not even have gone through the motions of discussing the NIEO agenda, as they did in the sixth and seventh special sessions of the UN General Assembly (1974–75), in the Conference on International Economic Co-operation (1975–77, sometimes known as the North-South Dialogue), and at successive sessions of the UN Conference on Trade and Development (UNCTAD) throughout the 1970s. Such ideas are taken less seriously now that many people in the North agree with Kaoru Yosano.

> YOSANO: The relative political importance of the Middle East will decrease in the next fifteen years, because we depended too heavily on the supply of crude oil from that region, but in the last ten years most industrialized countries have succeeded in changing their source of supply of energy to other sources like coal and nuclear, and at the same time we have found many oil wells which produce good and very cheap oil, and their [Middle Eastern oil producers'] political status has started to decrease, and this trend I think will continue, and at the same time the function of OPEC will never work well again.

But it is also true that the "moral offensive" of the Third World in the early seventies had a powerful impact on the liberal intelligentsia of America and Europe. Christians and Marxists alike—and above all, perhaps, those of us who had absorbed something of both those outlooks without necessarily becoming full adherents of either—felt it was wrong that some parts of the world should be conspicuously so much richer than others, and were predisposed to accept the idea that the plight of the latter must in some way be the responsibility of the former. For this was an idea very much in the Rooseveltian tradition: indeed, what was the New International Economic Order if not an updated version of the global New Deal that Roosevelt had hoped to see?[3] There is a continuity, unpalatable as it may be to some Americans, between the Rooseveltian beginnings of the UN and the Third World–oriented UN of today—a continuity symbolized by Brian Urquhart, who served both with equal loyalty.

URQUHART: The basic fact about the Third World which one has to understand, if one belongs to the Western world, is that these are mostly countries who missed the biggest economic boom in history: the Industrial Revolution. They missed it for various reasons, and they're in a hurry to catch up, and they're going to be quite unreasonable, and we're going to have to see what adjustments are going to be needed to deal with that problem.

But this benign outlook has become hard for the "Northern" industrialized countries to sustain in the harsher and more pessimistic world of today; especially hard, perhaps, for the world's greatest "have" power, the United States. As the American historian David Calleo puts it:

> Third World claims inconveniently pushed certain liberal ideals to their logical conclusions. An integrating liberal world, like an integrating liberal nation and state, presumably implied a bond of brotherhood and, somewhere in the distance, a common standard of welfare. As an outrageously rich society in a hungry, restless and straitened world, practical American interests hardly lay with radical world-income redistribution. Postwar liberals, counting on limitless growth to resolve all problems, had yet to face this issue. But as expectations of unlimited growth began to recede before Malthusian analysis, Americans who took these kinds of liberal egalitarian ideas seriously grew increasingly disabled.[4]

Certainly that is how Fouad Ajami now sees such ideas—as the last gasp of the old liberal international order.

AJAMI: I think they really believed it: I mean, if you go back to the United Nations special session on raw materials in 1974—which marked, if you will, the apex, the climax of this kind of New International Economic Order—that we have a set of demands, and that the producers of raw materials have some case against the consumers, and so on. I think that the Third World agenda, as it emerged out of this UNCTAD, and as it emerged out of this vague Third Worldist ideology, the critique of the Western powers and complaint that the manufacturing powers are unfair to the producers of raw materials—the Arabs did see themselves in the forefront of that movement. You know, they were the producers of oil, the most important commodity. The Algerians were very active: they were really probably one of the two or three most important states, if not *the* most important state, in the definition of the agenda of the Third World in 1974 and 1975. . . .

The New International Economic Order was part of a parliamentary world, if you will. . . . Now the world really is a raw place; and parliamentary procedures and discussions, and meetings of the UN, and arguments about how much of its income should the West channel to the Third World, and the access to the markets of the industrial world—all these seemed antiseptic after 1980–81, and we have a more gruesome agenda: we have not so much the man debating the price of raw materials at the UN, but we have the suicide driver. The terms of the encounter between the West and the Third World, or the West and the Muslim world in particular, became much harsher.

And you know, we now look back with great nostalgia. I mean, these were times of real banality, of tranquillity in the relationship between the West and the Third World, [when] people were talking about the prices of raw materials. All this, I think, has gone, and I think what we're witnessing is the end of the liberal international system which comes out of Bretton Woods and so on. I mean, here is the international system: the liberal terms were specified in 1945; and I think you now have, in my own interpretation of it, a double revolt against the Western liberal international system: it's a revolt by the West itself, a revolt by America in particular which has become an a-liberal power, and openly so—it doesn't even talk liberal symbolism; but it's also a revolt of the Third World. . . .

So I think that liberal internationalism, which had specified in some way the terms of the relationship between the West and the Third World, is the ideology of yesterday; and Americans in particular are no longer ashamed. . . . The people who represented liberal internationalism have either become neoconservative—that's what the whole neoconservative movement is, a rebellion against this liberalism—or just simply, even people much harsher than these neoconservatives. But so, too, on the other part of the divide, in the Third World (and in the Muslim world in particular), that generation which I call the generation of petitioners—people who petition the West, who come and say, "Look, these are our terms, what can we get out of you?" and "We're part of this system of states, the Western order of states"—I think that generation also is in retreat. But if you date Bandung* as the beginning

*The Afro-Asian Conference held at Bandung, in Indonesia, which marked the beginning of the Third World as a self-conscious entity.

—1955—and then 1979, the Iranian revolution if you will, as another arbitrary point, I think that you have a quarter-century where there was something of a liberal international system, and there isn't today; and the terms are not liberal terms any more. . . . There is really no constituency in America today for even a liberal relationship to Africa; and Asia, after Vietnam, is this kind of world which again is hostile, enclosed. I think by and large Americans have concluded that the ideas that they built the post–World War II world with, those ideas are discredited and dead.

Ajami, as an academic and something of a professional iconoclast, can describe all this with a certain relish and gusto. Olu Adeniji, as a diplomat and a United Nations man, has to be much more cautious. He, too, admits that "more and more one begins to get that impression . . . that it's getting to be an era of each country for itself," but he still hopes "that that is just a passing phase, then internationalism, multilateralism, would again come to be seen as an important factor for world progress." Adeniji mentions events like the UN General Assembly's special session on Africa in May 1986.

ADENIJI: . . . where the problems of a particular region are analyzed and where that region is really willing to engage in self-criticism, might persuade others that the requirements for international cooperation are genuine, and that it would be in their own interests, as well, to cooperate so as to ensure that no part of the world is put in a situation where it continues to be deprived. I think it's in the interest of us all to ensure that development is evenly spread all over, both in our national policies as well as in the international arena. So I would like to be optimistic in seeing this as perhaps a phase, which is the spillover of the economic difficulties which the developed countries themselves had encountered in the not-too-distant past, and that, with recovery, that sense of altruism, that sense of service, would hopefully come back again.

His political master, Bolaji Akinyemi, who is an academic by training, was blunter.

AKINYEMI: Personal achievement notwithstanding, I think by the middle of the 1970s I have tended to get this feeling that things weren't going right, that it was going to be a hard and long road to travel; and I started to wonder whether the early sixties, when one dreamed . . . were going to carry one through, and whether it's not just going to be, now, a question of mundane activities. By the 1980s I had started to wonder whether we even had objectives left, whether we had targets left.

The disillusionment of the Third World is not only with the response of the North to its demands, but also with its own leadership.

ADENIJI: . . . [leadership] that has been perhaps a little more selfish than nationalistic; and since these were people who are brought up in the Western ideas of government, to that extent people might feel—and still feel—that their background was responsible for what they had done or had not done in their individual countries. Of course, I suppose there are all kinds of local circumstances also which molded some of the ways the leaders behaved. I do not, quite frankly, believe in putting all the blames for one's ills on outside influences. I think one should also look inward and see in what areas one had failed. . . . The Africans are no longer shifting all the blame for their economic ills—and, quite frankly, our failures are mainly in the economic area, where many of our countries are worse off today than they were when they attained independence. Much of it has been due to the lack of vision on the part of many of the leaders: the kind of economic programs, the economic projects, which they found very attractive in the early days of independence, of course, were not the type which would permit of long-term growth.

And the disillusionment extends to the ideologies with which the leaders of the independence generation were associated.

ADENIJI: By and large in Africa, in Nigeria, there is a certain disillusionment with the political philosophies from the West, and East for that matter—from Europe generally—whether it's socialism, whether it's capitalism, whether it's democracy the way you see it, or democracy the way the Eastern Europeans see it. There is a feeling actually that we do have, or we did have, our own traditional system of governance, which perhaps with some reorganization may be found to be more relevant really to our societies than these imported systems of government. As you know, it's often said in some places jokingly that socialism is being given a bad name in some parts of Africa because of the way it's evolved, just as democracy has also been given a bad name, it's been said, in parts of Africa because of the way and manner it's been handled, the various changes of government that we've had. We in Nigeria have had two experiments in the democratic process—parliamentary democracy, so-called. The first ended with a military coup in 1966, and the second, which was a sort of presidential system based on the American model—almost a carbon copy, really, of the American system of government—also failed within four years.

And the disillusionment is shared by those in Europe—in France, particularly, who had hoped the Third World was going to lead the way to a fairer and more humane civilization. Pierre Lellouche remembers this as an important factor in his own breach with the radical left.

LELLOUCHE: The leftist groups, in which I was very active, were resolutely anti-Zionist and pro–Third World, pro-Palestinian, and saw the Third World as a great hope for humanity: they had translated the Marxist dialectic of the proletarian class as a liberator into the world scale, and saw the Third World as a force of liberation for all these lousy democracies [which were] lost in material values.

And then unfortunately I had this drive, which I still have, to go travel and look for myself. . . . I did some of my studies in the U.S., and I was still very leftist. I used to spend my summers traveling in Central and South America, and then I discovered what was the Third World and what was the problem, and my views became more and more different. . . . I saw how hopeless the situation was, mostly not only because of U.S. exploitation, or because our societies were bad, but because their societies are completely corrupt, fundamentally, and there is not enough of a middle class which is motivated enough to pull their country out of underdevelopment; and that you cannot rape history, you cannot bring a country from the Middle Ages to the twentieth century in one generation.

Jacques Toubon's romance with the Third World ended with "the deaths of those charismatic leaders [people like Tito, Gandhi, Nasser]. They were replaced by more efficient—really, I think so—but gray people, [who] were sometimes, unfortunately, kind of employees of the Soviet Union or other world powers."

And Jack Lang, the charismatic, tousle-headed French theater director who is President Mitterrand's minister of culture, now feels that his own generation expected too much from "these young countries."

LANG: Because they had no experience, they had no money—or no means—and we, European young people, expected them to achieve much more and better than us who had the experience of two or three centuries of democracy. . . . We were expecting through the revolution of these countries a new model, but at the same time many of these young people were very unfair with them because they did not understand that it was so difficult for these young countries to find the way, as you see the situation of Vietnam now. I don't approve of the political situation of Vietnam, but it is so difficult for this country which has been destroyed during thirty years of war.

That remark echoes the feelings of many of the rising generation in the Third World itself who feel, as Bolaji Akinyemi puts it, that their countries "never had that cocoon of protection which the United States or European countries had when they were developing, to fashion out their own systems, their own values, against superior forces externally."

AKINYEMI: We've just never been given that chance. If we had a corrupt leader and we wanted to deal with him, his being in power was of service to some superior political force externally, and so they were prepared to defend him. If we had a good leader, incorruptible, who has got his act together, the same forces come in and remove him because he wasn't going to serve their interests. . . .

I never really believed in my wildest dreams that it was possible for countries to engineer assassinations of heads of states of other countries, and the death of Lumumba* I think was my very first shocking experience. It took me a long time before I became persuaded that so-called civilized countries engineered the kind of thing that happened to Lumumba. It was an eye-opener. . . . At times the anger is directed at fellow Africans, at times it is directed externally, because I believe that if we'd been left alone, I mean Africans, we would have changed the bad leadership and got on with the job, but really we were never left alone.

In a similar way, the Arabs feel, as Fouad Ajami says, "that that generation was somewhat hopeful and strident, until its stride was broken in 1967" by the Six-Day War. This is confirmed by Prince Abdullah Bin Faisal Bin Turki, an English-educated junior member of the Saudi royal family, now head of the royal commission which administers the new Saudi ports of Jubail and Yanbu. Because of his good English and his relaxed, affable manner, Abdullah is often used by the Saudi government as a semi-official spokesman. He identifies

*Patrice Lumumba, left-wing nationalist prime minister of the Belgian Congo (now Zaire) at the time of independence (1960). He was overthrown in a coup d'état, arrested, and shortly afterward killed, in circumstances that have never been fully known.

the 1967 war as the international event of his lifetime that made the greatest impact on him.

> ABDULLAH: We used, of course, to listen to the radio stations and the news agencies from Syria, Egypt, and Jordan. We thought that the Egyptians were winning, and in six days we realized that the West Bank was lost, Golan was gone, Jerusalem was taken, of course, Sinai was taken. It's unbelievable how depressing that felt.

But what made a lasting impression on him was "the fact that the international community did not do much about it."

> ABDULLAH: They took the easy way out, and they did not feel that there is a responsibility to address the situation; and what affected me was that an aggressor was able to take the initiative militarily [and] able to use political action to avoid any loss of its advantage, to influence world opinion with regard to something that I felt was very unjust. I think this shook me, and I still feel it. Remember that, of course, in the late sixties a lot of the young people were driven by a resurgence of idealism, by a strong expression of this idealism, and the shock of it [came] when I felt the Middle East was slipping away to the background in world opinion, when very few people were taking the issue that we felt was very important—very few were taking it as part of their expression, in the Western countries. That was rather important to me.

And, according to Jorge Castañeda, Latin Americans of the same age were suffering a similar moment of truth at about the same time.

> CASTAÑEDA: All of a sudden in the late sixties, early seventies, when, in a sense, the older generation begins to transmit some of the levers of economic, cultural, intellectual power to the next generation, we realize in a sense that what they are handing over is not what we had expected. In other words it is not the relatively developed, relatively prosperous, relatively modernized—and relatively democratic, it's also important—societies which the long march of economic development of the twentieth century, and mainly of the postwar years, should have led to. All of this, all of a sudden it's not there: the poverty, the misery, the backwardness are all there, in a sense worse than ever; the enormous disparities in income and living standards, in nutrition, in education, in culture, are all there, within each country. All of these countries are essentially still very poor, backward, uneducated—and it wasn't supposed to be that way. So the reaction is, "Well, what has been

done wrong, and what can be done to do things right?" And you have a clear pointing of fingers at the international aspects, because there does not seem to be anything else that you can do internally, and so you start trying to look for causes, and solutions, outside.

So the Latin Americans, as much as if not more than the Africans and Asians, pinned their hopes on the New International Economic Order, and have been as embittered as anyone by the North's response.

CASTAÑEDA: The response has been nil, and the reaction to the response, if you will, has been, of course, very bitter and very disappointed. The fact is that in Northern countries—particularly the United States, because there are the "good" Northern countries: Scandinavian and some of the Western Europeans, etc., even the Canadians, which have responded in a much more positive, emphatic way to this entire problem since the early seventies—but the United States's reaction, and to the extent that it's identified with it the rest of the industrialized world's reaction, has provoked an enormous amount of bitterness. Essentially what the Americans have been saying over the past fifteen years is, first, "It really isn't our problem," secondly, "We're doing what we can, we can't do more," and now more recently, "If you would just be like us, you wouldn't have these problems in the first place!" . . .

But we have heard all of this many times before. It's not new. Reaganomics is not a new recipe for development in Latin America. We've been hearing this sort of thing for twenty, thirty, fifty, sixty years, and in many cases it's actually been tried with some success—sometimes with no success, but most of the time with a little success in applying this sort of recipe. What has happened is that the state has had to step in to correct—or promote, or encourage, or complement—what the private sector was doing.

"THE PROBLEM IS THE UNITED STATES"

And so America, that generous power that had always quite sincerely seen itself as the sponsor of decolonization, of progress and development, came more and more to be seen in the Third World as the main obstacle to the achievement of Third World people's aspirations for freedom and prosperity. In Latin America, of course—"Uncle Sam's backyard"—that goes almost without saying. The view of the United

States as an "imperialist" power may be confined, according to Jorge Castañeda, to the left.

CASTAÑEDA: [But] the mainstream opinion within the Latin American relatively politicized middle classes would be more that it's a sort of hegemonic, overbearing, overpowering presence, which is constantly creating problems, making things difficult—though at the same time, of course, it has all of the advantages for us that we all know of: it's fun to go to the United States to travel, to take the kids there; what would we do without all the American products which are produced in the Latin American countries and which we all do consume?, etc.—I think, then, it's an overbearing, overpowering presence, which is always there, with which we have to live—we don't want to live, but we probably could not live without.

As for the comparison between America and the Soviet Union, that—according to Castañeda—does not even arise.

CASTAÑEDA: The Soviet Union is not a threat in Latin America. It's not a danger in Latin America. In most cases it's not even a presence. Nobody that I know has ever been scared of the Soviet Union in Latin America honestly: there are people who will say they are, because that makes it easier to get more money from the Americans, and so you can have all the Latin American tinhorn dictators, mainly the Central American ones, who go around saying that the Soviets are coming, to squeeze more money from the Americans. But other than that there has never been historically a threat, presence, or danger for any Latin American country emanating from the Soviet Union. Most Latin Americans have never even seen a Russian. You must remember that most Latin American countries don't even have diplomatic relations with the Soviet Union, or have not had them until recently—the last ten or twenty years. So when you talk about the presence of the Soviet Union in Latin America you're talking about something that doesn't exist. Consequently there is no symmetry. The problem is the United States. The threat, the money, the danger, the idealized myth, is the United States.

And something must be done about the debt problem, he adds.

CASTAÑEDA: [If not,] relations are going to deteriorate enormously. Because every child who is born in Latin America, and who has malnutrition, who's not getting a decent—or any—education, who's not clothed, who has no shoes, who does not have any real future in front of him, knows one way or other, in a very intuitive, exaggerated way, that the problem is the United States, and enough people are saying so in Latin America for that child to be convinced that this is the case. When he will be eighteen or twenty or twenty-five and will find no job because there is no economic growth and because unemployment is enormous, and marginalization is enormous, that fellow will hate the United States: he will no longer dislike them, he will no longer have "on the one hand, on the other hand" type of views. He will have pure hatred in him.

But in Africa, too, where the image of America was so favorable in the early sixties, things have changed, according to Olu Adeniji.

ADENIJI: That image of a United States that is outward-looking, that is willing to do things for other countries, that is willing to help other countries, is no longer seen in that same light. More and more people tend to believe that the United States has become more inward-looking: it's rather what the rest of the world can do for the United States than what the United States can do for the rest of the world.

And this in more areas than one: because sometimes I think the area which has been creating problems in the relationship between the United States and many areas of the world, including even our own in Africa, is the perception that the requirements of our own security as small little countries are not being totally appreciated in Washington in some of the policy measures that are being taken there.

On the other hand [he adds diplomatically] I suppose those in Washington feel that small countries like ours which insist that there ought to be a reduction of the present level of armaments just do not understand what they are talking about: they do not recognize what it takes for a large country and a powerful country like the United States to feel secure. Now this conflicting view of the requirements of security in the world is a big stumbling block, no doubt, in the perception of the United States in other countries.

It's the same, of course, in the area of economic cooperation. . . . We are essentially countries that depend on, or should depend on, agriculture; and yet, if on the one hand there is talk about revamping our agriculture, and on the other hand there is some discouragement of our finance through the collateral of commodity prices, then it's very difficult for us to know where to go—and yet the United States is the one country that has consistently given the impression that it's not interested in organizations of commodity producers, which are meant to ensure that our farmers get remunerative prices. . . . As long as that is so, obviously our perception of the United States is likely to be one of a country that is no longer interested in others' welfare beside its own. . . .

At the United Nations it seems to be the policy of this present administration in Washington that any government that does not support American vision or American views on specific subjects should not expect to be embraced by the United States, and therefore should not expect cooperation or assistance from the United States. So I think in a sense it's a desire to make the United States the center of everything.

In the Arab world, of course, it is above all the American-Israeli connection that has altered the image of the United States, for Abdullah Bin Faisal Bin Turki as for many others.

ABDULLAH: I didn't go to the United States until 1978, but we [Saudis] had a long relationship with the United States, and we regarded them as friends and friendly people. . . . I think what shocked me later on is the influence the Israelis have on public opinion, on the legislature . . . on politicians and the media, which later on, of course, affected events in the Middle East. . . .

I still feel the same way about Americans—they're friends as people—but it certainly made me worry very much about the impact that that influence has on our area, and my main worry, if American policies continue as they are, is that the Middle East will be even more anti-American, and whatever friends they have remaining in the Middle East will regard them as a necessary evil—and that is not a very good thing, because I think the American people are well meaning, well intentioned. But one never knows how far this feeling might grow.

Like many Arabs, Prince Abdullah contrasts the action of President Eisenhower in 1956, who "gained a lot of popularity for the United States when he stopped the continuation of aggression by the British, French, and Israelis," with "President Johnson's acquiescence with what the Israelis did" in 1967, and with American support for Israel in 1973.

ABDULLAH: [And] later down the line, the bombing of Ozirak [the Iraqi nuclear reactor], the bombing of the schools in Lebanon, and then subsequently the 1982 invasion of Lebanon, the siege of Beirut, the bombing of the PLO headquarters in Tunis: all these things without the Americans putting a stop to it, without taking certain opportunities to put pressure on the Israelis to reduce this level of conflict. . . .

In Saudi Arabia, because of the oil business, we had a lot of American companies working . . . but now this has been reduced. We have less and less people studying in the United States and more and more studying in Europe.

As Fouad Ajami sees it, the Arabs have come "to understand that their own romance with America is unreciprocated"; and for him, too, 1967 was the moment when this first dawned on them, 1982 the moment when it was revealed in a blinding midday glare. From the former, he recalls the sudden disappearance, after the Six-Day War, of the language about "territorial integrity of all states" used by Lyndon Johnson before it; from the latter, "the sight of a great power that gave a green light to Israel."

AJAMI: [For them] . . . to go into Lebanon: and that for eighty days Beirut is shelled by land, air, and sea . . . and that, you know, there is really no illusion to be entertained about this power. Either it couldn't tell Israel what to do—and for a generation that always thought about the precedent of Eisenhower telling Israel what to do that was hard to cope with—or this great foreign power, America, was really a party to that war, which I think was much more the prevailing interpretation . . . that this wasn't just an Israeli campaign, it was really an Israeli-American campaign in the region. . . .

[Today] the entire Arab-American relation, to me, is a wasteland. I mean there's a great feud and a great misunderstanding between America and the Arab world, and it grows more intense as the Americanization of the Arab world, in many strange ways, proceeds. They're two sides of the same coin: the place gets more enamored with this foreign power, but more angry at this foreign power. The place grows flooded with American goods, but again it feels that it has to demonstrate its independence from this foreign power.

There's a great Arab hypocrisy, in many ways, in the relation to America: it's an affair, but it has to be under wraps. You see, it's like . . . all sexual affairs in the Arab world are secret, and so the affair with America also has to be secret. And so you on the one hand are enamored with America and you believe in America, but on the other you carry on this kind of angry relationship with America in public. And the Arabs in many ways have wanted the Americans to understand that: "Look, you know, Americans, we have an affair with you but we can't acknowledge it openly, because, you know, we've got all these mad extremists. We've got the Muslim Brothers in Egypt, we've got the radical Shi'a in Lebanon, we've got the fanatics in Saudi Arabia, and so on. So we have a relationship with you, we have an *amour* with you, we have an affair with you, but please don't make us acknowledge it in public. Let's have a secret relationship with America."

Well, it hasn't been working, because the Americans are not good at having secret liaisons. They like public affairs, and the Arabs can't have a public affair with America, and I think that really it's a large cultural problem for them: how to have a relationship with America that they can acknowledge and they can defend and they can live with —and they haven't been able to do it.

Take a look at the strange relationship between Egypt and America. In the early years of the Free Officers, Nasser, Sadat, and company had an open channel of communication to the Americans; and the Americans thought, through their romance with officers and military and modernization, that these new classes would come to power and the place would be modernized—you know, whether it's Latin America or the Middle East—through the military. So they had a relationship with the Free Officers, in 1950, 1951, 1952. And then, of course, we know what happened later on: Nasser and company became devoted and fervent enemies of America, so from, let's say, 1955, 1956, 1958 until 1974 you have a great feud between Egypt and the Americans.

And yet, in 1974 most of Egypt turned out to greet none other than Richard Nixon! You know, Richard Nixon was coming, and he was going to bring peace and prosperity to Egypt, and suddenly America became the Mahdi—the Messiah—for the Egyptians: all of a sudden, from devil to redeemer! And then, you know, after Nixon and Kissinger, who became, as Sadat always used to say, "my friend Henry Kissinger," this was the great new relationship and the great new romance with America, that Egypt experienced in 1974, 1975 and so on.

Then came Jimmy Carter, who became Sadat's "brother," and he was also going to bring the "Carter Plan," as Sadat used to say, for Egypt: he was going to develop Egypt. And so suddenly in 1974, 1975, and beyond, Egypt decided she will become America's ward and America's friend in the region, and here is the Egyptian regime that led the revolt against America in the region in the fifties suddenly becoming an American client—and Egyptians as of late have begun to talk about the American Raj in Egypt.

But it doesn't have the romance of the old Raj in India: it's a very different relationship. The Americans give the Egyptians two point some billion dollars a year, but they don't invest much of themselves in Egypt. They have no illusions about Egypt: they're stuck with Egypt as a client. They pay the Egyptians because there was peace between

Egypt and Israel under American auspices, but again there is no romance and no understanding. There is no Egyptian political class that has a good relationship to America and that openly acknowledges this relationship. So you have a regime in Egypt which is dependent on America economically but denies a relationship with America publicly.

And I think here in a nutshell, in this strange relationship between Egypt and America, lies the broader Arab-American problem. Because the Americans sustain the Egyptian regime, but without any cultural commitment—without any "affair" with Egypt, if you will—and the Egyptians take this money and then go around trying to demonstrate to themselves, to their own fundamentalist groups, to the wider Arab world, that "Well, we're really not clients of America"—and I think the difficulty of the relationship will become clearer in the months and years to come.

Now move over to Saudi Arabia: again, there, there's a regime that's supposed to be close to the U.S. Well, how close? Again there is an American economic interest in Saudi Arabia, there is a Saudi dependence in many ways upon the U.S., but there is no great romance there either. None of America's "self," if you will, its commitment to democracy, all these ideas that America holds dear—America cannot find itself in Saudi Arabia: there is not much of the American psyche invested in Saudi Arabia.

Underneath the monarchy there is a generation—princes and others—who are very much enamored with the American model. You know, people speak of a California mafia there: the University of Texas and the University of Southern California must have trained the bulk of the Saudi technocratic and managerial elite; and there is a kind of pro-American generation underneath, but it doesn't openly acknowledge its own relationship to America.

And so, you know, here is another key Arab society and another key Arab regime with a very problematic relationship to America . . . and, of course, for the Americans there is no great interest whatsoever in Saudi Arabia, I mean beyond the interests in oil and hardware. I mean, here is a relationship, if you really want to understand the aridity of this Arab-American relationship, which is symbolized by two great commodities: oil and arms, that's all. The traffic doesn't have anything else. Art, folklore, culture, ideas, books: they don't travel. And I think in this kind of aridity of this relationship you can tell plenty that's wrong about the relationship between America and the Arab world.

In Iran, a harsher view of what are now called North-South relations can be traced further back, to the great battle over the nationalization of the Anglo-Iranian Oil Company in the early fifties. Although Iran, too, had had its romance with America, as the supposedly disinterested power that would help Iran free itself from the endless machinations of Great Britain and Russia, that romance abruptly came to an end in 1953, when the nationalist government of Mohammed Mosaddegh was overthrown, and the shah restored to power, in what was widely realized even at the time to be a CIA-organized coup. "It was quite clear: everybody knew it," says Said Rajaie-Khorassani, the remarkably skilled diplomat who headed Iran's permanent delegation at the UN from 1981 to 1987. He remembers the excitement of collecting money to support Mosaddegh's government as a schoolboy, although, he says, speaking as a devout supporter of Ayatollah Khomeini, "there was also a sense of insecurity, because when the central government was weakened, then all sorts of corruption and thievery could be expected. It was not a real fundamental revolutionary movement in which all people participate and the whole social and moral atmosphere of the society are changed. . . . In that case people did not have the same sense of security and participation that we experienced during the Islamic revolution."

The result of the coup, as Rajaie remembers it, was "that the British went and the Americans came. They were, as a matter of fact, playing almost the same role in the administration of the country that the British were playing. Probably the British were playing it in a different manner: they were doing it somehow in a more covert way, but the Americans were so open—coming and going, opening our institutions and this and that, and American English classes going, with American uniforms walking in the street, some of them carrying arms."

Much later, during the Islamic revolution of 1978–79, Rajaie remembers "that the government of the United States was continuously supporting the shah, and they were very outspoken in that position."

> RAJAIE: . . . so we thought that without their support the shah could have fallen far, far earlier, and it was [thanks to] the support of the United States [that his troops were] still shooting at ordinary people in the streets. We also remembered that your foreign minister, the foreign minister of England [Dr. David Owen], made a statement, a very, I should say, untimely and wrong statement in support of the shah. I think that statement was absolutely unnecessary, when he could have just kept silent without any commitment to either side—to the revolution or to the shah: it would have been much wiser of him to have done

that.* But he probably had to say it because usually Great Britain is somehow associated with the United States in many aspects of their foreign policies, and this is the case now: I mean, you see what Mrs. Thatcher is doing, it's not very much different from the position of President Reagan, in many areas. However, that statement gave us the understanding that both the Americans and the British were responsible for the prolongation of this struggle, and consequently for a lot of shootings against the people.

WHAT "THIRD WORLD"?

A common resentment at the North's greater prosperity and a common anger at the North's apparent selfishness were, obviously, what brought the Third World governments together in such organizations as the Group of Seventy-Seven (the developing countries' lobby within UNCTAD) and the Non-Aligned Movement, despite their widely varying political ideologies and regional preoccupations. One might suppose, therefore, that the increased resentment and frustration bred by the lack of progress on development issues in the various North-South talking forums since 1974, and by United States policies in various parts of the world, especially under the present administration, would have reinforced the Third World's internal cohesion and unity.

ADENIJI: If one of the results would be greater cooperation between the developing countries, I would see that as a salutary influence. . . . Perhaps with what is now being seen in some areas as rejection by the West . . . the developing countries would seriously explore these alternatives.

But Third World unity, such as it was, was also based on hope. The program of the Non-Aligned Movement in the early seventies was, as we have seen, an expression of belief in the Rooseveltian world order —of belief that international justice could be achieved through multinational institutions and majority votes. The effort focused especially on the United Nations. But, as Brian Urquhart says, "the Third World

*Owen, however, is unrepentant: "It was never a Western interest that the shah should have been toppled. Quite obviously so. A very unpopular thing to say in 1978, but I said it publicly: it was not a British interest that the shah should be toppled. I also warned that what would follow would be far worse in terms of human rights than the shah, and sadly that prediction has been amply proved."

vastly overestimated the actual value of its overwhelming majority in the General Assembly, and voted through a whole series of resolutions which, in the long run, were extremely disadvantageous to them, and incidentally to the UN." The most famous of these was the resolution declaring Zionism a form of racism, passed in 1975, which greatly harmed the image of the UN in the United States, and to a lesser extent in Europe. Although the General Assembly is only one of the UN's organs, and in the Security Council, which has much more extensive powers under the Charter, the great powers retained their veto, the impression given to public opinion in the West was that the Third World countries had taken over the UN as a whole and made it their plaything. But that, of course, is not how *they* see it.

RAJAIE: On the contrary, it was those who are now disappointed who are manipulating the Charter in favor of their own interests and against the Third World, and since they are less able to continue with those manipulations any longer then they are unhappy and they are just misidentifying the role of the Third World. If the Third World is doing something contrary to the Charter of the United Nations, it can be stopped immediately according to the rules of procedure: any chairman, any president, will stop it. . . . On the other hand, we have to expect a little bit of modesty and understanding on the part of those who have been overpowering everybody in the United Nations, to be more objective and to realize that the scene of the globe has changed and they cannot exercise all those things that they used to exercise in the past.

But this is a purely negative value.

RAJAIE: As a matter of fact, many of us participate here in order to prevent the evil, not in order to achieve good, because we see that it's almost impossible to achieve good in the United Nations. . . . For instance, the Vietnam War was never solved in the United Nations; or the Iran-Iraq conflict—it has not been solved in the United Nations.* Even the Falkland Islands: you know, a resolution in the United Nations did not bring that to a final settlement. The Cyprus issue: United Nations has not been able to achieve anything. That impotence, incapability—inactivity, let's say—on the part of the United Nations can be and should be explained in terms of the composition of various forces in action in the United Nations, and that is the reality of the situation.

*Interview recorded in May 1986.

The Third World has, to a large extent, imposed its own agenda on the UN, consisting of the New International Economic Order, world disarmament, freedom for Southern Africa, and a homeland for the Palestinians. But it has not been able to persuade the North to take this agenda seriously: to all these demands the reply, often delivered in patronizing tones, is either that they are not within our power to give or that they are better discussed separately, in smaller and more private forums. Nuclear disarmament, in particular, is treated by the superpowers as an issue that concerns them alone.

> RAJAIE: Quite regrettably, unless other countries demonstrate that they, too, can use atomic weapons, then those superpowers—I don't like the term "superpowers" because this is their own invention—those powers who have access to nuclear power, nuclear energy, will not come to the understanding that they should sit down and consider the issue of atomic disarmament very seriously. . . . I think other people must have it, and only then these people will sit down and get rid of this danger which is threatening the entire globe.

This remark, from the delegate of the Islamic Republic of Iran, has fairly chilling implications when one thinks about it. Rajaie is a very skillful diplomat and did a remarkable job at the UN in presenting his government's positions—especially on the Iran-Iraq war—in terms acceptable and persuasive to the UN Secretariat and to other countries' delegations. His years in New York taught him to appreciate at least the negative value of the UN. But he did not blend into the cosmopolitan elegance of the UN scene, where his jacket and open-necked shirt marked him out, among so many carefully knotted neckties and sumptuous, flowing national costumes, as the representative of a revolutionary regime.

And his speeches could be very embarrassing to other Third World delegates—particularly those from Arab and other Muslim countries—for instance, when he insisted on challenging the credentials of the Israeli delegation, an issue most Arab governments prefer to fudge in order not to further alienate the United States. For the premises from which he starts are not those of the Rooseveltian world order, and the message of the revolution he represents is that Muslims—and by implication other non-Westerners, too—do not have to accept those premises, since they have an all-sufficient religion and culture of their own; that, moreover, it is no good for the "have-nots" to expect the "haves" to accommodate them in some comfortable global negotiation. If the "haves" are enemies of God, then violence will be their natural mode of expression and the godly must be prepared to respond in kind. (In traditional Islamic terminology, the whole world outside the domain of Islam itself is called "the house of war.") It is in this sense that, as Fouad Ajami puts it, "When Khomeini and company took on America and the West in their own way, that was the coffin of the New International Economic Order."

The Islamic revolution also cuts across the very notion of the "Third World," drawing attention to its artificiality and the element of condescension involved in reducing such a vast array of different peoples and cultures to a single category.

> RAJAIE: I have been very sensitive to these themes of "Third World," and I have always believed that it was not the right classification which could explain our country best: we thought that it was more or less preoccupied with certain economic criteria, and I believe that we had and we still have a very, very rich, profound and glorious cultural heritage at work—it is not in the museum, it is at work. . . . It is the poorest man in Iran who always memorizes the Koran: the beggars, in order not to be simple, professional beggars, went to the graves and recited the Holy Koran. It was a function—they did it as a job for others who came to pay a visit to the graves of their parents and their relatives. So the professional beggar was familiar with the Holy Koran, but the professional beggar in the West—I don't know how familiar he is with the Bible.

It is Islam, for Said Rajaie, that represents the real "third choice, between the Eastern political ideology and the Western political ideology." The Islamic revolution, he suggests, is "structurally" similar to the Non-Aligned Movement, but not similar in content.

> RAJAIE: What the Islamic revolution did was not to create something new: it was, as a matter of fact, a very important outcry which introduced to the rest of the world something already existing: Islam was there. Even if the Islamic revolution did not exist, and as a great scholar you would go to Islam and study it profoundly, you would come to the same conclusion, that Islam offers a third choice. So the actual ideology, the heritage, the system, regardless of the political events, the social events that it has created recently, the system has something to offer. But the Islamic revolution made the system better known to the public: it brought it up, it demonstrated it, and magnified it properly.
>
> So I think in this respect we have to make a slight distinction between the Islamic ideology as such and the political convention that certain countries came to in the Non-Aligned Movement. They thought, "Let's come together and let us handle our problems independently of the

East and of the West." That was a sort of convention. It was very constructive, very useful—I wish they had been able to continue with that good thought. But it was not an ideology which in itself had all these offerings and all these rich ideals in terms of politics, in terms of economics, in terms of moral philosophy. . . .

The Muslims—all the Muslims of the world—feel somehow betrayed by the promises of secularism, and they think that they have been, probably deliberately, kept deprived of their own Islamic identity. . . . So Muslims are refinding their own identity. They are returning to their own cultural background, to their own heritage, and they are becoming what they wish to be. You see, when they are treated as a secular Lebanese, as a secular Palestinian, as a secular something, in the West, they are always second-class citizens and they have nothing to stand on, but as Muslims now they have an identity which is at least equal to the identity of other nationalities and other subjects of various countries: they have something to identify with, something original, something which has been there for centuries, something rich, something decent, something constructive. So for them it is a very important cause, and they are returning to it.

MORTIMER: So is there an irreconcilable conflict between Islam and the West?

RAJAIE: If by "the West" you mean technology or science or construction, I think there is no conflict between Islam and that. . . . But if by "the West" you mean certain modes of life which we consider unhealthy, if cheating, gambling, drinking, womanizing, lust for money, materialistic ambitions, plundering other countries' properties, doing what has been happening in South Africa, doing all the injustice to the Palestinians—if all these things are okay in terms of Western values, I think it's very difficult to reconcile between Islam and these aspects of the West.

Of course, that is only one voice of the Islamic world, and one whose credentials many Muslims would dispute—among them Prince Abdullah, who said that if the Iranians wished to claim they represent the Islamic solution to the world's problems "then the first thing they should do is stop the war with Iraq, because it's not very Islamic the way they are pursuing continuation of military conflict with Iraq." The prince rejected the argument that punishing the aggressor is, according to Khomeini, itself a very important part of Islam.

ABDULLAH: No. Not like this. Not when you're killing hundreds of thousands on the way. They believe in God: they should leave it to God to punish whoever they claim did wrong. But to cause the death of hundreds of thousands and waste their country's resources, to continue having the situation when they're queueing for food in Iran, this is not the right way. There's nothing in Islam that says this.

But about the irreconcilable conflict between Islam and "what has been happening in South Africa," he heartily agrees.

ABDULLAH: Because in our religion, in our culture, in everything that we believed in, in our education, in our upbringing, to see apartheid implemented like this in a country that is recognized by the world community—by a lot of countries and by what is called the Free World—without any, well maybe not enough, effort put to end this apartheid, is remarkable. I mean, we feel very strongly that apartheid is, of course, wrong, not because we are part of the Third World or in sympathy with the African people, or whatever, but because it goes against everything that we believe in. Islam is very strong on this, on discrimination.*

In Latin America, according to Jorge Castañeda, the notion of the Third World was never taken all that seriously anyway.

CASTAÑEDA: There have been attempts by Mexican presidents, and by intellectuals, to portray Mexico as part of the Third World, to develop a sort of Third World solidarity between Mexico and Africa and Asia. I don't think it's worked very well, and I think in the last analysis what makes it not work is that there are enormous differences; and that which you can do in the best of cases is get the sort of solidarity between Mexico and, let's say, the Cuban revolution, or Mexico and Chile or Mexico and Central America for the last five or ten years, but the African and Asian thing simply doesn't work: it's too far. The obvious, evident differences are too great. The Mexican people just don't buy it. It hasn't worked. . . .

The idea of a Third World solidarity I don't think has taken root almost anywhere in Latin America. Perhaps in the Caribbean because of the racial question: Cuba, Jamaica, at one point perhaps Grenada, whatever—yes, because there is an African presence in those countries and there is a certain affinity. Brazil, perhaps, with the former Por-

*David Owen, interestingly, is prepared to concede that the Iranian revolution had an "impact on ethical and moral attitudes internationally which may even be beneficial. I mean, who can deny that some of the move back in terms of the reassertion of Muslim values is a thoroughly good thing? I mean, it's a very fine religion, and it's very important that we don't become anti-Muslim because of some of the more unattractive features of some of the Muslim revolutionaries. And if the Muslim religious value system was to come through in its full strength and genuineness, this could be a very beneficial influence in the world."

tuguese colonies in Africa—the language, race—perhaps, but not a great deal now.

And consequently, he says, Latin Americans do not take the noneconomic items on the Third World agenda very seriously either—with one, possibly significant, exception.

CASTAÑEDA: The government intellectuals will sign manifestos about them, and you will have the "six-country initiative" on disarmament, and you will have a lot of rhetoric, but I do not see anybody in Mexico or Latin America getting terribly excited about disarmament, about Palestine. South Africa *could* become something of great import, because there is a very important antiracist element latent in Latin America, because of important racial differences within the societies, and there's a sort of very noble antiracist streak in Latin America which could respond and be awakened by an exacerbation of the racial conflict in South Africa. The rest of these matters, frankly, I don't think are taken very seriously or are very close to home in Latin America. I think the North-South question, in Latin America at least, is essentially an economic issue.

So there seems to be some support from within the Third World itself for Newt Gingrich's view that the very term "Third World" is "one of the crippling intellectual devices of the modern world."

GINGRICH: There is no Third World. . . . I mean, India is radically different from Zaire, has no relationship. India represents the highest civilization of Hinduism and Buddhism and Islam; is a remarkably complex and developing country; is industrializing—it's now the tenth-largest industrial power in the world; has the English tradition of rule-of-law, free press, free elections; and is essentially a nontribal society. Zaire is a country that has two hundred languages, largely in the tribal tradition, is still essentially preindustrial, and is a single-despot dictatorship, because that's the system that seems to be evolving in large parts of Africa as a function of tribal societies. Now to lump those together in the "Third World" is simply to create an excuse for an anti-Western binary system—there's us and there's them. . . .

I would just suggest to you that the best thing we can do in the West is drop this concept of the Third World, because it cripples us.

But to many people *in* the Third World, such talk from a right-wing American will inevitably sound like "divide and rule." A great deal of human history, after all, can be written in terms of common grievances that have brought together people of otherwise very different outlooks and interests, and persuaded them to fight for a common cause. The growing gap between First World and Third World living standards could yet provide such a grievance, especially if we in the North appear indifferent to or complacent about it. And since South Africa is the one political issue outside their own area on which both Muslims and Latin Americans profess to feel strongly, it could be that the oppression of black by white in that country would provide the necessary stimulus of flagrant injustice that makes economic grievance boil over into violent political and military confrontation—if, that is, the West does not come down convincingly on the side of the blacks, and if the conflict reaches the kind of dramatic climax envisaged by Neil Kinnock.

> KINNOCK: It could be the great cauldron. Anybody who has taken an interest in the affairs of South and southern Africa since, say, the early sixties, which is what I've been doing, saw the process of decolonization—both the Portuguese and ourselves—saw a vacuum created in many respects in the wake of it, saw the existence of a prosperous and strong and prejudiced state in South Africa, and could see the incompatibility between the shift in expectation and the attempt by South Africa, especially the Afrikaners, to try and freeze history at the high tide that it reached in about 1952 as far as they were concerned. And the question all the time was, how is that basic conflict that's there going to be resolved? And . . . hitherto there has not been much hope for suggesting that there is any possibility other than huge destabilization, because that's what's gone on. Apartheid infects territories five hundred, a thousand miles north of the South African border, by the raids, by the constant conflict, by the implacable difference between people of different races that sustain that system of apartheid.
>
> Now, anybody looking at it knows that if it does break down, if the conflict comes, it will be a holocaust. Indeed the Eminent Persons' Group reporting to the Commonwealth in the spring [1986] said: take action or witness the biggest bloodbath since the Second World War. That's their words, and those words, because of the cautious and moderate language in which the Eminent Persons' Group report is generally couched, get greater authority.

Disappointment cannot, so far, be said to have solidified the Third World. It has made it embittered, but also more ragged, exacerbating its internal conflicts. As we shall see in the final chapter, that doesn't necessarily make it less dangerous for us in the comfortable North.

CHAPTER 13

An Untidy Village—and an Angry Policeman

AN ELECTRONIC NEIGHBORHOOD . . .

YOSANO: For instance, take rock music: what is popular in England, in your country, is popular in Japan simultaneously. . . . It's amazing, the things are happening simultaneously.

FABIUS: I am not thinking in terms of frontiers. My parents were thinking in terms of France, Germany, England, and I am thinking in terms of Europe as a whole, which is an enormous change—and it has something to do with many problems—the problems of ecology. Think about this nuclear accident in Chernobyl: it's sort of vivid proof that frontiers do not mean much today, and it is a new feeling.

GINGRICH: The modern era, I think, is totally different for all sorts of reasons. It's totally different, first of all, because Americans travel. We're probably par excellence the aviation nation. I mean, we Americans go and get on airplanes nowadays almost like people used to commute on trains from the suburbs into the central city. . . . Second, I think television makes us all one. We're now living in an electronic neighborhood, and we're all instantaneously together.

RAJAIE: I think this direct contact is somehow mutual. I think the West has had—or even the East, both of them—has had more direct contact with our people, and our people have had more direct contact with the West or with the East, thanks to the very important changes in the role of the media. . . . So this contact is a sort of change in the whole cultural setup of the globe.

If there is one thing that "FDR's children" have in common, right across the continents, it is this sense of wonder at being the first generation to live all its adult life in a single world society, in which every part of our planet is instantly visible and accessible to every other—what it has become a cliché to call the "global village." It is something that marks us off both from our parents and from our children, because it is something that has happened during our life-time—for the most part during our childhood and adolescence.

Most of us can still just remember a time when an aura of glamour and modernity surrounded the first jet airliners—the Comets. My own first flight—it was also my first trip abroad—was at the age of twelve, from Exeter to Paris, in a propeller-driven aircraft, or rather two, because it involved a change at Jersey. I was eighteen before I boarded a jet myself to fly to West Africa for Voluntary Service Overseas, and then I remember my father saying, "My goodness, we didn't have your opportunities!" or words to that effect. Now most jet aircraft don't even have names, only numbers—747, DC-10, etc.—and my teenage son flies to America for his summer holidays by Virgin Atlantic.

It seems extraordinary to think that in October 1943—two months before I was born—the seventy-two-year-old Cordell Hull, Roosevelt's secretary of state, boarded an aircraft for the first time in his life. Nowadays the secretary of state is hardly ever out of one. And it is not only grandees like him or professional globe-trotters like me whose lives have been transformed. Pakistani villagers visit their relatives in Bradford. Filipino maids in London save up for a three- or four-week trip home. Take a flight from Paris to Cairo in the season of the *haj,* and you will find it full of pilgrims from French-speaking African countries on their way to Mecca. Or take almost any flight from one Arab country to another: you have to fight your way on board through crowds of migrant workers and their families, most of them wearing heavy overcoats, however unseasonal, and carrying enormous transistor radios, presumably to avoid paying overweight. Often the one next to you will ask you to fill in his immigration form: he himself cannot read or write.

Of course, such journeys may represent the fruit of a year or more's savings. And not everyone who can afford it is free to travel where he or she wants. Some countries, like the Soviet Union, are very difficult to get out of. More and more countries are difficult to get into. And there are all too many whose own citizens, once out, do not go back for fear of political persecution. But they still have the use of the telephone. Most countries in the world can now be dialed direct from each other, and the habit of doing it has spread from business to private life. Fewer and fewer people seem to worry about the size of their phone bills. The Soviet authorities actually went back, for a time, to routing international calls through the operator, because so many well-wishers from the West were dialing direct to their favorite dissident. In September 1978 the Shah of Iran asked the Iraqi government to expel the Ayatollah Khomeini, thinking he would be less dangerous farther away. In fact, for all practical purposes, he turned out to be much *nearer* Iran in France than he had been in Iraq, because he had unrestricted access to the telephone, and to the world news media.

One consequence of this sudden shrinking of the world has been, for us in the North, what Christine Ockrent identifies as the major difference in world outlook between our generation and its predecessors: "the discovery of the South." She finds it even more pronounced among the next generation after us.

> OCKRENT: In France, for instance, it's very striking that among young people, according to polls, they are very much aware of hunger, much more than Communism, much more than East-West struggle or anything—and I think if politicians do not address themselves to that new form of consciousness of the world, they are in trouble.

Neil Kinnock, too, believes that our generation feels closer to the Third World than its predecessors.

> KINNOCK: It is a little bit superficial and a little bit of a cliché to say we are One World, but when I read of Mahatma Gandhi saying it, and when it is such a concept that's well understood now, I think that we'd be foolish to ignore the force and the truth of that idea, and then the obligations that it imposes on this generation and future generations of politicians in democracies; because we can recognize that and hope it'll go away, and do very little about it, or we can recognize that and try to be in partnership in control of those events; and that's why I say my attitude toward our relationships with the Third World is one entirely of partnership and not at all of patronage; and I suppose in some ways, with a few glorious exceptions, my generation is the first generation to really think in those terms about the Third World.

And this leads him to believe that a generous approach to the South can command popular support from a Northern electorate.

> KINNOCK: I think that it's a very substantial stratum of support because of the degree of anxiety that people regularly feel about the

deaths of millions in the agony of starvation. I think in addition, as part of that stratum or perhaps a little bit on top of it, there is a degree of the feeling of moral obligation, which is pretty profound in Britain—and we get knocked a lot, and we knock ourselves a lot, but on any private assessment of opinion this really does come through, and it's one of the great things about being British. . . .

Now I think that we've got to add to that constituency . . . and then add to it the understanding that there are huge material reasons, and major economic advantages, in treating the rest of the world as part of a human partnership instead of either neglecting it or abusing it. . . .

I'll just give you a couple of examples: I stood in Tanzania last July,* in the middle of a railway stockyard and engine repair shed; and alongside were scores of locomotives that had been cannibalized until they barely existed, in order to feed the locos that were kept on the track. In Britain, in that very month, we were shutting down railway engineering workshops because, allegedly, there wasn't enough work for people to do. Now there *is* that work to be done, and in the act of doing it there is simultaneously delivery from the evil of shortage and inefficiency in Tanzania, and delivery from the evil and massive expense of unemployment in this country.

That's just one instance: I could multiply it a thousandfold. . . . And so if we really understand we've got that moral obligation, but to that moral obligation can certainly be attached a material advantage which is a mutual material advantage both for the peoples of the Third World and for ourselves, then I think we make that constituency of relationship with the Third World much bigger, indeed absolutely dominant, in the political actions and the political psyche of the peoples of the Western World.†

A name that recurs constantly in discussion of this point is that of Bob Geldof, the Irish rock star who founded Band Aid and succeeded in galvanizing, or channeling, the conscience of the Western world into aid for famine-stricken Africa in 1984–85. We have already seen Christine Ockrent credit him with having "understood very well" that the younger generation in Europe today is "a generation that needs to give," and contrast his imagination and intuitive grasp of the popular mood with the politicians' lack of those qualities, in the context of

*This interview was recorded in July 1986.

†David Owen, somewhat similarly, believes that "there is a constituency that understands that the United Nations, for all its problems, is an organization without which the world would be a worse place; that therefore wants Britain to think in terms of international collective action, and is prepared to pay some price for it, and to put our money where our mouth is."

the need to inspire it with "a European crusade." Exactly the same point was made in a more general context by the Nigerian foreign minister, Bolaji Akinyemi.

> AKINGEMI: He showed that the human race could be a caring race, that the human race is not a selfish one, that there's a nobility in the soul of the human race that can be tapped. It is there, Bob Geldof showed that, so why can't political leaders tap this same kind of thing?

But it is generally understood that television played a crucial role in arousing the humane feelings that Geldof appealed to.

> OCKRENT: When the BBC showed those pictures of famine in Ethiopia—which was certainly no coincidence as far as the Ethiopian regime was concerned—we did not go for the political analysis at all. We didn't ask ourselves, "Why's bloodthirsty old Colonel Mengistu letting the camera crew in? Perhaps he wants these poor children filmed so that the world sends dollars to Ethiopia. . . ." We didn't think of that at all. We just were so appalled at what happened that a mixture of guilt and responsibility took shape: not political shape—it was not a political action, it was charity organizations, nongovernmental organizations, doctors' organizations—Bob Geldof, mainly.

Jacques Toubon goes so far as to call Geldof "a pure creation of TV," since "without TV there is no Band Aid, no Sport Aid"; and has no doubt that it is television that has made the human problems of the Third World so much more real for him and others in France, in spite of their disillusionment with its politics. So television, he thinks, can provide "one of the solutions to mobilize Western opinion in favor of this struggle for life." And Neil Kinnock likewise sees it as a great potential force for good.

> KINNOCK: Television is potentially, and in many ways currently, the greatest instructive medium that's ever been developed. The fact that you can back experience and knowledge with immediate illustration is the essence of good teaching in any case, in any set of circumstances. But to do it on that scale, and so graphically, gives television limitless opportunity for the movement and influence of opinion of people right across the world.
>
> So it's impossible to overestimate the impact of television. It doesn't even rely on literacy: it only relies on human perception. And consequently I think that it should very definitely be deliberately employed

as a force for good—and that doesn't mean any clamp-down or constriction of the direction of television. It does mean an emphasis all the time on the way in which television can deliver people from ignorance: and in doing that, of course, in my view, it then immediately becomes a force for good.

David Owen, too, thinks television has made an enormous difference, but more to the next generation than to his own.

OWEN: I think that it's the generation below us that felt the difference. I mean, I think nowadays a politician is very conscious of the fact that when he's talking about a subject, particularly international affairs, to an audience, they may well know more about it than he does: they've watched *Panorama* the night before, or *This Week,* * and there is a sense in which people are able to grasp, visually, complicated international political things.

Laurent Fabius believes that this makes it easier for us to understand and sympathize with the problems of other parts of the world—for instance, the problem of apartheid, and that this is why the South African government "has decided to stop and to forbid this sort of image, because it gave sympathy to the whole world, sympathy toward the anti-apartheid movement." But Jack Lang, a close political friend of Fabius who had actually visited South Africa with him not long before these interviews were recorded, was less sure.

LANG: I don't know. I am not a fanatic of television, and I am not sure that the best means to understand the situation is to give people shocking images. I think that sometimes it is better to speak to the intelligence of people, to the reason of people, to the heart of people, than to speak through emotive images. You forget rapidly, and these images give you the habit of seeing violence every day: you accept this violence, it becomes something normal—and this is terrible. I understand that television opens your doors on the world, but is this opening really an opening? That is the question . . . I speak only for myself, I don't speak for my political friends: I am not sure that TV is such wonderful progress.

Chris Patten feels a similar ambivalence.

*Popular current affairs programs on British television.

PATTEN: It's obviously extended, in a literal sense, people's horizons. I fear that it may also have blunted their sensitivities and their sensibilities as well to some extent. When one's seen a large number of horrors on one's television screen, as it were happening just down the road, I guess that perhaps one is capable of taking rather more, and that may not be a good thing.

In America, politicians' views of television tend to be even more jaundiced. As we saw in chapter 5, Richard Perle blamed television for the loss of Vietnam, while Larry Pressler felt it had made another large-scale conventional war impossible; but this might be a mixed blessing, since the alternative—guerrilla warfare—may involve "things that are hard for us to deal with." He thinks "we're going to face a new kind of war, that is, terrorism or something like that with nuclear weapons," and with live television coverage.

GINGRICH: We are much more aware, much more rapidly, of the surface of events, and much less aware of the substance of the mess: so that if next week's crisis is in Chad, we'll have nine television crews in Chad, and we'll all see five-minute live shots from Chad on the evening news, and we'll all see a map of Chad—which is somewhere in the middle of Africa—and we'll all say, "Oh, yeah, something must be happening there." But that doesn't mean very many Americans will delve into "Where *is* Chad? What are the tribal conflicts? What are the personalities? What's really involved?"—partially because, I think, of the information explosion. Our grandparents had relatively more mundane things to do—canning, cooking, sewing—but relatively less information per day. . . . You can know an enormously greater amount than your grandparents, and be more ignorant relative to what's available to know.

And Sam Gejdenson, at the other end of the political spectrum, is just as skeptical.

GEJDENSON: I'm not sure if there's enough depth in what we get on television, if enough of what's out there sinks in. If you take a look at previous generations, maybe a smaller portion got a substantial amount of information on what was happening in the world, but that small portion of the public that reads the *New York Times* or the *Wall Street Journal* or the *Boston Globe* or what have you—they had a much larger impact on our foreign policy decisions. Today there is much more of a direct relationship between popular desires and government actions, and much more of America's public is getting a very superficial amount of information, primarily through television: they're not reading papers, journals, they're watching television news programs—nightly news—and so much of it, you know, certainly in the local end, is covering, you know, the biggest car accident and fire rather than what's happening around the globe.

And what is true of America's image of the rest of the world may also be true of the rest of the world's image of America. Jorge Castañeda has no doubt that in Latin America, at least, television has exacerbated North-South tensions rather than increasing understanding.

CASTAÑEDA: On the one hand, it's true that you have a clearer vision in Latin America of what the United States is—or at least what American television says the United States is: I'm not sure that's what it really is, but certainly one view. But on the other hand, all of those aspects of the United States which many people in Latin America, among the middle classes particularly—not the politicized middle classes but the apathetic middle classes—have not wanted to know, or have not known, have been in a sense imposed on them by television over the past fifteen or twenty years: the bombing of Vietnam, the My Lai massacre, the fact that an American president, who was idealized as a somewhat mythical individual, in fact was forced from office because he was as corrupt, as thieving, lying, and foul-mouthed a politician as any Latin American dictator had ever been—one was elected, the other was not, but other than that they seemed to be the same—and so on. The fact, as of 1968—and this was of enormous importance—that large sectors of American society were rebelling against the established order in the United States, and in Europe also, undoubtedly had a very strong influence, for example, on the student movements which emerged throughout Latin America, and particularly in Mexico.

So I think that by presenting many things which are true of the United States, but which are not particularly favorable and not particularly positive, television has exacerbated things. It has made things more honest, but perhaps, as a consequence, more difficult to live with.

. . . OR A GLOBAL JUNGLE?

There, indeed, is the rub. Television and air travel may have brought us all closer together. But Joe Biden, who says he has "never been enamored with the notion that if I know you better I'm certain that I am going to have less conflict with you," has an important point: seeing someone in close-up doesn't always make them easier to live with. And if the United States as seen on television by Latin America's middle classes is on the whole unattractive, so is much of the outside world as seen from the American living room. The decolonized, multipolar world of today is not the tidy and harmonious place that Roosevelt and his advisers hoped it would be.

On one reading, this can be seen as the result of the breakdown of the victorious alliance of great powers that, in Roosevelt's mind, was supposed to remain in being, having won the war, to maintain and enforce the peace. That is still Alger Hiss's view.

> HISS: There could have been a greater unity within the umbrella of the United Nations than there has been, so that not only has the confrontation of the great powers resulted in enormous expenditures on armaments and economic strains, and the danger of atomic holocaust, but it has also meant that the Non-Aligned nations have not been able to participate in real aid on a multilateral, disinterested basis, bestowed on them by the other powers. There should be a harmony of nations: this was certainly the concept that those of us who worked on the establishment of the UN had in mind. That has not been possible, and as I say I think that's another deleterious consequence of the confrontation of the great powers.

Yet it now seems highly utopian to have supposed that the world ever could have worked like that; and this was not the only respect in which the Rooseveltian blueprint turned out to be based on false assumptions, as Brian Urquhart points out.

> URQUHART: The great emphasis in the [UN] Charter was on resisting aggression and threats to peace, and the notion of aggression wasn't quite as clear from 1945 on as it had been in the thirties with Hitler, Mussolini, and the Japanese, so that I think we started off with an oversimplified view of the problem to be tackled in avoiding another world war. . . . I mean, aggression in the way we had experienced it in the 1930s wasn't the normal mode in the 1940s: the normal mode in the 1940s was spheres of influence, and influencing governments to go one way or another, to become satellites and so on.

And the "normal" mode of the 1940s has become if anything more "normal" in the decades since. Clear-cut cases of one country attacking another and seizing its territory are the exception. The "norm" is provided by disputes over internal arrangements within countries, in which outside powers intervene either "at the request of the legal government" (sometimes clearly spurious, as with the Soviet interventions in Czechoslovakia, 1968, and Afghanistan, 1979, sometimes less so) or with the proclaimed purpose of rescuing an oppressed population where legal government has been subverted or violently overthrown (India in Bangladesh; Turkey in Cyprus; Tanzania in Uganda; the United States in Grenada; Syria, Israel, etc., in Lebanon) or has become intolerably, quasi-genocidally oppressive (Vietnam in Cambodia). In none of these cases have the frontiers of the invaded territory been directly challenged. Where they are, the issue is confused by arguments about the appropriate modalities for granting the right of "self-determination"—a concept proposed by President Wilson during the First World War to solve European frontier disputes, and carried over into the Rooseveltian global order—in colonial or ex-colonial territories: what size of territory should qualify (Western Sahara, East Timor, etc.) and whether the right extends to settler populations (Israelis, Falkland Islanders) or only to autochthonous inhabitants.

Perhaps the notion of a world divided into neatly self-contained nation-states was always an illusion. Manifestly it has become so since 1945, as the Chernobyl disaster of April 1986 reminded us all, in a particularly telling and unpleasant way.

> URQUHART: The fact of the matter is that we have now spilled over the national borders in so many fields of human activity that you're going to have to try to start thinking of institutions that could manage a very overcrowded planet afflicted with a whole new series of problems.

But while that may indeed be a good argument for a multilateral system of some sort, it could be said to make an anachronism of the United Nations in its present form, namely, that of a trade union of national governments each of which is assumed to enjoy undiluted sovereignty over a given area—and in many cases a very small area—on the world map. Brian Urquhart says that he sometimes feels—and it is hard not to agree with him—"that the UN was a beautiful Western concept constructed to deal with the problems of the early 1930s, and in this beautiful Rolls-Royce we're now bumping over all sorts of uncharted and unexpected terrain, with a whole lot of problems which the vehicle wasn't constructed for at all."

But part of the trouble is that this very period that has seen such a burgeoning of transnational activities and problems has also seen the birth of over a hundred new "nation-states" for whose rulers the trappings of national sovereignty, however ill suited to reality, are much too new and precious to be belittled.

BIDEN: We've got about a hundred nations in the world that are literally raising themselves out of the ashes of colonialism: they haven't figured out who they are, they haven't figured out where they're going. They are literally in a process of defining what their statehood is, what the nature of their nationhood is.

And this anachronism becomes all the more frightening, when—as seems to be gradually happening—the possession of nuclear weapons comes to be seen as a necessary attribute of national sovereignty, alongside such relatively harmless items as a flag, an army, and a national airline. It is a thoroughly unwelcome development, needless to say, to those who hitherto enjoyed a monopoly on nuclear weapons. "The general feeling is," says George Will, "let's not have more: more is worse as far as nuclear fingers, as it were, are concerned." But how can the West prevent it?

WILL: Well, it can do lots of things about materials, and the training of nuclear physicists, and discouraging it diplomatically—and every once in a while the Israelis may have to bomb something, and then we'll deplore the Israelis for doing what we're awfully glad they did. That's the division of labor in the world: the Israelis do it, and we deplore the Israelis.

This is all very well, but one cannot help being reminded of the remark of Kurt-Georg Kiesinger, the West German chancellor at the time of the Nuclear Non-Proliferation Treaty, that it was like "a bunch of notorious drunkards inviting everyone else to sign the pledge." At least Norbert Gansel, as a parliamentarian in a state that has itself forsworn nuclear weapons, has some moral credibility.

GANSEL: [I'm] among those who don't see the biggest danger for peace and East-West military confrontation in the middle of Europe, but I think the dangers of the Third World War are coming from the Third World. We are irresponsible enough to give to them the most modern weaponry instead of helping to solve their social problems; we are giving them nuclear power stations which are not even absolutely

> secure in our society; and they are developing the capacity of producing atomic weapons and chemical weapons, and I'm afraid if these arms will be used they will be first used in the Third World.*

Newt Gingrich identifies four "major conflict areas of the twenty-first century" to which "we have not yet invented solutions," namely: terrorism; "transnational conflict—the fights in Afghanistan, in Angola, for example, where you have a Cuban colonial army, Soviet equipment, Soviet training, and a Soviet general, but it's not technically a Soviet colony"; "information warfare"; and "finally there's what I would call "cultural warfare": I find it amazing that, in most of Latin America, the United States [intervention] in Nicaragua in 1933, and the United Fruit Company, which no longer exists as a real company, are more important realities than that the Soviet empire invaded Afghanistan in the 1980s—that people get more emotionally upset describing a fifty-three-year-old event than they do describing this morning's news."

Of these four, terrorism was the one that most preoccupied both Americans and Europeans during the summer of 1986. "Hostages could be captured any day of the week," said Larry Pressler. "We could have a terrorist incident in the center of New York City. You can carry an atomic bomb across the Mexican border in a suitcase and nobody would see you. We're vulnerable to a lot of things that just haven't happened [yet]." He declared himself a supporter of "what happened in Libya" (the U.S. bombing raid), but felt that "we can't depend too much on that kind of thing." Also the United States needed to have other "legal tools" to deal with international terrorism —tools of which it had deprived itself in the post-Watergate reaction during the seventies, when the CIA was emasculated and "there was an executive order making it illegal for the CIA to engage in any assassinations, which means that the president has to do things like bomb whole villages if we're after somebody like Qadhafi—if indeed we are . . ."—although, he added as an afterthought, "it also protects the lives of the president and vice-president, in the sense that if we're not out doing that sort of thing, then our guys probably won't get killed either—because I think in the backs of a lot of people's mind

*Chemical weapons had already been used (by Iraq) against Iranian forces, according to a UN report published in 1985. In March 1988 Iraq again outraged world opinion by using chemicals against the Kurdish population in an area of Iraq that had just been occupied by Iranian forces. Gas was used, of course, in Europe during the First World War. Alleged evidence that chemical weapons had been used by Communist forces in Afghanistan and Southeast Asia appears now to have been discredited: the "yellow rain" turned out to consist of bee feces! Defoliants were used extensively by U.S. forces in Vietnam.

the Kennedy thing might have been a retaliation for the Castro assassination attempt. It's never been proved."

In spite of this awkward point, he felt that in the situation now "we're realizing, as a practical matter, that some of that is necessary. . . ."

PRESSLER: We may have to create structures and organizations within our government that we find somewhat repulsive, to deal with terrorism. . . . We hope we can deal with things in a kind of a remote, clinical, mechanical way, but that means that we have to get right down into the gutter, so to speak, and slug it out with the terrorists. And if the terrorist movement continues as a way of countries expressing themselves, it means, for example, that the U.S. will have to re-create a unit, in the military or the CIA or someplace, where they're given a list of five guys who've killed Americans—without a jury trial . . . you go out and kill these guys.

Now that's a pretty big change. That's repugnant to our system. But we had such a law, where we could engage in assassinations, up until the 1970s, and it was used: it's part of history. I'm not advocating that, but I'm saying that if American citizens keep being killed, right now the only recourse the president has is to do a military strike on some military bases—and so we may have to do some things that will be very controversial.

Richard Perle, however, seemed to have fewer qualms about the bombing of Libya, reserving his scorn for the European reaction to it.

PERLE: The terrorist activity has been carried out on European soil, and I must say we are not only troubled but even puzzled as to the inability of these governments [in Europe] to do the obvious thing and close down these "People's Bureaus" that are really nothing more than forward bases for terrorist activity, in which your citizens and your territory are the subject of attack. Mrs. Thatcher was singularly courageous in the position she took, and I gather that she's suffered for it in the polls in the U.K.* And yet the irony is that, despite all of the predictions that the kind of action that the United States took would lead to a new outburst of terrorism, we now find the Syrians running round the world proclaiming that they're not involved in terrorism, and Qadhafi hasn't been seen since the raid took place;† and I don't think

*Opinion polls. The affair had faded from the headlines by the time of Mrs. Thatcher's third general election victory in June 1987.

†Interview recorded in May 1986.

we've seen the end of terrorist activity, but I think we have, for the first time, associated a price with that activity, and if we're going to discourage it, you have got to demonstrate that there's a price to be paid when it takes place.

In fact, European reaction to the raid was not uniformly hostile. Christine Ockrent, who supports military action as a response to terrorism, pointed out that "when President Reagan decided to bomb Tripoli, the official reaction in France was "Oh, we wouldn't let the American planes fly over France because we're so independent," but polls did show that not only were a majority of the French in favor of the American raid over Tripoli, but they wanted it to succeed more, and they said, "Why didn't the Americans bomb more heavily?"

Pierre Lellouche perhaps echoed that public feeling when he condemned the raid as a "very stupid act," but on purely tactical grounds. He shares Pressler's view that "other means" should be available.

LELLOUCHE: I mean, suppose I want to get rid of Mme. Thatcher or Mr. Mitterrand: I'm not going to bomb London or Paris, would I? I wouldn't. I would use other means—there are other means. The question is, we had not been able to do it collectively in NATO—why? Once again, because people are making a buck with those countries, selling weapons: we have thousands of Europeans in Libya and so on, it paralyzes our government. This is going to be a long-term threat: we're going to have to deal with it in probably as dirty a way as they do it to us; but you have to be dirty in a clandestine fashion. This is not a big public-opinion war, and with spectacular action like Tripoli what you do is, you transform it into a big public-opinion affair, in which the Americans accuse the Europeans of being cowards to the terrorists.

But the West German approach to the terrorist problem tends to be considerably less "gung-ho"—which is interesting because West Germany has had to confront a serious internal terrorist problem over the last fifteen years or so, and has done it with a fair measure of success.

ADAM-SCHWAETZER: From our own experience I think we must say that there is a danger of sacrificing democratic standpoints and democratic traditions, if you are faced with a threat like terrorism. It is a threat, there is no doubt; but we never thought that force, under peaceful conditions, might or should be answered by force. We said, "If you wish to do away with terrorism, you have to dry it out."

> Terrorism lives by the support of other people, who are just standing between our democratic society and terrorism: these people are giving shelter; they are giving support; they are writing in newspapers; so they really make up the bases which terrorists can live on, and you have to dry out that. You have not to force more people into that field around terrorism, but you really have to convince people who are there, on the border, to stay with democratic values, and this you can only do if you don't use force, but if you use tactics such as discussion, thinking over your own positions, trying to define your own position, trying to explain why you are doing what, and just convince people not to associate with terrorism, not to give the bases for terrorism, but stay in democratic values.

She feels that this approach, of drying up the water in which terrorist fish might swim, is equally applicable "on a national basis as on an international basis."

> ADAM-SCHWAETZER: If you could get all the other countries now clandestinely associating with Libya and Qadhafi—if you could get these countries not to do that anymore, but associate [them with] yourself and your ideas about international cooperation, I think the way would be far better.

And she agrees that this means showing a greater understanding for Arab political grievances—for instance, making more effort to solve the Palestinian problem—in order not to "push Arab countries to solidarity with Qadhafi," and that there is a clear difference between Europe and the United States in the priority they assign to these different methods.

> ADAM-SCHWAETZER: I think it's understandable because the United States is such a big country . . . but still I find it absolutely necessary that even a very powerful country should think of how to handle smaller countries, in order to better understand their reactions.

In fact, of course, a degree of force *was* used against West German domestic terrorism, and Karsten Voigt wryly recalls being "accused in the United States, when we were fighting the Baader-Meinhof gang, that we again were symbolizing our authoritarian methods; and they were accusing us for being too tough and too authoritarian against these terrorists."

Therefore, he stresses, in the argument over Libya the difference was not whether one should fight terrorism but whether the American strategy was right. Norbert Gansel draws a distinction between domestic terrorists of the Baader-Meinhof type—"the children of the best-off, not of the better-off but of the best," who acted out of a mixture of frustration and perverted utopian idealism—and the terrorism that comes from conflicts in the Third World, with which he is able to sympathize to some extent without actually approving it.

GANSEL: I think the whole Arab world, the whole Islamic world—which is nearly the same but not exactly the same—is in a process of search for identity, and this is a very painful process for themselves, also for us, and there are military conflicts in this area—the Iran-Iraq war for instance—there are social tensions, there is a suppression of religious and ethnic minorities, the miserable situation of the Palestinian people—and actually it is no surprise that they try to carry their fights from their territories to our territories, where they believe people are, powers are, who are responsible for the situation. For whether you like it or not, modern terrorism is, to a certain degree, the partisan with a credit card and access to the timetables of modern air traffic.

And, lest anyone should think the French are any more monolithically militarist than the Germans are pacifist, let us add that Jack Lang, the Socialist minister of culture, takes a very similar view.

LANG: You know, few people are terrorists for the pleasure. I don't approve of terrorism but, if you want to analyze a situation with objective eyes—if it's possible—you are obliged to say that terrorism is not something abstract, it is in relation with a concrete situation; and when during a long period oppression has been organized against a minority, this minority sometimes is obliged to take terrible means. I don't approve this situation: I want to explain, and probably we have to be more generous, we have to be more open, more imaginative, to find new solutions, to give peace—to these different people.

A plea echoed from the Arab world by Prince Abdullah:

ABDULLAH: There's a lot of talk and discussion and study of terrorism, [but] very few people have taken the trouble to look into why, for example in the Middle East, out of a group of two to three thousand, some people successfully recruit small teams to carry out violent attacks. Nobody has taken the time: they were looking at the political and the remedies sides of it rather than why would such

> numbers of people be influenced to carry out these . . . I think neither you nor I can feel the same way as those people who have been born in a refugee camp, looking across to their own homes occupied by strangers, or that their rights were taken away from them, or that their lands were taken by force, aggression, or fraud. It is impossible for me as a Saudi, or for you, or somebody else, to feel the same way that for example the Palestinians feel, or the Africans feel in South Africa, or in some other countries.

But he complains that Western attitudes toward the Arabs in general have hardened since "some Palestinian groups started some violent acts to bring attention to their plight." After that, people in the West "tended to look at the Arabs as terrorists, and that all the Arabs were either terrorists or oil sheikhs and there was nothing in between. I think that was rather an unfortunate situation, and of course we thought that this has gone, and now in the eighties—because again of certain acts by small numbers of people—that impression is even increased, unfortunately."

AMERICA AT BAY

It is true that those Westerners who are prepared to react to terrorism in the patient, understanding manner of Norbert Gansel and Jack Lang are diminishing in number, while those who are inclined to lump all Arabs together or even to lose patience with the Third World as a whole are getting more numerous, especially in the United States. America itself, thanks to its geographical distance from the Middle East, may be physically on the receiving end of less terrorism than Europe, but its forces, representatives, and even ordinary citizens in other parts of the world are frequent targets, and it certainly gets the lion's share of the verbal abuse.

We tend to think of modern high-speed transport and communications as having made the world "smaller," but this is, of course, a figure of speech. What has really happened is that the world we all have to cope with in everyday life has got much larger, more diverse, more difficult to cope with, and often more dangerous. Air travel and television, in particular, have brought us all closer together. But the former makes us more vulnerable to other people's quarrels: aircraft and airports are favorite targets of international terrorism, and it is air travel that brings other targets in the prosperous "North" within the reach of desperadoes from the alienated "South" (though one might say that is only historical justice, after centuries in which Europeans interfered more and more with the lives of people in other continents but there was very little traffic the other way). And the latter, television, makes us more aware of quarrels in other parts of the world, in all their ugliness, and more sensitive to the fists being shaken at us by people far away.

Americans, especially, are constantly being reminded by their TV screens that much of the world no longer loves them, and is less amenable than it once was to their control—or, as they might prefer to put it, less responsive to their leadership. "It seems almost institutionalized that anything the United States is for the Third World seems to be against," complains Joe Biden. Americans would not be human if they did not resent that. And the degree of their resentment is proportional to the generosity of the intentions with which they started out. Some of them felt the snub of the Third World reaction very early on—Newt Gingrich, for instance, when his schoolboy initiative of collecting books for Ghana drew a cold response from the Ghanaian government.

> GINGRICH: They wrote back and very huffily pointed out to me that in fact they had plenty of books, and they were a proud nation, and all that—which I found sort of bizarre, because clearly they are not that rich and they don't have that many books. But . . . we've educated them into believing that if their government bureaucrat doesn't talk to our government bureaucrat to get our government dollar, so their bureaucracy can buy new books, clearly it demeans them just to accept commonsense practical solutions.

Pat Schroeder, however, acknowledges that if American good intentions were "misinterpreted" in the Third World, it was often because they were "channeled in incorrect ways."

> SCHROEDER: For example, I spent a lot of time in refugee camps in Southeast Asia, and there would be huge boxes of things coming in from America filled with Snoopy dogs and things like that: these children had no idea what they were. I mean, you knew that people meant very well sending the Snoopy dogs, but they would have really done much better sending money and they could have bought the diets that the people wanted. . . . I understand the compassion that goes into Americans loading up stuff in the boxes in the church basement and sending it off somewhere, but it's not always the best way to go in dealing with the Third World, and I think that's a real challenge to our generation to try and explain that and get that goodwill that's there going in a way that's more effective.

She also suggests that American feelings about the Third World are colored by fears about the influx of Hispanic immigrants—"We have got Third World–type problems right here in our hemisphere that are very troublesome to us"—something that may be equally true of feelings about Arab North African immigrants in France, Muslim Turks and Kurds in Germany, or Asians and Afro-Caribbeans in Britain. But the point she comes back to is the failure of the Third World to respond to American aid in the way that Europe did to the Marshall Plan.

SCHROEDER: It worked in Europe because Europe had a certain education level, had a certain infrastructure level: all you had to do was infuse some stuff on the tap and get it all rolling, and boom, it went like Gangbusters! You go into a Third World country that doesn't have the education level, doesn't have the infrastructure, and try and do the same thing, and it gets ripped off; and then people get sour and angry. If you try and go in at another level, you have to be very careful that you don't come in and do all the wrong things. In Africa we went over and taught men how to drive tractors and do all sorts of things in agriculture, only to find out that in those countries men didn't do agriculture—we never thought to check that—women do. So we didn't make any progress. . . . So Americans tend to get frustrated: they want to help, but they get frustrated. They are not too sure the bureaucracy helps; they are a little frightened by the figures; and they are not quite sure how to respond.

Inevitably, a major subject of American concern is the misuse of American money by Third World governments. "The United States has pumped so much money into Haiti it's unbelievable," says Schroeder, choosing a particularly flagrant example.

SCHROEDER: Where did it go? I think probably Switzerland. I mean, you have the leader of Haiti living a much more elegant life than the president of the United States: Americans would never tolerate that, a leader living like the Duvaliers lived. That makes me really angry.

And Elliott Abrams broadens the point to take in the Third World as a whole: there has been, he says, "an awful lot of American money thrown in, and in return for it we have gotten an awful lot of abuse of the United States."

ABRAMS: [As a result] there is a kind of developing impatience, in the United States, with being asked to throw resources to people who have been unable to use them very well. . . .

Foreign aid is not a right. I mean, I understand that this concept has virtually been approved in the United Nations—the right to foreign aid, which is after all what the "right to development" means, I think. But we don't believe in that. I mean, this is taxpayers' money, whether it's Japan or the United States or Germany or Britain, and we have to make a decision that we're going to take some of this hard-earned money and not spend it at home but rather give it away to people abroad. To do that there are certain requirements.

Alas, the United Nations itself has come to be seen by many Americans as no more than a particularly flagrant example of this misuse of American money by Third World governments. It is, in the view of Brian Urquhart, the world body's faithful servant, "ironical that one hears the sort of talk one hears now in Washington about the terrible Third World which is supposedly—I think quite wrongly—that it is supposed to be anti-American and Marxist—not my experience of it at all, but nonetheless it's widely believed. This in fact, is the direct result of the U.S.'s—I think correct—enthusiasm for decolonization: something which belonged to the mood of the century and was ethically right."

The effect, Urquhart explains, was that the UN General Assembly ceased to be "the playground of the West," in which "they had an absolute surefire, automatic majority and they were bound to win, they couldn't lose," and which they had therefore enabled to override the Security Council (where the Soviet Union could use its veto) by adopting the "Uniting for Peace" procedure.

URQUHART: It then became clear to the U.S. that sooner or later they were going to have to come back to the Security Council and rely on the veto themselves, because they began to lose the majority in the Assembly; and of course the final loss of that majority was in 1971 when the Assembly finally voted to seat the People's Republic of China as the representative of China in the UN.

But Urquhart concedes that it was not only the loss of their automatic majority that alienated the Americans but also "the strident and sometimes, to me, extremely foolish sort of punk anti-American tone of much Third World oratory."

URQUHART: The British were the great scapegoat in the first ten years of the Organization: the British were used to this kind of thing. But the U.S. wasn't. They violently resented the idea that, because they were powerful, rich, and benevolent, in some way they were a sort of natural scapegoat for the poor and the dispossessed . . . and that, I think, has created a very considerable reaction already.

A third thing was that it became increasingly clear that the Security Council could not really take forceful action, and that was a great disappointment to many people, especially in the West. And on top of that, of course, we had the effect of all of these developments on the UN attitude toward Israel. . . . That began to change with the swing in the voting balance in the Assembly, in the Third World or Non-Aligned group, where decolonization was the main sort of glue that kept the group together: Israel began to be regarded as a colonial power because it was occupying territory thought to have belonged to the Palestinians and even parts of other Arab states—and this created a tremendous shift in American opinion.

I think we have to be very honest about this: it has had a huge effect on the way not only the Congress and people in Washington, but also the American public at large, view the UN. From having been the great electric train of the U.S., this wonderful idea which *they* had put on the road, it began to show signs of acting up and even in some cases being hostile.

Americans don't like to admit that they are sensitive to the kind of language used about them in the General Assembly, but their own language gives them the lie. "There isn't really much resentment," says Elliott Abrams, "because we don't take it all that seriously. Disgust and contempt are probably more the reactions that we have." And Newt Gingrich, as usual, expresses those reactions with particular force.

GINGRICH: A United Nations in which some local army sergeant, who takes over power and declares himself supreme president and dictator for life, has one vote, and France has one vote, is nonsense. I mean, what is the meaning of the vote? The concept of representation inherently, in the Western tradition, starts with the notion that you represent *someone:* and you can't just represent the latest boy to shoot his way into power. . . .

If the average citizen in Europe or America saw two weeks of the UN on television, they would vote for withdrawal, because it's outrageous: we send our money to some weak and irrelevant minor dictatorship so it can then afford to send its ambassador to New York, where he works for the Secretariat—which is paid more than 40 percent more than the American civil service—in order to have a forum in which they beat up on the country which gave them the aid money so that they could send the ambassador. Now that's dumb, and there's no reason for us to do it, and there's no reason to pretend it morally has any meaning: it has *no* meaning if sixteen minor random dictators collectively vote that Qadhafi's a good guy, and Western Europe and America are bad because we don't think terrorism is a nice thing. It's just nonsense, and I think the average American's attitude is "Why do we pay for non-sense?"

George Will claims not even to hear when Third World countries use the word "imperialist" to describe the United States.

WILL: I don't hear it: just tune out. It's part of a sort of audio wallpaper of being an American to hear that stuff in the background—a sort of buzz in your inner ear. But I don't think it obsesses Americans. If anything, they say, "Well, that's good: if they can't like us let them fear us."

Pat Schroeder does hear, but says she feels "that it's just rubbish."

SCHROEDER: You know, that's for home consumption. They talk about us as an imperialist power, and the next day they get on the plane and come over here and they say, "Can we go over the Andrews Air Force base and kick tires? We would like five of these and seven of those—and you'll give them to us, of course—and we'd like nuclear submarines and . . ."—you know, they come over with their shopping list, it's like they treat us almost like we are a parent. You know: you yell and scream and holler at the parent, trying to make them feel guilty, and then you run over and say, "Now if you want to stop feeling guilty you could give me all this!" Yeah, I think it's that they want to be treated as equals, but they act more and more like juveniles. That's too bad. That's really too bad!

She also regrets that Third World leaders have not emulated the self-restraint of an earlier anticolonial hero, George Washington, and said no "when someone said, 'Maybe you should be king,' or 'Maybe you should be the dictator"—though she admits rather charmingly that she herself might have constructed a rationale for accepting "if someone came to me and said, 'Pat, you really should be queen'!"

Clearly the lack of internal freedom, in countries whose freedom from external control America had championed, is another important factor in American disillusionment with the Third World. It was generally thought, says Elliott Abrams, "that decolonization meant freedom. It hasn't: it has meant national independence, but for the most part it hasn't meant freedom. I mean, if one asks how many genuine democracies there are in Africa, the answer is, not a lot."

> WILL: We believed that we knew how to administer foreign aid to elevate these countries, that it was just a matter of time before we planted democracy like so many potted plants around the world. . . . Nowhere has the sobriety of the last part of the twentieth century been more visible than in the thinking about the Third World. We don't know how to bring prosperity and free institutions to most of these countries. The economic infrastructure, the moral and intellectual prerequisites of democracy, aren't there, and we don't know how to export them. Those are not export goods that we're really good at!

And in the American mind it goes almost without saying that the lack of political freedom is connected with the lack of economic freedom. Although Joe Biden says that he cares "much less about whether a country as its path to nationhood or stability attempts to choose capitalism or socialism" than he does "about what they do in terms of alignment, in terms of geopolitics," he contrasts this with "the view that's held by many in this country—and in yours as a matter of fact—that what the ideological disposition of the leader in question is has more to do with how we should respond to that country than anything else."

Elliott Abrams would no doubt be counted among those "many," and gives the rationale behind that view.

> ABRAMS: A lot of what has gone wrong can be attributed not to anything that we in the West did wrong but rather to poor government in a lot of Third World countries. . . . I mean, the joke is to blame the London School of Economics, but there is an element of that—it happened in Latin America, too, under different auspices—that we have lived for thirty years with some version of good old-fashioned state socialism and a theory of what's good economics, and that has brought disaster and ruin to a lot of countries. . . .
>
> When I look at the difference in the rate of growth, let us say—just taking economic growth and putting politics aside—of countries like, take the Ivory Coast and compare it to Tanzania, it isn't because of aid:

Tanzania's got a lot more aid per capita than the Ivory Coast, and it hasn't grown as well—and the reason is internal economic policies. We should not be asked to subsidize failing development models.

Newt Gingrich, too, thinks the West has itself to blame for indoctrinating Third World leaders with a bureaucratic "socialist" approach to government. Indeed he seems to be one of those who believe the whole business of foreign aid to be a well-meaning but disastrous left-wing conspiracy.

GINGRICH: I think there's a real relationship between the left-wing education of black African leaders in the fifties and sixties and the fact that Africa is the only continent in which the standard of living has dropped in the last ten years. . . . [It] has nothing to do with the drought. When you take countries that have not had a drought, the average income in Africa has dropped, and it is the only continent that's true of. It is also the continent that has the most people who believe in sort of a left-wing intellectual socialist approach to life, and it's just been incredibly destructive.

I think we should take some responsibility for that, because when we have the foreign aid program, and we send the foreign aid minister, and we send the foreign intellectual, and they sit down with the African leader and say, "To really develop, you ought to do A, B, and C" (which sets up a government bureaucracy), "and you set up this planning system . . . and your entrepreneurs don't matter and your tax rate doesn't matter," etc., and they listen to us because we are giving them the $100 million loan, then to that extent we've had a peculiar combination of three things: a neo-socialist value system among foreign aid planners, a bureaucracy of the government, and an intellectual, academic involvement of people who don't know anything about economic growth except what they've read—and those three groups have truly helped make Africa sick.

Anti-Americanism, dictatorship, socialism: to these three sins the Third World majority in the UN General Assembly adds the least pardonable of all, in the eyes of at least some Americans: anti-Zionism. According to George Will the most important event in the progressive disillusionment of his generation of Americans with the UN was unquestionably the "Zionism is racism" resolution of 1975.

WILL: . . . because the American-Jewish community is articulate, important, and at that point certainly liberal, and the UN will never get it back, that kind of aura it had up to the point when it passed that resolution, because American Jews said that the United Nations "is an enemy of reason," and that was a very important constituency to lose.

Otherwise, he added, disillusionment springs from "just the general feeling that huge wars erupt—the Soviet Union invades Afghanistan and you can't get them to condemn the Soviet Union; you have one of the major wars of the modern era between Iran and Iraq and the UN is absolutely impotent—that it's just not serious. . . ."

The former point was true in the letter but perhaps not entirely in the spirit: since 1979 the General Assembly, although not condemning the Soviet Union by name, had repeatedly voted by overwhelming majorities in the teeth of Soviet opposition for the withdrawal of all "foreign" troops from Afghanistan. The latter point, by contrast, was true in spirit but overstated: the UN had not, of course, been able to stop the war between Iran and Iraq—it could do so only if the great powers acted in concert to enforce the Charter as originally envisaged—but the Secretariat had helped to negotiate *de facto* arrangements by which both sides desisted, at least for a time, from bombing each other's cities.*

If anti-Zionism is the worst of the Third World's crimes, it is not surprising that the general American disillusionment with the Third World often turns to positive antipathy when attention focuses specifically on Arabs and Muslims. Fouad Ajami claims that even the present secretary of state, George Shultz, "after the defeat of his scheme of May 17, 1983, of bringing about peace between Lebanon and Israel under American auspices—excluding Syria of course— . . . developed a great resentment against the Arab world, and a great distance, a great aversion, to all things Arab and to all people Arab."

Iran, of course, since the hostage crisis of 1979–80, excites even stronger hostility—which Said Rajaie-Khorassani predictably attributes to the efforts of the media "in smearing the face of the Islamic revolution and the face of Iran in the United States"; and Elliott Abrams confirms that "militant Islam is connected in the minds of most Americans with Arab terrorism, and that has tended, I think, to be confused together and to make people quite unsympathetic. Throw

*Belatedly in 1987 the Security Council did embark on a serious attempt to end the war, which bore fruit a year later, when Iran suddenly accepted its terms, apparently to forestall imminent defeat.

in the ayatollah and Iran and the hostages, and you've got a real lack of sympathy!"

Small wonder, then, that the disclosure of his clumsily clandestine dealings with Iran was to prove such a disastrous turning point in President Reagan's political fortunes!

Lack of sympathy with militant Islam in particular, with the prevailing political order in the Third World in general, and even more generally with the way the world as a whole has turned out is clearly something shared by American politicians of my generation almost irrespective of their other political views. What, then, do they think has gone wrong? On the right, at least, the diagnosis is very clear: America has been weak; and the prescription—America must be strong again—follows inevitably from it. (Or is it the other way around?) The "turmoil and confusion" in America during the late sixties and seventies, says Newt Gingrich, "cost us a considerable amount: it frankly cost the people of Vietnam, and Cambodia, and Laos, and Ethiopia, and Afghanistan a lot more."

> ABRAMS: When there was a withdrawal of American power, did things go better or worse? And our answer, of course, is they went worse, and you had Soviet gains all over the place from Angola to Nicaragua, and then in a place like Iran you just had a general decomposition of whatever modernization had taken place—worse in every possible way. And the lesson we drew from that was that American power is not the problem: American power is the solution. . . . When we walk away things tend to go very, very badly, and not just for us but for the people there.

Having been in Iran myself during the Islamic revolution and witnessed the extraordinary mobilization of millions of Iranians and the strength of anti-American feeling, I am always astonished by the readiness of Americans to regard this event as caused essentially by the weak and misguided policies, if not by a positive decision, of their own administration—"We went and turned it over to that maniacal fanatic," as President Reagan said in his foreign policy debate with Walter Mondale in October 1984. Americans, it seems, have a truly imperial disposition to take responsibility, positively or negatively, for whatever happens in almost any part of the world. Whatever people in Iran may decide to do, it is assumed to be within the power of the United States to prevent it and therefore, as Abrams puts it, "inaction is a form of action."

ABRAMS: It is our feeling that if we withdraw any vacuums are likely to be filled by the Soviets.* This is precisely what we think happened in the seventies when the United States did tend to withdraw in the aftermath of Vietnam. The openings were filled, and every single time they were filled things seemed to go worse. I can't think of an example where Americans would agree that our withdrawal tended to produce more freedom.

But in the case of the United Nations the trouble goes back further: Richard Perle believes that America "made the mistake in the immediate postwar period of concentrating unduly on building institutions but without the power to back them up," while Newt Gingrich detects a "grudging realization that we made a major mistake in the way we founded the UN—that we frankly should not have allowed dictatorship in." For Elliott Abrams the conclusion is bleak.

ABRAMS: The UN is a discredited institution to most Americans: there is a desire that it could be better, there is no desire to junk it, but I think there's a kind of general view that all of those great international institutions we set up after the war with high hopes—the UN, the World Court†—are just not working. They have failed.

George Will thinks this has happened because "the ideological premise of the UN is false, which is that there is a community of nations. In no useful sense of the word 'community' is there a community of nations. No shared values."

In which case, asks Newt Gingrich, why not a new-model UN, restricted to those who *do* share our values?

GINGRICH: You're going to see the beginning of a real argument that maybe we need something like the Strasbourg European Parlia-

*The Soviet view, on the other hand, as expressed by Sergei Plekhanov, is that American policy-makers will sooner or later "have to come to terms with a new world which is now in existence, and that's a world which is clearly not bipolar: it's multipolar. It's a world which is much too crowded for the use of military force. [Could this be a lesson the Soviet Union has learned in Afghanistan?] It's a world which cannot afford even a conventional war of any serious size and scope in a place, for instance, like Europe. . . . All these realities are there, and the Americans will have to adapt their own behavior and thinking to those realities, just as they will have to adapt their own thinking to the fact that the United States had diminished stature in the world economically. It's still the strongest power, but it's not the dominant power."

†The International Court of Justice was in fact set up before the First World War but—especially no doubt since Nicaragua sought redress from it for the American mining of her harbors—has come to be seen as just another of the shackles of postwar multilateralism from which America now needs to break free.

> ment,* maybe we need an association of nations which you can only get into if you're free—elections and the rule of law, etc.—and that's the assembly we ought to take seriously, and then keep the UN around essentially as a place for people to chitchat with each other, but we recognize that a lot of the thugs we're chitchatting with are in fact thugs. . . .
>
> The most populous single nation at that assembly would be India: India is a democracy. By contrast, although Pakistan's more pro-American, President Zia would not be in that assembly: he's a dictator.

A touching thought, but one can hardly imagine India agreeing to join this admirable new club; and it misses the point of the United Nations as conceived by Roosevelt, which was that problems of world peace were too important to be discussed only with those who shared your own values and system of government. The relationship between democracy and good international behavior is in any case not a simple one, as Prince Abdullah—member of the ruling family of one of the few states in the present world that has the grace not to *pretend* to be democratic—points out.

> ABDULLAH: Well, I mean, how did Hitler get to power? Didn't he use a democratic process? Didn't Marcos have elections? . . . What right do certain people have to make moral judgment on issues that people themselves have to make, in each society, in their own way, in whatever form, and with whatever urgency they feel they have to express it? . . . I don't believe that a society can make a moral judgment for the rest of the world, just because whatever they have on appearance looks better, or that they feel their checks and balances are better than other countries.

But moral judgments clearly *are* important in American foreign policy, whether foreigners like it or not. For Elliott Abrams the essential continuity between the immediate postwar age and the present is provided by the mission "to protect certain values . . . not simply peace, but peace and liberty." Jimmy Carter in his time was accused (by Europeans, notably) of trying to conduct too moralistic a foreign

*Probably a reference to the Council of Europe—an association of European democracies set up in the late forties, whose institutions in Strasbourg include a parliamentary assembly (composed of delegates from the parliaments of member-states) and a Court and Commission that administer the European Convention on Human Rights. The European Parliament, which also meets in Strasbourg, is an institution of the European Community, whose members are directly elected by the citizens of the twelve member states.

policy, but the criticism of his administration by its successor, through Abrams's mouth at least, is the opposite.

ABRAMS: One way of summarizing the distinction between the Carter period and the Reagan period, I think, in American life—or, if you will, the seventies and the eighties in American life—is that there seemed to be a view in the seventies that if you would compromise on these principles with the Soviets, this was the path to peace, and in the Reagan years I think there's more of a consensus that that's wrong, that you never get to peace by compromising on these fundamental principles. You just have to fight for them. And if you're going to fight for them—economically, diplomatically, militarily—then you have to be strong.

AMERICA TRIUMPHANT?

In this mood, Americans still feel able to offer the world leadership, and still feel confident that it will be accepted. There may be, says Richard Perle, "some surface manifestations of criticism from the left, from a part of the intellectual community," but "I don't know where one is looking if it is not to the United States."

PERLE: I notice, for example, that throughout Western Europe, despite the controversies and the criticism, the realization exists that the American economy performs as well as it does because it is unencumbered by the kinds of restrictions that exist in Europe—and one government after another is moving to eliminate those restrictions. You see it in Germany, you see it in France, you see it in the Netherlands, in the United Kingdom. The notion that innovation and energy and progress and scientific achievement can only take place in a system of relatively unencumbered individual enterprise, in which talented individuals are given an opportunity to perform because there's capital available and because work is going on in universities and in industry —one sees that being emulated all over the world, with enormous success in the Pacific, for example, where one country after another is achieving real success in its political and economic institutions, largely by emulating the United States and often in collaboration with the United States.

ADELMAN: I think there is a kind of momentum of freedom around the world. When I compare the situation today with the situation in the 1970s, I see, myself, that freedom is very much on the march and not on the run. We don't have a succession of countries falling to Marxism like we had in the seventies with Vietnam, with Afghanistan, with Cambodia, with Laos, with Angola, Mozambique, with Ethiopia: none of that is happening nowadays. Nowadays all the opposition movements around the world are fighting Marxist governments. Now I wish them well. I hope they overthrow the Marxist governments myself. But I am saying that when you look at the flow of history—to use Marxist terms—you realize that the flow of history is against these Marxist governments, and very much *for* Western-leaning governments.

And Elliott Abrams, too, believes that the Third World is now beginning to be more appreciative of the American model.

ABRAMS: I have the sense that there is a kind of intellectual revolution going on: I see it most clearly in Latin America, but I think it is true in Africa as well, that there is a greater and greater sense that, first, the leaders of a country are responsible, not some international system —they are responsible for development; but that, secondly, the way they can probably best do it is to get out of the way.

He believes, moreover, that Reagan's America can speak to the Third World in the same language that Kennedy's did, and that if Third World leaders like Bolaji Akinyemi are less responsive now than they were then, "what has changed is not us but them."

ABRAMS: Kennedy's vision, remember, was "America's watchmen on the walls of freedom. . . . Bear any burden, pay any price, for the survival of liberty." Kennedy was speaking at a period in which liberty was the key issue, and Kennedy was a central figure in the Cold War and the desire to resist Soviet expansionism. One of the things that many Third World leaders are now saying is that they do not wish to concentrate on liberty because many of the people who are speaking to you do not have it in their countries and do not wish to permit it in their countries. So I would, in a sense, throw Kennedy in their teeth and ask them if they can beat the standards which he set. I would ask them to join us in a great struggle for development and for liberty—and in many cases they have been more concerned with achieving personal power and state power, and less with the development of their countries and the development of institutions within those countries that reduce their personal power.

But there is progress, he insists—even on such an apparently unpromising issue as nuclear proliferation.

> ABRAMS: Do you know, ten years ago if you'd asked people whether there'd be a fantastic amount of proliferation in the seventies and eighties, probably people would have said yes—and there hasn't been. Some of the efforts we've made to reduce it or check proliferation have been working. So I'm an optimist on these questions.

The change in Indian economic policy under Rajiv Gandhi is seen as particularly encouraging by apostles of free enterprise like Jack Kemp and Newt Gingrich.

> KEMP: Here's India beginning to grow, beginning to establish an economic vitality. Their markets are beginning to respond, there is a dynamism returning, the stock market's rising, the rupee is strengthening, and people are beginning to see capital come into India. It can happen anywhere.
>
> GINGRICH: India's now the tenth largest industrial power in the world. India's making it, because it's getting more and more commercial and less and less socialist. Now you know the French are discovering this: Mitterrand tried the left, it was a disaster, he's now shifting to the right—whether or not he has help from the French conservatives is beside the point. The point is that the French looked to what America was doing—creating ten million jobs; what French socialism was doing was killing jobs—and gave up. It's only in the political and intellectual communities that people say, "I don't care how bad my cooking is, I'm going to keep doing it this way even if it produces the worst breakfast ever!" In the rest of the world people say, "Why don't we do what works?" And what works is regulated free enterprise.

George Will sums up this sense of rediscovered self-confidence by comparing the America of today with the America he grew up in in the fifties.

> WILL: It's hard to recapture, although I have a feeling in the 1980s people are beginning to recapture it, the sense that we had as young people in the United States in the 1950s that our country was at the wheel, the wheel of the world. I was born in 1941: began reading newspapers and becoming aware of the wider world in the 1950s when Eisenhower, this avuncular figure, was presiding over a quite placid

peace and prosperity—which was his campaign thing—and there was no doubting the sense that the United States was the dominant force —politically, economically, culturally—in the world. That was shattered in the 1960s, reduced to rubble in the 1970s—and what you're beginning to see now in the 1980s is a recapturing of that. I mean, it's easy to caricature Ronald Reagan saying, "America's back and standing tall," but a lot of people feel that way, and I have a feeling that people who are ten, twelve, thirteen right now are going to have some of the same experience that the American people had when we were young in the 1950s.

How seriously should one take these claims of an American renaissance? They certainly don't cut any ice with Bolaji Akinyemi.

AKINYEMI: To call what is going on in the United States today a "renaissance" is to take liberties with the language. There's no doubt that there is a resurgence of something. I'm not sure—it's not the best either for America or for the rest of the world. There is nothing wrong with developing pride in oneself, in one's society, but not at the expense of others. . . . Defining pride and effervescence in a particularistic kind of way, at the expense of a larger whole, is never a testimony to the nobility of the human soul. Never. . . . I don't think it's true to say that a renaissance is going on anywhere in the world. I don't see any evidence of that. I see evidence of narrow selfishness, narrow nationalism, all over the world. I see an inability on the part of leaders to overcome their own petty egos, and that kind of thing. I see a world that seems to be waiting for its soul to be reawakened, to continue on its journey.

But how "particularistic" is America's current burst of "pride and effervescence"? Is it really a form of "narrow selfishness" expressed at the expense of the rest of the world? In America's own political vocabulary the charge is one of "unilateralism" or "isolationism"—the attitude that led the Republican-controlled Senate to reject ratification of the League of Nations Covenant in 1920; against which Roosevelt fought in the thirties and early forties to convince Americans that their fate was bound up with that of the European democracies; and which Truman and his advisers overcame, with the help of Senator Vandenberg, at the time of the Marshall Plan and the North Atlantic Treaty. According to Elliott Abrams, the present attitude cannot be equated with the old unilateralism because the goals of the Truman period have not been abandoned.

ABRAMS: I think what's happened in this country in the eighties, that is to say, the Reagan years, is that we have become persuaded that the values [the defense of liberty] are more important than ever and that the institutions have failed to protect them, and that they can be best protected by a strong America. That isn't unilateralism because the goals are, if you will, multilateral. . . .

I think that in an odd way there is a growing reapproachment between the view of the immediate postwar generation that America had awesome global responsibilities and that a strong America was crucial to the meeting of those responsibilities, and—after a chasm of a number of years—the advent of a new generation that actually believes the same thing.

But Arthur Schlesinger, speaking with the triple authority of a member of "the immediate postwar generation," a historian, and a former adviser to President Kennedy, disagrees. He feels that the crucial innovation of the Roosevelt-Truman period—the belief in working through alliances—has "been lost in recent times." "We practice," he says—picking up the phrase popularized by the neoconservative polemicist Irving Kristol—"a kind of global unilateralism" that is not really different from the old prewar isolationism.

SCHLESINGER: Isolationism historically never meant the United States's withdrawal from the world. . . . What isolationism has meant historically is insistence on American freedom of action in foreign affairs. This meant a rejection of what Jefferson called "entangling alliances"; and I think that old isolationism has been reborn in the unilateralism of the U.S. today: an insistence on doing things our own way without consultation with allies, without belief that allies matter very much. "We'll do it and they'll come along. A bit too bad, their bad luck, if they don't." As Reagan said after they got the hijacked plane down,* he said "We did it all by our little selves!"—and it's this go-in-alone thesis which is historically the essence of isolationism and which is the essence of American foreign policy today, but which was rejected by foreign-policy-makers in the great period of the 1940s.

George Will, a supporter of the new attitude, is not afraid of the word "unilateralism"—interpreting it as "a belief . . . that America is special, has special powers, special responsibilities, no one else can

*In October 1985 American aircraft forced an Egyptian plane carrying the hijackers of the Italian cruise ship *Achille Lauro* (who had murdered an American passenger) to land at an American base in Sicily. The men were taken off and handed over to the Italian authorities.

do them, the world's better for our undertaking them and we have to do them alone." And while he considers this quite different from the old isolationism he warns that "one can quickly become the other" if America's benevolent interventions continue to be spurned and obstructed (as in the case of the raid on Libya) by those in whose interests they are supposedly undertaken. On the Democratic side, Joe Biden does not think unilateralism could ever reach the point where "a dedicated attack on Europe" would not be considered as an attack on the United States, but adds, "What you may see is unilateral *action* on the part of the United States over the next twenty years, to say 'We're going to make a judgment as to how best we will meet that requirement of being protective of you' "—for instance by basing American F-111 aircraft at home rather than in England, where their use for such purposes as bombing Libya is subject to veto by the British government.

The new unilateralism (if that *is* its right name) does not enjoy full bi-partisan support among "Roosevelt's children," however. While some Democrats such as Pat Schroeder may be more ready than Republicans to envisage reducing America's commitment to Western Europe, they tend at the same time to advocate a more multilateralist approach to the world at large, and take a more forgiving line toward the foibles of the UN. "Regrettably," Schroeder says, "we have tended to use the UN for lectern-pounding and screaming and Third World–bashing: they bash us, we bash them, and maybe everybody feels better when it's over. But it certainly doesn't do anything for the world. It doesn't do anything for what the UN is supposed to be doing."

She fears, moreover, that the cuts in government expenditure will fall on foreign policy commitments in the Third World, rather than "on the developed world [Europe and Japan] which can take care of itself. I think for my children and my children's future there is much more trouble if we take it out on people who can't fight back or can't stand on their own two feet. Unfortunately I'm afraid that's where it will come. Our European allies, our Japanese friends, are very good at making their case. The Third World really isn't, because they are not into that advocacy yet, and I think the next generation will wake up and say, "What did you people do?' "

One observer of American foreign policy who is not convinced by the "global" or multilateralist pretensions of the present administration is Fouad Ajami.

AJAMI: American conservatives, if I read them right and if I follow their debate, really don't say that this model that they have applies to all the Third World. American conservatives have never taken part of themselves and said "Okay, we are going to test the validity of our model in foreign lands." They're not really "travelers," if you will. The liberals were. They traveled much more, metaphorically. I mean they really took their ideas, and their self, and implanted it in other places, and wanted to see it grow. I think American conservatives don't have this belief: they're not looking for New Frontiers. . . . If you buy this American package of private enterprise and democracy and it works for you, good. If it doesn't—well, you know, there's not much we can do for you.

Americans today really don't believe that they are to go outside and be crusaders for anything. I think the crusading instinct is at its weakest today, and I think that Reagan—part of him—when he tries to be a crusader is unpersuaded. You know, Nicaragua is an easy one: fine, we'll see what we can do there. But should there be a setback in Nicaragua, I mean this country can walk away from Nicaragua without great pain.

Certainly the Reagan administration walked away with amazing nonchalance from Ajami's own country of origin, Lebanon, in 1984, after investing a great deal of Cold War rhetoric and the lives of several hundred U.S. Marines. It showed greater tenacity in Nicaragua, in the teeth of strong congressional and public opposition, but without taking the crucial step of deploying U.S. forces there. Yet even its obsession with that small Central American country could be taken to support Ajami's point: what is at stake there is not really America's global mission or her image of herself, but the good old-fashioned issue of control of the "backyard," which every president has concerned himself with, no matter how isolationist, from Monroe onward. And Richard Burt, Reagan's ambassador to West Germany, can be quoted in the same sense: "The rest of the world has to gradually become used to the fact that the United States cannot be the superpower that it was in the 1940s and 1950s—that we have to protect our interests, just as other countries have to protect theirs."

Even the would-be globalists like Elliott Abrams admit that they "still consider the East-West struggle to be central" and that this is a source of difficulty with at least some Third World countries.

ABRAMS: It is the most important thing about international life to us, the struggle against the expansion of Communism, and to a number of Third World leaders that seems to be a peripheral issue and one which uses all our resources and our attention and takes it away from them, and they don't like that. I mean, I can understand why, if you're dealing with fantastic rates of poverty and illiteracy and disease in a very poor country that needs help, and we're all concerned with the Soviets, that looks like it's a mistake and it's a misuse of resources. But, of course, from our point of view that's just wrong.*

It is indeed a matter of "attention" as well as physical and financial resources. Saudi Arabia is hardly in need of the latter, but Prince Abdullah, like every other Arab who wants to be friends with the United States, still complains bitterly about the seeming American obsession with the East-West conflict to the exclusion of issues more immediately important to people in the Middle East itself (meaning the Palestinian problem and perhaps the Iran-Iraq war):

ABDULLAH: They act as if they are almost at war with the Soviet Union. You know they already have an agreement with the Israelis on medical facilities, on storage facilities, on Star Wars, on this and that —you know you'd think there's a war that's going to break out in the Middle East, or the Middle East front is where the Third World war is going to start. But with regard to our own issues they seem to be wasting their time on tactical things, rather than important strategic issues and the long-term relationship between a very important block of countries [the Arabs] and the American nation.

Whether one emphasizes the global or the unilateralist ingredient in the mix, it is clear that an important aspect of current American doctrine is willingness to use force if necessary and determination not to be restrained from doing so by multilateral obligations—whether it be injunctions from the World Court not to mine Nicaraguan harbors or entreaties from European allies not to exacerbate tension in the Mediterranean by bombing Libya. And this aspect of Reaganism, too, comes in for criticism at home.

*I asked Sergei Plekhanov how far this preoccupation with the East-West balance was reciprocated on the Soviet side. He replied: "Well, we view the world as a very diverse and multipolar entity, and we are not inclined to view it in just East-West terms, but the East-West terms are sometimes imposed by the situation, or by the will of some governments. For instance, as a result of viewing the Nicaraguan situation—Central American situation—in East-West terms the United States is now conducting an undeclared war against that country and is planning an invasion, is sending units there to fight against the government, to kill civilians and so on. In that sense the East-West context is artificially brought into the picture, and when we think about the Nicaraguan situation there's no way that we can really see it independently of what the United States does. So when one power views a local situation in terms of East-West conflict, then that imposes its logic on the situation, so it's a very contagious thing."

GEJDENSON: Sadly enough, the Reagan administration has sent some of the wrong signals in the sense that the Reagan administration has been too cavalier with its use of force and ended up embarrassing the United States in several instances: moving the Marines into Lebanon and trying to use World War II kind of offshore power ended up being a tremendous failure, embarrassing the United States and making us more one of the combatants rather than someone who could come in and help establish the peace process—we've basically lost an opportunity for peace in the Middle East. In Central America we've used force in the wrong way again, in financing the *contras*: there is now no contrast between our actions against the Nicaraguan government and the Soviet action against the government and people of Afghanistan. So I think they've used force which sends a message the United States is ready to do so—rightly so in Libya, but all too often in the wrong way.

Along with this goes the jingoistic patriotism that has become known as Ramboism, after the cinema hero played by Sylvester Stallone and publicly praised by Reagan himself. To the outsider, and to some more reflective Americans, all this talk of American strength seems to protest a little too much. The comparison with the 1950s, when American strength was largely taken for granted and did not have to be asserted so stridently, seems telling in a way that George Will does not intend it to be. Larry Pressler, the thoughtful Vietnam veteran, takes a refreshingly detached view of it all.

PRESSLER: I think it comes from an American spirit that we'd like to believe in—as in the 1950s: "American know-how, we're the best, we're the greatest." We'd *like* to believe that. We'd like our leader to be the man who "if anybody crosses us, we take care of him quickly," and we like to see American businessmen succeed—and athletics. I think the [1984 Los Angeles] Olympics is an example of that: we had a very successful Olympics, but if you think it through a lot of fine athletes weren't there for one reason or another. The East German team, for example, probably would have won the Olympics had they been there: you don't hear that very often. . . . It was a great celebration, very much a part of this era. I think that those Olympics sort of caught the spirit: they were red in the crest, everything worked out well, and it's great on TV, but still, the fact of the matter was the competition wasn't there. . . .

Self-congratulation over the Libyan raid (which he supported) was, in Pressler's view, equally excessive: "It's highly publicized, but if you really look at it what did we do? We raided a little tiny country somewhere, showed that we could shoot down all their planes with heat-seeking missiles." And he thinks that if it came to "a situation where people are drafted into the military and made to go fight . . . we'd have a hard time doing that."

It is difficult to know whether America's allies should be reassured or alarmed by that thought, though it does seem to strengthen the case for Europe taking a bigger hand in its own defense. If Europeans are willing to do that, they could also be reassured by Pat Schroeder's point that what she and others are asking for in NATO is a more genuinely multilateral approach, with the allies taking a bigger share both in the burdens and in the decisions; and we must all hope that she is right when she says that Americans in general "really understand that we need a more multilateral approach in the whole world. That's part of your responsibility if you are going to have a free and open world: with that freedom comes responsibility."

Sergei Plekhanov, who—unlike all the Americans quoted, except Adelman—had the advantage of speaking after the "Irangate" scandal broke in November 1986, opined that "the American government cannot continue on its unilateralist course for a long time without inflicting great damage on the United States and the rest of the world; and so I think that there will be, after this painful and recalcitrant stage in American foreign policy, another period of coming to terms with the world—of adaptation to the world. In fact, some of the signs of that adaptation are already visible."

Time was—and for some people no doubt still is—when the very fact of a Soviet commentator taking comfort from the troubles of an American president would have caused dismay in a Western listener. Yet I found myself sharing Plekhanov's hope that the bursting of the euphoric bubble of Reaganism would induce a return to sobriety and realism in the American approach to international problems. At the same time, though, I feared it was equally likely to provoke a new fit of American moroseness and impatience with foreign entanglements of all sorts.

CONCLUSION

Of Management and Muddle

I asked Alger Hiss, who helped draft the UN Charter, and Brian Urquhart, who worked for the UN from its very beginnings in 1945 until 1986, to sum up what they saw as the main differences in outlook between their generation and mine. Although Hiss has been banished from the counsels of the great since 1948, when he was accused, before the House Committee on Un-American Activities, of involvement in a Communist cell,* whereas Urquhart continued to deal personally with the leaders of great powers and small until his retirement, their answers were very similar.

> HISS: I think the difference that most impresses me is a loss of hopefulness, a loss of idealism, about the world as a whole. I have found the modern, young leaders so anxious to know all the answers, and to appear before their respective publics as strong competitive figures, instead of as collaborators with the rest of the world. I have been discouraged by the recrudescence of naked, narrow nationalism.
>
> I think that's the difference. My generation, after all, grew up in the shadow of World War I and the hope for the League, went through the terrible devastation of World War II, and thought: there must be a better solution, there must be a better world that we can devise. . . . The present generation has been removed from that. There've been great constructions—in this country [the U.S.], in Europe—of new

*Hiss denied the charge on oath, and was convicted of perjury in 1950, in a trial strongly influenced by the anti-Communist hysteria of the time. His accuser, Whittaker Chambers, himself an admitted ex-Communist, has since been shown to have been a highly unstable character—but was nonetheless honored posthumously by the Reagan administration.

factories, new methods of enjoyment: we've become a consumer world, and a complacent world.

URQUHART: I think people are much more concerned with short-term, self-interested matters, and are sometimes quite myopic about the results of the sort of things they're setting out to do. . . . I hope that it will be possible to break out of this kind of national provincialism and sort of "I'm all right, Jack" approach, before we have a disaster which makes us break out—and one can think of quite a number of disasters which can do that. I personally think it terrible if the only incentive to make political progress on the international scene is dependent on disasters . . . because one day we'll have a disaster which will be so bad there won't be too much left to put together again, and I don't think that that's any sense—but having said that, I must say I don't feel too encouraged about that prospect at the minute. I think there is a terrible propensity to put your head in the sand, to take short cuts, to have completely simplistic ideas about what world problems are, whether they're political, economic or social or technological or anything, and to simply try to ignore them. I think that's very bad—and we've done it before, God knows, and I don't see why we should have to do it again.

Some representatives of my generation, in their more unguarded moments, plead guilty to these charges.

WILL: My generation doesn't quite understand the costs of life—hasn't had the fundamental seriousness of things borne in upon it in the way my parents did. My parents were young during the Depression, and remember the war, and the world seemed a less hospitable place. We who were young in the 1950s, the world was our oyster, so there's a kind of sense that life is easier than in fact it often is for people.

But [he is quick to add] the good side of that is a kind of confidence and cheerfulness that I think's very important to the functioning of democracies.

When it comes to the specific point that most concerns both Hiss and Urquhart—the loss of faith in multilateral institutions—it is not only Americans who plead guilty. A West German like Irmgard Adam-Schwaetzer can say quite cheerfully, "The attitude in my generation toward these institutions has changed."

ADAM-SCHWAETZER: We are not that optimistic anymore on what they could do, at all. . . . We see that they are necessary, that they do their good deed in handling international problems, but we don't overestimate anymore what they can do. So maybe this is the reason for the fact that we are not that eager anymore to develop them any further, but just take them as something you need. . . . I don't believe in new institutions, and I blame the old ones for the bureaucracy they did get into. . . . Only by bilateral talks you can develop really the understanding for the other one, his specific needs: you can never do that in a big meeting with two hundred people. . . . It's just statements exchanged, but the real decisions are taken in other channels.

That is part of the story. Another is the loss of confidence in government itself as an instrument for dealing with human problems. Joe Biden explains this in the American context.

BIDEN: To my father's generation, government had the answer. It answered the Depression. It answered World War II. It answered the economic growth of the fifties. My generation started off thinking government was the answer, because we saw the civil rights movement as a vehicle by which we could change things. But then Vietnam came, and it shattered our confidence and our abilities and our judgment. Then along came Watergate, which shattered our somewhat idyllic notion of our institutions. Then came the energy crisis that government did not manage at all well, and on the heels of that came this phenomenal inflation. . . .

Quite clearly, this phenomenon is not confined to the United States. In Europe, too, the intellectual tide has turned, in the last ten to fifteen years, spectacularly against the growing role of the public sector in national economies; and latterly, partly through the insistence of foreign aid donors, a similar change has affected developing countries as well. No doubt this reaction was necessary and healthy, given the inflationary effect of the expectations about state action that so many socioeconomic groups had developed, all over the world, by the 1960s; given also the frequent inefficiency, not to say insensitivity to human feelings and aspirations, which big organizations tend to develop in the absence of competition, especially when they are draped in the authority of the state and are therefore imbued with the belief that by their very existence they are doing a public service; given, finally—though on this point the libertarian argument is to my mind much less clearly proven—the debilitating effect on human creative energies that the narrowing of economic choice and of the gap between success and failure is widely believed to have. The question that arises now is whether we have not swung too far the other way and developed, as Chris Patten says, "a ludicrous overconfidence in market forces"; or, as Prince Abdullah feels, from his vantage point in a traditional Islamic society seeking to adapt to the modern world without sacrificing its core values, an excessive "emphasis on economic performance and profitability, at the expense of employment and social services."

Yet one could hardly suggest, on the basis of these interviews, that complacency is the dominant characteristic of my contemporaries in the world political elite. The resurgent confidence of the Reaganites —expressed in this book by Elliott Abrams, Kenneth Adelman, Newt Gingrich, Jack Kemp, Richard Perle, and George Will—clearly does, or at any rate did, pre-Irangate, reflect the mood of a majority of the American public: so much so that a Democrat like Joe Biden had to associate himself with it to have any hope of being taken seriously as a presidential candidate. But even he admitted to being worried by the dangers of a nuclear cataclysm.

> BIDEN: [These dangers] come most strongly in terms of a miscalculation: as we move to more and more sophisticated weapons, as we reduce the response times that each nation has to respond to the warning of a nuclear attack, we put the world on a hair trigger. We run the risk of literally yielding the fate of the world to the malfunction of a computer—and that's disastrous for all mankind. We also run the risk that some madman like Qadhafi will do what he attempted to do not long ago—purchase a nuclear weapon—and then we get into the double-think game: was that a nuclear weapon that was detonated, was it a weapon that in fact had the sanction of the Soviets* or the sanction of the United States for it to be done? . . . which is dangerous territory to tread when you're in the nuclear side of the equation.

The same fear, that "a mistake today can mean the end of civilization," is expressed by his fellow Democrat Sam Gejdenson, who places it in the general context of East-West relations.

> GEJDENSON: Each side its own rhetoric, building mistrust. The regional wars come into that: they heighten mistrust. . . . It's hard to conceive of a situation where you can reach agreement on the nuclear

*Precisely such a scenario for the opening of a terminal nuclear conflict—an Egyptian attack on the United States with Soviet-built missiles is assumed to be an attack by the Soviet Union itself—was drawn more than thirty years ago by the Australian writer Nevil Shute, in his novel *On the Beach,* which threw me into acute anxiety and depression when I read it as a schoolboy.

weapons issue if there is so much mistrust over regional conflicts. If the United States feels that it's under siege by Soviet attempts to take over the Western Hemisphere—if the Soviets appear to be expansionist here in the United States—it's hard for the United States to move forward; and certainly the Soviets have their view of our actions.

They do, and they have also had a recent opportunity to contemplate the destructive power of nuclear energy, as the Ukrainian Viktor Mironenko recalls.

MIRONENKO: I have been to Chernobyl several times. I worked there during the accident at the Chernobyl atomic power plant, which you know about. I have seen how serious can be the consequences of just one accident on one power block of one atomic power station. That does not mean that I am advocating closing down atomic power stations: so far we do not have another way—science does not know it—and mankind needs energy. What I mean is, if just one reactor on a peaceful atomic plant can bring so much misery, so much unhappiness, think what may happen as a result of even a limited nuclear exchange—or even as a result of a willful destruction of atomic power stations, without the use of nuclear arms: that is not excluded.

Gejdenson also expresses anxiety about the North-South issue.

GEJDENSON: I think that that has been before us from the sixties, seventies, and we still haven't addressed it. Now when you take a look in this hemisphere—a country like Haiti, which has as much as 50 to 60 percent of its population unemployed, 80 percent illiteracy, an average yearly income of around $300, a fast-rising population: we have a crisis here not unlike Calcutta, and the United States and much of the world ignores it. When you go through Central and South America, Mexico: the poverty, the illiteracy, the population growth, are things that threaten world stability and cause incredible human hardship, and I think that whether you look at South America, Africa, Asia, that is still a growing problem that we have not addressed. . . . It seems that we are not able to focus our attention on a region unless there's an explosion.

Even the Republican Larry Pressler feels acute anxiety about the world economy and the Third World debt problem, as we saw in chapter 11, while Richard Burt, perhaps infected by the German *Weltanschauung,* expresses a more generalized angst.

BURT: I sometimes am concerned that we take this extended period of peace for granted, and that sometimes we are in danger of forgetting what the fundamental foundations of that peace are. I think that we could face another major conflict in our lives—that there are threats, real threats, to our well-being. They may not be traditional threats: maybe resource shortages, widespread terrorism . . . We have to guard against becoming too fat and happy.

In Japan, as noted in chapter 10, the phenomenal economic success of the postwar era has not really cured deep-seated anxieties about the vulnerability of the country and its dependence on imported raw materials. One effect of this is, perhaps, that the Japanese are a little less prone than others to bother themselves with apocalyptic fears about the fate of the planet as a whole; but Kaoru Yosano at least, relaxed and humorous as he is in his personal manner, expressed worries both about a collapse of the world economy caused by Third World debt and about the exploding world population.

YOSANO: I think on this earth we have about 4.5 billion people living, that is to say eating and sleeping, and in the year 2000 if the current trend continues we will have about seven billion people the earth has to feed. I worry very much whether this is possible or not, and especially the explosion of population happening in the developing countries—and this will lead to further poverty or starvation of those countries, which will induce instability of the other areas.

In Europe, besides the Conservative Chris Patten with his generalized "constructive pessimism" and fear of the "time-bomb behind the sofa," there is the Socialist Laurent Fabius with *his* fear.

FABIUS: There would be a tendency in every country to keep on saying, "We have lived up to now like that, it can keep on," without raising the question "Is it possible to keep on this way?" . . . There comes a point where it is no longer possible, and especially in terms of armaments, and divisions between North and South. You must never put people, and especially billions of people, in a situation where they have nothing to lose. . . . I think people don't choose to be either Communist or this or that. If people have no choice, if they have to make revolution if they want to eat, if they have to go to Communism if they want to have freedom—thinking (which is rubbish) that Communism can bring freedom—then you bring them to solutions which are no good, which they don't want really, but which are the only ones.

. . . If some people have the feeling that with a Communist regime they can have a chance, and they cannot have a chance with another regime, maybe they will choose that one; and afterward they will be disappointed, but it will be too late.

MORTIMER: So that's your greatest fear?

FABIUS: No, it's not my greatest fear—but it's a mistake, because if you can avoid it, why not? No, my greatest fear is the fear of war.

But, he adds, the one can lead to the other, especially with nuclear proliferation: wars in the Third World can lead to the Third World War (the same fear expressed by his fellow Socialist Norbert Gansel).

FABIUS: The problem is, the issues are worldwide, but the capacity of mastering the issues is a national one. Therefore you have a contrast, and even a contradiction, between the nature of the issues, which are on a world scale, and the instruments politicians have to answer the questions: the instruments are not efficient on a worldwide level. . . . We have a growing tendency to have international problems, and to bring to international problems national solutions.

Ingrid Matthäus-Maier fears that if we do not solve the problems of the Third World, we shall experience a new barbarian invasion.

MATTHÄUS-MAIER: [An invasion of] people walking—is that the word?—to the north, as two thousand years before they went and overthrew Rome, because they said, "We are the new people, and we want to eat and to live." We have known this problem a bit now, when we had these thousands of people who wanted asylum, or the Mexicans going to North America. Of course, they go there for economic reasons. They say, "We want to live, too, and we want to have enough to eat, and education for our people." And if we don't solve these problems, I think that there'll be terrible ones for us, and for these people, and for our children.

And in the Third World itself, of course, there is no lack of leaders anxious to wake the North up to the dangerous consequences that complacency might have.

AKINYEMI: Of course they are in danger. They may not see it. They may not wish to admit it. But if the system disintegrates, if somehow we blunder into an atomic war, there will be nothing left. There'll be no victors, and—who was it once said?—that's when the alive will envy the dead. What kind of a victory would that be? What kind of a security is that to anybody? . . .

I do believe that if we're not careful, it is going to start in the Third World, in the sense that that is often where a vacuum is perceived, and a vacuum is the most dangerous thing within an international system that is made up of competing forces, because then the forces tend to throw themselves into trying to fill that vacuum before the next man gets there. I was discussing with a foreign minister of one of the superpowers, and I was trying to persuade him of the need for more direct intervention by his government in the problems of southern Africa, and I was trying to show him that I wasn't making a moral argument: I pointed out to him that if the kind of violence and cross-border military attacks that we have witnessed in the past few months* continue and in that whole region disintegration sets in and there's a perception that the pieces are up for grabs, then in fact, if his country's not careful, that's where a world war may start.

Similarly, Prince Abdullah seeks to refute the view that the Middle East is no longer an area the world needs to worry about, now that the oil shortage seems to be over.

ABDULLAH: Well, aren't we part of the world? I mean, we are one of the most important regions in the world. We've got about 150 million people in the Middle East. There are very important strategic considerations: the Middle East is bordering the Soviet Union. . . . On the contrary, this is when they need to worry about the Middle East, with all the conflicts that are going on: the Palestinian problem, the Iran-Iraq war, Afghanistan. On the contrary, I think this is when they need to work even harder toward some solution for each of these problems.

And even Fouad Ajami, for all his cynicism about his fellow Arabs, sees dangers "in an international system where the preeminent power, the Americans, are much more reluctant to define their interests in a very viable way and to care about the rest of the world."

AJAMI: I mean, there are all kinds of dangers; and even short of danger I think it's a poorer place, in a way, intellectually—I mean, to just consign large parts of the world to irrelevance . . . and to say that the way that nations will have to enter this international system is they

*Interview recorded in May 1986.

have to crash through the gates. This is really, if you will, the main danger: to tell people out there, I mean, to leave them open to the kind of message that Ayatollah Khomeini and others will be delivering, that this is an unjust international system, and that you can't really get anything by appealing to anyone or petitioning anyone. . . .

There is always a danger when you live in a world where the dominant view is that we should have no illusions—that this is a world in which justice is not attainable. And so even though the liberal myth may have been a myth—that there would be an improvement in the terms of trade and there would be an improvement in the position of nations in the world—to wake up to an international system where dominant voices in the world, intellectual and political voices, are saying to people that this is an unjust international system, that there are really no superior powers, there are no arbiters, there are no referees in this world, that "just do what you will, run afoul of all the rules, and if you crash through the gates you'll do very well and you can get what you want," the ascendancy of this new philosophy today that the world is open for all and that people could just simply smash at its limits, and if they win they win, if they lose, well, too bad, no tears will be shed for them—that to me is a great retrogression.

Perhaps the problem is not so much complacency as resignation. One almost gets the impression that this generation of leaders is divided into the Reaganites on the one hand—who believe, or affect to believe, that everything will go right with the world so long as America keeps up its military strength, sets a good example of economic freedom, and above all goes on believing in itself—and everyone else on the other hand, hoping that the worst will not happen but not sounding as though they thought they themselves could do much to stop it. The Germans tend to sound a bit more optimistic about the future of Europe than the British or French, but the only European who sounds at all optimistic about the Third World is Neil Kinnock.

KINNOCK: [The Third World is] just about the central challenge to the world over the next few decades, mainly because we now have the means to prevent that poverty engulfing thousands of millions of people—because that's the scale we're talking on—and by so doing engulfing the whole world. If we didn't have the means, then perhaps we'd have to rely on the power of prayer, or just the management of international relationships, but now that the economic and technological means exist, the means of communications exists, for us to really

> combat the sources of poverty, I think we must; and it's getting a consensus around that, and getting the action that comes from it—in terms of debt scheduling, in terms of political futures, the improvement of systems, the partnership between North and South—they make an agenda that would last most political systems for at least four or five years.

That has an authentically Rooseveltian ring to it—and Kinnock has latched onto Roosevelt's New Deal as a precedent for the domestic policies he proposes as well. But Kinnock, as his opponents never tire of pointing out, has no experience of actually being in government. The contrast between his tone and that of Laurent Fabius, who had just emerged from five bruising years of ministerial office, is obvious—and painful.

Apart from Perle's criticisms of Yalta, and of those who built institutions "without the power to back them up," Roosevelt's children seem on the whole grateful for their inheritance. Jacques Toubon no doubt speaks for most Europeans of his age—or Western Europeans, anyway—when he remarks: "Just fifty years ago people said that the normal situation of the world was war between Germany and France, between France and Britain, or between Germany and Russia, because that was history. Now . . . we believe—and I think we are right—we believe that the normal history of humanity is peace and not war."

Newt Gingrich would give the builders of the postwar world "probably an A": for saving as much as realistically could be saved from Stalin's clutches in Europe—though he thinks "we might have done slightly better in saving Czechoslovakia"; for managing decolonization of the British and even, on balance, of the French empire, "reasonably well, at a reasonably human cost—it's easy to go back, frankly, and find ways it could have collapsed, rather than ways it could have been dramatically better"; for building the European Common Market; and for democratizing Japan. He concludes that "if Franklin Roosevelt and Winston Churchill could be alive today, and could survey the world they left behind, they would feel pretty darned good. They would feel like on balance more human beings are prosperous, and more human beings have a decent standard of living, than at any time in the rest of the history of the human race. And that ain't bad!"

To which Elliott Abrams, whom we asked how he would like *our* generation to be remembered by its children and grandchildren, adds a rider that Gingrich would surely accept.

> ABRAMS: I think that the gift that we were given was liberty, and that it is for a whole variety of reasons under attack in large parts of the world, including by one of the most powerful countries in the world, and I would like them to look back and say that we received this gift of liberty and we passed it on.

But only Chris Patten seemed to sense clearly that this is not something to be achieved by simply soldiering on as we are.

> PATTEN: Either we will reestablish, for the future, the sort of structures which were set up in the 1940s and helped us to an unparalleled period of prosperity and peace; or else either protectionist pressures, or the Third World debt problem, or the unemployment consequences of both economic factors and a change of industrial generation—one of those things will, if not blow us to pieces, at least make it much more difficult to run parliamentary democracies in the civilized and rational way in which they should be managed.

He understands, in other words, that those structures are no longer there. Bretton Woods is gone. Marshall Aid is a distant memory. The UN, in which such enormous hopes were placed and to which such strenuous efforts were devoted—especially by the United States—in the early years, is now treated with open contempt, and performs no more than a marginal role in power politics. The Third World is disillusioned with Western leadership and even with its own capacity to achieve a fairer share of economic and political opportunities in the world order. NATO *is* still there, but its foundations have been rotted by the long calm on the eastern front and the increasingly sour view that Americans and Western Europeans take of each other's leaders and policies. The postwar international system, in short, is like an aircraft that is still airborne, but whose motor has conked out. Skillful piloting may keep us aloft for a time, but unless we either repair the engine or replace it we are sure to hit the ground sooner or later.

To suppose that the engine can be repaired and made to run again as did in the forties and fifties is surely beyond hope, because that system in all its aspects reposed on one essential, if not always clearly stated, premise: the overwhelming, dominant power of the United States. The dollar was a world currency in which everyone had unquestioning confidence. America had saved Asia from Japanese domination, and had saved Western Europe from the grim alternative of Nazi or Soviet control. It was natural for Western Europeans and East Asians to look to America both for protection and for help in rebuilding their economies, and America was well able to respond. It was natural for America to take the lead in establishing and running the United Nations, and no one outside the Soviet bloc seriously questioned her right or her ability to do so. It was natural for nations struggling to be free from European colonialism to look to America for moral support in that struggle and for economic aid in establishing their new states, and the postwar generation of Americans was eager to respond to that appeal.

Whatever the state of collective euphoria that Ronald Reagan and Rambo and the 1984 Olympics may have induced, at least for a time, in the American people; whatever the productive capacity developed by supply-side economics since 1981 and supposedly still to be unleashed on the world market, it is just not credible to me, or, I think, to most other even partially detached observers of the world scene (until we go and live on other planets full detachment from that subject is no more possible for us than it was for Archimedes two and a half millennia ago), that America is going to recover that position of overwhelming and largely unquestioned dominance. In fact most people expect its *relative* decline to continue, even if it will for the foreseeable future remain the single strongest country.

> KOMORI: Certainly the United States will be playing a less significant role in world politics. Looking at the dwindling or diminishing state of the American economy I think that's unavoidable.
>
> AKINYEMI: I don't think the United States will ever run out of ideas, but the kind of gap that exists between the United States and other countries is bound to be diminished.
>
> BIDEN: The United States will be the strongest power in the world, but it will not be the absolute power in the world like it was after World War II.
>
> PRESSLER: We're on a high, we're on a roll now, and I think things are going to be much tougher in the eighties and nineties: just the law of averages. I think our economy is going to struggle. I think we're going to get into sticky situations in Central America and elsewhere. . . . There's a lot that can go wrong.

Those were the considered views in the summer of 1986, of the best Japanese commentator on U.S. and international affairs, of the foreign minister of the most important black African country, and of two U.S.

senators of opposite parties. They have surely been confirmed rather than invalidated by more recent events.

So it would be chasing a will-o'-the-wisp to try and rebuild the international system as it was in the 1950s. And yet, as Brian Urquhart says, many of the things that have happened since 1945 make the concept of a central world system of some sort "rather more valid than it was then." Fewer and fewer of the problems that society has to face can be solved within the frontiers of one nation-state without reference to what is happening elsewhere. Urquhart hopes that the current crisis of the United Nations—which, as he says, is in fact "a conceptual crisis, not a financial crisis: the sums of money are peanuts by comparison with what any defense department spends before breakfast"—may lead "to governments really having a look at the international system they so happily set up in 1945 and deciding what it should do and what it shouldn't do, and how they also can do a little better in making it work. . . ."

> URQUHART: It has been a really very revolutionary forty years . . . and I think the reaction in the sort of established world has sometimes been one of nostalgia and of trying to believe that if you keep on the way you always did some of these other rather disturbing phenomena may go away. I think that's very shortsighted. I don't think it'll work. Furthermore, I don't think it's any fun. I mean, it seems to me the future ought to be something to look forward to, not to dread.

No doubt in the last resort it *is* governments that will have to take the decisions. But another of the lessons of this century is perhaps that international affairs are too important to be left to governments, that citizens have to take a hand. If governments are unwilling to adopt imaginative policies in the international field, it is mainly because they conceive their political constituency (whether elected or not, every government depends on some sort of wider backing for its survival) exclusively in national terms. If the domestic public shows itself to be thinking in international terms, sooner or later governments will have to take note, and many of the actual or potential government men and women interviewed in this book sound as though they would be glad enough to do that. The crucial battle, therefore, is to develop a coherent multinational public opinion in favor of a coherent multinational system.

But this time it will have to be more genuinely multinational than in the past, in the sense that there will no longer be one dominant power to which everyone else can look for leadership and which—

perhaps more important—everyone else can blame when things go wrong. A few Americans understand that—like Sam Gejdenson, who thinks "we need to develop programs that are multilateral rather than bilateral. We need to work with our friends around the world to come up with a coordinated policy to a far greater degree than we have."

Perhaps even fewer non-Americans really understand it. As Yoshi Komori says, "It's so easy to just criticize the United States." It is also easy, especially when one is not in power, to indulge in fantasies about national independence and telling the Americans to go to hell. It is very much harder to work out ways of managing the world in which America will, inevitably, continue to play the largest single part in most respects, but in which others will contribute their due share of wisdom, their due share of resources, their due share of sacrifice, and accept their due share of responsibility for the results.

In Europe, I think this must mean bearing a larger share of responsibility for our own defense—in financial terms, in manpower terms, in equipment terms—and this can only be done if we work together more closely as Europeans, including—for Britain and France at least—in the development and deployment of nuclear weapons.

In the world economy, it must mean establishing a greater degree of monetary stability: an effort by both deficit and surplus countries to correct imbalances and, I would suggest, a new international unit of account, possibly adapted from the SDR, based on national currencies in proportion to the importance of the nations in question in the world economy, and managed by a multinational body: presumably the IMF. All currencies should have an official value expressed in terms of that unit of account, and all governments, including that of the United States, should undertake not to change that value, and not to let the market rate of their currency in terms of other currencies vary from it by more than an agreed margin, without first going through a set of agreed procedures. But it is no good pretending that such a system can work unless nation-states are prepared to surrender a part of their sovereignty in economic policy, into the hands of the multinational body that issues and manages the new international currency. Anodyne communiqués issued by occasional meetings of national finance ministers are clearly not enough.

At the same time a new, multinational Marshall Plan should be launched to write off the outstanding debts of Third World countries, to which countries disposing of large financial surpluses—Japan and West Germany, especially—should make the largest contribution. The Northern industrial countries should also be prepared, in return for undertakings from Third World countries to maintain a free market for goods and capital, to keep their own markets open to Third World products, including manufactured products; and public opinion in all industrialized countries has somehow to be convinced of the truth, clearly apparent to most economists and stock markets, that barriers to trade damage the economy of the country imposing them as much as—often more than—that of the country whose products are targeted. (Contrary to the prevailing opinion in Europe and North America, it is by no means certain that Japan is the worst offender in this respect.)

America's allies have to be prepared to play a bigger role in both deciding and implementing alliance policy outside the NATO area, especially in places where freedom is genuinely threatened by direct or indirect Soviet encroachment. This should make possible a genuine East-West dialogue on regional issues as well as arms control, which in turn might open the way to a reform of the United Nations itself, including perhaps: a revision of the permanent membership of the Security Council—it would make sense, for instance, for the European Community to have one seat instead of Britain and France having two; the development of a real enforcement mechanism to impose peace in places where the great powers can agree—such as the Iran-Iraq war; and an increased role for nongovernmental organizations dealing with some of the many problems, from space research through the environment to the free circulation of people and ideas, which increasingly escape the control of national governments. The latter are, after all, only a stage in the development of human society. We must hope, but we should also strive, to ensure that they are not the last.

All that begins to sound very starry-eyed and utopian. I cannot say I feel particularly sanguine that it will happen, or very certain that in detail it is precisely what is needed. All I am trying to do is to think on the scale that people thought on in the 1940s—a habit that political leaders and thinkers have almost lost. Of course, it is more difficult now, because then, as I said in the Introduction, war had put vast energies at the disposal of political leaders and had made populations ready to accept extreme measures involving considerable sacrifices. They knew, from direct and horrifying experience, what the alternative was. Our generation does not have that sense of urgency, because we were too young to share that experience. But a repetition of that experience for pedagogic purposes is a luxury none of us can afford. It is high time we used our imagination instead.

CHRONOLOGY OF EVENTS

1919		Treaty of Versailles. Establishment of League of Nations.
1931	Sept.	Britain abandons gold standard.
1933	Jan.	Roosevelt becomes president.
		Hitler in power in Germany.
	March	United States abandons gold standard.
1939	Aug. 23	German-Soviet Non-Aggression Pact.
	Aug. 25	Anglo-Polish Alliance.
	Sept. 1	German invasion of Poland.
	Sept. 3	Britain and France declare war on Germany.
	Sept. 17	Soviet invasion of Poland.
1940	June 22	Franco-German armistice.
1941	June 22	German invasion of Russia.
	Aug. 12	Atlantic Charter agreed by Roosevelt and Churchill.
	Dec. 7–8	Japanese attack on Pearl Harbor and the Philippines: U.S. enters the war.
	Dec. 11	Germany declares war on the United States.
	Dec. 12–20	Eden (British foreign secretary) in Moscow.
1942	Jan. 1	"Declaration of the United Nations."
1943	Oct. 18–30	Moscow foreign ministers' conference: Hull, Eden, Molotov.
	Nov. 22–26	Cairo conference: Churchill, Roosevelt, Chiang Kai-shek
	Nov. 28–Dec. 1	Teheran conference: Churchill, Roosevelt, Stalin.
1944	July	Bretton Woods conference.
	Aug. 21–Oct. 7	Dumbarton Oaks conference: UN Charter drafted.
	Sept. 11–16	Quebec conference: Churchill and Roosevelt accept Morgenthau Plan.
	Oct. 9–18	Churchill in Moscow ("percentage" agreement with Stalin).
1945	Feb. 4–11	Yalta conference.
	Apr. 12	Death of Roosevelt. Truman becomes president.

	Apr. 25	Soviet and U.S. forces meet at Torgau on the Elbe.
	Apr. 25–June 26	San Francisco conference: foundation of UN.
	Apr. 30	Death of Hitler.
	May 2	Berlin surrenders to Russians.
	May 7–9	Unconditional surrender of Germany.
	June 26	UN Charter signed at San Francisco.
	July 16–Aug. 2	Potsdam conference.
	July 26	Churchill and Eden replaced by Attlee and Bevin.
	Aug. 6	First atom bomb dropped on Hiroshima.
	Aug. 8	Russia declares war on Japan.
	Aug. 9	Second atom bomb dropped on Nagasaki.
	Aug. 15	War ends in Far East ("VJ Day").
	Aug. 17	Indonesian independence declared; Communist-led
		Viet Minh seize control in Vietnam.
	Sept. 2	Japan signs unconditional surrender in Tokyo Bay.
	Dec.	First East-West crisis, over Soviet troops in Iran.
1946	Jan. 5	Truman's rebuke to Byrnes: "I'm tired of babying the Soviets."
	Jan. 10	First session of UN General Assembly opens in London.
	Feb.	Kennan's "long telegram" warns of Soviet designs.
	March	Churchill's "Iron Curtain" speech at Fulton, Missouri.
		French troops return to Vietnam.
		Inaugural meeting of IMF and World Bank.
	May	Soviet troops withdrawn from Iran.
	Aug.	Dardanelles crisis.
	Dec.	Vietnam War starts between France and Viet Minh.
1947	Jan.	Marshall replaces Byrnes as U.S. secretary of state.
	Feb.	Britain tells U.S. it can no longer sustain Greece and Turkey.
	March	"Truman Doctrine" proclaimed.
	June 5	Marshall's Harvard speech.
	June 27–July 1	Bevin, Bidault, Molotov confer in Paris.
	July 1	Molotov withdraws.
	July 4	Bevin and Bidault invite twenty-two states to Paris Conference on European Economic Co-operation.
	July 12	Conference opens with sixteen members.
	Aug. 15	Independence of India and Pakistan.
	Sept. 22	CEEC presents "shopping list" to U.S.

	Oct. 5	Establishment of Cominform.
	Nov. 29	UN General Assembly votes partition of Palestine.
	Dec.	Last four-power foreign ministers' conference adjourned *sine die.*
		Truman requests $17 billion Marshall Aid from Congress.
1948	Jan. 22	Bevin calls for consolidation of Western Europe.
	Feb. 25	Prague coup.
	March 17	Brussels Pact (U.K., France, Benelux), including collective self-defense.
		Truman promises U.S. help for European defense; calls for reintroduction of universal military training and Selective Service.
	April 3	Truman signs European Recovery Act ($13 billion).
	April 16	OEEC established in Paris.
	April 28	Canadian prime minister St. Laurent publicly advocates NATO.
	May 14	State of Israel proclaimed.
	June 11	Senate adopts Vandenberg Resolution recommending U.S. involvement in collective defense system.
	June 18	Western powers introduce reformed currency in West Germany.
	June 24–28	Berlin blockade starts.
	July 2	Truman orders implementation of Vandenberg Resolution.
	Nov. 12	Close of trial of Japanese war criminals in Tokyo.
1949	Jan.	Acheson replaces Marshall as secretary of state.
	April 4	North Atlantic Treaty signed in Washington.
	May	Council of Europe set up.
		Communist victory in China.
	May 11	Berlin blockade ends.
	May 23	Federal Republic of Germany established.
	Aug.	First Soviet atomic test.
	Sept. 17	North Atlantic Council formed.
	Oct. 7	German Democratic Republic proclaimed.
	Oct. 17	Greece and Turkey invited to join NATO.
	Dec. 27	Indonesian independence recognized.
1950	Jan. 27	Truman approves NATO defense plan (but Germany left out).
	June 25	Outbreak of Korean War.
	Sept.	Acheson proposes German rearmament.
	Dec. 18	North Atlantic Council agrees to integrated military force under U.S. general.

1951	Jan.	Eisenhower sets up headquarters (SHAPE) at Versailles.
	March	Iran nationalizes Anglo-Iranian Oil Company.
	April	Foundation of European Coal and Steel Community.
	Sept. 8	Signature of peace treaty with Japan, and U.S.-Japanese Security Treaty.
	Oct.	Conservatives return to power in Britain.
1952	May 27	European Defense Community agreed.
	July	Nasser comes to power in Egypt.
	Nov. 1	First hydrogen bomb test.
1953	Jan.	Eisenhower becomes president.
	March 5	Death of Stalin.
	June	East German rising.
	Aug.	Mosaddegh overthrown in Iran.
1954	July 20	Geneva accord: France withdraws from Indochina. Vietnam divided into north and south.
	Aug. 30	EDC rejected by French National Assembly.
	Oct. 23	Agreement to admit West Germany to Brussels Pact (renamed WEU) and NATO.
	Nov. 1	Outbreak of Algerian War.
	Dec. 29	German admission to NATO and WEU ratified by French parliament.
1955	April	Asian-African Conference at Bandung.
	May 9	West Germany joins NATO and WEU.
	May 14	Warsaw Pact signed.
	May 15	Austrian State Treaty signed.
	July	Four-power summit in Geneva.
1956	Feb.	Twentieth Congress of Soviet Communist Party (Khrushchev's "secret speech" denouncing Stalin's crimes).
	April	Bulganin and Khrushchev visit Britain.
	Oct.–Nov.	Hungarian uprising. Suez crisis.
1957	March	Independence of Ghana
		EEC and Euratom founded (Treaties of Rome).
	Oct.	Russians put first satellite in orbit (Sputnik).
1958	May–June	De Gaulle returns to power in France.
	July	U.S. Marines land in Lebanon.
	Dec.	End of European Payments Union.
1959	Jan.	Castro comes to power in Cuba.
1960	May	Abortive four-power summit in Paris (U-2 incident).
	June	Independence of Belgian Congo (later Zaïre)
	Oct.	Independence of Nigeria.
	Nov.	Kennedy defeats Nixon.
1960–61		Sino-Soviet split.
1961	Jan.	Kennedy inaugurated.

	Feb.	Murder of Patrice Lumumba.
	Apr.	Unsuccessful attempt to invade Cuba at Bay of Pigs.
	Aug.	Building of Berlin Wall.
	Sept.	First Non-Aligned Summit at Belgrade.
		Death of UN secretary-general Dag Hammarskjøld.
1962	July	Algerian independence.
		Kennedy announces "Grand Design" for two-pillar Atlantic Community.
	Oct.	Cuban missile crisis.
1963	Jan.	De Gaulle vetoes British entry into EEC; signs Franco-German Friendship Treaty with Adenauer.
	May	Organization of African Unity founded.
	June	Kennedy in Berlin (*"Ich bin ein Berliner"*).
	July	Test Ban Treaty signed in Moscow.
	Nov. 22	Kennedy assassinated. Lyndon Johnson president.
1964	Oct.	Fall of Khrushchev. Brezhnev and Kosygin in power.
		Wilson's Labour government in Britain.
	Nov.	Johnson defeats Goldwater.
1965		Large-scale U.S. forces engaged in Vietnam.
	Nov.	Unilateral Declaration of Independence in Rhodesia.
1966	January	First military coup in Nigeria.
	February	Overthrow of Kwame Nkrumah's regime in Ghana.
	March	France leaves NATO command structure.
	April	Beginning of Cultural Revolution in China.
	Dec.	"Grand Coalition" (CDU-SPD) comes to power in Bonn.
1967	May–July	Nigerian civil war begins.
	June	Six-Day War in Middle East.
	Nov.	Devaluation of pound.
1968	Jan.	Alexander Dubček comes to power in Czechoslovakia.
		Tet offensive in Vietnam.
	March	Creation of "two-tier" gold market.
		Agreement on IMF special drawing rights.
	March 31	Johnson suspends bombing of North Vietnam, announces he will not seek reelection.
	April 4	Assassination of Martin Luther King, Jr.
	May	Vietnam peace talks start.
		"The events" in Paris.
	June 5	Assassination of Robert Kennedy.
	July 1	Johnson signs Nuclear Non-Proliferation Treaty.

	Aug.	Chicago Democratic Convention.
		Soviet invasion of Czechoslovakia.
	Nov.	Nixon defeats Hubert Humphrey.
1969	Jan.	Nixon becomes president.
	March–Aug.	Clashes on Sino-Soviet border.
	April	De Gaulle resigns.
	June	Georges Pompidou elected president of France.
	Oct.	Willy Brandt chancellor of West Germany.
1970	Jan.	End of Nigerian civil war.
	June	Heath becomes prime minister in Britain.
1971	Aug. 15	Nixon breaks dollar-gold link.
	Oct.	Communist China admitted to UN.
	Dec.	Smithsonian agreement sets new parties, but U.S. accepts no responsibility for maintaining them.
		India intervenes in East Pakistan: independence of Bangladesh.
1972		Publication of Club of Rome report *Limits to Growth.*
	Feb.	Nixon's visit to China.
	May	Nixon and Brezhnev sign SALT I in Moscow.
	Nov.	Nixon reelected, defeating George McGovern.
	Dec.	Basic Treaty between two Germanies.
1973	Jan.	Britain joins EEC.
		U.S. agrees to withdraw from Vietnam.
	March	End of fixed exchange rates.
	Sept.	Overthrow of Allende in Chile.
		Algiers Non-Aligned Summit calls for New International Economic Order.
	Oct.	Yom Kippur War.
	Dec.	Fourfold increase in crude oil prices.
1974	Feb.–March	Heath defeated. Wilson returns to power.
	April	Death of Pompidou.
		Revolution in Lisbon starts decolonization of Portuguese empire.
	April–May	Sixth Special Session of UN General Assembly, on raw materials and development.
	May	Helmut Schmidt replaces Brandt as chancellor.
		Giscard d'Estaing president of France.
	June	Nixon's Middle East tour.
	July	Turkish intervention in Cyprus.
	Aug.	Nixon resigns. Ford president.
	Nov.	Arafat speaks in UN General Assembly.
1975	March	Fall of Phnom Penh to Khmer Rouge.
	April	Fall of Saigon to Viet Cong.

	July–Aug.	Helsinki Accord on European security and cooperation.
	Sept. 17	Seventh Special Session of UN General Assembly adopts resolution on development and international cooperation.
	Nov. 10	UN General Assembly passes "Zionism is racism" resolution.
	Nov. 11	Angola becomes independent under Soviet-backed MPLA government.
	Nov. 15–17	First Western economic summit at Rambouillet, France.
	Dec.	Indonesia annexes East Timor.
		Opening of Conference on International Economic Co-operation ("North-South Dialogue") in Paris.
1976	Feb.	Morocco annexes Western Sahara.
	June	Syrian forces enter Lebanon.
	Sept.	Death of Mao Tse-tung.
	Nov.	Ford defeated by Jimmy Carter.
1977	Jan.	Carter becomes president.
	June–July	Ethiopia, invaded by Somalia, turns to Russians for help.
	July	Zia ul-Haq seizes power in Pakistan.
1978	July	Bonn economic summit.
	Sept.	Camp David Accords between Egypt and Israel.
	Dec–Jan '79	Vietnam invades Cambodia, overthrows Khmer Rouge.
1979		"Second oil shock."
	Feb.	Khomeini in power in Iran.
	April	Idi Amin of Uganda overthrown by Tanzanian forces.
	May	Margaret Thatcher becomes prime minister in Britain.
	June	Carter and Brezhnev sign SALT II in Vienna.
	July	Sandinistas come to power in Nicaragua.
	Nov.	U.S. diplomats taken hostage in Teheran.
	Dec.	Soviet invasion of Afghanistan.
1980	Aug.	Solidarność formed in Poland.
	Sept.	Iran-Iraq war starts.
	Nov.	Carter defeated by Ronald Reagan.
1981	Jan. 20	Reagan becomes president. Hostages released in Iran.
	May	François Mitterrand elected president of France.
	June	Israel bombs nuclear reactor in Iraq.
	Dec.	Martial law in Poland.
1982	April	Argentina seizes Falkland Islands.

	June	Israel invades Lebanon. Britain recovers Falklands.
	Aug.	Mexico announces moratorium on debt repayment: beginning of Third World debt crisis.
		PLO leaves Beirut under protection of U.S.-led Multinational Force.
	Sept.	Multinational Force returns to Beirut after massacre of Palestinians at Sabra-Shatila.
		Christian Democrats return to power in West Germany, with Helmut Kohl as chancellor.
	Nov.	Death of Brezhnev. Andropov comes to power.
1983	March	Reagan announces Strategic Defense Initiative ("Star Wars").
	May 17	American-sponsored agreement between Israel and Lebanon.
	Sept.	Crisis over Soviet shooting-down of Korean airliner.
	Oct.	Nearly three hundred U.S. and French troops killed in Beirut by Shiite suicide bombers. U.S. intervention in Grenada.
1984	Feb.	Andropov dies. Chernenko in power.
		Multinational force withdraws from Lebanon.
	March	Lebanon denounces agreement with Israel.
	Oct. 31	Indira Gandhi assassinated. Rajiv Gandhi prime minister of India.
	Nov.	Reagan reelected, defeating Walter Mondale.
	Nov.–Dec.	Bob Geldof launches Band Aid for Ethiopian famine.
1985	March	Chernenko dies. Gorbachev general secretary of CPSU.
	Sept.	Group of Five finance ministers meet at Plaza Hotel, New York, and agree on action to drive down dollar.
	Oct.	Israel bombs PLO headquarters in Tunis.
		Palestinians hijack Italian liner *Achille Lauro.*
		Americans force Egyptian plane carrying hijackers to land in Sicily.
	Dec. 12	Reagan signs Gramm-Rudman-Hollings Act, mandating balanced federal budget by 1991.
1986	Feb.	"People Power" revolution in Philippines, backed by U.S.
	April	Maekawa report advocates measures to open up Japanese economy.
		U.S. bombing raid on Libya.
	May	UN General Assembly Special Session on Africa.

	Oct.	Reagan-Gorbachev summit at Reykjavik.
	Nov.	"Irangate" scandal breaks.
1987	Feb.	Finance ministers meet in Paris and agree on package to ensure exchange-rate stability.
	Oct.	"Black Monday"—spectacular crash on world stock markets.
	Dec.	Reagan-Gorbachev summit in Washington: INF Treaty signed.
1988	April	Signature of accord on Soviet withdrawal from Afghanistan.
	May–June	Fourth Reagan-Gorbachev summit, in Moscow.
	Aug.	Iran and Iraq cease-fire, on terms proposed by UN Security Council.
		Death of Zia ul-Haq.

DRAMATIS PERSONAE: PEOPLE INTERVIEWED

"FDR'S MIDWIVES"

Valentin Mikhailovich Berezhkov. Soviet translator, journalist, and historian. Born Petrograd, 1916. Education: University of Kiev; three-year course in English, German, and Spanish. Engineer in navy—Pacific fleet (Vladivostok), 1938. Moved to general staff of navy, 1939. Sent to Krupp factory in Germany, 1940, to inspect deliveries of artillery, etc. Then assigned to Foreign Trade Ministry under Mikoyan. November 1940: interpreted for Molotov in talks with Hitler. Moved to Foreign Ministry. December 1940: sent to Berlin as first secretary in Soviet embassy. June 22, 1941: went with ambassador to see Ribbentrop, who read them the German declaration of war. Assistant to Molotov, then interpreter to Stalin and Molotov 1941–45. Executive editor, *New Times,* 1945–69 (reported Geneva summit 1955, etc.). Founder and editor-in-chief, *USA* (monthly journal of the Institute of U.S. and Canadian Studies of the Academy of Sciences of the USSR), 1969–78, and since 1984. Ph.D. (history), Institute of U.S. and Canadian Studies, 1974. Represented the institute at Soviet embassy in Washington, 1978–83. Author of *History in the Making* (English edition, 1983).

Edward M. Bernstein. U.S. economist. Born 1904. Academic economist until 1940, after which he served in the U.S. Treasury Department as principal economist (1940–41), assistant director of monetary research (1941–45), and assistant to the secretary of the Treasury (1946). Chief technical adviser and executive secretary of the U.S. delegation at Bretton Woods. Director of research and statistics, International Monetary Fund, 1946–58. President, EMB (Ltd.) Research Economists, 1958–81. Chairman, Review Committee for Balance of Payments Statistics, Bureau of the Budget 1964–65. Member, Advisory Committee on International Monetary Arrangements, U.S. Treasury ("Dillon Committee"), 1965–68.

Sir Alec Cairncross. British economist. Born 1911. Education: Glasgow and Cambridge universities. University lecturer, 1935–39. Civil servant, 1940–45. Director of Programmes, Ministry of Aircraft Production, 1945. Economic Advisor Panel, Berlin 1945–46. Economic adviser to Board of Trade, 1946–49; to Organization for European Economic Co-operation, 1949–50. Professor of applied economics, University of Glasgow, 1951–61. Director, Economic Development Institute, Washington, D.C., 1955–56. Economic adviser to H.M. Government, 1961–64. Head of Government Economic Service, 1964–69. Master of St. Peter's College, Oxford, 1969–78. Chancellor, Glasgow University, from 1972. Author of *(inter alia): Intro-*

duction to Economics (1944), *Monetary Policy in a Mixed Economy* (1960), *Essays in Economic Management* (1971), *Control over Long-term International Capital Movements* (1973), *Inflation, Growth and International Finance* (1975), *The Price of War* (1986).

Maurice Couve de Murville. French public servant. Born 1907. General secretary to General Giraud (de Gaulle's rival) in Algiers, March–June 1943. Member, French Committee for National Liberation, June–November 1943. Member, Italian Advisory Council, 1944. French ambassador to Italy, 1945. Director-general of political affairs, French Foreign Ministry, 1945–50. Ambassador to Egypt, 1950–54; to U.S. 1955–56; to West Germany, 1956–8. Foreign minister, 1958–68. Finance minister, May–July 1968. Prime minister, July 1968–June 1969.

Lord (formerly Sir Oliver) Franks. British public servant. Born 1905. Taught philosophy at Queen's College, Oxford, 1927–37. Professor of moral philosophy, University of Glasgow, 1937–45. Temporary civil servant, Ministry of Supply, 1939–46 (permanent secretary, 1945–46). Provost of Queen's College 1946–48. Chaired Paris Conference on European Economic Co-operation, 1947. British ambassador in Washington, 1948–52. Chairman of *(inter alia):* Lloyds Bank Ltd, 1954–62; Commission of Inquiry into Oxford University, 1964–66; Committee on Official Secrets Act, Section Two, 1971–72; Falkland Islands Review Committee, 1982. Provost of Worcester College, Oxford, 1962–76. Lord Warden of the Stannaries and Keeper of the Privy Seal of the Duke of Cornwall since 1983.

Lord Gladwyn (formerly Sir Gladwyn Jebb). British diplomat. Born 1900. Entered diplomatic service, 1924. Served in Teheran, Rome, and Foreign Office. Appointed to Ministry of Economic Warfare, 1940. Acting counsellor in Foreign Office, 1941; head of Reconstruction Department, 1942; Counsellor, 1943: in that capacity attended conferences at Quebec, Cairo, Teheran, Dumbarton Oaks, Yalta, San Francisco, and Potsdam. Executive secretary of Preparatory Commission of UN, August 1945. Acting secretary-general of UN, February 1946. Under secretary of state and UN adviser, 1946–47. UK representative on Brussels Treaty Permanent Commission April 1948. Deputy undersecretary 1949–50. Permanent representative of UK to UN, 1950–54. Ambassador to France, 1954–60. Deputy leader of Liberal party in House of Lords and Liberal spokesman on foreign affairs and defense, 1965–88.

Ernest A. Gross. U.S. public servant. Born 1906. Chief of Economics Section of Civil Affairs Division, War Department General Staff during World War II. Legal adviser to State Department under Secretary of State George C. Marshall (1947–48), then assistant secretary of state for congressional relations. Member of U.S. delegation at five sessions of UN General Assembly. Deputy U.S. representative to UN, 1949–53. Special counsel to UN secretary-general Dag Hammarskjøld, 1953–61. In international legal practice since 1954. Chairman of UN Development Corporation.

Alger Hiss. U.S. diplomat. Born 1904. Secretary and law clerk to Supreme Court Justice Holmes, 1929–30. Legal assistant to Senate Committee investigating munitions industry, 1934–35. Assistant to assistant secretary of state, 1936. Assistant to adviser on political relations, 1939–44. Executive secretary of Dumbarton Oaks conference, 1944. Special assistant to Director's Office, Far Eastern Affairs, 1944; director, 1945. Attended Yalta conference. Secretary-general of UN Conference on International Reorganization, 1945. Principal adviser to U.S. delegation to UN

General Assembly (London), 1946. President, Carnegie Endowment for International Peace, 1947. Accused by Whittaker Chambers of espionage for the Soviet Union, denied charge on oath, 1948; convicted of perjury, 1950; has fought ever since to clear his name.

Paul Nitze. U.S. public servant. Born 1907. New York investment banker, 1929–40. Financial director, Office of Coordinator of Inter-American Affairs, Department of State, 1941–42. Chief of Bureau, Board of Economic Warfare, 1942–43. Director of Bureau, Foreign Economic Administration, 1943–44. Vice-chairman, Strategic Bombing Survey, 1944–46. Deputy director, Office of International Trade Policy, 1946–48. Deputy to assistant secretary of state for economic affairs, 1948–49. Director, Policy Planning Staff, Department of State, 1950–53. Assistant secretary of Defense for international security affairs, 1961–63. Secretary of the navy, 1963–67. Deputy Secretary of defense, 1967–69. Member, U.S. delegation to strategic arms limitation talks, 1969–74. Head of U.S. delegation, Intermediate-Range Nuclear Forces, 1981–84. Special representative for Arms Control and Disarmament Negotiations, 1984–86. Ambassador-at-Large since 1984. Author of *U.S. Foreign Policy, 1945–1954.*

Jacques Polak. Dutch economist and IMF official. Born 1914. Economist, League of Nations, Geneva and Princeton, 1937–43. Netherlands Embassy, Washington, 1943–44. Attended Bretton Woods conference. Adviser, UN Relief and Rehabilitation Administration (Washington) 1944–46. IMF from 1947: Chief, Statistics Division 1947–48; assistant director, Research Department, 1948–52; deputy director, 1952–58; director, 1958–79; economic counselor, 1966–79; adviser to managing director, 1980; executive director (representing Cyprus, Israel, Netherlands, Rumania, and Yugoslavia), 1981–86.

Sir Frank Roberts. British diplomat. Born 1907. Entered Foreign Office, 1930. Served in British embassy, Paris, 1932–35; Cairo, 1935–37; in Foreign Office (London), 1937–45. Chargé d'affaires to Czechoslovak government-in-exile, 1943. Attended Yalta conference. British minister in Moscow, 1945–47. Principal private secretary to foreign secretary (Ernest Bevin), 1947–49. Deputy high commissioner in India, 1949–51. Deputy under secretary of state, 1951–54. Ambassador to Yugoslavia, 1954–57. UK permanent representative on North Atlantic Council, 1957–60. Ambassador in Moscow, 1960–62, in Bonn, 1963–68.

Arthur Schlesinger, Jr. U.S. historian. Born 1917. Office of War Information, 1942–43. Office of Strategic Services, 1943–45. U.S. Army 1945. Consultant, Economic Co-operation Administration 1948; Mutual Security Administration, 1951–52. Associate professor of history, Harvard, 1946–54; professor 1954–61. Adlai Stevenson presidential campaign staff, 1952 and 1956. Special assistant to Presidents Kennedy and Johnson, 1961–64. Schweitzer professor of humanities, City University of New York, since 1966. Author of *(inter alia): The Age of Roosevelt* (3 vols., 1957–60); *A Thousand Days: John F. Kennedy in the White House* (1965); *The Imperial Presidency* (1973).

Sir Brian Urquhart. International public servant. Born 1919. British army: Dorset Regiment and Airborne Forces, North Africa, Sicily, and Europe, 1939–45. Personal assistant to Gladwyn Jebb as executive secretary of preparatory commission of UN

(London), 1945–46. Personal assistant to Trygve Lie, first secretary-general of UN, 1946–49. Secretary, Collective Measures Committee, 1951–53. Office of under secretary-general for special political affairs, 1954–71. Assistant secretary-general, 1972–74. Executive secretary, first and second UN conferences on peaceful uses of atomic energy, 1955, 1958. Active in organization and direction of UN Emergency Force in Middle East, 1956. Deputy executive secretary, Preparatory Commission of International Atomic Energy Agency, 1957. Assistant to secretary-general's special representative in the Congo, 1960. UN representative in Katanga (Congo), 1961–62. Under secretary-general (in charge of peace-keeping operations and special political assignments), 1974–86.

"FDR'S CHILDREN"

H.H. Prince Abdullah Bin Faisal Bin Turki Al-Saud. Saudi Arabian official. Born 1951/2. Nephew of present king. Educated in England, at boarding school, then University of Nottingham (B.Sc., production engineering and management—a "sandwich" course including several months' practical experience on the factory floor). Head of Industrial Security, Royal Commission for Jubail and Yanbu (new ports on Gulf and Red Sea), from 1979. Secretary-general of the commission since 1985. Has headed several Saudi delegations in Europe and frequently addresses gatherings of foreign businessmen on economic and industrial subjects.

Elliott Abrams. U.S. under secretary of state for inter-American affairs. Born 1948. Education: Harvard; London School of Economics. Admitted to New York bar, 1974, to Washington, D.C., bar, 1979. Attorney, Breed, Abbott & Morgan (New York City), 1974–75. Assistant counsel, U.S. Senate Permanent Subcommittee on Investigations, 1975. Special counsel to Senator Henry M. Jackson, 1975–76; to Senator Daniel P. Moynihan, 1977–78; chief of staff, 1978–79. Attorney, Verney, Liipfert, Bernhard & McPherson (Washington), 1979–80. State Department: assistant secretary for international organization affairs, 1981; for human rights and humanitarian affairs, 1981; present post since 1985.

Irmgard Adam-Schwaetzer. West German politician. Born 1942. Trained as pharmacist. Holds doctorate in natural sciences. Joined Liberal party (FDP), 1975; became party chairman in Aachen district and was elected to Bundestag (federal parliament), 1980. General secretary of the party, 1982–84; treasurer, 1984–87. Minister of state for foreign affairs since 1987.

Kenneth Adelman. Director of U.S. Arms Control and Disarmament Agency, 1983–87. Born 1946. Education: Grinnell College, Iowa; Georgetown University (Ph.D., 1975, for thesis in political theory researched in Zaire). Served in Department of Commerce, 1968–70; Office of Economic Opportunity and VISTA, 1970–72; Agency for International Development, 1975–76. Assistant to secretary of defense, 1976–77. Strategic Studies Center, Stanford Research Institute (Arlington, Va.), 1977–81, writing extensively for *Foreign Affairs, Foreign Policy,* etc. Deputy permanent representative of the U.S. to the UN (number 2 to Jeane Kirkpatrick), 1981–83. Led U.S. delegation at UN Second Special Session on Disarmament, 1982.

Oluyemi Adeniji. Nigerian diplomat. Born 1934. Education: University College, Ibadan; University of London. Training officer, Nigerian Foreign Ministry, 1963–64.

Acting high commissioner in Ghana, 1966–67. Head of Africa Division, Foreign Ministry, 1967–70. Minister, Permanent Mission to UN (New York) 1970–73. Director of international organizations (Foreign Ministry), 1973–76. Ambassador to Austria and governor of the International Atomic Energy Association, 1976–77. Ambassador to Switzerland and permanent representative to UN offices in Geneva, 1977–81. President, UN Conference on Certain Conventional Weapons, 1979–80. Chairman, Ad Hoc Committee, UN General Assembly Second Special Session on Disarmament, 1982.

Fouad Ajami. Arab-American scholar. Born in southern Lebanon, 1945. Went to school in Beirut. Came to U.S. in 1963 to study at University of Washington (state). Ph.D. in political science, 1972. James P. Warburg fellow, Consortium of World Order Studies, Princeton, 1973–75. Assistant professor of politics and faculty associate, Center for International Studies, Princeton, 1975–80. Research fellow, Lehrman Institute (New York) 1978–79. Director of Middle East Studies, School of Advanced International Studies, The Johns Hopkins University (Washington, D.C.) since 1980. MacArthur Prize fellow, 1982–87. Majid Khadduri professor of Islamic studies since 1985.

Akinwande Bolaji Akinyemi. Minister of external affairs, Nigeria, 1985–87. Born 1942. Education: Temple University (Philadelphia); Fletcher School of Law and Diplomacy (Tufts University, Medford, Mass.); Trinity College, Oxford. Instructor in politics of developing nations, Northeastern University (Boston), 1965–66. Visiting professor in African studies, De Pauw University (Greencastle, Indiana), 1969–70. Director-general, Nigerian Institute of International Affairs (the Nigerian government official "think tank" on foreign policy), 1975–83. Professor of political science, University of Lagos, from 1983.

C. Fred Bergsten. U.S. economist. Born 1941. Education: Central Methodist College (Fayette, Mo.); Fletcher School of Law and Diplomacy (Medford, Mass.). International economist, Department of State, 1963–67. Visiting fellow, Council on Foreign Relations, 1967–68. Assistant for International Economic Affairs, National Security Council, 1969–71. Senior fellow, Brookings Institution, 1972–76. Assistant secretary of the treasury for international affairs, 1977–81. Founder and director, Institute for International Economics (Washington, D.C.), since 1981.

Joseph R. Biden, Jr. U.S. senator from Delaware (Democrat). Born 1942. Education: University of Delaware (Newark) and Syracuse (New York) University College of Law. Trial attorney in Public Defender's Office, Wilmington, Delaware, 1968. Founder of Biden & Walsh law firm, Wilmington. Member New Castle County Council, 1970–72. U.S. Senator since 1972, serving as member of committees on the budget, foreign relations, and the judiciary, and the Select Committee on Intelligence. Member of Democratic Party Steering Committee. Chairman, Senate Judiciary Committee, and vice-chairman, Foreign Relations Committee, since 1987.

Richard Burt. U.S. ambassador to West Germany. Born in Chile, 1942. Education: Cornell University; Fletcher School of Law and Diplomacy. Research associate, then assistant director, International Institute for Strategic Studies (London). Defense correspondent, *New York Times.* Director, Bureau of Politico-Military Affairs, Department of State 1981–82. Assistant secretary of state for European and Canadian affairs, 1982–85. Present post since 1985.

Jorge G. Castañeda. Mexican political writer and foreign policy expert. Born 1953. Son of former foreign minister. Education: Princeton, Ecole Pratique de Hautes Etudes (Paris). Ph.D. in economic history, University of Paris. Professor, Graduate School, Department of Economics, National Autonomous University of Mexico, 1978–82; Department of Political Science, 1982–85. Adviser on Central America and Caribbean Affairs to Mexican Foreign Ministry, 1979–82. Political journalist for *Proceso* (Mexican weekly), *Le Monde Diplomatique* (Paris), and Radio Canada since 1982. Author of *Nicaragua: Contradicciones en la Revolución* (Mexico, 1980); *Los Ultimos Capitalismos* (Mexico, 1982); coauthor of several other books on Latin American politics and economics; contributor to *Foreign Policy, Foreign Affairs, Washington Post, New York Times, Los Angeles Times,* etc.

Laurent Fabius. French Socialist politician. Born 1946. Education: Lycées Janson de Sailly and Louis-le-Grand, Paris; Ecole Normale Supérieure; Institut d'Etudes Politiques. Trained at Ecole Nationale d'Administration, 1971–73. Auditeur, Conseil d'Etat 1973. (Maître de Requêtes 1981.) Senior assistant to mayor of Grand-Quévilly (Rouen) since 1977. Member of parliament for Seine-Maritime, 1978–81, and since March 1986. National secretary of the Socialist party in charge of the press from 1979. President, Regional Council of Upper Normandy, 1981–86. Minister-delegate for budget, 1981–83. Minister of industry and research, 1983–84. Prime minister, 1984–86. President of the National Assembly since June 1988.

Norbert Gansel. Social Democratic (SPD) member of West German parliament. Born 1940. Served in Bundesmarine, 1960–62. Studied history, political science, and law at University of Kiel, 1962–69. Joined SPD, 1965. Member of party council from 1968 (deputy chairman). Deputy chairman of Young Socialists, 1969–70. Member of Parliament for Kiel since 1972.

Sam Gejdenson. U.S. congressman from Connecticut (Democrat). Born 1948 in Germany (of Lithuanian parents). Education: Mitchell College, New London; University of Connecticut. Farmer. Chairman, Bozrah (Connecticut) Town Committee, 1973. Member of Connecticut House of Representatives, 1974–78. Coal broker, 1978–79. Legislative liaison, Connecticut Office of Policy and Management (Hartford), 1979–80. Representative from 2nd Connecticut District in U.S. Congress since 1981. Member of Foreign Affairs, House Administration, Interior, and Insular Affairs committees, and Select Committee on Hunger.

Newton Leroy ("Newt") Gingrich. U.S. congressman from Georgia (Republican). Born 1943. Education: Emory University, Atlanta; Tulane University, New Orleans (Ph.D., 1971). Taught history at West Georgia College, Carrollton, 1970–78. Representative from 6th District of Georgia in U.S. Congress since 1979. Member of committees on House administration, public works and transportation, and the Joint Committee on the Library.

Josef Joffe. West German political commentator. Born 1944. Education: Swarthmore College (B.A.), Johns Hopkins University (M.A.), Harvard University (Ph.D. in government). Senior editor and director of "Dossier" department, *Die Zeit,* 1976–82. Taught international relations at Johns Hopkins School of Advanced International Studies (Washington, D.C.) while a fellow at the Woodrow Wilson Center for Scholars and a senior associate of the Carnegie Endowment for International Peace, 1982–84. Foreign editor and columnist/editorialist, *Süddeutsche Zeitung* (West Germany's largest quality paper) since 1984. Contributor to many American and Israeli publications; frequent panelist and commentator on U.S., Canadian, and British television. Author of *The Limited Partnership: Europe, the United States, and the Burdens of Alliance* (1987).

Koichi Kato. Japanese politician. Born 1939. Education: Tokyo University Faculty of Law; Harvard. Entered diplomatic service, 1963. Served in Japanese embassy in Taiwan, 1964; in U.S., 1966. Vice-consul, Consulate-General in Hong Kong, 1967. China Division, Asian Bureau, Ministry of Foreign Affairs, 1969. Member of House of Representatives since 1972. Vice-chief cabinet secretary, 1975. Director of House Rules and Administration Committee, 1980; of Agriculture, Forestry, and Fisheries Committee, 1981. Director, General Affairs Bureau, Liberal Democratic party, 1983. Minister of Defense, 1984–86.

Masao Katsurauma. Japanese industrialist. Born 1941. Education: Kyoto University (B.A., economics). Entered Toray Industries, 1963, in Accounting Department, Shiga Plant. Finance Department, Head Office, 1964. Comptroller of Textile Alliance Ltd., 1973; of Lukyex (Thailand) Ltd., Bangkok, 1974—both Toray affiliates. Corporate Planning Department, Head Office, 1978. Manager, International Finance Department, 1983. Manager, Comptroller's Department, since 1985.

Jack F. Kemp. U.S. congressman from Buffalo, N.Y. (Republican). Born 1935. Education: Occidental College; Long Beach State University; California Western University. U.S. Army Reserve, 1958–62 (active duty, 1958). Professional football player for thirteen years. Cofounder (and president, 1965–70) of American Football League Players' Association. TV and radio commentator. Public relations officer, Marine Midland Bank of Buffalo. Special assistant to Governor Ronald Reagan of California, 1969. Representative from 38th District of New York in U.S. Congress since 1970. Leading advocate of tax cuts, "supply side" economics, high defense spending, and support for anti-Communist insurgents; also of return to fixed exchange rates. Chairman, House Republican Conference. Member, congressional delegation to SALT negotiations; committees on appropriations and the budget, and Select Committee on Children, Youth, and Families. Unsuccessful candidate for Republican presidential nomination, 1988.

Neil Kinnock. Leader of (British) Labour party. Born 1942. Education: University College, Cardiff (history and industrial relations); chairman of Socialist Society 1962–65; president of Students' Union, 1965–66. Tutor-organizer in industrial and trade union studies, Workers' Educational Association, 1966–70. Member of Parliament since 1970. Parliamentary private secretary to secretary of state for employment (Michael Foot), 1974–75. Member, National Executive Committee of Labour party, since 1978. Chief opposition spokesman on education, 1979–83. Leader of Labour party and leader of the opposition since 1983.

Iwao Koga. Executive of Nippon Oil Company. Born 1945. Education: Keio University, Tokyo (B.A., economics). Joined Nippon Oil Company, 1967. Nippon Oil Delaware Ltd. (New York), 1971. Corporate Office, 1974. London office, 1981. Manager, Corporate Finance Section, 1984. Manager, General Accounting Office, 1986.

Andrei Afanasievich Kokoshin. Adviser to Soviet foreign minister. Born Moscow, 1945. His father was "an active participant in World War II, being at the front from the very first day until 1944, inside the German circle round Leningrad." Graduated 1969 from Moscow Higher Technical School (engineering and radio electronics). Since then has been at the Institute of U.S. and Canadian Studies of the Academy of Sciences of the USSR, successively as postgraduate student, research fellow, executive secretary, head of department, and, since 1984, deputy director. Chairman of the Political-Ideological Commission of the Central Committee of the Young Communist League since 1983. Visits U.S. practically every year.

Yoshihisa Komori. Japanese journalist. Born 1941. Education: Keio University, Tokyo (B.A., economics); University of Washington School of Communications (graduate study in journalism). General news reporter and diplomatic correspondent, Mainichi Newspapers, 1964–72. Saigon correspondent, 1972–74; bureau chief, 1974–75 (UPI Vaughn Prize for outstanding international reporting). Diplomatic correspondent, 1975–76. Washington correspondent, 1976–82. Senior associate, Carnegie Endowment for International Peace, 1981; Japanese Newspaper Publishers and Editors Association award for best reporting of the year, for an interview article on former U.S. ambassador to Japan Edwin O. Reischauer's remarks about nuclear-armed American vessels visiting Japan. Senior political correspondent, Mainichi Newspapers (Tokyo), covering Japanese foreign and security policy, U.S.-Japanese relations, etc., 1983–87. London correspondent, Sankei Shimbun, since 1987. Author of *Vietnam Coverage, 1,300 Days: The Demise of a State* (1978: Kodansha Non-Fiction Prize); *Japan Lobby* (1980); *Structures of U.S.-Japanese Distrust* (1981); *Have Nuclear Weapons Been Introduced?* (1982).

Jack Lang. French Socialist politician. Born 1939. Education: Lycée Henri Poincaré, Nancy; Faculty of Law, University of Paris; Institut d'Etudes Politiques (Paris). Director, Nancy University Theatre, and founder-director, World Festival of University Theatre, 1963–72. Director, Théâtre du Palais de Chaillot (formerly Théâtre National Populaire), 1972–74. Professor of international law, 1976. Director, Law and Economics Department, University of Nancy, 1977. Elected to Paris Council, 1977. Special adviser to the first secretary of the Socialist party (François Mitterrand) from 1978. National delegate of the party for culture, 1979–81. Minister of culture, 1981–86, and again since May 1988. Member of parliament, 1986–88.

Pierre Lellouche. French defense expert. Born 1951 in Tunis. Education: Faculty of Law, University of Paris; Institut d'Etudes Politiques; Harvard Law School. Graduate student fellow, Harvard Program for Science and International Affairs, 1974–75. Editor, *Défense et Diplomatie,* 1976–79. French army, 1976–77. Consultant to Palme Commission on Disarmament and Security Issues, 1979–80. Associate director, Institut Français des Relations Internationales. Columnist: *Le Point; Newsweek* (International edition). Associate editor, *Politique Etrangère.* Lecturer, Ecole Nationale d'Administration, French War College, etc. Consultant to French Defense Ministry. Main areas of work: East-West and European security issues; arms control; nonproliferation. Author of *L'Avenir de la Guerre* (1985); *L'Initiative de Défense Stratégique et la Sécurité de l'Europe* (1986); many influential articles and papers.

Ingrid Matthäus-Maier. West German politician (Social Democrat, formerly Free Democrat). Born 1945. Studied jurisprudence in Giessen and Münster. Involved in student politics and member of Humanist Union, 1966–69. Joined FDP, 1969. Federal chairman, Young Democrats, 1972. Member of FDP Land (North-Rhine-Westphalia) and Federal executives. Administrative judge, 1976. Member of Bundestag, 1976. Chairman of Bundestag Finance Committee, 1979–82. Resigned from FDP and from Bundestag, 1982, after FDP switched from coalition with SPD to coalition with CDU-CSU; joined SPD. Reelected to Bundestag as Social Democrat, 1983. Member of Finance Committee. Deputy chairman, SPD parliamentary group working party on the world economy and currency policy. Member, "Third World" working party of SPD party executive.

Viktor Ivanovich Mironenko. Soviet youth leader. Born Chernigov (Ukraine), 1953. Worked as tool operator in chemical textile factory, 1970–71. Studied history at Chernigov Pedagogical Institute. Graduated, and took up teaching post in history at University of Chernigov, 1975. Joined Communist party in that year, becoming secretary first of district committee, then for region. From 1980 worked at Central Committee of Komsomol (Young Communist League) of Ukraine, successively as head of department, second secretary, and first secretary. Candidate member of the Central Committee of the party, First secretary of the Central Committee of the Komsomol of the USSR, and member of the Presidium of the Supreme Soviet, since 1986.

Tadashi Nakamae. Japanese economist. Born 1938 in Hiroshima. Education: Tokyo University (B.A. agricultural economics). Senior economist, Daiwa Securities (Tokyo), 1962. Chief economist, Daiwa Europe Ltd (London) 1973. Chief economist, Daiwa Securities Research Institute (Tokyo), 1985. Founder and president, Nakamae International Economic Research, May 1986. Author of *Inflation and the Japanese Yen,* 1979. Columnist on *Nihon Keizai Shimbun* (financial paper), contributor to *Euromoney,* the *Guardian,* the *Times,* etc.

Kazuhiko Nishi. Japanese tycoon. Born 1956. Education: Matriculate in Machinery Division, Industrial Department of Waseda University (Tokyo). Founded ASCII Publishing Inc. (later renamed ASCII Corp.), 1977, and assumed title of director in charge of corporate planning. Published *ASCII,* a personal computer magazine. Executive vice-president, ASCII Inc., 1978. Executive vice-president and director, Microsoft (U.S.A.), 1979. Researcher, SRI, Stanford University, California, 1981. Assistant professor, Broadcasting Training Development Center, Broadcasting University, Japan, 1984. Resigned from board of Microsoft, 1986. Combines business with positions as committee member or researcher for various government committees and corporations.

Christine Ockrent. French broadcaster. Born 1944 in Brussels. Education: Collège Sévigné (Paris); Cambridge University; Institut d'Etudes Politiques (Paris). Journalist in EEC information office, 1965–66. Researcher, NBC News, 1967–68. Producer/reporter, CBS News (New York), 1968–77. Editor and presenter of news programs, Radio Europe 1 (Paris), 1980–82. Similar position at Antenne 2 TV (Paris), 1982–85. Assistant managing director of TF1 (France's newly privatized first TV channel) since 1987.

Yutaka Ohtaka. Japanese executive. Born 1938. Education: Hitotsubashi University, Tokyo (B.A., commerce). Career: Shell Sekiyu K.K., 1961–71. Shell Eastern Petroleum Co. (Singapore), 1971–76. Subsidiary Relations Department, Shell Kosan K.K., 1976–79. Director, various Shell subsidiaries and affiliates, 1979–81. Director, Showa Shell, 1981–85. Managing director, Showa Shell Sekiyu K.K. since 1985.

Dr. David Owen. British politician (Social Democrat, formerly Labour). Born 1938. Education: Sidney Sussex College, Cambridge; St. Thomas's Hospital, London (bachelor of medicine, bachelor of surgery, 1962; M.A., 1963). House appointments at St. Thomas's, 1962–64; neurological and psychiatric registrar, 1964–66; research fellow, Medical Unit, 1966–68. Member of Parliament for Plymouth since 1966. Parliamentary private secretary to minister of defence (administration), 1967. Parliamentary under secretary of state for defense (Royal Navy) 1968–70. Opposition defense spokesman, 1970–72—resigned 1972 when Labour withdrew its commitment to British membership in European Community. Parliamentary undersecretary of state, 1974, and minister of state, 1974–76, Department of Health and Social Security; minister of state, Foreign and Commonwealth Office, 1976–77. Foreign secretary, 1977–79. Opposition spokesman on energy, 1979–80. One of "gang of four" Labour leaders who broke away to form Social Democratic party (SDP), 1981; leader of the party from 1983 to 1987, when he resigned after majority voted to merge with Liberals. In March 1988, after the merger had gone through, a separate SDP was relaunched under his leadership. Member, Trilateral Commission, Palme Commission on Defence and Disarmament, etc.

Christopher Patten. British politician (Conservative). Born 1944. Education: Balliol College, Oxford (M.A., history). Conservative Research Department, 1966–70. Cabinet Office, 1970–72. Home Office, 1972. Personal assistant to chairman of Conservative party, 1972–74. Director, Conservative Research Department, 1974–79. Member of Parliament for Bath since 1979. Parliamentary private secretary to leader of the House of Commons, 1979–81; to secretary of state for social services, 1981. Parliamentary under secretary of state, Northern Ireland Office, 1983–85. Minister of state, Department of Education and Science, 1985–86. Minister for Overseas Development since September 1986.

Richard N. Perle. U.S. assistant secretary of defense for international security policy, 1981–87. Born 1941. Education: University of Southern California; London School of Economics; Princeton. Came to Washington in late sixties to work for Paul Nitze, then for Senator Henry "Scoop" Jackson (Democrat, Washington), a leading opponent of Kissinger's détente policies. Staff of U.S. Senate, 1969–80. Department of Defense, 1980. Still a card-carrying Democrat, but regarded as an ultra-hawk on arms control and East-West issues. Revels in his nickname "the Prince of Darkness." Resigned 1987.

Sergei Mikhailovich Plekhanov. Soviet political scientist—head of political and social studies, Institute of U.S. and Canadian Studies of the Academy of Sciences of the USSR. Born Moscow 1946. Education: Moscow State Institute of International Relations (graduated, 1968). Ph.D. (American history), 1975. Main publications (monographs): *Modern Political Consciousness in the U.S.A.,* 1980; *Right-Wing Extremism and U.S. Foreign Policy,* 1986; articles: "The George Wallace Movement," 1974; "Shift to the Right in the U.S.A.: Imagined and Real," 1979; "American Society and Foreign Policy," 1986.

Larry Pressler. U.S. senator from South Dakota (Republican). Born 1942. Education: University of South Dakota; Oxford (Rhodes Scholar); Harvard (Kennedy School of Government; Harvard Law School—J.D., 1971). Delegate to 4-H Agricultural Fair, Cairo, 1961. Lieutenant in U.S. Army, Vietnam, 1966–68. Member, U.S. House of Representatives, 1975–79. Senator since 1979. Chairman (until 1986), European Affairs Subcommittee of Senate Foreign Relations Committee; Business, Trade and Tourism Subcommittee of Commerce Committee; Family Farm Subcommittee of Small Business Committee. Also serves on Committee on Environment and Public Works, and Special Committee on Aging.

Said Rajaie-Khorassani. Iranian politician. Born 1936. Education: Tehran University (B.A., Islamic philosophy); American University of Beirut (M.A., philosophy of education); Durham University, England (Ph.D.). High school teacher, Kerman, Iran, 1960–62. Assistant professor of philosophy, Tabriz University, 1970–78; director, Department of International Relations, 1977–78; vice-chancellor, 1978–79. Chancellor, Kerman University, 1978–79. Director, Radio of the Islamic Republic (for three months). Joined Ministry of Foreign Affairs, 1980. Head of delegation to Third Committee, UN (New York) 1980. Representative to 36th Session of General Assembly, 1981. Permanent representative of the Islamic Republic of Iran to the UN, 1981–88. Member of Parliament since April 1988. Author (in Persian): *Science and Religious Knowledge* (1978; 5th edition, 1982); *History of Moral Philosophy among Muslims* (1987).

Volker Rühe. West German politician (Christian Democrat). Born 1942. Studied German and English philology at University of Hamburg. Joined Christian Democratic Party (CDU), 1963. Secondary school teacher, Hamburg, 1968–76. Member of Hamburg City Parliament, 1970–76; of Bundestag since 1976. Deputy chairman, CDU-CSU parliamentary group. Foreign affairs spokesman of the party; adviser on defense and East-West relations to Chancellor Helmut Kohl.

Patricia Scott Schroeder. U.S. congresswoman from Colorado (Democrat). Born 1940. Education: University of Minnesota; Harvard. Admitted to Colorado bar, 1964. Field attorney, National Labor Relations Board (Colorado, Wyoming, and Utah), 1964–66. Practiced law in Denver, 1966–72. Hearing officer, Colorado Department of Personnel, 1971–72. Faculty, University of Colorado, 1969–72; Denver Community College, 1969–70; Regis College, Denver, 1970–72. U.S. House of Representatives since 1973. Rocky Mountain whip and chairman, Congressional Caucus for Women's Issues, from 1976. Member of Democratic Steering and Policy Committee. Member of House committees on the armed services, the judiciary, the post office, and civil service, and the Select Committee on Children, Youth and

Families. Chairman, Gary Hart campaign for Democratic presidential nomination, 1984; explored possibility of running herself in 1988 after Hart's withdrawal, but decided against it.

Hitoshi Seki. Japanese executive. Born 1956 in Washington, D.C. Education: Keio University, Tokyo (B.A., political science). Research staff, Social and Economic Congress of Japan, 1978–82. Program coordinator and Japanese-English simultaneous interpreter, U.S. office, Japan Productivity Center, 1982–86. Project officer, International Cooperation Department, JPC, since 1986.

Hajime Shinohara. Executive of Bank of Tokyo Ltd. Born 1940. Education: Tokyo University (B.A., liberal arts). Joined Bank of Tokyo, 1965. London office, 1968. Singapore office, 1974. Corporate Office, 1979. Deputy general manager, Planning Division, until 1988, when he was appointed general manager, Kuala Lumpur office.

Jacques Toubon. French Gaullist politician, right-hand man of Jacques Chirac. Born 1941 in Nice. Education: Faculty of Law and Institut d'Etudes Politiques, Lyon. Trained as civil servant at Ecole Nationale d'Administration (Paris), 1963–65. Ministry of Interior, 1965. Directeur du cabinet of prefect of Basses-Pyrénées, 1965–68. Chef de cabinet of secretary of state for Overseas Departments and Territories, 1968–69. Technical adviser to secretary of state for parliamentary relations, 1969–71. Worked in private office of Jacques Chirac as minister for parliamentary relations, 1971–72, Minister of agriculture, 1972–74. Minister of the interior, 1974. Prime minister, 1974–76. Director, Claude Pompidou Foundation (of which Chirac was treasurer), 1970–77. Assistant secretary-general, Gaullist party (RPR), 1977–81. Member of parliament for Paris since 1981. Mayor of 13th Arrondissement of Paris since 1983. Secretary-general of RPR 1984–88.

Karsten Voigt. Foreign affairs spokesman of Social Democratic party of Germany (SPD). Born 1941. Studied history, German, Scandinavian languages in Hamburg, Copenhagen, and Frankfurt. Member of SPD Subdistrict Executive in Frankfurt from 1968. Chairman of Young Socialists, 1969–72; of Control Commission, International Union of Socialist Youth, 1973–75. Member of Bundestag since 1976. SPD representative on Select Committee of Bundestag; member of the executive of SPD parliamentary group. Author of *Roads to Disarmament* (1981); *Nuclear Weapons in Europe* (in English, 1983).

George F. Will. U.S. political columnist and news commentator. Born 1941. Education: Trinity College, Oxford; Princeton (Ph.D.). Taught politics at Michigan State University, University of Illinois, University of Toronto. Congressional aide to Senator Allott of Colorado until 1972, when he became Washington editor of the *National Review.* Political columnist for *Washington Post;* columnist, then contributing editor, *Newsweek* magazine. Author of *The Pursuit of Happiness and Other Sobering Thoughts* (1979), *The Pursuit of Virtue and Other Tory Notions* (1982), *Statecraft as Soulcraft: What Government Does* (1982). Participant, "This Week with David Brinkley," since 1981. Commentator, "World News Tonight," since 1984. Won Pulitzer Prize for Commentary, 1977. Named a "Young Leader American" by *Time* magazine, 1974.

Matthias Wissmann. West German politician (Christian Democrat). Born 1949. Studied law and politics in Tübingen and Bonn, 1968–76. Political assistant, Bundestag, 1970–71. Chairman, Young Christian Democrats of Germany, 1973–83. President, European Union of Young Christian Democrats, from 1976. Member of CDU Executive Committee from 1975. Member of Bundestag from 1976. Economic policy spokesman of CDU/CSU parliamentary group since 1983.

Kaoru Yosano. Japanese politician. Born 1938. Education: University of Tokyo (LL.B.). Employed by Japan Atomic Power Generation K.K., 1963. Head of office of Yasuhiro Nakasone, 1968. Private secretary to Nakasone as minister of defense, 1970. Member of the House of Representatives for Tokyo (District 1) since 1976. Deputy chairman of Diet Affairs Committee and deputy director-general of International Bureau, Liberal Democratic party, 1983. Parliamentary vice-minister of international trade and industry, 1984. Acting director-general of LDP International Bureau and acting director of Commerce and Industry Division, LDP Policy Research Council, 1986.

NOTES

INTRODUCTION

1. See Edward Mortimer, *France and the Africans 1944–1960* (New York: Walker Brothers, 1969).

2. See Edward Mortimer, *The Rise of the French Communist Party* (London: Faber and Faber, 1984); also Martin McCauley, ed., *Communist Power in Europe, 1944–1949* (London: Macmillan, 1977).

CHAPTER 1

1. Television interview with Baroness Asquith of Yarnbury by Kenneth Harris on April 13 1967. Quoted in John W. Wheeler-Bennett and Anthony Nicholls, *The Semblance of Peace—The Political Settlement after the Second World War* (London: Macmillan, 1972), p. 290.

2. Keith Sainsbury, *The Turning-Point: Roosevelt, Stalin, Churchill, and Chiang-Kai-shek, 1943. The Moscow, Cairo, and Teheran Conferences* (New York: Oxford University Press, 1985), pp. 277–79.

3. Herbert Feis, *Churchill, Roosevelt, Stalin: The War They Waged and the Peace They Sought* (Princeton, N.J.: Princeton University Press, 1957), pp. 367–73.

4. Ibid., pp. 538–39.

5. Sir Llewellyn Woodward, *British Foreign Policy in the Second World War* (London, 1962), pp. 469–70, cited in Wheeler-Bennett and Nicholls, op. cit., p. 228.

6. Feis, op. cit., pp. 619–20.

7. Wheeler-Bennett and Nicholls, op. cit., pp. 271–75.

8. Harry S. Truman, *Year of Decisions, 1945* (London: Hodder and Stoughton, 1955), pp. 251–52.

9. Ibid., p. 181.

10. Winston Churchill, *The Tide of Victory* (London, 1954), p. 198.

11. Wheeler-Bennett and Nicholls, op. cit., pp. 94–95.

12. Sainsbury, op. cit., pp. 273–80.

13. Feis, op. cit., p. 572.

14. Feis, op. cit., pp. 583–96; Wheeler-Bennett and Nicholls, op. cit., pp. 252–55.

15. Feis, op. cit., pp. 584–85.

16. Truman, op. cit., p. 275.

17. Ibid., p. 331.

18. Ibid., p. 342.

19. Ibid., pp. 492–93.

20. Quoted in Dean Acheson, *Present at the Creation* (London: Hamish Hamilton, 1970), p. 228.

21. Acheson, op. cit., p. 233.
22. Wheeler-Bennett and Nicholls, op. cit., pp. 574–75.
23. See Edward Mortimer, *The Rise of the French Communist Party* (London: Faber and Faber, 1984), pp. 358–9.
24. Wheeler-Bennett and Nicholls, op. cit., p. 576.
25. Ibid., pp. 576–82.
26. Harry S. Truman, *Years of Trial and Hope, 1946–1953* (London: Hodder and Stoughton, 1956), p. 254.

CHAPTER 2

1. Armand Van Dormael, *Bretton Woods—Birth of a Monetary System* (London: Macmillan, 1978), pp. 5–6.
2. Ibid., p. 26.
3. Ibid., p. 28.
4. Ibid., pp. 34–35.
5. Ibid., p. 40.
6. Ibid., p. 43.
7. Ibid., p. 45.
8. Ibid., p. 72.
9. Ibid., p. 246.
10. Ibid., pp. 169, 254.
11. Ibid., pp. 260–61.
12. Ibid., pp. 266–85.
13. Ibid., pp. 200–203.
14. "Anglo-American Financial Relations," lectures given by Paul Bareau at the London School of Economics, quoted in Van Dormael, op. cit., pp. 301–302.
15. Van Dormael, op. cit., pp. 306–307. There is no truth in the story that White committed suicide; see David Rees, *Harry Dexter White* (London: Macmillan, 1974), pp. 416–17.
16. David P. Calleo, *The Imperious Economy* (Cambridge, Mass.: Harvard University Press, 1982), pp.17–18.

CHAPTER 3

1. John W. Wheeler-Bennett and Anthony Nicholls, *The Semblance of Peace—The Political Settlement after the Second World War* (London: Macmillan, 1972), pp. 537–38.
2. Evan Luard, *A History of the United Nations,* (London: Macmillan, 1982), vol. 1 p. 39.
3. Ervand Abrahamian, *Iran Between Two Revolutions* (Princeton, N.J.: Princeton University Press, 1982), pp. 228, 244.
4. Luard, op. cit., pp. 271–72.

CHAPTER 4

1. See Strobe Talbott, *Deadly Gambits* (New York: Alfred A. Knopf, 1984), p. 158.

CHAPTER 5

1. See Paul Kennedy, *The Rise and Fall of the Great Powers* (London: Unwin Hyman, 1988), passim.

CHAPTER 6

1. Riccardo Parboni, *The Dollar and Its Rivals: Recession, Inflation and International Finance* (Milan: Etais Libri, 1980; tr. from Italian, *Finanza e crisi internazionale,* 1980); quoted by Susan Strange, "Interpretations of a Decade," in Loukas Tsoukalis, ed., *The Political Economy of International Money* (London: Royal Institute of International Affairs and SAGE Publications, 1985), pp. 34–35.
2. David P. Calleo, *The Imperious Economy* (Cambridge, Mass.: Harvard University Press, 1982), p. 113, and table, p. 216.
3. Jean Denizet, *Le Dollar* (Paris: Fayard, 1985), p. 64.
4. Calleo, op. cit., p. 18.
5. Denizet, op. cit., pp. 72–74.
6. Calleo, op. cit., p. 22.
7. See table in Calleo, op. cit., p. 210.
8. Ibid., p. 201.
9. Calleo, op. cit., p. 29.
10. Ibid., p. 106.
11. Ibid., p. 143.

CHAPTER 7

1. John W. Wheeler-Bennett and Anthony Nicholls, *The Semblance of Peace—The Political Settlement after the Second World War* (London: Macmillan, 1972), p. 499.

CHAPTER 9

1. *The Military Balance, 1985–1986* (London: I.I.S.S., 1985), p. 170.
2. *The Economist,* April 26–May 2, 1986, p. 61.
3. Ibid., pp. 61–62.

CHAPTER 10

1. John W. Wheeler-Bennett and Anthony Nicholls, *The Semblance of Peace—The Political Settlement after the Second World War* (London: Macmillan, 1972), p. 502.
2. Ibid., p. 520.
3. Giles Merritt in the *International Herald Tribune,* August 28, 1986.

CHAPTER 11

1. See Jean Denizet, *Le Dollar* (Paris: Fayard, 1985), pp. 156–57.
2. Loukas Tsoukalis, "The New International Monetary 'System' and Prospects for Reform" in *The Political Economy of International Money* (London: Royal Institute of International Affairs and SAGE Publications, 1985), p. 302.
3. Denizet, op. cit., pp. 145–155.
4. Tsoukalis, op. cit., p. 294.

5. "Deficits and the Dollar: The World Economy at Risk—Summary," *Policy Analyses in International Economics* 14 (December 1985), p. 3.

6. Harold Lever and Christopher Huhne, *Debt and Danger* (London: Penguin, 1985), p. 11.

7. Bruce Nussbaum, *The World after Oil: The Shifting Axis of Power and Wealth* (New York: Touchstone Books, 1984).

8. David Stockman, *The Triumph of Politics: Why the Reagan Revolution Failed* (London: The Bodley Head, 1986), p. 420.

9. See Philip Stephens, "There is nothing to fear but the lack of fear itself," in *Financial Times,* April 8, 1988.

CHAPTER 12

1. See David P. Calleo, *The Imperious Economy* (Cambridge, Mass.: Harvard University Press, 1982), pp. 110–14.

2. Gwyneth Williams, *Third-World Political Organizations* (London: Macmillan, 1981), pp. 56–58.

3. See Willard Range, *Franklin D. Roosevelt's World Order* (Athens, Ga.: University of Georgia Press, 1959), chapter 10.

4. Calleo, op. cit., pp. 120–21.

INDEX